Human Conflict

Human Conflict

Disagreement, Misunderstanding, and Problematic Talk

C. David Mortensen

ROWMAN & LITTLEFIELD PUBLISHERS, INC.
Lanham • *Boulder* • *New York* • *Toronto* • *Oxford*

ROWMAN & LITTLEFIELD PUBLISHERS, INC.

Published in the United States of America
by Rowman & Littlefield Publishers, Inc.
A wholly owned subsidiary of The Rowman & Littlefield Publishing Group, Inc.
4501 Forbes Boulevard, Suite 200, Lanham, Maryland 20706
www.rowmanlittlefield.com

P.O. Box 317, Oxford OX2 9RU, UK

British Library Cataloguing in Publication Information Available

Library of Congress Cataloging-in-Publication Data
Mortensen, C. David.
  Understanding human misunderstanding / C. David Mortensen.
      p. cm.
  Includes bibliographical references and index.
  ISBN 0-7425-2729-8 (hardcover : alk. paper) — ISBN 0-7425-2730-1 (pbk. : alk.
paper)
  1. Interpersonal communication. 2. Miscommunication. I. Title.
  P94.7.M674 2005
  302.2—dc22

                                    2005007833

Printed in the United States of America

♾™ The paper used in this publication meets the minimum requirements of
American National Standard for Information Sciences—Permanence of Paper
for Printed Library Materials, ANSI/NISO Z39.48-1992.

To our precious twins: Dana and Kara

Contents

Introduction

The study of human interaction can be analyzed from any number of productive vantage points. It is important to know how complex projects, activities, habits, and routines of sense-making practice work or function when things go smoothly and everything turns out right and also what happens when things go badly or get out of synch. The basic distinction between effective and faulty forms of face-to-face interaction is a central concern. The study of applied social knowledge may be designed to show how mutually accessible clusters or networks of individuals manage to move into or out of varying states, degrees, or gradations of difficulty and perplexity with one another.

An initial presumption provides a useful starting point. Literate human beings are typically sensitive to the larger issue of what transpires when things go well or badly across a diverse spectrum of social contexts and divergent cultural settings. By this standard, effective social encounters occur whenever someone (observer) interprets what someone else (participant) is able to express in a clear, cogent, and coherent manner. A favorable atmosphere promotes an opportunity to construct a wide spectrum of agreements and understandings as the shared basis for an enduring working consensus. In contrast, an unfavorable climate promotes a collective sense of mutual misinterpretation and a wide array of chronic disagreements and serious misunderstandings. A central task is to identify the basic dynamics at work within and across a wide spectrum of face-to-face interactions that somehow fall short of some standard or miss the mark in a particularly telling or striking manner.

The opportunity to interact with other people does not ensure that an abiding state of mutual understanding will be achieved. Sometimes, people make reasonably good sense of other people, places, and things. At other times, the very same people, places, and things may well make little or no sense at all. In fact, we know that sense-making efforts do not always make good sense. Much depends on how well the personal vocabulary and idiom of one person can be readily translated, interpreted, and integrated into the vocabulary and idiom of any other. One may say, in a manner of speaking, that someone understands the expressed behavior of someone else. It is, in other words, a distinctively human enterprise that is at stake. Successful communication is a collective achievement of the highest order.

There may be as many diverse ways to grasp and comprehend the complex actions of other people as there is the number of observers who construe what transpires from a unique position or place within a larger social system. Of central concern is the sheer complexity of forces and factors that make things turn out the way they do, for better or for worse. Three broad issues surface. First, as literate beings, we can search for the inclusive genetic potentialities that make human understanding possible. Second, we can observe what transpires as unfolding social possibilities when a condition of mutual understanding between separate entities is fully accomplished. Third, we can study the actual personal effects that various states of mutual agreement and shared understanding can produce on a short- or long-term basis. Hence, the basic movement shifts from largely inherited abstract potentials transformed into selectively actualized possibilities, which in turn have distinctive behavioral outcomes.

The subject is timeless. The possibilities are endless. The central implications are far-reaching. In a seminal statement, John Locke completed the most celebrated treatise on the subject of human understanding ever published, *An Essay Concerning Human Understanding* (1659). Since that time, social philosophers have produced millions of words of dense commentary about his controversial "correspondence theory" of human truth. Unfortunately, few academic critics have actually attempted to address the sweeping and pervasive subject with greater vigor or more depth, either in the spirit of an extension and elaboration of the classic statement or as a major corrective addressed from an alternative theoretical or paradigmatic stance. Part of the problem is not the technical accuracy of academic criticism of Locke's proud dogma but rather the unwillingness of qualified social critics to link the critical question, What makes it possible for human beings to understand each other? with careful analysis of the sheer magnitude of applied social knowledge that is required to deal effectively with chronic communicative difficulties between one person and another.

After all, fundamental human concerns about troublesome and disquieting acts of conflict, miscommunication, and problematic talk often transcend small-scale notions of syntactical irregularity, semantic slippage, or pragmatic failure in conventional language use. Success or failure registers on a dramatic human scale in the fulfillment of complex intentions, multiple objectives, and collaborative goals in complex public settings. An efficacious conception of communicative competence involves three major domains of functional consideration: personal recognition of current communicative difficulties; mutual willingness to acknowledge, confront, and deal with any unresolved communicative issues; and viable methods used to cope with relevant communicative concerns in a fresh, innovative, or inspiring manner.

Specifically, it is possible to identify what transpires in complex social settings where a distinctive climate of agreement, disagreement, understanding, or misunderstanding prevails. The essential progression is from abstract matters of applied social knowledge translated into specific spheres of contested negotiation and social deliberation. The first chapter examines common sources of miscommunication in daily life. Consider social situations in which the participants appear to interact for the sheer sake of appearances, as in dramatic acts or prolonged episodes of sophistry, pretense, and pseudocommunication. Pretending to communicate is an expedient substitute for an authentic achievement. In surface manifestations, speaking subjects may act on the presumption that everything is fine and nothing is wrong. At times people act as if they are infallible or absolutely certain in what they claim to know, without a hint of doubt, qualification, or reservation. Personal styles qualify as being omniscient insofar as an aura of infallibility is predicated on the use of imperial proclamations, universal declarations, and sweeping claims of objective certitude about absolute truth. A purified myth of "perfect communication" is perpetrated insofar as speaking subjects present themselves as being flawless, free of error, bias, or deception.

Extreme perfectionists are known to favor inflated egocentric comparisons; invoke absolute standards that leave little or no room for less-than-optimum outcomes; and, even worse, manage to stifle dissent, debate, or divergent responses. Moreover, some types of competitive negotiation over perplexing social issues do not readily lend themselves to flawless exercises in rigorous civic deliberation. Speaking subjects may discover that the force of intangible feelings, sensitive issues, and chronic conflicts do not necessarily lead to precise quantitative analysis or compelling metaphoric verification. Ordinary conversation remains, to some extent, a matter of hit or miss, trial and error. Some interpretations may be right on the mark while others may well be misinterpretations and miss the target all together. Even reasonably accurate interpretations often incorporate two broad types of mistaken identification. One may read too much into little things (false positives) or leave too much out of bigger things (false negatives). The determined pursuit of outstanding personal accomplishments or distinctive social achievements requires a stance of resolute persistence in spite of mistake, miscue, or miscalculation. Likewise, strong social bonds enable, rather than disable, the fulfillment of idealized personal strivings and demanding social goals. In effect, making sense together requires hard work, regular practice, and considerable tolerance of the constraining influences of miscommunication, strategic ambiguity, and confusing impact of problematic talk. The margin of upside opportunity cannot be so easily separated from the magnitude of downside risk. What is at stake is how well or poorly the respective parties are able to reason together, despite whatever problems, issues, or concerns stand in the way.

Human interpretations are based on the progressive integration of complex cognitive appraisals, value orientations, and social identifications. Chapter 2 explores certain basic interpretive dimensions of individual and collective performance specified in pragmatic and functions terms. When we interpret the observed significance of people, places, and things, we must, of necessity, make use of scarce material resources, acquired cognitive abilities, and derived social skills. Strategic success in goal-directed behavior depends, therefore, on naive notions about what types of strategic activity in given public situations will most likely produce or reproduce the desired effects. Matters of gain and loss, success and failure, register as scaled social comparisons arranged in multiple scales, alignments, or hierarchies based on exclusionary standards of preference, privilege, and priority. In other words, social interactants do not simply become aware of what transpires but rather must actively construct the very standards by which their own personal constructs are judged, evaluated, and measured.

Intentional expectations are subject to multiple tests of validity and reliability that must be fashioned in an uncertain and precarious world. Baseline levels of friction, strife, and strain qualify as subversive forces and factors because virtually all supportive, caring, and constructive endeavors can be neutralized or undermined by the force of unknown, uncertain, or unpredictable factors that give rise to diverse states of prolonged discomfort or acute distress. In effect, personal appraisals provide multiple standards of critical assessment; produce a positive or negative hedonic tone or slant; and reproduce a convergent or divergent outcome, result, or effect.

Human language is heavily value laden. Chapter 3 shows why it is so routinely difficult to define what transpires on a factual level without making implicit value judgments on an evaluative level. We know that critical appraisals vary widely across lines of gender, class, and culture. Moreover, various sexual orientations shape the initial formulation of assumptions, attitudes, beliefs, and moral outlooks about human relations in general and the acquisition of intimate relations in particular. The pervasive impact of gender inequality and all manner of cultural bias, bigotry, and prejudice also greatly complicates the time, energy, and effort required to deal effectively with contentious, polarized social viewpoints and reconcile incongruent or incompatible value orientations between competing advocates.

Communal orientations qualify as being prosocial insofar as the respective participants are able to adopt emotion-laden vocabularies based on frequent reference to the prevalence of certain core values—respect, honesty, and trust. In contrast, subversive personal influences may well promote escalated levels of tension, conflict, and distress that undermine the shared production of constructive social valuations and thereby give rise to implicit rumination, suspicion, and accusation over multiple signs of disrespect, dishonesty, and mistrust. Incompatible value orientations are truly difficult to negotiate and often prove to be virtually impossible to reconcile. A harsh legacy of strong disagreement and serious misunderstanding entails hidden costs and unwanted side effects. As always, the subject of loss is never far away.

Cognitive appraisals and enduring value orientations are deeply embedded in negotiated matters of social identity. Chapter 4 examines certain interactive factors associated with the stability and consistency of personal identity. It is not always easy to accept other people for who they are and what they do. Narrative descriptions, the telling and retelling of personal stories, enables speaking subjects to explore unshared history, clarify current events, and strengthen relational ties. However, prevailing conceptions of personal identity are also subject to destabilizing influences. Narrative capacity often deteriorates among discredited and disadvantaged groups who lack sufficient resources, abilities, and skills to preserve a unified and coherent sense of personal identity over the life course.

Postmodern critics underscore the rapid erosion of personal, social, and ethnic identities in rapidly changing cultural settings where pervasive technological innovations lead to the massive proliferation of new social identities as well as the rapid disintegration of traditional habits in everyday life. Miscalculations occur as persons from diverse ethnic and cultural backgrounds make faulty attributions to outsiders' personality traits and unusual situational factors that resist reciprocal identification. In addition, reactive individuals tend to become defensive in response to observable signs of risk or threat. Defensive reactions often escalate in contested social situations characterized by chronic disagreement and mutual misunderstanding. Social skill defects hold people back, prevent mutual understanding, and keep them from fully functioning with each other.

Arguments pose special difficulties for opposing advocates. Chapter 5 examines tests of reason and rationality taken as valued cultural assets. It is one thing to argue well. It is quite another to become argumentative over a severe clash of polarized arguments. Advocates qualify as being argumentative when they cross the line from advancing constructive arguments to indulging in hostile personal attacks. The main finding provides an affirmation for the traditional standard that skill in argument is inversely related to the amount of reactive defensiveness and character attack that takes place. A study of narrative themes associated with debate, dispute, and dissension provides solid evidence that argumentative persons are likely to adapt rigid and inflexible styles based on argument for argument's sake, stubbornness, closed-mindedness, and resolute determination to prove who is right and who is wrong. The potential for constructive conflict resolution diminishes among steadfast advocates who refuse to give in or give up the futile struggle.

It is possible to compare and contrast what transpires when working agreements proliferate and chronic disagreements dissolve. Chapter 6 identifies salient features of what animated speaking subjects feel, think, say, and do when they work well together to promote the routine reproduction of constructive human dialogue. Chapter 7 outlines what transpires when speaking subjects turn negative and disagreeable. There are stark differences in the type and slant of emotional vocabularies that are employed across a broad spectrum of convergent or divergent settings. Mutual constructions of working agreement generally produce strong positive sentiment (love, care, joy, happiness, interest, and excitement), whereas social constructions of chronic dispute and prolonged disagreement promote equally strong negative sympathy (anger, fear, and sadness). Both agreeable and disagreeable dispositions qualify as stable personality traits that resist major change and significant alteration but in opposed ways.

The central finding is that agreement-making activity is amicable, attractive, and desirable while disagreement-making activity is agonistic, unattractive, and unstable. Specifically, tentative working agreements are fashioned out of mutual recognition of personal intent and strategic engagement. Emphasis is placed on congenial spheres of perspective taking, stable social identities, similar interests, compatible values, and considerable consensus over the quality of interaction. Tentative disagreements, in contrast, emerge from fleeting states of inattention, denial, and refusal to recognize steady reproductions of petty complaint, minor grievance, and trivial distinction. Gradual escalation of tension, stress, and strain is linked to high levels of ego involvement over contested relational matters. Emphasis is placed on the persistent misrecognition of intention, divergent perspective taking, contested social identity, repeated verbal abuse, and, in extreme cases, dangerous fights or violent assaults. To make matters worse, the escalation of serious disagreement is inversely related to the mutual ability to grasp and understand what goes wrong and the shared willingness to make things right.

Chapters 8 and 9 outline relevant comparisons of familiar social situations that are well understood with certain direct encounters that are poorly understood or otherwise infiltrated with deliberate confusion and strategic ambiguity. It is important to recognize that acts of miscommunication and episodes of problematic talk may be viewed as a missed opportunity or a strategic achievement. Social agents, after all, do not always strive for the maximum or ultimate fulfillment of optimum conditions, as equated with enduring achievements of mutual understanding that stand the test of time.

Sometimes, it is considered socially desirable to settle for shallow or superficial communication or none at all. Nonetheless, strong social strivings are associated with heavily value-laden claims of authentic disclosure, empathy, synchrony, alignment, convergence, accuracy, and fidelity in the acquisition and cultivation of secure relationships. In contrast, serious modes of human misunderstanding arise from personal ambiguity over appropriate boundaries, inauthentic disclosure, empathic failure, asymmetry, misalignment, and insecure relational ties. Furthermore, verbal references to matters of hurt and harm are rarely mentioned under conditions of agreement and understanding but are frequently employed under conditions of disagreement and misunderstanding. One implication is striking. Those speaking subjects who produce the least amount of hurt and harm are generally able to repair minor violations or major transgressions in small doses and thin slices, whereas speaking subjects who produce the greatest amount of hurt and harm are often unable or unwilling to do anything about the collateral damage.

Chapter 10 examines damaged human relations in view of discordant respondent claims of hurt and harm in relation to tactical matters of repair, renewal, and restoration. Emphasis is placed on corrective or remedial efforts to restore or renew more favorable conditions for direct human encounter. Past mistakes, mishaps, and miscues can become objects of conversation as well as causes for concern and consternation. There is also wide allowance for realignment or readjustment of prevailing standards for sorting out messy and complicated gradations of success and failure specified in terms of an upside promise of improvement (making things better) in relation to a downside risk (making things worse). Remedial tactics, repair mechanisms, and compensatory strategies vary widely in frequency of occurrence, degree of reciprocity, and functional effectiveness. Personal excuses are commonplace. Special pleading has certain appeal as a means to cover up or deny harmful intentions.

On core issues of personal accountability, there is a broad tendency for alleged perpetrators to shift attention toward mitigating circumstances that must be taken into account. It is tempting to engage in self-exoneration as a means to minimize further blame and accusation. Mutual efforts at reformation of troublesome or disquieting episodes of face-to-face interaction require reciprocal modes of behavioral adjustment and shared speech accommodation. Overt acts of reconciliation often require a period of healing and recovery. Acts of apology, pardon, and forgiveness have been most extensively examined in academic studies of peace making and conflict resolution, but such acts of contrition or confession are rarely identified as badly degraded outcomes of chronic disagreement or prolonged misunderstanding among engaged social agents.

Much of the healing of invisible wounds takes place during brief periods of silence and private contemplation among speaking subjects. Respondent accounts identify an ingenious repertoire of unspoken gestures to provide temporary relief from the disruptive influence of incessant talk, chatter, and phatic distraction. Some stop talking until things cool down. Others refuse to speak. Still others withdraw or resign. Chilling effects are common, and stonewalling at times works as a means of last resort. Constructive silence is effective when there is a widely distributed sense of guilt and responsibility for previously unacknowledged violations and transgressions.

ACKNOWLEDGMENTS

Colleagues in the Department of Communication Arts at the University of Wisconsin, Madison, are a source of inspiration as part of the larger collaborative quest for more exacting, rigorous, and sensitive methods of textual appraisal. Graduate coordinator Linda Henzl contributed to the preparation of a computer transcript containing sixteen hundred personal accounts of reconstructed modes of face-to-face interaction. Morgan Mortensen offered verbal support and unspoken encouragement. Linda Hadenfeldt, acquisitions editor, provided guidance and direction on important matters. Finally, the privilege of waking up to the orange glow of the rising sun over the magnificent eastern shores of Lake Mendota made up for the grind, grit, and gruel that accompany the privilege of working things out along the way.

1

Misconstruction

My knowledge of everyday life has the quality of an instrument that cuts a path through a forest and, as it does so, projects a narrow cone of light on what lies just ahead and immediately around; on all sides of the path there continues to be darkness.

—Peter L. Berger and Thomas Luckmann,
The Social Construction of Reality

It may be helpful, then, to remember that any portion of reality with which we deal stands always with the encompassing silence of all that is. . . . There is no truth that does not rest ultimately upon what is evident to us in our own experience.

—William Barrett, *The Illusion of Technique*

Fallibility is part of the human condition. Any view which denigrates reason, and the possibility of truth, and which even doubts our identity, is in fact saying that there is no way in which we can be mistaken, either individually or collectively. Each epoch will have its own views, its fictions and even that view will be fiction. Even the notion of fiction collapses, since there will be nothing left to contrast it with. If we cannot be right, we cannot be wrong, and if we cannot be wrong, we cannot be right.

—Roger Trigg, *Rationality and Religion*

What we learn from considering cases of mistakes is just how unformed our understanding is of how mind mixes with the world to form language, of how little we understand how to make sense of our making sense or even our failure to do so.

—Paul A. Roth, "'Mistakes'"

FALLIBILITY

The primordial question of what it means to be a human being cannot be easily settled in the abstract or simply resolved on narrow theoretical grounds. Over the life span, each person is endowed with the greater potential to be located somewhere when something happens, to discover something that matters, and to test the magnitude of desired effect against the cumulative margin of unwanted error. What is affordable is an unspecified measure of contingent, tentative, uncertain, and provisional opportunity to participate in the composite features and dense textures of everyday life.

In the preliminary stages of inquiry, innovative interpretive devices may be readily activated as a means to define, typify, and explain the inclusive meaning of whatever is disclosed or concealed from greater public view. Strategic human encounters qualify as survival-oriented, reality-testing exercises that follow in line with their intended or unanticipated consequences (Mortensen 1991). Likewise, the interior workings of living organisms are designed to facilitate rapid and reliable detection of the slightest degree of environmental change and then to react accordingly.

Productive inquiry requires an intentional, purposeful, and strategic commitment to the fulfillment of complex tasks, projects, and routines in a material world that is brightly illuminated by intricate webs of elaborated significance. We are, after all, thrown into the world, as Heidegger (1962) says, but not necessarily one of our own ideal choosing, to make whatever we can of people, places, and things. We strive to make sense of complex daily events without any instructive benefit of a complete prior understanding but rather as exercised through our species' distinctive endowment in the illuminating power of social performance. The primacy of practice is prior to, and necessary for, a lifetime of socialization (Archer 2000).

The reality of everyday life can be approached from two radically different types of functional paradigmatic premises. On a local scale, vague presumptions of human infallibility may arise from intuitively appealing notions of what transpires in a complex public sphere as being somehow free of any error, mistake, falsehood, or deception. Infallible subjects may presume to know everything there is to know about a given subject. On a regional scale, competing groups may produce "true believers" who presume their distinctive worldviews to be infinitely superior to any alternative conception currently available on a human scale. Zealous advocates proclaim one certain way as the only possible way to seek ultimate truth, wisdom, or glory worthy of emulation and worship with resolute conviction. On a global scale, a condition of sacred infallibility may be collectively attributed to some higher force, a supreme being, a god, or the cosmos, as defined in abstract theological terms. A religious exemplar occurs in solemn prayers directed toward a personal deity (higher power) who supposedly knows all things, hears all things, sees all things, and reveals all things to finite mortal beings through an infallible method of devine revelation.

Sacred ceremonies may be infused or imbued with spiritual force, magical power, and resolute belief in timeless truth, beyond further change or subsequent alternation. True believers profess abiding faith in the literal interpretation of sacred documents. Religious fundamentalists around the globe worship sacred texts where unconditional presumptions of sacred infallibility are taken as a matter of supreme faith in sweeping claims and inerrant dogma that seek to transcend all manner of personal doubt. An inspired sense of divine revelation may be a source of primordial comfort in precarious or troubled times for the faithful who can imagine or envision their own lives as being subject to a theocratic master plan. True believers, after all, are free to worship at the sacred throne of faith, which passes all human understanding.

At the other end of the immense aesthetic spectrum are located far more secularized versions of human infallibility. Human subjects may be viewed as sources or objects of evaluative categorization fashioned along lines of who is best qualified as being pure, uncontaminated, and flawless in performing a difficult or demanding social task or, conversely, who is to be disqualified as impure, contaminated, and flawed by one standard or another. In this regard, sacred valuations are based on a principle of hierarchy and a superior (above/beyond) versus inferior (below/within) dualism, whereas secular virtues are derived from a lateral principle of equality in human encounters (Donskis 1998).

The stark clash between sacred and secular outlooks resonates in the value-laden tendency of some persons to organize their core senses of social identity according to a master theme of "redemption" and "contamination" with moral, ethical, and aesthetic overtones. Redemptive acts transform bad into good. Contaminative acts transform good into bad. It matters greatly whether a succession of negative events will precede or follow a sequence of positive events. When bad things happen to good people, primordial sources of behavioral contamination may be redeemed, transformed, salvaged, and purified by the strength of personal narrative alone into subsequent and radically altered objects of goodness and light (McAdams et al. 2001). Generative adults strive to promote decisive and critical goals in everyday life that transcend narrow egocentric fulfillment and contribute to the larger welfare of society through steadfast commitment to a positive, constructive legacy that will outlive them. Psychosocial generativity promotes personal concern with legacies and the preservation of succeeding generations. Over their life spans, generative adults strive to produce satisfying endings for their life stories, distinctive legacies of symbolic immortality, envisioned as abiding faith in the worthwhileness of human life. In contrast, stagnating individuals endure pervasive feelings of self-absorption and suffering in impoverished interpersonal relations (Bradley and Marcia 1998).

Fuzzy distinctions between the presumably perfect/imperfect modalities and flawless/flawed domains of human encounter may give rise to inspiring utopian fantasies of mortal beings who strive to achieve a state or condition of "perfect communication" with one another. When judged by a standard of redemption over malignant forces, a superior performance may be viewed in positive, lofty, elevated, and rarified terms. When judged by a standard of contamination over purified forces, an inferior performance may be viewed in negative, lowly, fallen, and deteriorated terms. By implication, comparative social standards qualify as personal constructions based on inflated ascriptions and deflated attributions of credit and discredit, valuation and devaluation, qualification and disqualification. An awe-inspiring vision of perfect communication requires not only a flawless performance but also a flawless reception. Likewise, a lofty vision of a human world without any visible signs of miscommunication or problematic talk implicates the magical sense that everyone would somehow express themselves clearly and interpret others accurately, without a hint of noise, distortion, disruption, or interference.

A universal language system would enable engaging speaking subjects to interact in a clear, coherent, and transparent manner, without disabling modes of memory distortion, cognitive lapse, emotional blockage, forgetfulness, transference, or subversive sense of anything being hidden, lost, misplaced, or left out of sorts. Likewise, speaking subjects would not make mistakes in translation, interpretation, or valuation along the way. By implication, there would be no need to repeat, clarify, or explain anything to anyone anymore. There would be no cause nor reason, therefore, to question or doubt any speaking subject or given subject matter, because virtually everything would be well understood by everyone else without a flawed secret to hide, hidden agenda to conceal, or false impression to manipulate, deceive, or mislead.

Omniscient styles arise from a false presumption of selective personal access to a domain of infinite knowledge or a singular demonstration of one's unlimited power, force, or influence. Imperial proclamations and universal declarations strive to invoke exalted invocations of unwavering commitment, conclusive proof, absolute truth, and objective certitude of one's own purity and piety before others. After all, an ascendent aura of infallibility imposed by a self-righteous subject implies a descendent stance of fallibility on the part of other members. Likewise, resolute appeals to cultural purification tend, as Harris (1990) suggests, "to fear or scorn what is mixed or apparently impure" and thereby reinforce massive bias into "a self-righteous cult, a self-righteous polarization, a self-righteous ghetto" (175). Messianic leaders of charismatic cults strive to manipulate quasi-religious themes and binary op-positions between good and evil, sacred and profane, saint and sinner in or-der to conquer and transform malignant secular forces (Smith 2000).

Charismatic authority depends on a profound shift from a state of mun-dane understanding of ordinary kinship ties to a radical or transformed un-derstanding of a selected or chosen person as one having superhuman or su-pernatural power over speaking subjects. A charismatic leader acquires power and authority derived from consensual faith in future visions of col-lective purification cast in an articulate and inspirational manner (Dorian et al. 2000). Prophetic visions must cast a magic spell that stands the test of time. If an awe-inspiring demonstration is severely disrupted, some loss of plausibility is implied. A charismatic person who assumes an extraordinary calling depends on growing validation of some special gift, remarkable achievement, or supernatural communication. Failure to deliver the ex-pected sense of wonder and awe means that witnesses "rapidly decline and disappear" (Finlay 2002, 549). In effect, inspired faith in charismatic salvation is precarious and fragile. The search for purity and light is cast against a murky background of binary opposition from hidden sources of contamina-tion and damnation.

The superior–inferior distinction—whether defined, classified, or ex-plained in fully explicit and literal terms or left as tacit inference and as mere implication—is nonetheless added to the mix of multiple intentions, per-sonal strategies, social tactics, short-term outcomes, and long-term effects of human encounter. Here, the ideal exemplar is the singular speaking subject who alone presumes to know—that is, the one who is always right, the one who rises above the common idiom no matter what occurs, for better and for worse. Hindsight bias magnifies the confidence of the all-knowing subject who professes to have known it all along (Winman, Juslin, and Bjorkman 1998). It entails the after-the-fact sense that some plausible outcome was likely to happen, as readily predictable, even though the actual occurrence was not predicted beforehand (Harley, Carlsen, and Loftus 2004). In contrast, foresight bias presumes that one will soon know it all. If hindsight and fore-sight bias are highly salient, then expansive conceptions of past, present, and future events may blur together in lofty, inspired visions of one's own exag-gerated sense of power in the human world. An omniscient style may also inflate the degree of hindsight and foresight confidence to an extreme or rad-ical point where someone claims to know everything completely and simul-taneously about someone or something (Morreall 1994). The combined force of hindsight and foresight bias provides a convenient source of double dis-tortion. Omniscient overtones register as pervasive bias against any deliber-ate public display of egalitarian assumptions and as that redirected toward a singular interpretive slant based on standards of selective deference, down-ward comparison, distancing maneuver, and implied disparagement toward others. Fortunately, the unacknowledged consequences of omniscient public drama may be fleeting and transitory.

The know-it-all-along effect is pervasive, robust, and difficult to eliminate in enduring social arrangements and traditional institutional affiliations (Hoffrage, Hertwig, and Gigerenzer 2000). By implication, the omniscient style is embodied in the steadfast refusal to acknowledge *any* possibility of error before others. Likewise, the desire to achieve an omniscient mode of human understanding requires, as a matter of principle, direct recognition and uniform validation before others. On a larger, dramatic, and mythic scale, resolute human belief in the cosmic significance of omnipotent, omniscient, and benevolent forces has deep historical, cultural, and psychological roots that enable people to mistakenly conclude that "someone or something other than themselves has engineered their fates" (Gilbert et al. 2000, 591). Nonetheless, illusionary confidence in the power of external agency provides psychic protection from the greater acknowledgment that human creatures, like other animals, are material beings who are all subject to decay, deterioration, and death (Goldenberg et al. 2001; Schimel et al. 2000). Illusions of all-knowing insight provide a magical means for persons to alter and transform suboptimal outcomes for unchangeable daily events into pretentious, subjective convictions that serve to deny and distance threatened individuals from their primordial connection with other animals and all living things (Goldenberg et al. 2000; Landau et al. 2004).

Delusions of grandiosity promote an inflated sense of personal knowledge based on massive deception and disparity between reported success and actual life circumstance (Meloy 2002). Grandiose self-enhancement is symptomatic of self-aggrandizement and fantasized proclamations of one's unlimited ability, knowledge, power, and skill (Stucke and Sporer 2002). Individuals who pretend to know it all are prone to manufacture protected and cherished beliefs because they simply refuse to admit anything as a potential source of falsification or disconfirmation (Leeser and O'Donohue 1999).

An illusion of personal infallibility interferes with the modest ability to recognize or even admit to the possibility of holding a mistaken belief about the world at large. The wide array of errors we make about our mental states affects the veracity of what we say and do before others (Wiland 2003). The presumed superiority of an omniscient person rules out the potential value of systematic testing for errors, omissions, and mistakes, both as a means to further discovery and as a rationale for devising new tests or subsequent refinements in reality-testing procedures to gain a better understanding of anomalous, incomplete, idealized, or misdirected efforts in complex goal attainment (Elliott 2004).

Inflated feelings of egocentric superiority are typical of self-serving and self-righteous persons who hold charitable views of themselves and harbor cynical views of their peers. Overly charitable social evaluations may give rise to emotional blind spots, profound delusions, and overlooked factors that can arise quickly, easily, hastily, or unconsciously (Pronin et al. 2001). While personal fantasy is integral to healthy functioning as a vital, adaptive mechanism in daily life, extreme fantasy proneness is implicated in maladaptive difficulty in distinguishing fantasy, imagination, and play from the reality of everyday life (Waldo and Davis 2000). Moreover, the alluring fantasy of flawless communication may well preserve surface appearance while disguising the fact that the depth of mutual understanding is misplaced or gone. Illusionary estimates of superior personal ability may be adaptive in the short term but only at a delayed cost of decreased sense of self-esteem and well-being in the long term (Robins and Beer 2001).

Perfectionistic self-idealizations may be designed to prevent any greater tolerance of what Berman (2000) describes as the "unavoidable imperfection" of every individual and, in so doing, permit or justify harsh but unspoken judgmental attitudes or punitive disqualifications of others who fail to measure up to implausible standards of ultimately successful interaction. By dividing the human species into higher and lower domains of worth, significance, or valuation based on collective appeal to rather arbitrary and fabricated standards of moral qualification and ethical disqualification, new meaning is given to the old adage that many are called but few are chosen.

The perfectionistic fantasy of the new, reborn, purified, and sanctified individual acquires a lofty and ultimately privileged status in religious or rebirth rituals of eternal salvation, monastic aspirations for pure spirituality, national liberation movements (to transcend oppression by all means necessary), and authoritarian dynamics of cohesive groups with rigid and self-righteous devotion to inspirational ego ideals imposed on subordinated members cast as mere supplicants (Berman 1998). Spiritual purification is predicated on transcendental visions of salvation, redemption, and heroic transformation of regressive upheaval and chronic tribulation into progressive and liberative movements toward wholeness and integration (Washburn 1990). Here the utopian exemplar consists of true believers, the chosen few, who impose what they alone take as devine intervention upon other people, thereby overriding any appeal to secular authority, will of the majority, or binding force of community standards. Zealous, compensatory conviction provides transitory relief from troubling uncertainty (McGregor and Marigold 2003). On a larger scale, zealots and fanatics strive to generate a readiness for self-sacrifice, irrespective of the doctrine or program, with what Hoffer (1951) describes in terms of "enthusiasm, fervent hope, hatred and intolerance . . . blind faith and singlehearted allegiance" (1).

A resolute stance of idealized impression management, appearing as though "holier than thou," is symptomatic of the widely erroneous expectation to think that one will behave far more admirably, or saintly, than what one actually would—if only put to a moral test (Epley and Dunning 2000). Pretensions to holiness invite moral hypocrisy—appearing moral to oneself without being so. False piety appears moral insofar as individuals seem to take others welfare into account yet still bring benefit only to themselves (Batson, Thompson, and Seuferling 1999). Sanctimonious behavior prevails when self-interest overpowers any desire to act morally before others (Batson, Thompson, and Chen 2002). A perfect facade produces self-deception through duplicitous means that make real hypocrites hard to find (Statman 1997). Self-serving persons employ pretense and pretension to take credit for success and to deny responsibility for collective failure (McGlynn 2001).

Severe moralistic conflicts that unfold on a secularized but global scale are often difficult to manage, negotiate, or resolve by purely holy means, particularly where sacred values (infinite or transcendent significance) are pitted against secular values (relative or comparative worth). In contrast, secularized perfectionistic strivings explore ultimately valued considerations about what a good life means to each member of the wider human community. However, personal abilities and social skills "differ too much for all of us to want to realize them in quite the same balance" because "persons differ not so much in basic values as in their capacity to realize them" (Griffin 1990, 70).

The potential for human misunderstanding is magnified insofar as members of society must struggle to protect their cherished sacred values—which preclude trade-off, concession, or compromise—from pervasive secular encroachments led by mainstream societal trends toward consumption, gratification, and materialism (Tetlock et al. 2000). Secular movements are emblematic of intense historic conflicts over the liberation of personal and public life from repressive or regressive forms of religious indoctrination and the forced imposition of dogmatic, infallible declarations (Dallmayr 1999; Sommerville 1998). Likewise, fleeting and transitory presumptions of personal infallibility may infiltrate the ebb and flow of daily tasks, habits, and routines insofar as heavily engaged groups of people indulge in multiple illusions and purified fantasies of obtaining ascendent and exalted states of unsullied perfection with each other. Pride and vanity can give way to intense strivings to project a stance of omniscience, righteous indignation, an insolent hubris, that anyone else could possibly doubt the veracity of one's most outlandish pronouncements.

Dogmatic declarations and categorical imperatives leave little or no room for added personal scrutiny or subsequent social rejoinder—"It's true because I say its true." Perfectionistic people strive to perpetrate a dramatic illusion of supreme invincibility or project an aura of not being liable to fail in the completion of complicated personal projects, shared social activities, or rigorous cultural tasks. Rhetorical acts of sophistry, enacted for the mere sake of appearance, aim to extend the outer limits of stylistic embellishment by persons who presume that they and they only can do no wrong, and they are likely, therefore, to take refuge in a sweeping litany of minor complaints and petty bickering without hint of flaw or admission of any unsoundness of voiced opinion. Underneath such inflated impressions of personal perfection, an astute observer may discover a maze of weaknesses, shortcomings, and vulnerabilities masked by acts of pretense and shallow communication.

Idealized impression management entails both a strong need to appear perfect before others and an equally strong resolve not to reveal visible signs of imperfection in public life. Ultimate success depends, of course, on the willingness of speaking subjects to be subjected to the singular application of purified or rarified standards, without hint or sign of blemish, fault, lapse, or stain. The desire to obtain a flawless performance, a living embodiment of sheer perfection, is not easily defeated. Moreover, observers may attribute omniscient status to any idealized model of ultimate fulfillment, whether apparent in real or fictional forms. Personal distress occurs when dialectical tensions between the ideal (expectation) and the actual (performance) reaches a point where it becomes evermore difficult to manage a host of mixed messages and contradictory outcomes. Active promotion of a flawless ability, skill, or special gift requires at least a passive disavowal of implied nullities—shortcomings, liabilities, and weaknesses (Purdon, Antony, and Swinson 1999). The self-protective aspects of resolute perfectionism are regarded as defensive, avoidant, and ineffective in facilitating a more constructive view of relational ties (Flett and Hewitt 2002).

Extreme perfectionistic strivings promote repeated acts and chronic episodes of miscommunication and problematic talk insofar as strategic and tactical manipulations in social relations are based on aversion to risk that invalidates facades, reluctance to engage in mutual disclosure, compensatory defense against feelings of inadequacy, dishonest depictions of one's accomplishments, lack of authentic response, avoidance of sensitive issues, diminished satisfaction, and lost intimacy (Sherry et al. 2003). It is an open question whether the aversive consequences of setting "high" personal standards outweighs the subversive impact of setting "low" social standards or none at all.

It is important, nonetheless, for aspiring, exceptional achievers to know the real magnitude of difference between the lifetime pursuit of perfection and the temporal quest for excellence. Extremely perfectionistic individuals are vulnerable on several fronts at once. They construct dichotomous notions of the difference between success and failure; invoke absolute standards that leave no room for submaximum or suboptimum outcomes; engage in major attribution errors in a global tendency to envision self, others, or society as the exclusive cause or ultimate reason for whatever prevents one party from achieving superior rankings; and decide to suffer in silence. Still at issue is whether the larger quest for perfection and glory qualifies as being healthy or unhealthy in daily life. Positive adaptive modes of perfectionism may facilitate somewhat greater focus on matters of personal strength, inner resolve, and enhanced reinforcement as preparation for intensely competitive engagement in demanding feats and grueling daily tasks. Conversely, negative or pathological perfectionism promotes devalued traits, negative self-talk, and repressed fears of failure (Greenspan 2000; Wiebe and McCabe 2002).

Narcissistically infused perfectionistic cravings thrive on an exaggerated sense of personal importance, entitlement, exploitation, exalted need for admiration, and zealous pursuit of personal glory (Wallace and Baumeister 2002). Narcissistic conversations also promote the use of inflated language, willingness to exploit others, exhibitionistic urges, and avoidance of intimacy (Vangelisti, Knapp, and Daly 1990). Dysfunctional social strivings qualify as being maladaptive insofar as egocentric subjects seek to appear flawless in competitive situations; indulge in extreme, deceptive, or calculating styles; and avoid risky settings where their self-glorifying actions are subject to close scrutiny by others. In general, social maladaptation promotes performance-avoidance goals while social adaption generates performance-approach goals (Barron and Harackiewicz 2001).

Self-critical perfectionism is negative, maladaptive, harsh, evaluative, and critical. Personal inability to derive real satisfaction from desired social outcomes, mixed with chronic or anxious concern about the lofty or idealized expectations of other engaged parties, is associated with the frequent occurrence of minor stressors, depressive symptoms, nagging hassles, and lingering helpless orientations in daily life (Dunkley 2003). The maladaptive style confers a greater sense of vulnerability to risk, threat, danger, and anxiety (Riskind et al. 2000). Those who are quickest to blame or condemn themselves for a wide succession of faulty social performances are vulnerable to chronic preoccupation with their own hidden shortcomings, deficiencies, and liabilities. Critical perfectionists underestimate the total magnitude of support available in times of great stress, and they may find themselves unable or unwilling to turn to others for help to share their unspoken anguish or acute distress (Dunkley and Blankstein 2000).

In contrast, perfectionists who focus on the responses of significant others shift attention away from their own imperfections and toward the imagined or attributed imperfections of other people, as in cases of turning the tables. Common maladies include a pervasive lack of trust, feelings of hostility, and difficult interpersonal relations (Flett and Hewitt 1998). However, socially derived standards of perfectionism may be imposed on speaking subjects who are unable to satisfy or live up to the lofty expectations of significant others (Hewitt and Flett 1991). Whether the self, other, or society is directly implicated, constant striving for exalted status of ultimate perfection may become a compulsion or obsession, particularly where the quest for excellence is confused with the far greater opportunity to fulfill more realistic aspirations, standards, objectives, and strategic goals. The courage to be imperfect can be a salutary antidote to the incessant urge to reach an elevated state of superiority and endless adulation. In daily life, not only is perfection impossible, but the actual cost to "those who seek it is inordinately high" (Pacht 1984, 390).

The mystifying desire of obtaining an infallible or flawless social performance is important because it is such a risky standard to impose on our daily interactions with other people. It does not actually matter whether perfectionistic strivings are predicated on working assumptions of devine intervention (revelation) or exceptional measures of spectacular secular success (achievement). Whenever strategic rivals hold themselves accountable for flawless social performances, they may unwittingly set themselves up to struggle in vain against what are implausible, impossible, or unobtainable standards of personal strivings, social expectations, or societal goals. At issue is all manner of small-scale allowances for corresponding difficulties in recognizing, sorting out, ranking, cross-checking, and honoring the critical distinction between what can be subject to falsification and what cannot be settled one way or another.

Adherents of fallabilism must struggle with the timeless need to learn from personal experience and to distinguish between better and worse claims to know this or that about one thing or another (Gomory 2001). If we as human beings qualify as fallible creatures, we should, as rational agents, acknowledge this fallibility and treat ourselves and others accordingly (Evnine 2001). Fallabilism requires keen and steady awareness of one's own flawed conceptions of daily life as well as broad tolerance of others' flawed notions of what transpires. Oddly, the secular study of human fallibility leads to broader recognition of just how intricate, unworkable, or unsuitable the formal analysis of social agents' behavior may prove to be.

For strategic purposes, living beings *must* measure things on a scale of relevance. Whatever qualifies as a "measurement" of a given person, place, or thing will entail an element or trace of mismeasure left behind. After all, only mythological, gothic, or deified figures in the cosmic drama are left to entertain presumptive notions of living up to utterly infallible standards for fallible creatures like us. An infallible transmission of meaning would require a perfect replication from an initial point of origin to a final point of destination, without hint of error, mistake, or miscalculation. Alas, only mechanical devices can produce a "perfect" replication, as in cases of cloning, electronic music, or robotics. In contrast, each speaking subject is an "imperfect" measuring device for all manner of individual and collective consciousness (Marks 1999). On a human scale, whatever works to improve conscious experience implies greater promise for an enhanced sense of well-being (Henry 1999).

Perplexing social issues may not be construed as those suitable for close public scrutiny. Other sensitive matters may be ruled out in advance as being intangible or immeasurable and, therefore, not subject to precise quantitative analysis or metaphoric verification one way or another. An inspirational or miraculous dream, resplendent and luminous in the darkest hours of the night, dissolves into superficial trivia or banter when recalled by a bewildered dreamer the next morning at breakfast with a friend. Other possible courses of impending action may be discredited, disqualified, or dismissed in advance as being too speculative, hypothetical, or unobtainable. Still other plausible options may be rendered inaccessible or unavailable for analytic purposes of close observation, careful scrutiny, or detailed inspection. Difficult hidden issues may be rendered null and void insofar as they are viewed as being impenetratable, as those beyond the ordinary scope of human comprehension. Partially obscured objects—people, places, and things—may not be amenable to rapid detection or instant recognition, because, for intrinsic reasons or extrinsic factors, they cannot even in principle be subject to reliable or valid comparison due to what remains incommensurate, out of balance, fleeting, or transitory.

The study of miscommunication examines the mismeasure of measure, or the magnitude of error that is attributed to the faulty performances of speaking subjects or their adverse circumstances. Complicated human environments are not always easy to read, construe, figure out, or size up. Unanticipated, unknown, or uncertain personal concerns may be consigned to the caldron of indeterminacy, the scope of all that resists the impact of interpretive appraisal. Also relevant are complex public confusions where the prevailing conditions of aesthetic density, inefficacy, and mythos reveal that each participant knows what transpires globally without knowing exactly what transpires ever so quickly (Scharfstein 1993). In effect, there is a broad spectrum of entangled relational conditions in which the common linguistic idiom of any one person does not, and will not, translate neatly into those adopted by anyone else who is accessible and close at hand (Grace 1987).

Because no one person has complete access to the lived circumstance of anyone else, it is necessary to factor in a constant—an X factor—an element of noncommunication between separate entities who lack the means to exert any measure of direct influence over one another. Prevailing assumptions about implicit conditions of noncommunication (no influence) or explicit states of incommunibility (no possibility) may be predicated on little more than a common ability or inability to express, convey, or impart something sensibly to someone else (Mortensen 1979). Specifically, it is possible to know that one does not know anything about a speaking subject, spoken text, or amorphous social setting.

TRIAL AND ERROR

Two basic ecological principles apply in simple learning trials. One, articulate human beings express themselves, and respond to the animated expressions of other human beings, for the short-term effects they have on the others. Two, they repeat specified things for the very sake of the long-term effects that they may have on others. Early, unsteady initial exchanges among unacquainted strangers are grounded, by definition, in a surplus of uncertain intentions, concealed strivings, and hidden aspirations. By this standard, some interpretations might be right on the mark (consensual standards) while alternative interpretations might miss the target (idiolectical standards). Human errors are valuable, therefore, as correctives or countermeasures for misconstructed, misconstrued, or misdirected modes of social inquiry.

Two derivative principles apply in complex learning sequences. One, the process of trial and error partially registers at higher levels of conscious awareness and cognitive control but also at lower levels of mechanical, automatic, and habituated activation. Two, human choices reflect their anticipated outcomes. Speaking subjects must learn to make connections and disconnections in rapidly changing public circumstances not only on the basis of broad plans and abstract working outlines but also in heuristic terms of short-term effects, results, and successive outcomes gained from multiple contacts with other people. By these standards, the establishment of strong, vital, and close ties with others requires a great deal of focused, determined, and concerted effort to achieve, regulate, and maintain constructive expectations, whereas an assemblage of weak connections and distant ties permits greater levels of autonomy and indeterminacy among separate entities. The greater potential to make a determination means to be in a position to "figure things out," while a state or condition of indetermination means to be constrained, restricted, or limited in methods to "figure things out" under complex or perplexing interpersonal circumstances.

One measure of mismeasure involves the imprecise calculation of the magnitude of estimated error. Few human observations qualify, after all, as being free of bias, noise, or static. Personal accounts of complex, confused, or conflicted episodes of social encounter may be rendered somewhat more inaccurate or imprecise insofar as prevailing environmental constraints remain poorly defined or badly unspecified in observational terms. Human judgments rendered under uncertain or unusual circumstances often contain an uneven mix of hit and miss in the alternative definitions of what qualifies as a matter of interpretive accuracy. The former consists of false positives (mistaken identification); the latter involves false negatives (missed detection). We may, in other words, make a false or mistaken identification of something (type one error) or fail to recognize something else (type two error). Thematically, one may "read too much" in, or leave "out too much" of, what occurs. It is difficult to minimize positive and negative mistakes simultaneously because deliberate effort at reducing the probability of one necessarily increases the likelihood of the other (Haselton and Buss 2000).

Interpretive misconstructions occur when complex personal decisions, through reflection and rumination, comprise imagined alternatives to what transpires in daily life. Retrospectively, real-world events can be compared, contrasted, and reformulated into an imaginary, mythical, or fictional form. Thematically, one may wonder what questionable events would, could, should, ought, or might have turned out differently if only the source in question could go back and relive personal decisions over complicated events that were unusual, less than optimum, or otherwise closed off other choices, options, or remedial actions (Landman and Manis 1992). In general, prior events are subject to counterfactual reconstruction with emphasis on the abstract features of the distant past and greater stress on far more specific details of recent events (Semin and Smith 1999).

Spontaneous counterfactual disclosures are more often generated after personal failure than after social success, after a negative outcome than a positive outcome, and after a missed opportunity than an actualized opportunity. While one cannot literally undo what has already been done, he or she can convert sharp or abrupt deviations from prevailing social expectations, rules, and regulations from exceptional antecedent conditions into a more ordinary, normative, or average sense of social consequence (Roese 1997). Hindsight bias exaggerates the imagined certainty that things had to turn out the way they did. Counterfactual slants reveal the tension between bias and benefit, as if another feasible outcome almost happened instead of what actually transpired. However, counterfactual examination of excluded social alternatives may intensify sensitive feelings of regret, guilt, and blame (Boninger, Gleicher, and Strathman 1994). These contradictory effects are beneficial (higher striving) and aversive (lower feeling) at the same time. Alternative versions of past events are, by definition, contrary to established fact.

Upward-directed counterfactuals pose an alternative standard as being better than actuality and imply ascendent aspirations (making things better), whereas downward-directed comparisons are construed as something worse than actuality and imply descendent strivings (making things worse). After social success, downward comparisons are reflected in greater enjoyment and positive moods; after social failure, upward comparisons are reflected in negative moods and higher determination to prepare better or improve next time (Sanna, Meier, and Wegner 2001). Moreover, downward social comparisons are often based on a given observer's vulnerability to another's negative outcomes. A study by Lockwood (2002) indicates that high levels of perceived vulnerability are likely to deflate self-evaluations, whereas low levels of perceived vulnerability are more likely to increase one's motivation to avoid the negative fate of someone else.

Decision avoidance arises from the partially unconscious tendency to deny a difficult current choice by postponing it or finding an easy way out. Unspoken reactions to troubling aspects of prior events may lead to choice deferral, status quo bias, omission, and inaction (Anderson 2003). Central themes include "I was not almost wrong but I was almost right" (Tetlock 1998); "I wish things had turned out differently but I cannot do anything about it now" (Latridou 2000); "If I had only done the right thing at the right time, things would not have turned out as badly as they did" (Thompson and Byme 2002). Counterfactual statements compare fulfilled actions to failures to act. Selective focus helps one to identify the causes and reasons for less-than-optimum outcomes; it promotes greater learning about mistakes; and it generates affective knowledge of regret, guilt, blame, and responsibility (Byrne and McEleney 2000).

The process of learning from the recognition of one's worst mistakes and major miscalculations entails greater reflexive scrutiny of what goes wrong as well as enhanced sensitivity to what goes right. By observing the short-term consequences and long-term effects of their concerted strategic strivings, determined social agents may adopt more favorable stances so that they can consider (or reconsider) how to strive to do things better the next time around. Small corrective measures, when enacted swiftly with little risk, lead to somewhat-improved conditions for the pursuit of higher-order achievements.

When calculative errors are based on multiple appraisals of social failures that register at low levels of personal aspiration, the comparative distinction between what qualifies as success or failure can be dismissed as being insignificant, irrelevant, or meaningless. In effect, it hardly matters how things turn out, one way or another, where one construes the stakes as being trivial or inconsequential. Generally, we would expect a set of small-scale performance errors to be more easily tolerated if successful outcomes matter little or not at all. Petty mistakes are easily tolerated as being mostly innocent or benign. After all, the novice is simply learning to play the game. Small-scale difficulties may go unnoticed or simply ignored. However, at moderate levels of personal aspiration or collective striving, the relative distinction between success or failure in complicated goal attainment acquires greater salience when being judged by a standard of relevance. Those at intermediate levels of achievement become far less forgiving of once-tolerated major unskilled errors. Finally, at the highest levels of personal aspiration or collective striving, the increasingly refined distinction between what qualifies as a gradation of success or failure now becomes critical up and down the scale of affordable measure. Hence, there is hardly any margin of tolerable error. In short, the pursuit of personal perfection entails resolute persistence in the face of ever smaller and smaller gradations of mistake, miscue, or miscalculation. At all times, tolerance of success commingles with intolerance of failure.

GOODNESS OF FIT

Principles of trial and error facilitate greater modes of incremental learning about the scaled gradations of stable and settled conditions when construed outcomes (payoffs) are favorable. Slowly repeated learning trials give rise to embedded critical tests that evolve into more refined modes of inquiry, along with greater individual sensitivity to what it takes to stabilize, neutralize, or diminish the cumulative margin of error. Not all personal decisions or social consequences are consistent with optimizing achievements. Individual learning approaches optimum conditions only if current responses to feedback are optimal, but direct access to such favorable levels of social alignment is strict and only infrequently rendered possible. Incomplete feedback means that social agents are not able to determine the probable consequences of whatever actions are not chosen or otherwise excluded from consideration.

Moreover, learning directly from current experience may not provide the supply of elaborated information required for accurate and effective mastery to take place. Also relevant is broad recognition that inattentive interactants will likely notice the observed impact of verbal relations but not the implicit, unspoken effects themselves. From the standpoint of utility, learning from direct experience is flawed because (1) some errors or mistakes in decision, evaluation, and judgment go unrecognized; (2) inflated confidence in treating a course of action is thought as being the best possible when, in fact, it is not; and (3) judgment provides no evidence to compare current outcomes with the effects of alternative options originally viewed and dismissed as being inferior (Gresham and Elliott 1989).

The lived circumstances of speaking subjects may be construed as being mutually accessible and commensurate or, conversely, incommensurate and inaccessible to one another. The process of commensuration entails the rapid transformation of disparate, divergent, and disjunctive features of personal assessment into a single common scale, metric, or standard of assigned appraisal. Espeland and Stevens (1998) stress that commensurate endeavors are fundamentally relational; involve transformation of imprecise qualities into somewhat more precise quantities; reduce and simplify disparate information (analogical ambiguity) into global (digital) units that can be more easily compared and ranked; provide public outlets for discarding information and reordering or rearranging what remains into new shape, substance, or form; and increase opportunity for radically changing the world by generating new conceptual and linguistic categories and then backing them with the totalizing weight of prevailing norms. On a smaller scale, a state of local incommensurability in personal ranking systems presumes partial exclusion of certain subject matters, or taboos, as those lacking in personal value or social relevance (Simmons 1994).

MAKING SENSE

Sustained public activities based on patterns of trial and error—the imprecise logic of certain intentional choices mixed with uncertain unintentional consequences or unwanted side effects—slowly acquire definition and direction via the acquisition of active and passive patterns of expressive initiative and interpretive response. A favorable mix of active and passive states of sustained interactive orientation facilitates gradual acquisition of necessary personal abilities and social skills to link abstracted, categorical notions with specific social circumstances. Multiple considerations of nodal points of convergence and divergence in perspective taking are at stake here. Closely interrelated are small-scale baseline distinctions between effective and faulty steps, moves, or alignments among speaking subjects. Heuristic conditions must take into account (1) what works, what is useful, and what makes things better and (2) what fails, what is not useful, and what lets things become worse.

Human encounters may be progressive or regressive in respect to current short-term effects or long-range outcomes. Progressive movement serves to enhance, enable, and add to the elaborated process, whereas regressive movement works to subvert, neutralize, and subtract from the larger equation. Progressive communication, by implication, is sensible, coherent, complicated, and generative of solid connections and enduring commitments. Regressive communication, in contrast, is reactive, restrictive, and resistant to progressive change. Regressive groups are often unable to address conflict, encourage dissent, or confront negative attitudes and destructive behavior that remain outside of conscious awareness of individual members (McClure 1994). Similarly, regressive communication in intimate relationships is repetitive, charged with negativity, and as a consequence leads to disjunctions and breaks in connection and commitment (Sheftel 2002).

Face-to-face interaction is labor intensive. Making sense of the complex conduct of other people requires a great deal of time, energy, and effort. The collective effort to make sense of things takes place at two levels: the strategic level (intentional, conscious, and purposeful) and the automatic level (unintended, unconscious, and mechanistic). The process entails determinated modes of meaning and significance, those explicit (observable) and implicit (inferential). The distinction between meaningful sense and meaningless nonsense matters greatly. Speaking subjects are constantly in a position, whether favorable or not, to absorb an array of particulars into a enduring sense of relational history.

Making sense of social interaction either occurs or does not, but the differences between success (fluent, clear, coherent) and failure (inarticulate, confused, incoherent) are a matter of degree (more-or-less rather than all-or-nothing). There is constant interplay between digital and analogical modes of meaning production and meaning reception. Three basic issues surface: whether people are capable and willing to make sense; what type of significance is established; and how various personal accounts either evolve or remain much the same in daily life. To interact simply means to be there when something happens (activity); to communicate means to discover something that matters (achievement). In other words, the larger process gives rise to the possibility, but not the necessity, of finding something that has any distinctive communicative value (relevance). In effect, each source of reference must entail multiple points of view to make any real connection at all (Mortensen 1972, 1991, 1998).

Social interaction can be expected to produce an array of shifting reference points, as well as a confluence of affordable positions and places (occupied or abandoned) from which to engage in multiple perspective taking and multiple perspective sharing. Speaking subjects make use of background knowledge, situational context, and memory of past interaction in shared attempts to accomplish reasoning tasks. Therefore, the operational definition of a given social situation is simply that of all individual definitions combined. What is produced is a meshed pattern of possible actions, an embodied conceptualization, and a reformulative and sequential transformation in systems of conceptualization that evolve as accessible patterns and configurations of possible actions (Glenberg 1997).

Direct encounters that promote close ties with other people are the most frequent sources of meaning in life (Debats 1999). The meaning of life may be envisioned as a quest, a journey, and an arduous process of constant probing, questioning, and testing generated by all the tensions, contradictions, triumphs, and tragedies of everyday life. The search for greater meaning qualifies, therefore, as a universal motive, as a means of belonging, as a pathway to worthwhile endeavor, and as a fundamental way to understand one's place in the world (King 2004). Sophisticated reflection about one's encounter with predicaments, quandaries, and contradictions is a condition of the good life (Cheung 1998). Likewise, one's sense of meaningful engagement is also a vital factor in preserving a coherent worldview and strong sense of well-being over the life span (Moomal 1999). In effect, a life worth living implies one's abiding commitment to achieve states of optimum fulfillment sustained by an inclusive sense of significance, worth, and valuation. In contrast, concern about the inability to find meaning in life may mask a broader clinical syndrome (depression, compulsion, addiction, or stress disorder) or may produce problems in living with obstacles, barriers, false starts, and resistance to worthwhile endeavors (Bergner 1998). Excluded or rejected individuals may enter into a defensive state that avoids all meaningful thought, feeling, or awareness and retreats instead into lethargy, listlessness, and slow reaction (Twenge, Catanese, and Baumeister 2003).

Making sense of productive social outcomes requires the capacity and willingness to put certain matters to the test of direct exposure to multiple perspectives and alternative standards of critical personal assessment. We know from studies of symbolic interaction that individuals are prone to infuse their public performances with dramatic gestures and narrative scenarios with a confirmatory aura. Insofar as the slant of personal presentation comes to be accepted as being sincere, genuine, and accepted, it thereby acquires tacit status as something that qualifies as being real. Therefore, the more skillful the appraised performance, the greater is the likelihood that some observers may be unwittingly placed in a position to be duped or misled. Simple words and gestures can provide layer after layer of symbolic cover for duplicitous tricks of the trade in which one uses "word magic" to construct a brief but convincing illusion of the apparent presence of something that is not really there. Manipulative performers strive to misrepresent, mishandle, and misdirect the wider search for common ground, turn everything upside down, and leave everything in a total muddle.

PROBLEMATIC CIRCUMSTANCE

A succession of high-order achievements facilitates personal appreciation of the distinctive communicative value of what takes place. Favorable conditions presumably have a broad range of secondary benefits. These include, among other things, greater personal sensitivity to the expenditure of scarce resources, willingness to contribute good ideas, faith in personal goals as being worth the cost, and an enhanced sense of satisfaction. In contrast, unfavorable conditions include any harsh, unsafe, degraded, unhealthy, or otherwise unsuitable environments for human language to multiply and flourish.

In effect, face-to-face interactions have the greatest value when the vocabulary of any one person can be readily translated into the vocabulary of any other person. Skilled speakers are best prepared to engage in repeated acts of mutual influence in which the ground rules of situated knowledge are clearly specified or well known in advance. Routine interactions take place insofar as the respective parties in question are able to rely on a stable tradition of prior interactions for tacit guidance and direction in deciding what to do in the present and in the future. However, under unusual or uncertain circumstances, there may be a greater measure of difficulty coping with issues of complexity, complication, and possible loss of personal control.

Studies of faulty decision making show that personal estimates of probability and forecasting can result in unacknowledged errors and misjudged mistakes in comprehension because spontaneous representations of uncertain conditions are somewhat vague and imprecise and because individual lexicons vary widely in ways likely to induce or evoke an illusion of validity (Karelitz and Budescu 2004). The tendency of speakers to overestimate what listeners know (to talk over their heads) or underestimate auditor knowledge (talk down to them) often produces common misjudgments that "work against effective and efficient communication" (Nickerson 1999, 737). Personal problems soon pile up, one after another, without an equal number of solutions in sight.

Problematic human encounters produce complicated, difficult, and perplexing questions. A problematic issue registers as an archaizing concern that does not lend itself to an apparent or self-evident means of articulation, course of action, or satisfactory mode of resolution. The declared value of a specific problematic issue corresponds broadly with the magnitude of what is still at issue or construed as being outstanding, unresolved, unsettled, or unknown. It is, in other words, a matter of a collective capacity to attend to the complete accumulation of unfinished business. In solving problems, we test our own ability and willingness to compare possibilities, to discriminate between good or bad decisions, to tolerate better or worse outcomes, and to improve our condition by making selective choices that enable us to feel better or avoid feeling worse (Overskeid 2000).

Problematic situations promote performance errors. Goal planning, after all, is a stressful, complicated, and labor-intensive activity. Personal inflexibility has a negative impact on the broad design of strategic planning as well as specific aspects of performance, such as guiding assumptions, selected procedures, attention to detail, recognition of relevant causal variables, timing, estimates of problems in execution, and forecasting of plausible consequences. Error rates increase when multiple goals are contradictory; when decisions are self-confirming, oversimplified, or premature; and when tactics are biased by futile searches of irrelevant information (Mumford, Schultz, and Van Doorn 2001). At times of great confusion or intense commotion, there is a tendency to repeat the same types of "interactive mistakes" without end. People become stuck in a litany of poor performances, with no way out or no better way to alter the faulty parameters of a failing system. Where there is little evidence of further learning, the probability of correcting chronic errors, mistakes, and omissions is low (Fritz et al. 2000).

The study of miscommunication and problematic talk holds great promise as a means to understand the resilient but fragile process. It is possible to establish what makes strategic human encounters so repeatedly and so deceptively prone to the regressive or subversive influence of inadvertent error, unwitting mistake, or deliberate distortion. Salient standards for evaluating the efficacy and resilience of strategic personal conduct may be rendered explicit rather than unspoken, tacit, or covert. Moreover, after being subject to further negotiation, performance standards may be deemed as those set far too high or way too low for specific purposes. Careful and sober reflection provides a powerful means, therefore, to determine what makes things "better" or "worse" in the muddled course of daily life.

2

Cognitive Appraisal

There can be no dialogue, no communication unless beliefs, values, commitments, and even emotions and passions are shared in common. . . . There is no communication, understanding, interpretation, or reading that is not also open to miscommunication, misunderstanding, misinterpretation, and misreading.

—Richard J. Bernstein, *The New Constellation*

If we fail to know or understand another person it is because the task is just too difficult, not because it was doomed to failure from the start through some kind of metaphysical necessity.

—D. W. Hamlyn, "Person-Perception and Our Understanding of Others"

Our characterizations of people's utterances and actions, like our perceptual statements, can always be defeated.

—H. J. Glock, "The Indispensability of Translation in Quine and Davidson"

Much of communication occurs in situations where failure brings a high cost.

—Michael Oliphant, "The Learning Barrier"

We have good reasons to believe that we know many things about how the world is and how it works. Without doubt we ignore more than we know. However, the question is to what extent we manage our ignorance.

—Anna Estany, "The Thesis of Theory-Laden Observation in the Light of Cognitive Psychology"

It is a sobering recognition. Simply because literate people interact with one another, it does not follow that they will be able or willing to make clear, cogent, and coherent sense out of what transpires between them. There is what Fischer (1988) calls "an overwhelming amount of evidence" that communication between individuals, even under ideal circumstances—with identical levels of information and interpretive-processing capacity, unlimited time, sufficient resources, mutual goals, and lack of outside interference—will "almost unavoidably, within some reasonable time span, eventuate in misunderstandings, misinterpretations, different conclusions, different cognitive adaptations and variations, and disparity of perception in certain domains" (194). Stated bluntly, "the more complex the system, the more uncertain of its state an observer necessarily must be" (Platt 1989, 655). Similarly, Wilden (1980) acknowledges that "no communication can be properly defined or examined at the level at which it occurs" (11). Hence, there is simply "no assurance that communication will be certain or even relatively trouble free" (Fish 1989, 42).

At issue is whatever can be achieved by one source among many in a mutually sustained environment. The critical task of each entity is to take into account scarcely noticeable changes in complex relations with other entities. For each expressed act, there is some opportunity for multiple forms of interpretive response. As a corollary, each source constructs a frame of reference from a unique position and place within the larger social system. What is subject to question is a distinctive style of personal presentation that cannot be duplicated or replicated by any other source. In effect, separate yet related entities construct unique versions of what transpires between them. The personal conduct of each source is constrained by the expressive freedom and interpretative slant of every other source. Therefore, in collaborative matters, any notion or presumption of "complete" or "total" communication is precluded as a matter of principle.

GAIN AND LOSS

Living, interactive systems do not produce rigid structures. Dynamically stable processes are subject to a wide range of destabilizing or disintegrative social influences. Any sudden, novel, unfamiliar, or unpredictable turn of human events can make it more difficult for individuals to comprehend the underlying meaning of what transpires. Ordinary language qualifies as being indecisive or indeterminant when messages are construed as being ambiguous and obscure and when the stream of words and gestures can be interpreted in any number of ways with no basis for deciding between them. Mutual comprehension of complicated speech acts can be perplexing when there is heavy reliance on irony and deceit and when episodic or chronic failures to communicate are more difficult to handle than what transpires in successful situations. Interpretive clashes and linguistic entanglements often proliferate when speaking subjects not only sense that others are misconstruing their speech acts but do not know how to repair failed signals associated with marked discrepancies in message production and message reception. What qualifies as a given "loss" or "gain" (small scale) ostensibly corresponds with matters of "success" and "failure" (large scale).

Specific goal-directed failures are conspicuous across the life course and across diverse cultural settings (Poon and Lau 1999). One develops sensitivity to comparative matters of "success" and "failure" in complex goal attainment early in life as a consequence of failed efforts at initiating interaction, exposure to ambiguous provocation, and avoidance of potential trouble or harm from others (Erdley and Asher 1999). Moreover, failure to thrive is an early warning sign of severe risk with grave consequences for health, growth, and development (Black 1995). In daily life, children make global attributions of success and failure on the basis of others' intent, strategic knowledge, social expectations, and performance issues (Erdley and Asher 1999). It is important for them to distinguish their true beliefs from awareness of other people's false beliefs (Knoll and Charman 2000). Learning to explain misinterpretations of false beliefs can make it easier for young children to recognize ambiguous situations in which acts of miscommunication are likely to occur. However, when faulty communication takes place between children and adults in formal educational settings, the impact of being seriously misunderstood is more profound for the youngest speakers due to the disproportionate power of authority figures (Crago et al. 1997).

Strategic success for aspiring adult speakers is based on naive notions about "what behavior" in "given situations" will likely produce or reproduce the desired effects. Psychological forecasts based on diffuse sensations, feelings, thoughts, and moods vary widely in degree of accuracy and voracity over short time frames (Totterdell and Reynolds 1997). Because people are unable to recapture the tenor and tone of prior events perfectly, implicit notions of past and future are useful in determining whether routine predictions are accurate or influence the shape of current activities. Key issues are complicated by conflicting evidence that shows how failure prompts some individuals to give up and others to try even harder. Chronic attributions to low ability or low effort may give rise to hidden feelings of incompetence, shame, guilt, or anger. Negative mood changes are greater if chronic or protracted failures are more difficult to justify than if they are easy to justify. Similarly, anxiety buffers mitigate against negative thoughts after repeated collaborative failures. Uncertainty of outcome, prediction of failure, and lack of control intensify feelings of helplessness in respect to the anticipated consequences of important social events with strong aversive stimulation (Cramer and Nickels 1997).

Promotion of success requires prevention of failure. Distinctive goal-oriented strivings may produce the desire for success (need for achievement) or the desire to avoid failure (fear of failure). Persons high in success motivation are disposed toward the open possibility of generating positive, constructive, and progressive outcomes. Persons high in fear of failure focus on the possibility of incompetence and thereby use self-regulative devices to avoid negative outcomes (Elliot and Sheldon 1997). Repeated failure, in the absence of sustained success, is linked to diminished goal expectations, reduced confidence in one's ability to perform the necessary actions for a difficult task, and lower persistence or amount of effort expended in complex goal attainment (Spieker and Hinsz 2004). Moreover, a prolonged cycle of repeated failure followed by renewed effort may implicate a "false hope syndrome," characterized by unrealistic assumptions, aspirations, and expectations regarding the total magnitude of time, energy, and effort required to promote constructive change (Polivy and Herman 2002). In contrast, minimal discrepancy between prior success and current goals promotes personal belief in self-efficacy, commitment, and performance attainment (Bandura and Locke 2003; Locke and Latham 2002).

In tactical terms, there is a significant difference between playing to win and playing to prevent loss. Competence-based aspirations orient engaged individuals toward greater success. Conversely, performance-avoidance goals activate fear of social failure, rejection, or exclusion; apprehension about poor performance; or deep-seated concern about one's inherent value or worth as a relational partner (Elliot 1999). Individuals who chronically question their natural talent or innate ability may appear, paradoxically, to undermine their own performance standards. Sometimes distressing implications of failure far outweigh the need or desire for success. Generalized goal avoidance is linked to deleterious consequences in competence-based measures of performance, persistence, intrinsic motivation, task involvement, well-being, and life satisfaction (Elliot and Sheldon 1997, 1998). Performance failure may lead to feelings of incompetence, powerlessness, lowered self-esteem, and lack of enthusiasm for the task at hand (Deppe and Harackiewicz 1996).

Persons who rely on performance-avoidance goals are prone to indulge in self-handicapping maneuvers that involve the intentional withdrawal of effort along with low persistence following failure (Grant and Dweck 2003; Wolters 2004). The purpose of self-handicapping is to create fabricated impediments to success so that one may excuse or rationalize poor performance for reasons other than lack of ability or competence (Urdan 2004). Persons may seek psychic protection in advance of demanding tasks that limit accountability for failure and inflate responsibility for success. The tendency to ruminate over negatively anticipated outcomes is often related to denial, disengagement, and poor adjustment (Zuckerman, Kieffer, and Knee 1998). Chronic self-handicapping qualifies as habitual self-defeating behavior. However, there is a certain payoff when anticipated failure is construed as being due solely to insufficient effort, which is somehow less threatening because self-handicapped persons usually believe they will do better the next time around by simply investing greater effort (Martin et al. 2003).

Avoidance goals have negative but indirect effects on the flexibility and flow of ordinary conversation. General conversational failures promote a diffuse, often nagging sense that something has gone wrong, whereas specific pragmatic failures implicate the inability or the unwillingness of someone to understand what someone else meant by what was stated in explicit terms. Nondeliberate disparities and discrepancies in interpretive slant may diminish the clarity of expression: misrepresentation, mishearing, misconstrual, misquote, or talk at cross-purposes. Likewise, when it seems that "nothing is wrong" on the surface of mundain conversation, there still may be a great deal of misinterpretation or miscommunication that registers at deeper levels of defensive personal reaction.

At issue is the willingness of speakers and listeners who routinely misread one another to detect and repair signs of verbal or nonverbal discord. Where there is no evidence that miscomprehension or misunderstanding has occurred, as when a listener fails to hear something clearly stated, such small-scale failures may go unnoticed. On a larger scale, complex linguistic failures among adult speakers are linked to tactical exploitation, deceit, unexpressive reactions, and persistent inability to grasp literal or intended meanings (Airenti, Bara, and Colombetti 1993). Unless linguistic ambiguities work to disrupt the flow or pace of conversation, personal difficulties in complex discourse comprehension may go unnoticed or may be ignored and may thereby generate greater levels of mutual misunderstanding than what one actually discovers. To make confused matters worse, an uneven balance of badly mismatched or conflicting interpretations may be rationalized, denied, or disguised to preserve the appearance of mutual understanding.

When engaged in routine encounters, human beings reveal rather mundane predictive capacities. Literate people are good at predicting how others will react in general terms or what significant others will say or do under anticipated conditions that cannot be forecast or planned in advance. Far more difficult to handle are the largely unanticipated considerations that preclude trade-off and resist shared effort to find the values of two different things that appear to be more comparable. Although most people can describe what transpires on the surface of conversation, some are unaware of their actual experiences and rely on concatenated, shorthand, and brief summaries, all of which can produce major discrepancies between what transpires and what is desribed as transpiring. Therefore, small-scale social failures in planning and execution often invite, even demand, use of glossary-type descriptions and crude explanations rendered after the fact before others. Retrospective accounts of "what went wrong" or "turned out bad" may be designed as rationalization or excuse in attempted legitimation and biased justification in anticipation of reproach from others.

Personal predictions occur in an often uncertain and precarious world. People's distant memories of responses to serious social failure often trigger strong emotions, affect sense making, and distort reason (Cannon 1999). Chronic failures, moreover, are most resistant to outside therapeutic intervention (Kincanon and Powel 1995). Therapeutic failure occurs when there is no change in working through pressing relational concerns (Bell 1999). Personal explanations for persistent social failures in matters of therapeutic intervention include faulty technique; inappropriate detachment; unrecognized signs of depression; worsening difficulties; intense negativity; and clients feeling criticized, attacked, abandoned, neglected, dismissed, or misunderstood (Macaskill and Macaskill 1999). Also relevant are sources of weakness and vulnerability among troubled family members that resist coherent identification and then become toxic to outside empathic intervention. Protracted failures associated with the obligations, burdens, and demands of caregiving are pervasive in society (Lefley 1997).

COPING WITH STRESS

There is great potential for mistake, miscue, and miscalculation in critical appraisals to occur along both sides of the immense emotional spectrum. Here the slant of affect-laden outlook is decisive. In general terms, what registers as being positive and optimistic is taken as a measure of pleasure, whereas what registers as being negative and pessimistic is construed as a sense of displeasure. Complex acts of mutual negotiation, governed by the imprecise logic of trial and error, are subject to all countervailing forces—progressive refinement (forward) and regressive alteration (backward). Moreover, baseline levels of tension, friction, and strain are subject to rapid change, even over the course of brief episodes of troublesome deliberation. At issue are complex links between cognitive appraisals and disquieting personal orientations that emerge under stress or duress. Stress-related appraisals relate with a sense of optimism, coping, and adjustment in a formula in which optimism adds validity in predicting adjustment beyond that deriving from appraisals and coping skills alone (Chang and Strunk 1999). Unrelieved stress reportedly prolongs discomfort and acute distress. Maladjustment has been linked with diminished sense of resilience, less clarity in self-concept (Treadgold 1999), resource loss (Wells and Papageorgiou 1998), and stress-related pathology (Amirkhan 1998).

Strategic personal encounters interact with aggregate life events to shape the strength of association of chronic stress to one's vulnerability to depression and resource depletion (Ingram and Hamilton 1999). Perceived stress apparently stems from depressive symptoms and lower life satisfaction (Chang 1998). Drawing on transactional linkages, Wells, Hobfoll, and Lavin (1999) associate anxious activity with cognitive appraisals rendered under great duress and conclude that worries are activated in anticipation of external threat; a complex variety of negative scenarios may be generated in short time frames; chronic worry and apprehension are accompanied by an implicit sense of uncontrollability; negative beliefs proliferate; and overt responses to the initiatives of others exacerbate intrusive thinking.

Social anxiety disorders promote escape behavior that in turn impairs planning, work, family relations, and quality of life (Fong and Silien 1999). The transmission of anxiety is pervasive in society (Thompson and Bolger 1999). In this equation, anxiety emerges as undue sensitivity to threat, risk, danger, worry, and fear (Hunt 1999). The magnitude, scope, and salience of distress are associated with repeated or prolonged exposure to uncontrollable events with adverse consequences (Larsen and Gillman 1999). Stressed, anxious, or distressed individuals are often dissatisfied with their social relationships. They are vulnerable on a number of fronts, including diminished activity; lack of involvement; few, if any, close relationships; inflated estimates of hostile reactions from others; less support from friends; negative, self-critical personalities; and major deficits in social skill. Moreover, they are susceptible to rejection from others, loneliness, and fear of intimacy. Because complex emotional states are manifestations of preconscious cognition, it is not always easy to determine why others are hurt, angry, or sad.

Personal negativity implicates a lingering sense of unhappiness, low self-esteem, dissatisfaction, and sensitivity toward the adverse reactions of others. Personal negativity correlates with maladaptive responses, negative reactions from others, low reputation, and poor self-image (Furr and Funder 1998). A pessimistic attribution style has been linked with negative affect, depressed mood, and emotional distress (Luten, Ralph, and Mineka 1997). The general tendency to explain bad events with stable and global causes has been shown to be related to reports of hassles that in turn appear related to stress and poor health status (Dykema, Bergbower, and Peterson 1995). Finally, the troublesome effects of self-focused rumination over troublesome feelings are predictive of a negative bias in the personal interpretation of hypothetical events, pessimism about positive future events, and ineffective solutions to interpersonal problems (Lyubomirsky and Nolen-Hoeksema 1995).

SUPPORT FROM OTHERS

Critical appraisals acquire definition as synthesizing structures that integrate emergent cognition (evaluations, expectations, and beliefs) and motivation (needs, desires, intentions, strategies, and goals) with affect (physiological arousal) and action (expressive motor responses). The potential for cognitive reappraisal is contingent on the magnitude of risk (threat or sanction) in relation to the magnitude of support (comfort or reassurance) available. The spectrum of possibilities is anchored at one end by a condition of unconditional or unqualified support and at the other by a condition of total discredit or complete disregard. The opposite of support (credit) is subversion (discredit). Hence, when supportive communication is present, it becomes a powerful force to sustain and preserve an existing state of affairs—conversely, when inadequate and defective, it undermines and subverts an existing state.

Supportive conditions include acquired benefits derived from secure connections, stable member satisfaction, consistent level of daily success, and tolerance of disruptive difficulties when close connections are lacking, ambiguous, or insecure. Attachment security is closely linked to greater tolerance of periods of separation and avoidance (Weaver and de Waal 2002). Secure human attachments promote positive working models, strong empathetic assertion and response, contributions to each member's sense of well-being, and inhibition of personal distress. In contrast, insecure, avoidant, or anxious attachments foster negative working models, weak empathetic reactions, a tendency to avoid closeness, and significant others being taken as unavailable, unresponsive, or uninterested (Collins and Feeney 2000). Unwelcome, unwarranted, and unwanted insecurities are associated with less generous working viewpoints and low ratings of social satisfaction (Murray, Holmes, and Griffin 1996).

Available social support comes and goes from family, peers, and communal ties, as does attachments to people, places, and things. Support, comfort, and care are related to one's willingness to provide aid to peers who are faced with major stressful conditions. Moreover, a measure of personal support provides warmth and comfort to compensate for deep-seated feelings of disappointment and distress (Rogers and Holmbeck 1997). Firm emotional support is a fundamental component of the acquisition and maintenance of close social and personal relationships. Men and women, despite distinctive stylistic differences, are in consensus concerning the strategies they regard as being most sensitive and effective (Kunkel and Burleson 1999). What matters is how well, or badly, chronic feelings of distressed or disturbed members are acknowledged and elaborated in the course of ordinary conversation.

A generous supply of social support knowledge apparently contributes to prosocial orientations, tolerance of mutual interdependence, and trust (Feeney and Collins 2001). Sophisticated comforting strategies link to greater involvement with distressed others and their difficulties, neutral forms of personal evaluation, awareness and sensitivity to stressful feelings, acceptance and validation of others' distress, and clear explanations for the urgency of another's condition (Burleson 1994). Supportive persons provide intangible gains—warmth, reassurance, help, assistance, and aid for troubled times. Resilient support entails effective use of positive emotions to bounce back from negative emotional experiences (Tugade and Fredrickson 2004).

There is an important connection between accessible levels of social support and matters of good health and physical well-being. Health and illness are a composite reflection of the way one lives his or her daily life. Global conceptions of social support help shape the personal sense of being worthy of help, care, and assistance from others. Support availability includes a general sense of care as well as specific orientations toward significant persons seen as caregivers. There is, in effect, great potential for diverse measures of social support to be given or taken away. Both effective and faulty efforts to minimize discomfort and distress have serious consequences for the maintenance of the social and personal relationships in which they take place.

STANDARDS OF ASSESSMENT

The pursuit of multiple strategic goals may give rise to serious dialectical tensions for which constraining influences and restraining boundaries are weighted against the magnitude of opportunity for productive and generative social encounters. By these standards, four distinct domains of evaluative and comparative critical assessment exist, wherein cognitive appraisals are presumed to be: positive in hedonic tone, giving rise to a state of mutual agreement; negative in hedonic tone, giving rise to a state of mutual disagreement; convergent in cognitive slant, giving rise to a state of mutual understanding; and divergent in cognitive slant, giving rise to a state of mutual misunderstanding.

The central issue is how engaged social agents construct complex pathways and diverse functions that work to either affirm or deny the definitional and directional implications that emerge and erode over time. The approach is to ask a large group of young adults to provide reconstructive accounts of common daily interactions that take place in their current social and personal relationships. Four hundred respondents who were enrolled in undergraduate communication classes at the University of Wisconsin, Madison, completed an "Interaction Profile." The instructions were as follows:

> Make a mental inventory of the people you encounter on a frequent basis. Now select the one person you would rank as having achieved the highest level of

personal agreement of anyone on the list. Second, select the one person you would rank as having achieved the strongest level of personal disagreement of anyone on the list. Third, select the one person you would rank as having achieved the highest level of personal understanding of anyone on the list. Fourth, select the one person you would rank as having achieved the strongest level of personal misunderstanding of anyone on the list. Notice that the same person may show up on one or more of the categories, i.e., a person who shared the highest level of agreement may be the same one you would rank as having established the strongest level of understanding as well. Provide a detailed account of the actual types of face-to-face interaction that have taken place in each of these different types of human interaction. Describe each category with as much detail as possible.

The respondents were to focus not so much on matters of physical appearance or personality traits but instead on the central matter of what had transpired during a short episode or a long sequence of direct and/or mediated forms of strategic human encounter. Participation was voluntary, with assurance that anonymity would be preserved by deleting any personal references. The participants signed release forms granting permission to include their personal accounts in published documents. The university-sponsored Human Subjects Committee offered steady guidance and firm direction to ensure the personal anonymity of those who participated in the study reported here.

The participants were encouraged to emphasize the larger process of what transpires in the course of daily life. They were given a sufficient period of time to define, describe, and explain what transpires in terms of intention, interpretation, strategy, tactic, and outcome. Ordinarily, it takes time for critical reflection about the immediate impact and larger significance of current events. Spontaneous behavior is prephenomenal only while it is taking place, whereas it becomes phenomenal only afterward, when it can be viewed retrospectively in a certain reflective light. A month later, the four hundred personal accounts were transcribed verbatim to form a computerized master text that facilitated the reconstruction of a minidictionary of the "just noticeable" things that individuals feel, think, and say and do in strategic efforts to achieve, or thwart, the pursuit of multiple and complex types of goal-directed aims. Computer software (Nudist) was installed to engage a series of search operations designed to take into fine-grained account the defining features and detailed attributes of personal relations for which a distinctive climate of agreement, disagreement, understanding, or misunderstanding prevails. Computerized word counts of relational states were calculated as follows: agreement (99,341), disagreement (94,953), understanding (83,703), and misunderstanding (86,823). Such a rich database makes it possible to trace the resources, abilities, and skills that enable social agents to achieve a working consensus and establish common ground.

Personal accounts can be compared on the basis of scale, relevance, coherence, and frequency of occurrence. The first task was to complete a list of critical terms that could be applied objectively and uniformly across the main conditions: agreement, disagreement, understanding, and misunderstanding. Through a multiple series of one-word computerized search operations, the exact number of accounts containing a given term (verb, noun) provided the basic unit of analysis. On the subject of personal criticism, for example, relevant references consisted of all sentences containing one or more of three terms: criticism, evaluation, and judgment. Likewise, on the topic of personal conflict, the relevant entries included all sentences containing at least one mention of three terms: debate, fight, and argue. Each search operation scanned the entire computerized transcript. However, a few entries were disqualified from final tabulation on the basis of excessive ambiguity or idiosyncratic usage. All cited material was taken verbatim except that some lengthy responses were shortened or condensed in presentation for the sake of brevity. Finally, distinctive patterns, trends, and scenarios were viewed in light of recent social science research findings that operate at the cutting edge of human knowledge.

Relevant entries designate an *S* for the one who wrote the account and an *O* for the other participant (or participants). A word of caution: The letter *S* is intended to signify one *source* but not a *self*, and *O* as an *other* person (or other persons). This nominal distinction avoids the pejorative implications of arcane academic jargon where *individual* and *self* are used interchangeably in a misleading implication that social interactants possess an internal center of self-representation (little man inside the head) that filters input and output so that human reality is mediated rather than directly apprehended. A false notion of individuals as owners of inner or interior compartments reifies the metaphor of mind as container of a self. The term *self* is misused in too many ways in far too many abstract and nebulous theories, which can only lead one into a trap of terminological confusion (Katzko 2003). Therefore, the notion of self as container is worthy of dismissal as sheer fiction (Dunne 1996).

PERSONAL CRITICISM

Some forms of cognitive appraisal are revealed in single acts or multiple episodes of direct personal criticism. Along one dimension of salient considerations is a broad spectrum of elaborated speech acts in which critical assessments and personal appraisals are directed at contested aspects of substantive issues. Along another dimension is the equally broad spectrum of speech acts in which critical assessments are directed at problematic aspects of interpretive performance. Criticized persons may be tempted to reach into their own bag of tricks: invalidate the critic, counterattack, deny, cover up, feign innocence, turn tables, change subject, play dumb, distract or deflect attention, play mind games, engage in selective justification driven by self-protective urges, or dismiss wholesale the entire bill of particulars as being simply absurd. Personal accusations often arise from a motivated threat or derogation of another person's sense of integrity, coherence, or worth.

A general stance of judgmental orientation is predictive of moral intolerance and diminishes the potential for the acquisition or maintenance of close personal ties with other people (Beck and Miller 2000). Critical persons often adapt a negative style that appears to others to be disagreeable, introverted, controlling, and with elevated vulnerability to depression and loneliness (Besser, Flett, and Davis 2003). Moreover, perfectionistic criticism is often demanding, harsh, and narrowly concerned with performance aspirations at the expense of interest in, and sensitivity to, enduring emotional needs (Rice and Mirzadeh 2000). In addition, self-critical persons are vulnerable to feelings of inferiority, guilt, and diminished esteem as a result of a tendency to aspire to absolute standards of perfection (Besser, Flett, and Davis 2003).

Harsh criticism, however well intended, is risky, particularly when blame, fault finding, excuse making, and accusation emerge as central narrative themes. Critical persons are inclined to assign too much acclaim or credit when things go well and attribute too much blame or discredit when things go badly (Moon and Conlon 2002). Highly judgmental critics are prone to blame individuals who arouse strong negative emotion or confirm unfavorable expectations, thereby exaggerating others' volition or control over adverse outcomes (Alicke 2000). Judgmental bias produces small-scale communicative failures based not only on participants' differing assumptions, skills, and goals but also on listeners' false inferences and erroneous implications where none were intended or their failure to notice intended meanings (Slugoski and Wilson 1998). Protracted criticism and resentment increase when victims of unjust or unfair actions are construed as being culpable for misfortune, failure, loss, or hardship (Johnson, Rehan, and Mulford 2002; Mikula 2003). Persons who subject themselves to unrelenting criticism may strive to internalize the deleterious effects of blame and accusation, thereby intensifying feelings of loneliness, anxiety, or low self-esteem. Some forms of self-condemnation may arise from a strong need to prevent error, draw attention to failure, strengthen resolve, or provide reassurance (Gilbert et al. 2004).

Consequential aspects of cognitive appraisal crystallize around biased or selective ascriptions of severe personal criticism. Relational issues come into play in an opposing manner, as a function of whether the quality of interaction works to promote the shared pursuit of a working set of initial agreements and tentative understandings (sufficient to establish a sense of common ground), or else move in the opposite direction, where a climate of disagreement and misunderstanding prevails. By examining in the computer transcript each sentence with specific reference to acts of "criticism," "evaluation," or "judgment," one can trace complex alignments between the specific domain or slant of shared activity in question with its underlying relational implications. Under conditions of agreement/understanding (a/u), narrative themes clustered around three categories of critical assessment: taking things in stride, making use of nonjudgmental attitudes, and demonstrating enhanced capacity for constructive criticism. Under the conditions of disagreement/misunderstanding (d/m), narrative themes clustered around three categories of cognitive assessment: adapting hasty evaluations, rendering harsh judgments, and indulging in personal attacks.

Taking Things in Stride

In the a/u conditions, critical cognitive appraisals are largely undertaken in a constructive and generous spirit. Here the major themes invoke a host of favorable social conditions in which the respective parties possess the resources, ability, and skillful willingness necessary to maintain a fluid and flexible style of social interaction during extensive time frames. There is great pleasure in knowing that fulfilling personal encounters can be maintained without any unwelcome criticism, judgment, or evaluation.

S/O are never critical of one another.
S/O can express their strongest personal opinions without being too critical.
S/O know they will not ever judge each other for the things they say, think, and do.
S/O know that being right does not mean the other must be criticized as being wrong.

Participants revealed a great deal of confidence in their collective willingness to prohibit the emergence of negative evaluations all together or at least to deal with unsettling matters in an productive and efficacious manner. There was a considerable margin of tolerance for reciprocity and virtually no mention of anomalies or counterexamples. Furthermore, there was a significant number of repeated mentions of social support and positive slant, as well as a rich surplus of tender virtues: trust, care, acceptance, openness, disclosure, vulnerability, and mutual refusals to pass judgment. Participants expressed joy and delight in being able to sustain such remarkably fluid sequences of sustained social exchange. Those who talked freely without undo tension and worry avoided the many pitfalls associated with unspoken inferences and implications over incongruent, mismatched, or contentious struggle regarding issues of interpretation, meaning, and valuation.

Nonjudgmental Attitudes

S/O accept what one another may have to say without passing any un-needed or unwelcome judgment.

S/O do not challenge each other to make points; they agree to disagree gently, without judgment.

S/O are not critical of each other; they are never worried about being judged harshly by the other.

S/O restrain from creating snap judgments of contested actions but still supply useful and noncritical advice.

S/O do not pass judgment on each other—most paths walked have been seen or pardoned before.

S/O do not judge or assume the worst until the other party has a chance to explain.

S/O are never judgmental or rude—they can talk about anything.

S/O's conversations are approached with open minds, free of judgment.

S/O say what is wrong, and the other listens without passing judgment.

S/O can tell each other anything and know that the other will never judge.

S/O can talk about anything and never judge one another for any reason.

Interactants who invoke or convey nonjudgmental attitudes share similar basic interactive qualities of those who place greatest emphasis on the mutual ability and the individual willingness to take things in stride. Shared features include the prohibition of urges to pass premature judgment; a strong sense of reciprocity; a distinctive positive slant; fluid and flexible sequences of social exchange; abundant supply of social support; and tender virtues—gentle responses, consideration, open-mindedness, care, comfort, concern, respect, honesty, and freedom to deal with sensitive issues in a congenial manner. There are, however, distinctive features of emphasis: absence of put-downs, heavy score keeping, or the desire to one-up or challenge the veracity of an-other's claims; receptivity to suggestion, advice, and counsel; strong sense of validation, use of repair mechanisms, willingness to give another the benefit of the doubt, and a refusal to hold grudges without end. These conditions en-able, rather than disable, mutual effort to integrate low or moderate levels of cognitive appraisal into the larger flow of emotional experience.

Constructive Criticism

S/O find that praise and criticism can be given freely; they try to refrain from judging.

S/O can talk and listen with open minds, add support, and offer construc-tive criticism.

S/O offer constructive criticism, but no personal feelings are ever hurt.

S/O offer criticism without ever feeling the need to change the other.

S/O know constructive criticism is welcome—they never judge or condemn.

S/O trust each other, and they do not take personal criticism personally.

S/O do not hesitate to speak openly—criticism is not taken in a bad way.

S/O are open to constructive criticisms, which they both volunteer a lot.

S/O never feel judged or criticized; they both know that constructive criticism is only meant to better the personal welfare of one another.

S/O respect each other's suggestions, opinions, and criticisms as being constructive and fair-minded.

S/O can engage in a great deal of constructive criticism without ever making each other feel inferior.

Individuals who are most tolerant of constructive criticism share similar interactive features of those who place greater emphasis on the ability to take things in stride and avoid the urge to impose judgmental attitudes on contested issues. However, there is a sharper edge and somewhat more confrontative style at stake. Participants are more willing to engage in critical appraisals and actively seek out and welcome the suggestions, advice, and judgments of the other parties. Critical considerations revolve around shared tolerance and mutual appreciation of corrective activity without taking such efforts personally, negatively, or defensively. Personal styles can be straightforward, even blunt, in dealing with constructive criticism without sensitive feelings getting hurt or egos getting bruised. Alternative views can be approached, discussed, evaluated, and integrated into the larger flow of daily experience. There is emphasis on the ability to take critical comments in the right way as mechanisms of problem solving and conflict resolution without indulging in condemnation or personal attack. Because the truth can hurt, S/O deem it important to find constructive ways to use criticism as a means to make things better without risk of making them worse.

A climate of strong disagreement and mutual misunderstanding produces a divisive social climate. Instead of personal evaluations being construed in a measured and deliberate way, they are often taken in a hasty and thoughtless manner. Instead of personal judgments being taken in an understated way, they are viewed as being harsh and unduly severe. Finally, instead of personal criticisms being handled in enabling and promoting more constructive response, they are treated as being destructive and disabling for one person or another.

Hasty Evaluation

S/O are always quick to criticize but never quick to praise.

S/O's interactions are about as deep as a shot glass; S thinks O is quick to judge.

S/O are too quick to judge the situation, sometimes without even thinking about it.

S/O disagree over the hasty evaluations they make of one another on a daily basis.

S/O are given to quick and premature judgments while jumping to the worst of conclusions.

The defining features of hasty social evaluations are important, as much for what is sorely lacking as for what is conspicuously present. There are literally no references to constructive matters being played out in fluid and flexible styles of social interaction with strong positive slant, social support, tender virtues, and routine use of repair mechanisms. There is, however, an atmosphere of bickering, quibbling, and complaint. Participants are seen as being impatient and quick to criticize for not measuring up to someone else's expectations or demanding standards. Tension, worry, and stress are closely linked with defensiveness, jumping to false conclusions, and premature judgments. There is frequent mention of power struggles, competition for attention, vulnerability over hurtful mistakes, and generalized willingness to write people off or put them down. Critical evaluations are imposed on unwelcome subjects who actively resent or passively resist the underlying flow of disturbing or discredited implications. Finally, many rivals who maintain a begrudging or contentious spirit cannot find a way to repair the damage or forgive and forget the endless stream of slights and noxious pinpricks.

Harsh Judgments

S/O are constantly criticizing each other.

S/O jump at each other for little things—this only makes matters worse.

S/O censor what they say to avoid being judged by one another.

S/O make harsh judgments about what they mean by every move and word.

S/O cannot express themselves freely, because what they say might be judged harshly.

S/O are critical and invalidate everything the other says or does.

S/O make critical comments, judgments, and change topics on whim.

Participants who indulge in harsh judgments lack many of the same constructive qualities found wanting among those who engage in hasty evaluations. There are no references to taking things in stride or expressed confidence in the mutual ability to deal with contested issues. Nor is there a positive slant, perceived support, or effort to establish major repair mechanisms in a forgiving manner. Many interact in disjointed and incoherent sequences of misconstrued exchange that consign them to positions that are out of synch and poorly aligned. If patience is a virtue, it is in short supply. Intolerance abounds in slights and indignities that pile up in nasty clusters of emotional baggage that, more often than not, are left unresolved from one social setting to another. These are the same linguistic conditions that are predictive of a flight from intimacy to even greater risks of relational deterioration.

Personal Attacks

S/O interrupt, criticize, and invalidate what one another has to say.

S/O contradict and criticize constantly—they blow things out of proportion.

S/O criticize almost everything, and this makes S feel bad.

S/O criticize, downgrade, and make fun of each other's ideas.

S/O express malice through criticism and judgmental attitudes.

S/O know O will personally criticize and humiliate S in front of others.

S/O find that criticism is blown out of proportion as a personal attack.

S/O disagree, argue, judge, defend, accuse, and have heated arguments.

Sometimes personal attacks emerge from failed efforts to curtail the spread of hasty evaluation and harsh judgment. Participants whine and complain about disruptive tactics, the severity of negative slant, or unwillingness to take the other party seriously. Opposing and polarized viewpoints are subject to discredit and devaluation. When individuals can no longer separate the person from the problem, the style of interaction is likely to shift from a cooperative enterprise to an adversarial relationship. Personal attacks differ from hasty evaluation and harsh judgment in important ways. It is one thing to protest and undermine a particular viewpoint, belief, or attitude. It is quite another to subvert the process and degrade or invalidate the opposition along the way. Damaging effects from aggressive and unrelenting attacks on character and personality are attributable to a total sense of alienation or estrangement. Some malcontents do not stop at attacking objectionable aspects of other people but indulge in verbal assaults on the integrity of those who are under sharp scrutiny. Extremists agitate for permanent criticism (Feldman 1999). Dehumanizing moral condemnation may be so savage and brutal as to leave nothing out.

3

Value Orientation

To breathe is to judge.

—Albert Camus, *The Rebel*

One forgets that judgment takes place every moment, because existence judges you every moment you live, inasmuch as to live is to judge oneself, to be open.

—Søren Kierkegaard, *Works of Love*

It is difficult for social inquiry to keep cultural meanings and moral values at arm's length when they are the very stuff of human life (including the lives of social scientists).

—Frank C. Richardson, Anthony Rogers, and Jennifer McCarroll, "Toward a Dialogical Self"

For humans, values are a central part of reality . . . Although humans do seek truth for the sake of truth, they above all seek it as a means to improve their lot in life. Values have two interrelated spheres: the relations of humans to each other, and their relations to the universe.

—Ira Gollobin, "Dialects and Wisdom"

The study of human values has been a source of acute embarrassment to social scientists and a vexing problem to philosophers alike. In the traditional view, it was considered important to dichotomize the distinction between fact (description) and value (evaluation). If only people could be taught to express themselves in clear, descriptive terms, the risk of greater misunderstanding could well be diminished as a consequence. After all, it was thought, the willingness to confine oneself to matters of clear definition and transparent description would surely keep one out of serious linguistic trouble because simple factual statements, in contrast to value-laden claims, can specify their intended objects of reference (in the "real" world), which in turn can be further quantified, classified, and verified by an impartial observer or third party. Overlooked was the possibility that speaking subjects can and do make good and bad use of fluid acts and integrated sequences of words and gestures that are "factual" and "metaphoric" at the same time. Hence, appeals to a singular standard of procedures to sort out the "value-laden" attributes from the "facticity" of observation would, by definition, fail (Tang 1999). Admittedly, there would be nothing to fight about or fuss over if discrete speech acts could be narrowed to specific objects of relevance or reference that anyone could verify one way or another. What is at stake is the ability to read between the lines and take such tacit factors of sense-making efforts into full account. To do anything less is to miss the point.

THE FACT–VALUE DISTINCTION

Social encounters based on strict adherence to simple statements of fact would in principle minimize or eliminate protracted communicative difficulties, whereas messy valuations and fuzzy notions could only be expected to provoke or exasperate them. As a consequence, well-reasoned appeal to the facts (and nothing but the facts) could be elevated to the superior status of an objective domain with matters of social value being relegated to an inferior sphere of a murky subjective caldron. If the outside world is treated as an objective material environment while the inner realm of human experience is consigned to a vague subjective status, then speaking subjects are faced with a tough conundrum that creates more difficulties than it solves. For if my insides invoke only subjective modes of physical activation (sensation) while my outsides are construed as being objective (perception) and verifiable (conception) by other people, a new dualism is introduced that smuggles an implicit sense of valuation in the back door.

Lost in the shuffle is the humble acknowledgment that the nominal distinctions between outer and objective or inner and subjective domains of human experience are a rather arbitrary, fabricated, and artificial means of social construction. Such perverse dualisms are misguided because they are based on false, contradictory, and reductive metacognitive premises. Moreover, the superior–inferior distinction does not need to be cast in stark dualistic terms. What matters is the broad type of interpretation or perspective at issue. A subjective viewpoint emphasizes what it feels like to observe someone or something from an immediate first-person position in a dynamic social setting, whereas an objective viewpoint entails a comparison of alternative viewpoints about someone else or something else. Competition among participants regarding alternative viewpoints and simultaneous possibilities arises only when, as Evnine (2001) states, "one of them makes a claim to offer a complete picture of reality" (170). In complex matters of contrasting or clashing social viewpoints, signs of strategic ambiguity and oppositional miscommunication emerge as a collaborative struggle to reconcile each individual viewpoint with the total weight of all the collective viewpoints at work.

Human beings are biologically designed to be integrated, holistic, and synthetic organisms. Therefore, it is a mistake to start carving up or segmenting our shaky conceptions of what it means to be a human being. In the absence of direct social verification, one's fleeting thoughts and idle ruminations remain transitory, random, and ephemeral. However, once acknowledged by others as part of the larger reality, an array of diverse thoughts, feelings, and valuations may acquire the status of objective reality. In this spirit, Hardin and Higgins (1996) describe a condition of strong objectivity not as a pure, unsullied, impartial, or value-free domain of public inquiry but rather as a product of productive and generative enterprises that promote less-partial and less-distorted beliefs among kindred spirits.

Academic efforts to restrict scientific terminology to whittled-down matters of fact and facticity have all ended in bittersweet failure. In an important chapter dealing with the dynamic interplay of communication, rhetoric, and values, Ehninger and Hauser (1984) trace the broad outlines of impassioned academic effort to eliminate appeals to valuation and judgment from rational discourse. To be sure, salient human values may give rise to intangible valuations, whereas hard facts evoke more tangible associations. Although observed facts may be measured in standard units, core values permeate the social fabric, but without any uniform or standard means of sorting them out. No wonder the traditional notion of a detached, unbiased observer has taken such a heavy pounding in current academic literature. There is a growing recognition that norms, judgments, and values shape the aims and methods of social inquiry (Bradley and Schaefer 1998). There are no brute facts, because human observers must depend on the perspectives that are adopted by the observers themselves. In effect, there are, as Little (1993) notes, no perspective-independent facts. Hence, the separation of fact and value is problematic (Pickering 1999).

The scientific study of human interaction, under the guise of a value-free neutrality, favors a passive, disengaged, anonymous voice, which is conducive to the production of an automaton-like image of people. When rarified academic discourse is leveled, diluted, or sanitized, social researchers are likely to adapt a dull, drowning, or dispassionate style, one that critics have characterized as a straightjacket that constitutes the intellectual equivalent of foot binding (Josselson and Lieblich 1996). To the contrary, the language of social science is deeply enmeshed with Euro-American values that champion rational, liberal, and individualistic ideas (Kane 1998). Comfortable dichotomies that once made simple sense (objectivity–subjectivity, fact–value) now break down under sharp scrutiny. To a startling degree, what are taken as presumed facts are our creations and imposed values that are pervasively woven into the fabric of the human world. According to *A Dictionary of the Social Sciences*, efforts to determine the validity of values—that is, their correctness or true relevance—cannot be assessed solely as the products of empirical observation (Becker 1964, 743–45).

The field of communication science provides the basic premises for social inquiry: facts are value laden; values express selective orientations toward shared experience that shape the unfolding sequence of explicit choices and implicit consequences; conventional language is not a transparent or neutral instrument but functions as a somewhat mechanical and automated medium of social control and interpersonal influence; language provides a unique slant on personal experience taken from a distinctive point of view; all forms of verbal interchange are laden with implicit valuations; and both facts and values must be articulated (reality tested) in contested public settings if they are to survive in credible form. In effect, human values are an important source of personal credibility and social currency. As Hart (1984) concludes, "It is impossible to discuss human communication without discussing matters of value" (751). People assign great importance to their cherished values and will vigorously defend them (Maio and Olson 1998).

A preliminary issue, one often overlooked, also deserves careful consideration. Try to imagine a hypothetical domain in which the members of a viable speech community did strive to reach the goal of concrete description without messy evaluation. Suppose that a uniform method could be devised whereby matters of fact could somehow be neatly separated from notions of fiction. As a consequence, human discourse would be sharply neutralized and weakened as a result. Moreover, complex aspects of spoken interaction would not require active participation or sustained inquiry but would merely serve as mechanisms of inert or passive modes of translation, as in the manner of a rote bean-counting exercise. By definition, much of the richness, subtlety, sloppiness, and imprecision of human discourse would have to be leveled, diluted, flattened, or ruled out. As a consequence, much of what makes us distinctively human would be sacrificed in the condensed process. Although such a reductive procedure might well minimize exposure to fuzzy or unspecified spheres of social reference, we would, as Burke (1957) claims, remain woefully ignorant of the very things we most need to know: how others feel about what we say and in turn how we respond to them; how much it matters whether we care or not what happens to ourselves and others in public life; and how important the need is to preserve an abiding sense of passion, drama, and mystery in human affairs.

Human values provide salient standards for inspection, scrutiny, and reappraisal of changing social circumstances among speaking subjects.

Critical values serve as guiding principles in daily life and provide tacit motivation for ascendent personal strivings and enduring collective aspirations. It is a mistake to perpetrate reductive notions of values as mere products of internalized subjectivity. To the contrary, the heavily evaluative dimensions of cognitive appraisal, evaluation, and prescription serve as implicit guides for strategic modes of social activity that limit which potential courses of action are even conceivable, possible, desirable, tolerable, forbidden, or unattainable. Human conceptions of people, places, and things surely qualify as value-realizing dimensions of public performance. Matters of harmony, integrity, and respect for the freedom of others (equality) are modified in light of pervasive personal concerns over issues of competition, order, and discipline (security) between competing groups and diverse cultural networks.

Because speaking subjects have vested interests in assessing gradations of personal responsibility for faulty social outcomes, there is a risk of bias in the coproduction of multiple judgments, mixed evaluations, and disturbing appraisals. Most common are inflated estimates of personal contributions to desirable social outcomes and diminished personal appreciation for the efforts of others toward those same ends. Here the process of truth telling presumes a sense of responsibility for what one displays before others with a minimum of omission (concealment), contradiction (falsification), or evasion (deception). No motivation for intentional fabrication is more compelling than the possibility of getting away with it. Psychological methods for judging the veracity of multiple value-laden claims vary widely as a result of the sheer complexity of behavior, knowledge, and implication that must be activated to render coherent explanations of truthfulness or establish violations that raise suspicion, doubt, or question.

GENDER CONSIDERATION

Critical valuations are subject to multiple forms of close public scrutiny. Questions of reproduction, sexuality, and gender figure heavily in the larger equation. The same principle applies for matters of personal, social, and cultural identification of salient gender-related differences and similarities. Genetically determined matters of age and sex qualify as the two main anatomical and physiological markers (morphs) of the human species. Cognitive appraisals based on comparative social valuations depend mightily on the shifting array of positions and places occupied by men and women in culturally stratified networks of affiliation. As always, what it means to be a woman or a man, a female or a male, cannot be neatly sequestered from the ultimate primordial consideration—namely, what it means to be a member of society who must navigate through a sustainable ecological landscape with other members who may or may not be able or willing to speak and listen in the same lexicon, idiom, or code.

From an ecological standpoint, privileged gender valuations arise from mating preferences, sexual activity, and sexual role identity (Schmitt 2002). Both men and women place a great deal of value on the direct recognition of certain functional and pragmatic virtues associated with stable traits of adaptability, sensitivity, concern, care, kindness, attractiveness, loyalty, generosity, humor, and practical intelligence (Okami and Shackelford 2001). Principles of mate selection and sexual attraction underscore a sweeping, pervasive, and robust scale of preferences in favor of valued modes of efficacious performance in applied matters that involve great practical intelligence, emotional stability, and a resolute spirit. People from diverse social, political, ethnic, and cultural settings show a great deal of agreement concerning the application of three broad dimensions of gender-related evaluations in social roles: valence (positive vs. negative), potency (strong vs. weak), and activity (lively vs. inactive; Kroska 2001).

Distinct gender differences are well documented in cognitive appraisals of sexuality, sex roles, and alternative sexual orientations. Nowhere is the importance of gender more decisive than in the domains of human sexuality and procreative potentiality. Autoerotic arousal resonates in fantasy; and visual erotica, often in a subtle but seductive manner. Men, on average, report more frequent private engagement in erotic and sexual fantasies than do women, who, on average, prefer to integrate themes of romance and affection into their vicarious sexual fantasies (Geer and Manguno-Mire 1996). Similarly, men report more permissive attitudes, opinions, and beliefs about the sensual value of extramarital intercourse, premarital intercourse, and masturbation than do women, but the magnitude of difference has narrowed in recent decades (Oliver and Hyde 1993).

In matters of sexual satisfaction, there are few differences in the verbal reports of women and men, but the main results are still inconclusive. In general, men and women value multiple aspirations toward sexual intimacy rather highly, but men construe sexual intimacy as a means to increase emotional intimacy, whereas women view emotional intimacy as a way to be sexually intimate (Greeff and Malherbe 2001). There are as many valid reasons for interest in sex as the number of women and men who produce verbal accounts: to produce deep, sensuous pleasure; to express a desire for closeness, intimacy, or warmth; to relieve sexual tension; to experience a sense of conquest; to reproduce; to find solace in the darkest hours of the night; to provide nurturance, care, and concern; to submit, yield, or surrender; to feel valued by a partner; to retreat from the cares of the day; to betray or avenge; to fulfill a secret longing; to feel dominated and possessed; or to share love, devotion, or passion.

Social motivations are complicated by contested, ambiguous, and confused sex roles; crude stereotypes; and lack of consensus about what it means to be masculine, feminine, or androgynous. Salient considerations include devalued symbolic associations with the gradual decline in marriage; sharp rise in the frequency of nonmarital cohabitation; and growing societal visibility of alternative sexual relations, alignments, and value orientations (Bozon 2001; Hoffman 2001). Nontraditional gender ideology provides strong evidence for a demise in the stability and the consistency of cultural category systems based on traditional sexual identification and a dramatic rise in feasible ways to calculate what matters decisively in societal discourse about the sensuous and erotic domains of intimate relations (Kroska 2001). It is reasonable to assume, from one culture to another, that matters of sex and age are weighted with diffuse cultural meaning, become salient over time, and will be taught often (Best 2001).

Women and men prove to be remarkably similar in the capacity and willingness to distort confusing, conflicting, or coercive types of messy social transactions in a self-compensatory and self-serving manner. Each gender prefers to emphasize its own erotic needs and often seeks to disguise or mask hurtful sexual feelings. Moreover, both genders seem equally adept at lateral or reciprocal acts of rationalization or denial of responsibility for adverse erotic outcomes. Biased modes of self-justification or self-exoneration are surely no respecter of gender. A study of close relationships by Kenny and Acitelli (2001) revealed little or no evidence for gender differences in comparative estimates of accuracy and bias. Men and women both appear to be adept at tactical engagement in the mindless and sometimes endless game of blame and one-sided accusation. As a case in point, troubled couples often produce strained, belabored, and dramatic descriptions of the other's behavior as being inexplicable, incomprehensible, or illogical (Schutz 1999).

We know that gender consideration makes a critical difference in the social construction of miscommunication and problematic talk. Contentious issues pivot on disparate and divergent accounts of scaled matters of privilege, domination, advantage, and discrimination that can be pitted against factors of subordination, disadvantage, and discredited social status. People often construe credible and compelling presumptions of collective bias as unacceptable or intolerable departures from an impartial model of egalitarian relations. Conversely, for every public clamor over gender-based bias, there is an added measure of civil opportunity for dismissive sets of counterclaims to follow (no "sexism" here). Fortunately, concerted public deliberation about gender based-claims of bigotry, prejudice, or discrimination can become a powerful catalyst for reparative, restorative, or progressive social change (Cameron 2001).

Certain gender-related issues reflect the widespread presumption that women prefer social valuations involving reasoning about matters of care and concern with a focus on themes of need and sacrifice, whereas men prefer social valuations involving reasoning about matters of justice with a focus on themes of fairness, equity, and rights. Key differences in moral reasoning and aesthetic judgment arise from contrasting and divergent variations in current life situations that are linked to stable gender traits. There is some evidence that women prefer to invest in close, often dyadic social bonds, whereas men prefer to invest more heavily in larger group affiliations (Gabriel and Gardner 1999).

Sociologists have provided dense documentation for several sweeping cultural considerations. In postmodern society, males occupy more advantaged social positions and obtain, on balance, better institutional outcomes than do females. On a larger scale, distinctive gender differences occur across all literate societies; they reflect the daily interplay of varied interpretive practices, rituals, and routines at work across conjugal contexts. There is a leading tendency to view males as being somewhat egocentric, focused, assertive, controlling, status conscious, and aggressive, whereas females are somewhat framed in terms of affiliation based on measures of striving, caring, nurturing, and attentiveness to others, as well as empathy, sympathy, and sensitive response to core relational considerations (Gove and Malcom 1997). In a study of the gender-interaction system, Ridgeway and Smith-Lovin (1999) raise important questions concerning how encounters between males and females mold personal experiences and narrative accounts that confirm and verify—or else serve to neutralize, subvert, or undermine—the credibility or currency of unstated assumptions, expectations, opinions, attitudes, or beliefs: persons regard gender differences as being commonplace, typical, and pervasive; studies of persons with equal power and status reveal fewer gender differences in conjoint behavior; and gender negotiation occurs in dynamic contexts.

Heated competition for preferred access to desired mates is predictably intense among adult males, who, due to evolutionary and genetic modification, appear on average to be large, strong, forceful, coercive, and aggressive compared to adult women. In power struggles, verbal aggression is more common among males than females (Halpern 2000). Biased social ranking systems shape the groundwork of contentious sexual relations and intimate alignments (and misalignments) between men and women (Eagly and Wood 1999). Women are annoyed by aggressive or relational threats, while men are sensitive to annoyances from issues of freedom and autonomy (Ter Laak, Olthof, and Aleva 2003). The feminist movement has documented the regressive effects associated with biased perpetuation of various limitations, constraints, and barriers produced by the uneven treatment of men and women in society. Oppression of women by men justifies paradigmatic concern with the material struggle of women to acquire the means to achieve greater autonomy and control in their daily lives (Ahmed 1996). Gender inequities vary according to issues of race, ethnicity, and social class. Large-scale production of cultural inequities exacerbates perpetuated unfairness in gender-related hierarchies when factors in age and wealth are factored into the larger equation (Cotter, Hermsen, and Vanneman 1999).

Congruent value systems are associated with strategic indicators of personal adjustment and shared speech accommodation. Incongruent value profiles, in contrast, are far more difficult to reconcile, owing in part to the broad tendency for sexually motivated social interactants to interpret their own erotic behavior in terms of competence (success or failure) but to interpret others' behavior in terms of morality (good or bad) (Skaldeman and Montgomery 1999). Compatible personal relationships are likely to promote greater latitudes of agreement and understanding, whereas incompatible personal relationships are likely to produce greater latitudes of disagreement and misunderstanding in daily life:

Agreement. S/O are a romantic couple who agree on social issues; they resolve disagreement quickly by compromising; sometimes S needs coaxing to open up, and O will persist until she does; they respect each other, feel comfortable sharing opinions, ask a lot of questions, and share the same values—if they fail, there is a cushion; if they succeed, they give each other support and move on.

Agreement. S/O have engaging conversations that are full with no uncomfortable silence—they support each other's life, share mutual respect, and agree about all facets of life; they think alike about most issues, interests, and values; they rarely have contrary views; they count on each other to listen and sometimes feel a psychic connection.

Agreement. S/O enjoy each other's company; they are comfortable because they agree about core beliefs and values; when they do not agree, they try to respect the other's view; they value happiness over money because if they are always working, there's no time to play; it is not that they agree about everything, but they agree about most fundamental issues of life.

Disagreement. S/O see each other for all the wrong reasons; they fight because they cannot agree on anything; biggest disagreements involve clashing values; S was raised with religious beliefs that men and women do not live together before marriage, but O simply refuses to believe S, who complains that O treats her like a little girl (she is nineteen; he is twenty-four) and O acts so macho and stupid; she also complains that he likes her for the wrong reasons and does not really know her at all; so, she becomes fed up with men like O, who knows only the "little girl" he wants a woman to be; he does not treat her with the respect she thinks she deserves; she wants to be heard, but he does not want to listen.

Disagreement. S/O are close friends who find their troubled friendship is on shaky ground; they have been having problems because they seem to have different views of what a strong friendship entails; these feelings are felt more strongly on her part, and all of it has come to a recent head; she thinks the friendship has become extremely suffocating—acts of kindness are seen as a "one-for-one" ratio; he feels that he does not have to live up to what she expects from him and that she is asking a lot; when he wants to do something kind, he feels it should be appreciated as kindness, not a payback; he feels that she wants to monopolize his time and actions; he recently told her that he needed a little space and more room; she was hostile because she could not understand his point; therefore, they have heavy disagreements that stand before them.

Understanding. S/O let their guard down, and their interactions venture where they would not normally go; there is a great deal of mutual self-disclosure; sensitive topics that would not be articulated elsewhere are discussed fully; S/O value openness, security, and trust—many mediocre conflicts are overlooked because they are not given any priority or they are subject to quick resolution; S/O have a great deal of influence over the core personal beliefs of one another.

Understanding. S/O understand each other so well because they are both under a great deal of social stress; they share similar interests and values; they enjoy frequent conversation, feel comfortable talking, share personal problems without hesitation, and get a lot out of each successful encounter.

Understanding. S/O are soul mates; because they express themselves so openly, they are able to agree and understand each other better than any of the other people they both know; if they are not in agreement, they at least understand or learn why; they know each other's motives and feelings behind most actions without even discussing them; they share the same values and solve small problems quickly.

Misunderstanding. S/O come from different cultural backgrounds, deal with feelings and emotions differently, and often misinterpret each other due to different personal styles, language use, and value systems; S/O are expert ballroom dancers; he places a lot of value on dancing as a form of expression that he wishes to share only with those who are closest to him, but she has no problem in dancing with others; because their value orientations are not the same, interactions are seriously affected.

Gender considerations do not easily or readily reveal their inherited legacies or hidden secrets. On a larger scale, cognitive appraisals and core value orientations shape and form the basis of blended social identities based primarily, but not exclusively, on the basis of sex, age, status, and power in diverse relational alignments and intersecting institutional affiliations. Gender-based disagreements and mutual understandings often arise out of alternative ways of detecting, classifying, and ranking of consensual and idiomatic signs of affiliation, affection, and involvement. Equally discriminating is mutual recognition of consensual and idiomatic signs of disaffiliation, disaffection, and detachment.

CORE VALUES

Social interaction has considerable potential to generate intricate and elaborated valuations or subvert or undermine frank discussion over topics of questionable or indeterminate status. Much depends on the value placed on the opportunity or obligation to share one's honored value orientations with other people and to respond in kind to their cherished value orientations. Core evaluative considerations are reality tested on a fluid, moment-by-moment basis. At issue are the relative merits associated with various modes of public inquiry: why we value our own knowledge; why we value other people's knowledge; why we value the exchange of personal insight; and why we devalue or discredit more remote sources of valuations that appear foreign or alien to our own. Presumably, personal knowledge is valuable because it serves critical functions that cannot be easily satisfied when people are not in the presence of others (Jones 1997). Applied social knowledge requires direct verification, which in turn fosters greater participation, involvement, and commitment to the pursuit of shared interests. Social encounters in which self-verification occurs have value in promoting positive responses, abiding commitments, strong attachments, and collective orientations (Burke and Stets 1999).

Communal orientations involve an implicit sense of personal nurturance and social sensitivity. The core values of respect, self-regard, and reciprocity are important individual indicators. Personal respect requires proper appreciation for the importance of being a certain person in the eyes of others. Conversely, the inability to recognize the dignity of others diminishes self-respect. Whereas self-esteem entails efficacious feelings derived from evaluation of one's own ability and skill, self-respect activates principles of knowledge and well regard for the integrity for all the persons that one encounters in daily life.

Respect is an intrinsic aspect of one's sense of being in touch with reality because it is rooted in principles of separation and tolerance of frustration. Its repeated disturbance leads to disdain, low self-esteem, and social withdrawal. Individuals who make comments in a respectful fashion show that they value mutual understanding and assume that the best way to make progress is through dialogue rather than moral exclusion. Strong commitments bind individuals to honor their agreements in a manner that evolves into an internalized personal norm. Strength of relational commitment is reportedly linked with high levels of congruence in partner's value systems (Kurdek and Schnopp 1997).

Respectful interchange provides added psychological insurance against the display of humiliating or contemptuous tactics before others. Similarly, the elusive concept of self-respect warrants privileged consideration as a prime virtue worthy of protection against the threat of loss and immeasurably enriched by the pleasure of being treated with appropriate consideration, care, and concern. It is possible to consider self-respect as a precondition of social valuation because an acquired sense of regard, dignity, pride, and esteem is each concerned with core issues of individual worth (Roland and Foxx 2003). Moreover, because a strong sense of regard is selective, exclusive, and particular, a strong sense of enduring respect is a valuable stabilizing force and a moral principle of balance and moderation. The ability to experience a wide range of constructive emotions influences both a coherence of value orientation and a strong commitment to the value of truth.

Attributions of honesty, trust, and respect are commonplace in polite and civil discourse. Honesty is associated with complex decisions and difficult choices that promote a strong prosocial orientation. However, distinctions between real and perceived honesty are not always easy or effortless to sort out. Ordinary language lends itself to deceptive practices that blur the distinction between truth and error. A preponderance of trust relative to mistrust has social currency because it mitigates against opportunism and counteracts certain basic costs associated with fear and greed in competitive endeavors. An abiding sense of personal trust presumably contributes to better self-rated health, greater life satisfaction, and frequent use of prosocial repair strategies in deceptive situations (Aune, Metts, and Ebesu-Hubbard 1998).

Trust emerges in distinctive patterns. Not only does it signal a stance of confidence and goodwill, but it also constitutes an intangible resource that is subject to further negotiation and regeneration. Mutual trust and shared commitment facilitate acts of self-verification, which in turn leads to more positive conceptions of personal identity, as well as more generous valuations of others (Burke and Stets 1999). High-trust individuals defend their sense of optimism and conviction about the security or integrity of their close relational bonds against external sources of potential risk and threat. Low-trust persons, in contrast, often amplify the tacit implications of another's negative behavior and ignore constructive inferences about possible positive actions (Rempel, Ross, and Holmes 2001). Personal trust is evaluated along broad dimensions of accommodation, interdependence, commitment, and readiness to sacrifice for the sake of the welfare of a significant other (Rusbult, Martz, and Agnew 1999).

A strong sense of mutual trust is necessary for affectionate personal relations to emerge in which abundant expressions of care and concern enhance an abiding sense of empathy, respect, and humanistic motives. Personal value systems that clearly cohere promote the cultivation of three core values: respect, honesty, and trust. Conversely, deficient or ineffective modes of social relationships often serve to discredit and replace these same qualities with an implicit sense of disrespect, dishonesty, and disrespect. A surplus of positive affects (love, joy, surprise) is gradually transformed into a more severe slant of negativity (anger, fear, and sadness).

It is possible to chart the evolution of prosocial value orientation under conditions in which states of agreement, disagreement, understanding, and misunderstanding are at issue. In the computer transcript, distinctive patterns emerge in the frequency of common social valuations. Across four main conditions, all sentences with explicit reference to any one of four core values— respect, trust, honesty, value—were tabulated (table 3.1).

Main results are consistent with several major themes. Personal accounts of obtained agreement and mutual understanding are heavily value laden, and they are usually cast in an affirmative mode of assertion or response. In descending order, affirmative valuations in the tentative formulation of working agreements cluster around displays of respect, value integration, trust, and honesty. Likewise, affirmative valuations in the understanding section are ranked in a similar manner—respect, honesty, trust, and value. Quite striking is the fact that there were no negative references (lack of value) in the agreement section and only 6 entries in the understanding condition. There were 174 mentions of positive value in the personal accounts of agreement and 210 mentions of constructive value in the accounts of understanding, for a total of 384 references. Clearly, when a constructive climate of working agreements and mutual understandings prevails, the emotional and affective vocabularies are likely to be heavily value laden. There were few exceptions to the positive slant.

The personal accounts of disagreement and misunderstanding contain few references to any socially desirable values. The distribution of negative mentions in the disagreement section are as follows: respect, honesty, value, and trust, for a total of just 23 references. The distribution of mentions in the misunderstanding section are even weaker: respect, trust, honesty, and value, for a total of just 9 references. Equally striking is the high frequency of negative references. Disagreement section: disrespect (26), lack of value (23), mistrust (9), and dishonesty (5), for a total of 63 instances. A similar pattern

Table 3.1. Respect, Trust, Honesty, and Value

	Agreement	Disagreement	Understanding	Misunderstanding
Respect	62	12	70	4
Trust	37	0	52	2
Honesty	33	7	58	2
Value	42	4	30	1
Total	174	23	210	9

emerges in the misunderstanding section: lack of value (13), mistrust (11), disrespect (10), and dishonesty (5), for a total of 39 references. In short, there were 23 references to positive values in the accounts of disagreement and only 9 in the misunderstanding section. In sharp contrast, there were 73 references to negative values in the disagreement condition and 41 instances in the misunderstanding section.

Emotional vocabularies based on disagreement and misunderstanding contained only 32 references to positive values and 114 references to their negative counterparts. In effect, the respective parties were sensitive to the thin layers of positive value reference and equally aware of the disquieting effects associated with a shared sense of disrespect, lack of value, mistrust, and dishonesty. There were few exceptions to the heavy negative slant. In sum, the total of 384 positive valuation in the combined a/u conditions is ten times greater than the totals for the d/m condition (32). Likewise, the combination of 114 negative references in the d/m sections is almost ten times greater than that of the a/u sections (12 instances). By examining the central themes that register across the four main conditions, it is possible to reconstruct the distinctive patterns contained in the respondents' own explanations (or rationalizations) for such dramatic contrasts in personal value orientation.

Respect

The highest-ranked value is the capacity and willingness to show respect toward others:

S/O treat each other with respect and dignity at all times.
S/O respect each other because neither one jumps to snap conclusions.
S/O show mutual respect for one another, regardless of the situation.
S/O have so much respect that they would rather die than hurt the other.
S/O treat each other with respect because they share the same values.
S/O respect each other so much that it is easy to accept each other's views.
S/O know that no matter what they will have respect for each other.
S/O respectfully listen to how the other feels about every little thing.
S/O share respect—there is no need to persuade the other of anything.
S/O respect each other's opinions, even when they are quite different.

When people express themselves in a civil and respectful manner, so many other things seem to fall into place. When viewed as a sign of admiration and regard, a state of mutual respect is most often taken as a requisite or precondition for the emergence of other types of constructive values. Moreover, the construct of respect is construed as a core value and a cherished virtue as well. The notion of respect occurs more often and in a greater variety of ways than any other value orientation. The range of free association is sweeping and inclusive. The style in question is rarely taken for granted in the manner of a mere presumption or entitlement. There is multiple reference to considerable respect for persons as individuals; for varied modes of expression or innovative, interpretive response; and for a broad spectrum of instrumental and terminal ends that are eagerly sought after and, once in place, preserved and sustained with great determination and shared resolve. The absence of such value–virtue pairings is quickly noticed in unsettled or troublesome episodes and thereby serves as an explanation or a rationalization for a wide assortment of psychological, linguistic, and social maladies. Virtually everything one might view as being socially desirable links to routine displays of personal deference and honorific demeanor.

A condition of respect or admiration is an important source of social currency. It is rarely presumed at the outset of personal engagement in the manner of a first impression. Rather, it is viewed as a valued resource that emerges slowly over extended, often protracted time frames. The emergence of a respectful manner is often described as a product of considerable shared effort and mutual regard. Once in place, respondents typically view its presence as a great virtue and a source of intrinsic merit. More than any other constructive value orientation, a condition of respect is couched in terms of mutuality and reciprocity. The emphasis is often placed on the sheer richness or surplus of reciprocity that can be sustained in a seemingly timeless way. There are abundant references in the data to the many ways of adapting or acquiring a strong stance of unconditional or unqualified respect. There are unmistakable religious overtones—when the desired quality is taken as a matter of unshakable faith, worthy of consideration as an ultimate virtue, something you can always count on, and fully apparent in all aspects of daily life. An attitude of mutual respect is ostensibly more important than winning and is a key ingredient in successful encounters.

A surplus of mutual respect among participants is credited with making effective communication easier to perform. Public display of deferential regard and preferential admiration also gives rise to a wide array of secondary associations: really caring about one another; revealing an attitude of sincerity, honesty, openness, tolerance, and trust in one another's thoughts, feelings, opinions, attitudes, choices, decisions, viewpoints, beliefs, morals, priorities, interests, judgments, and tastes; enhanced self-respect; greater regard for the uniqueness and individuality of other people; and the luxury of feeling safe and secure in speaking one's mind. Fringe benefits include a heightened sense of social support for the pursuit of diverse needs and wants; ease in valuing and gaining a greater measure of acceptance of another's point of view; and shared assurance that praise, advice, judgment, and criticism can be given freely and taken in an appropriate spirit. A related theme involves mutual sensitivity to the collective need to explore unresolved difficulties, issues, and personal problems in more depth and greater detail than would otherwise be possible. Finally, an implicit sense of mutual respect is viewed as having considerable preventive value. The surplus of strong virtue is taken as a form of psychological insurance that things will not degrade, relations will not deteriorate, communication channels will not be shut down or become a terrible mess, personal biases will not be carelessly imposed, no one will be looked down on, and confidences will not be betrayed in front of anyone else.

There is a widespread presumption that one good deed deserves another—that is, generous emotional reactions will follow in kind. Expectations of reciprocity are rather strong, at least so long as things go smoothly and the participants are willing to take their turns. The same logic holds for reactions to other core values, particularly for displays of honesty and trust. There is no simple formula for success. In fact, there is no broad consensus about what it means to treat others well, much less to respect and hold them in high regard.

Honesty

The second-most highly ranked value involves the capacity or willingness to be open and honest before others:

S/O are able to discuss difficult topics openly and honestly.

S/O become closer due to honesty and trust developed over time.

S/O share honesty, often blatant; they can tell each other anything.

S/O are not afraid to clarify mistakes and be totally honest.

S/O trust one another with everything; they are honest and hide nothing.

S/O are honest with each other; they look at the world in the same way.

S/O are open, honest, and trusting—they have no hidden secrets.

S/O discover honesty is not as black and white or straightforward as they once thought.

S/O conclude that honesty includes the willingness to talk about uncomfortable feelings.

S/O find keys to mutual understanding in openness, honestly, and lots of verbal feedback.

S/O are quite honest when it comes to dealing with annoyances or problems.

S/O promote mutual openness by responses that are honest and sympathetic.

S/O can see honesty, and this leads them to be able to speak freely.

Central theme: a small measure of initial respect leads to greater levels of mutual honesty later on. However, the value of honesty is more directly associated with a core set of communicative issues than basic matters of respect, which, in contrast, are mainly aligned with personal characteristics and traits that may or may not have direct relevance as variables of face-to-face interaction. After all, one person may respect another for reasons that have little to do with the way the two interact. In other words, the central theme is "honesty is generous." By examining each sentence with any reference to "honest" or "honesty," in contrast to mentions of "dishonest" and "dishonesty" in bonded modes of personal conduct, it is possible to reconstruct a litany of central themes across the spectrum of personal accounts. References to honest modes of interaction and honesty in relation to matters of personal identification reveal a robust theme. The style in question is often described as a state of unconditional honesty, without explicit mention of qualifiers or reservation. Honest activity is often envisioned as a constant, as evidenced in an all-inclusive reference to a presence that is whole and actively sustained. This cherished state may be taken in the manner of a solemn oath. A strict standard is invoked by which participants are viewed as being sufficiently honest to trust one another with anything—they hold no secrets. Such an idealized state enables persons to speak freely about anyone or anything.

There are inclusive, sweeping, and expansive references to convergent conditions in which relational partners always express themselves openly and honestly, thereby promoting even greater levels of mutual trust. The key component is a rich legacy of shared history. An honest style is manifest in detailed and complex explanations for things in life. It takes a great deal of honest effort to try to see things from others' perspectives and for others to try to see things from one's own viewpoint. It may be necessary to share honest personal feelings, issues, and concerns, even if they hurt. It often takes a long time to develop an abiding sense of honesty secured in the manner of an abundant, rather than a scarce, resource. Finally, what is so striking in the a/u sections is that there is virtually no references to "dishonest" or "dishonesty" on the part of anyone. It is quite simply a joyful and passionate celebration of what amounts to a shared achievement of the highest order.

Trust

A mutual sense of trust is the third-most frequently cited source of relational valuation:

S/O have trusted each other from day one.
S/O share everything and trust one another completely.
S/O talk often, and each time they trust one another more than before.
S/O trust one another with everything; they are honest and hide nothing.
S/O would not betray or cause the other to lose that strong sense of trust and respect.

S/O have created a strong sense of trust and comfort between them.
S/O share friendship that is built on complete trust and mutual respect.
S/O talk freely with each other about sex, love, commitment, and trust.
S/O have much in common; they understand and trust each other greatly.
S/O can tell each other anything and know that trust will exist.

A strong sense of mutual trust is idealized as a tender virtue. There is no sweeping consensus concerning what qualifies as a trusting style of self-expression. Note, this was not the case for the attributions associated with respect and honesty. If public displays of admiration and respect are taken as a cherished virtue and if those of honesty are construed as generous, then mentions of trust in action may be construed as being soft and fragile. Acts of unconditional trust deal more with the integrity of other people than the quality of human encounter per se. Central themes include the following: one knows that one can trust the other with anything; some establish a strong sense of mutual trust that is present at the outset; and sometimes the level of trust is so great that it slowly becomes a burden. There is also a strong component of mutual realization.

There is also an overarching sense of trust envisioned as a constant (always present, always affordable), as a given, as being complete, unconditional, and totally reciprocal. It is comforting to know that the other would not betray or cause a loss of trust and respect. Strong trust is idealized in several ways. It may be taken as a high honor to have been earned so slowly over time and with great effort from day one. Strong dyadic trust requires a reciprocal orientation, close emotional bonds, and interdependent strivings, whereas holistic trust underlies deep personal faith in institutions, society, and culture (Powell and Heriot 2000).

An implicit sense of mutual trust alters personal expectations and standards of cognitive appraisal across a number of distinct communicative senses. Conversations exhibit the values of respect, consideration, and trust in prosocial situations in which interactants expend a great deal in time, energy, and effort to learn how to trust each other. Trusting responses are what draw one to trust the other. It is generous to trust another with anything and to grant that person the psychological freedom to say and express anything freely, no matter what. When mutual trust is always there, it can never go away. The secondary associations are also diverse. In some cases, the mix of values is viewed as social glue or cement. Some participants find that understanding comes from trust and that trust comes from a good and healthy way of communicating. Others express themselves sympathetically. Still others share trust in one another and feel secure in themselves. In these metaphoric scenarios, an implicit sense of mutual trust mixes easily and well with other core values and cherished virtues. The level of compatibility could hardly be any stronger.

Value Integration

The fourth core value can be examined by charting all sentences (a/u) in which "value" or "value association" appears with a broad spectrum of constructively defined attributes:

> S/O value the same things: honesty, trust, self-worth, independence, and love.
>
> S/O understand each other's beliefs and values and express themselves so positively.
>
> S/O seem to have similar goals, ideals, and values and share a lot of respect between them.
>
> S/O have the same priorities—selflessness, respect, honesty, loyalty, and responsibility.
>
> S/O share the same values when it comes to talking about things that are important.
>
> S/O value little things they do for each other; when apart, they value them even more.
>
> S/O understand each other's way of thinking about moral and ethical values.
>
> S/O share common values, including hard work, honesty, loyalty, and truthfulness.
>
> S/O share their deepest, darkest secrets; they have the same values and rarely argue.
>
> S/O have shared ideals of what constitutes respect, self-worth, and mutual trust.
>
> S/O could never imagine having their trust in one another as confidants violated.
>
> S/O can see one another's point of view and respond with utmost respect.

There are three main narrative clusters of reference at work in social and personal relations based on compatible value systems. First, there is the relative absence of any stipulated reservations or qualifiers in the salience, scope, or scale of convergent value identification. Second, respondents use operational terms that specify how closely aligned value orientations emerge in structured patterns over extensive periods. Third, there is considerable emphasis placed on second-order associations with other core values, which in turn serve to strengthen and solidify relational commitments. Appeals to unqualified, reciprocated, or mutual forms of social identification are clear-cut, with little or no reason to doubt the veracity of shared presumptions that acquire unquestioned or privileged status. Salient clusters of free association are rich, vivid, and animated. There is a strong sense of symmetry in value orientations shared by kindred spirits.

DEVALUATION

Everyday injustice implies some form of disrespectful, dishonorable, devalued, or discredited source of behavior. A sense of unjustified experience in
daily life may arise from, among other things, wrongful accusation and one-
sided blaming; lack of recognition for great effort or high-order achievement;
violations of expectations, promises, or agreements; refusal to admit error;
bossing people around; treating others in a harsh, threatening, or inappropriate way; constant meddling and engagement in humiliating, ruthless acts;
betrayal of coworkers or illegal misuse or abuse of one's status and power
(Miller 2001). Signs of disrespect, injustice, anger, and aggression comport
well. It is not surprising that personal devaluation leads to demoralization,
often experienced as a persistent inability to cope, as a deprivation of spirit,
or as a reduction to a state of weakness, atrophy, or distress (Clarke and
Kissane 2002).

Acts of disrespect and injustice promote unpleasant, even painful, reactions, which appear as deprecating or depriving toward others' senses of entitlement. Countervailing factors include the rapid restoration of an offended
person's sense of esteem, worth, or identity in the aftermath of emotional exploitation; the struggle with an urge to retaliate against the offender as a form
of restorative justice; and the willingness to subordinate one's own immediate goals or objectives for the sake of the shared pursuit of some wider set
of communal aspirations, concerns, and goals. Far more difficult to reconcile
are personal entanglements in complicated relational imbalances that seem
to be well grounded in a profound moral dilemma, contradiction, paradox,
or profound perplexity. Salient issues include real-life decisions amid social
pressures that can be exceedingly difficult to address, much less confront,
overcome, and resolve. Both prosocial (care, justice) and antisocial (violation, transgression) tendencies must be weighed and reconciled against strict
relational standards—namely, priorities granted to uphold support for self,
other, or sheer magnitude of relational commitment.

When personal value systems seem quite incompatible, the most discouraged participants are prone to discount or devalue the opinions, beliefs, and
attitudes of one another as a means to preserve or maximize confidence in
one's own stand on sensitive relational issues:

S/O lose much respect for those who do not respect themselves.
S/O do not give full respect—they do not care enough to talk seriously.
S/O do not see eye to eye—they were brought up with different values.
S/O find that beliefs take over arguments, so they fight for mutual respect.
S/O often are easily hurt because their values are not the same.
S/O make wrongful assumptions—they see each other as not caring about
     sensitive matters.

S/O do not respect each other's feelings or know each other's feelings.

S/O have different values and reflect differences that will never be resolved.

S/O do not understand each other's cues, beliefs, values, or ideology.

S/O knock heads when it comes to discussions about opinions and beliefs.

S/O feel no bond, and they lose respect for each other after each failed conversation.

S/O do not have the respect to produce any sense of personal agreement.

S/O have different views on everything: friends, values, dreams, morals.

S/O have value conflicts so often that they are suspicious of each other's motives.

A surplus of constructive value enables engaged individuals to establish and maintain strong ties with others. Likewise, the lack or relative absence of positive valuation weakens strong ties and strengthens weak ties with others. In the d/m sections, references to acts of disrespect outnumber references to respectful actions more than two to one (36/16). Similarly, mentions of mismatched values are several times greater than references to matched values (36/5). Also, references to acts of mistrust exceed displays of trust several times over (20/2). A weaker pattern holds for the margin of dishonest conduct when compared with actions that are equated with honest intentions (10/9). The sum of the four negative values is much greater (in the d/m sections) than the number of constructive valuations by a ratio of 102 to 32. The surplus of negative valuation operates across two dimensions: what is viewed as lacking from the outset and what is present in the early stages of shared history but is subject to erosion or discredit along the way.

It does not take many isolated instances of disrespect to cause generalized doubt concerning whether given relational participants really do greatly respect each other. This pattern is striking when deliberations turn to issues of great magnitude or personal consequence. Likewise, a single act of disrespect may be all that is necessary to evoke a more generalized sense that the person in question would treat other acquaintances or even people in general the same way, at least when similar circumstances are present. A variation of the same theme occurs in the few instances in which one person fails to respect those acquaintances who do not seem to respect themselves. When core beliefs or fundamental differences are at stake, some persons feel compelled to engage in compensatory struggles that can be accurately characterized as a constant fight for mutual respect. Loss of respect is also troublesome, particularly when cast in the manner of a lament about what may seem to be a lost cause. It is often held up as an unobtainable standard that somehow must be regained as a way to ward off disturbing signs of relational deterioration and decay. After all, when respect is temporarily lost, people may be inclined to say things they do not mean and later regret.

When people see their efforts in bringing about corrective change as being futile or a waste of time, fatalism may enter the picture, rearing itself as addiction, racism, or self-neglect. Closely related is a stance of mutual resignation, as revealed in virtually all references to a total lack of respect that is entrenched and deeply ingrained and therefore thought to be highly resistant to unilateral efforts at constructive change. In some cases, resignation leads to indifference, detachment, or withdrawal. Finally, unwelcome or unwanted displays of disrespect may be tolerated, at least in close social and personal relations in which, despite the absence of a polite or deferential style of interaction, participants are willing to put up with such treatment because of other desirable or rewarding aspects of an enduring social bond.

Mismatched value systems are the most troublesome of all. They contribute substantially to misunderstanding, hurt, and upset feelings. The inability or unwillingness to take unspoken matters into account may lead to impasse and irreconcilable differences that are not amenable to resolution. When incongruent values are placed on too many things, there is apt to be tension, stress, annoyance, resentment, irritation, confusion, and struggle in misguided efforts to iron them out. There may be a sense that the interactants are from different worlds or embrace completely different realities. This makes it even more difficult to translate back and forth from one value system to another. Effective communication may break down until there is no longer any distinctive sense of personal bond. A major shift in personal values makes daily interactions much more difficult to sustain.

Participants complain of inconsiderate feelings and major tests of patience. In extreme cases, when contrasting viewpoints are cast in terms of polar opposites, engaging interaction may grind to a halt. Mutual efforts to restore a sense of semantic balance may cease if each party is suspicious of the other's motives. When conditions are so adverse, a mutual stance of impatience and intolerance is the order of the day. There is often pressure to avoid talk about the very things that matter most—family, friendship, relationships, morality, values, religion, or anything else that is deep, sensitive, or taken to be quite personal. There is virtually no mention of anyone's finding suitable mechanisms to alleviate the clash of moral valuations. With no way out of protracted communicative difficulties, and no options or better methods of translating back and forth, a case of linguistic gridlock is likely to be deeply ingrained with no viable solutions in sight.

4

Personal Identity

As a practical discipline, our essential purpose is to cultivate communicative *praxis*, or practical art, through critical study. All our work does, or should, pursue that purpose.

—Robert T. Craig, "Communication as a Practical Discipline"

The essential task is to study face-to-face interaction in a way that seeks to demonstrate how the conduct of various individuals, and the systems and structures that support or threaten their collaborative endeavors, are all historically constituted, both at the (micro) level of given types of exchange relations and at the larger (macro) level of the diverse institutional conditions in which they are embedded.

—C. David Mortensen, "Communication, Conflict, and Culture"

Individuals as actors negotiate meanings and self-identities within a broad social field on which larger social and cultural forces place both limiting constraints and creative possibilities.

—Robert G. Dunn, *Identity Crises*

There is no secure answer to the awesome mystery of the human face that scrutinizes itself in the mirror; no answer, at any rate, that can come from the person.

—Ernest Becker, *The Denial of Death*

What we see in the mirror of identity is not our own face, but the shadow of someone else's presence.

—Eduardo Mendieta, "Identity and Liberation"

71

Even simple acts of social praxis may give rise to more complex questions about embedded mechanisms of personal identity and social identification that are neither easy or effortless to unravel in anticipatory or retrospective accounts of direct or mediated forms of human encounter. The concept of human ability emerges as the life-span acquisition of a sufficient stockpile of social knowledge to implement scarce material resources in the pursuit of pleasure and the avoidance of pain (hedonic strivings). Higher-level aspirations incorporate an elaborated sense of meaning, significance, and well-being into the pleasure of greater achievement (eudaemonic strivings). From an ecological perspective, accessible material resources establish the greater potential for human understanding; personal abilities constrain the scale of possible achievement; and social skills provide opportunity for the actual discovery of meaning, relevance, valuation. In a global sense, a major question hinges on the issue of whether there are universal human skills that underlie, support, and promote social appreciation and opportunity for cultural diversity (Nelson-Jones 2002). Our understanding of social interaction is inextricably tied to the validity of our collective conception of humanity (Woods 2001).

RESOURCE ALLOCATION

Routine acts of social interaction rest on complex heuristic principles of resource allocation, maintenance, conservation, and loss. A fluid conception of communicative competence registers as the inclusive capacity to make things happen, make sense of what transpires, and address or scrutinize pressing issues or critical human concerns that unfold in a dynamic social context. Scarce linguistic resources provide implicit guidance in the rapid detection of error, mistake, or miscalculation in open-ended, flexible, and malleable relations among separate but autonomous entities. Personal resources facilitate recognition of common problems, tasks, and issues as a challenge and work toward persistence in the face of risk, crisis, or failure. In addition, personal resilience promotes greater stress resistance, well-being, successful influence, and goal fulfillment (Hobfoll et al. 2002).

The ability to obtain valued resources from others is a critical aspect of the power to effect change and exert direct modes of social influence. Personal reconstructions unfold in dramatic scenarios in which storytelling is the typical mode of social explanation. The retelling of personal stories enables people to forge connections to the past, bridge gaps in unshared history, and strengthen ties that bind. Narrative description helps a given social agent to clarify the definition and direction of personal experience; it gives greater coherence and meaning to public events; and it also reverses prior narrative failure. Defining memories, current activities, and future goals are linked by narrative themes to foster a sense of meaning and purpose, cast against the background of a world riddled with inconsistency, confusion, and tension between efficacy (doing well) and integrity (being oneself) in the course of real-life transactions (McGregor and Little 1998).

A performance is deemed successful when the behavior in question cannot be replicated by someone lacking in ability or skill. Proficient performance requires regulative sensitivity, task demand evaluation, viable options, proximal small-scale goals, incentives for demanding standards and taxing activities, stress management, and minimized intrusive ruminations (Bandura et al. 2001). The pursuit of optimal expertise requires rapid interpretation of what transpires into skillful coordination of relevant components of complex tasks with discrimination and sensitivity to matters of evaluated progress.

Narrative events require the inclusive ability to construe specific actions as observable aspects of a holistic perspective from which contrasting conceptions, their internal coherence and explicit interconnections, contribute to the establishment of functional standards of interpretive performance as being amenable to further scrutiny, monitoring, cross-checking, or successive refinement (Knight 1997). Confronting one's view with the contrasting views of other people opens the opportunity for strategic maneuvering and tactical devices that attribute desirable or favorable connotations in the best possible light. Conversely, deteriorated narrative capacity is revealed in unwelcome or unfavorable circumstances that destroy the systemic conditions required for one to maintain a continuous, unified, and coherent sense of personal identity over the life course. Personal identity disturbances arise from inadequate economic resources, unintended pregnancy, childbearing obligations, educational discontinuation, substance abuse, institutional dependence, negative images produced by dominant media, and insufficient parental socialization (Yancey 1992). It is a brutal fact of life that less-prosperous groups die sooner from most major categories of health (Watt 1996). Those who are most personally disadvantaged report more physical stress symptoms and signs of depression, whereas those who are collectively disadvantaged are more likely to become involved in collective redressive action (Hafer and Olson 1993).

On a global scale, an edgy sense of sociological crisis underscores contemporary preoccupations with the rapid erosion of personal, social, and ethnic identity in the most transitory segments and fleeting aspects of postmodern life. Technological innovations are disruptive of historical legacies and long-standing cultural traditions that enforce a strong sense of obligation, commitment, and renewal of close relational ties that typically are rather slow to change. Contemporary social movements, in contrast, promote trends of consumerism, individualism, demographic complexity, cultural diversity, global migration, and constant innovation in social knowledge and communication technology that can lead to a massive proliferation of new social identities and deconstruction of old social identities (Johnston and Lio 1998).

Broadly stated, pervasive cultural traditions decay, decompose, and disintegrate as the magnitude of societal change accelerates. In effect, it takes less and less time and space for more things to happen to more people. Hence, personal, social, and institutional spheres of sexual, ethnic, political, or cultural affiliation become evermore tentative, provisional, and precarious. Moreover, prevailing global changes serve largely to weaken strong ties among people and strengthen weak ties. Consequently, postmodernity produces mass-mediated depictions of segregated and autonomous individuals who are free to pursue their own self-interests without comparable levels of involvement in the welfare of others. Personal identity acquires an artificial, vicarious, fragmented, or incoherent quality.

Cynicism is pervasive. It is easy for postmodern critics to sneer at nostalgic notions of glorified individuals sitting on self-appointed thrones, puffed up, not only full of rationalization, excuse, denial, and self-enhancing bias but also fueled by an exorbitant drive for "certainty and security" in response to a sweeping materialistic sense of "fallibility and precariousness" (Dunne 1996, 138). Here questions of "personal" and "social" identity are not just destabilized, decentered, or dispersed but also effaced, reduced, or whittled down to nothing. Amid the clamor, noise, and din of contemporary life, sweeping radical disenchantment and disillusionment with "grand" theory (as mere fiction) are dismissive of any constructive appeal to a collective vision or cumulative hope for greater collective participation in a revitalized sense of human community. The constant press for technological innovation and the endless consumer demand for efficient and cheap mechanisms to copy, duplicate, or replicate material artifacts lead to the mindless proliferation of "virtual" or "vicarious" identities that compete with personal identities already established in the copresent world. Severe postmodern dialectics strive to atomize or dislocate segregated individuals so that each one appears to float freely in a massively incoherent landscape of fleeting and transitory textual materials.

The erosion of stable modern notions of personal and social identity has severely undermined the credibility and currency of all received cultural traditions and all-embracing schemes of decreed proclamation that pretend to put everything in its proper place (Bauman 1997). Solid, resilient, and immutable notions of personal identity have been pulverized by a series of cultural and global transformations: economic deregulation; collapse of occupational expectations; dislocating legal regulations; privatizing of societal concerns; disappearance of solidarity, cohesion, and celebration; and a pervasive sense of cultural anonymity with no stable ground for launching far-reaching life projects. In an age of stupefying complexity and profound technological transformation, personal projects can rarely be fully comprehended and must therefore be carried out with an abiding sense of openness, incompleteness, ignorance, and fragility in what Barnett (2000) has characterized as a world of "radical unknowability" (Curzon-Hobson 2002).

Human performance failures thrive with diminished concern for core moral, ethical, and aesthetic considerations. A bleak sense of spiritual, emotional, and intellectual impoverishment surrounds grim and relentless academic efforts to forever cast doubt on a strong belief in a stable, coherent, and secure ground of personal identity. The postmodern subject—decentered, dissected, destabilized, devalued, and demoralized—is resigned to a shallow identity in name only, suspended, immersed in the flux and flow of a world ever changing without fixed formula. The collapse of grand narratives signals widespread societal dissipation of trust in a "supreme court" of ultimate appeal for conflicted human deliberations. Anxiety and insecurity permeate all areas of contemporary life. In a biting review of central themes in postmodern criticism, Jarvis (1998) singles out unsympathetic assessments of facile eclecticism; aesthetic amnesia; delusions of grandeur; intellectual sabotage; self-defeating contradiction; rise of cynicism; grim dismemberment of meaning, place, and origin; triumph of nihilism in the face of declining identity, truth, and purpose; and, above all else, shrill insistence that all secular language is fatally contaminated by the fallible language system that is used to describe it.

If essential notions of abiding truth and firm foundation of applied human knowledge are put aside, and if the case for curt dismissal rests on the same system of suspect language and fictive communication that is presumed to be so fatally flawed, then there is really no justification for taking the dysphoric language employed in strident postmodern attack any more seriously than what is presumed to be defective about the conventional language practice it seeks to neutralize, subvert, deconstruct, or undermine. For in the absence of a rigorous and precise demonstration of the terrible stain of the human sign, there is no escape or feasible alternative but to continue to rant and rave in a bitter lament concerning proud pronouncements found to be so badly off the mark.

CULTURAL NARRATION

Personal narratives are socially enacted through a diverse succession of relational alignments, communication networks, and cultural practices. Autobiographical accounts provide a mundane and expedient way to define, reaffirm, or transform the distinctive identity claims of any one member against the identity claims of any other member of an active speech community. Speaking subjects employ an expansive and dramatic lexicon of words and gestures to shape the course of daily encounters with other speaking subjects. When individuals retell life stories, they may shift among first-, second-, or third-person perspectives that are at once expressive and responsive to the proliferation of alternative stances adapted by others who are present to observe what transpires.

It is a mistake to construe the concept of culture in a pure, unsullied, transparent, or self-evident manner. The term *culture* is, after all, an imprecise one in a double vexing sense—that is, what culture means and what it means to be a singular cultural subject and object of social mediation. Dense abstractions locate references to culture as an implicit set of instructive guidelines for life and living transmitted from one generation to another by large collectivities of highly integrated persons who share a distinct sense of legacy and inheritance (Bhui and Bhugra 2001). Culture influences individuals' use of collective interpretations and public categories that shape the greater personal ability to express and respond to shared language codes, schemes, and repertoires in a coherent and relevant manner (Eliasoph and Lichterman 2003). Anthropological debates, concerning one of our oldest academic concepts, underscore the dynamic, negotiable, endorsable, contestable, and ambiguous features of personal aspirations and collective sanctions across a spectrum of societal settings. Sweeping global changes pose a challenge to traditional notions of cultural stability. External connections cross over multiple spatial and temporal scales within a global ethnography in which speaking subjects are increasingly influenced by disembedded, pancultural, globalized influences (Gille and O'Riain 2002).

Some cultural comparisons entail implicit notions of a sweeping and inclusive social drama in which a collection of actors celebrate cultural models slanted toward a center stage on which the leading figures are autonomous, distinctive, and distinguished from the personal styles of other, far less prominent members. In contrast, alternative scales of dramatic cultural comparison work to displace the egocentric, individualistic spotlight so that each actor or agent can refocus on the roles of significant others, particularly in the enriching and sustaining themes of participation, cohesion, and solidarity (Pillemer 2001).

A great deal of systematic inquiry has addressed the central distinction between individualistic and collectivistic orientations toward the mutual exchange of cultural narratives. Cultural differences in emotional style underscore collectivism in systems of meaning, practice, and valuation that emphasize the relatedness of individuals to their common material surroundings and more generally to the world at large. Conversely, individualism is embedded in local meaning, practice, and valuation that emphasize the sense of specific persons as being bounded, unique, autonomous, and independent (Mesquita 2001). However, tension between individualistic and collectivistic standards is not easily resolved or precisely calibrated from one culture to another. Critics of assumptions behind the notion of individualism–collectivism have raised difficult questions about "unduly fixed" dichotomous categories that, despite widespread test, manage to conflate or discount complex distinctions, reveal little compelling empirical evidence, and afford very questionable explanatory power (Voronov and Singer 2002).

Underneath the neat and tidy surface of simplistic abstract distinctions lies a broad array of difficult complexities, contradictions, and conundrums. These transcend narrow dualistic comparison between those societies based on loose ties or causal connections among literate members who are trained to look after themselves and those societies based on close intimate ties whose representatives are trained to look after one another. Insofar as a plurality of collectivists act individually and individualists respond collectively, the sharp distinction breaks down. Furthermore, there is doubt about making sweeping or slippery societal comparisons because the totality of interactive effects outweigh single cultural dimensions in the magnitude of impact (Watkins, Mortazavi, and Trofimova 2000). Specifically, conflict styles are shown to be multidimensional for both collectivists and individualists alike (Cai and Fink 2002).

Intercultural encounters have potential to promote complex social constructions based on mutual affirmation, enrichment, and validation or, conversely, collective destruction based on relational confusion, conflict, disagreement, and misunderstanding. Initial contacts require broad tolerance for linguistic tension, stress, and strain (Chen 2002). Due to problematic factors linked with a second language or foreign culture, intercultural encounters often compound basic translation difficulties in deciphering different levels of personal involvement (risk); topic initiation; process coordination; uncertainty or anxiety; stylistic clash; lack of shared history; and code-switching mismatches, interruptions, and lexical disruptions in shared efforts at behavioral adjustment and adaptive speech accommodation (Li 2001). Intercultural communication requires that native and nonnative speakers of English remain alert to contextual cues of multiple linguistic systems and react in accordance with their unique value and distinctive traditional significance.

When individuals from diverse cultural backgrounds fail to react in an appropriate and deferential manner, miscommunication occurs, whether inside or outside of conscious awareness. Lack of speech adaptation, accommodation, and convergence remains dependent, among other factors, on cultural specific beliefs about speech acts and speaking styles, particularly matters of politeness, deference, and demeanor. Mutual awareness of cultural differences in interpretation tends to be viewed in slanted attitudinal terms. Pragmatic knowledge of the proper routines for making requests, complaints, and praise is required to promotes effective intercultural communication (Mei 2002). Contextual agreements and cultural disagreements can make a significant impact on the texture and tone of conversation. Personal accounts of intercultural encounters vary widely in the diversity and divergence of what transpires:

Agreement. S/O are best friends who are both 100 percent Polish descent; they find that their values match well; words seem to flow so easily because S is a good talker and O is a good listener; they complement each other well; they know how to disagree, refuse to discredit each other's values, and respect each other's ethnic identity; they care about daily events, they know each other's attitudes, they do not need to explain themselves at length, and they know that nothing that they feel could ever be wrong.

Agreement. S/O are coworkers; S thinks of O, an African American woman, as being "twice removed" from his own social sphere, yet they often interact, and they are able to see a different worldview; due to frequent conversation, he understands her perspective on issues in which he would normally have only a narrow, one-sided approach; they gossip—he tells her about whomever he happens to be dating, while she talks about her family; despite different personal perspectives, they still find themselves understanding most of what transpires—if they hadn't been willing to initiate daily interaction, they would have seen each other as just another anonymous coworker.

Disagreement. S/O are lovers who mean the world to each other; S's best friend (X) and O have strained interactions; X/O are strong willed, come from diverse backgrounds, and have different types of social expectations; S's girlfriend is African American who grew up in a working-class family that did not support her academic aspirations, whereas S's best friend grew up in a upper-middle-class family that was supportive; S feels caught up in the middle of X/O's differences; S hopes that he does not have to choose between his friendship and his lover—he would hate to lose either one.

Understanding. S/O are closest friends who live across the hall in a shared apartment; they knew that they were going to hit it off from the moment they met; O is from a large city and attended a high school in which, being black, she was a minority; S attended a high school that was half black and half white; yet, being Asian American, S was still in a minority, so, in effect, they shared similar experiences growing up; they were very accepting and respectful of each other; on many evenings, they would sit together in one of their rooms and talk for hours about their deepest feelings, needs, or wants; they confide in each other about many things, and they have come to be able to trust, yet they remain very accepting and understanding of their own ethnic differences; when they have a personal problem, they talk to each other about it; they always put themselves in each other's shoes; in public they stick together, and they never show any disrespect for each other in front of anyone else; they can say anything to each other—S can tease O about black stereotypes, O can tease S about Asian stereotypes, and they just laugh together; because both are from minorities, neither one takes offense to the ethnic jokes—you know how some blacks are totally comfortable calling each other a "nigger" as long as it's a black person saying it to another black? Well, O has gotten to the point where S is close enough to O that she will call S a "nigger" and would not care if S chose to use it in her direction; O has told other people that S is "her nigger," to mean that S is her close friend; O has used the term as S's title but just in close conversation—it is not meant to be degrading, and for O, it signifies an acceptance of S into her life and culture.

Misunderstanding. S/O start dating, but they are not really quite in sync with each other's personal styles; they have a lot of basic differences in the way that they look at the world; they are from different racial groups, which is a difference that fosters differing viewpoints, beliefs, values, language, and cultural norms; it also causes difficulties in their communicating with and understanding of each other; for example, he talks about gangs and family members in jail, friends and family that were murdered, being African American, and racial problems in U.S. society; he has trouble understanding what she is going through with finals, papers, classes, school anxiety, the severe illness of her mother, and the abrupt separation of her father; they have trouble expressing themselves—when they do not understand the other's past experience, they do not tell each other honestly how they are feeling in fear that they may be rejected or let down—they have so much interpersonal misunderstanding because they do not understand each other's movements, nonverbal cues, beliefs, values, or norms of family, culture, and ideology.

ATTRIBUTION/MISATTRIBUTION

In the study of human encounters, there is a fine line between the sheer necessity of engaging in complex attributional decisions and the possibility, or risk, of engaging in misattributed decisions for what transpires across the life span. Cognitive appraisals, personal values, and shared identities are coimplicated as being salient in both individual (separative) and collective (integrative) accounts of responsibility for jointly produced outcomes. Particularly relevant are the distinctive framing devices that individuals use to distinguish between gradations of credit or discredit assigned or imposed on matters of loss and gain in complicated matters of goal attainment. Heuristic considerations coalesce around strategic efforts to make sense of shared struggles to define, classify, explain, or justify what works well or badly or, in other terms, what makes things better or worse, effective or faulty, successful or unsuccessful, or worthy or unworthy of further consideration.

Miscalculations fit into distinct patterns, often repeated in a serial or repetitive manner. Blame for common disagreement, for example, falls heavily on unstable situational causes and on the partner's stable negative traits. When events are negative, social attributions to internal, stable, and global causes are broadly associated with depression, helplessness, distress, and a pessimistic explanatory style (Horneffer and Fincham 1996). Individuals who suffer from low-to-moderate depression are prone to make complex and multiple attributions for specific life problems. Likewise, studies of tension, stress, and strain have identified competitive attributions as important factors in personal efforts to explain the likelihood of success turned into failure: if ascribed to internal, unstable, and controllable factors, such failure arouses adaptive efforts to find solutions, whereas failures attributed to external, stable, and uncontrollable forces yield avoidant and escapist responses that may exacerbate distress and illness (Amirkhan 1998).

Misaligned attributions, beliefs, and convictions lead to greater personal distress and discomfort as relational partners become closer and more committed to the well-being of the relationship (Davis and Rusbult 2001). Cynical intuitions are usually badly skewed insofar as people assume others are more biased than themselves (Kruger and Gilovich 1999). Observers appeal to external circumstances when accounting for failure but internally in regard to success. Personal explanations are rather complicated, however, because conceptions of success and failure are mediated by rough estimates concerning effort, ability, task difficulty, luck, inference, and hindsight bias.

The potential for misattribution is as great as the opportunity for attributional activity to go wrong, be wide of the mark, or miss the point. Virtually anything that triggers implicit associations may be subject to unspoken influences that are quite incidental or undetectable. This realization situates the focus of implicit knowledge squarely in the center of what eludes or limits the specific use of words and gestures as stable reference points for shared action that operates at the periphery of conscious awareness. After all, people do not have privileged access to why they think, feel, and behave as they do. Implicit assumptions guide explicit assertions, claims, and declarations. One's first presumption is that the responses of other people do not just happen randomly, with no relation to anything. Human responses are about something rather than mere references to nothing in particular. Second, responses are specific and concrete, formed in relation to a particular thing or case in point. Third, responses are reactions to distinct objects of observation. Therefore, they guide an implicit quest for causation or control.

When dealing with complicated social matters, it is easy to misidentify the real source of something with a phantom, trace, or shadow. Moreover, there is a pervasive tendency to hang on to enduring category systems well after they have outlived their functional usefulness. Striking is the finding that people often believe what they have said simply because they heard themselves say it. The believability of fictional accounts tends to increase as perceptual or emotional detail is added to narrative description (Johnson, Bush, and Mitchell 1998). Concerted effort to establish complex causes for a single response is subject to countervailing forces that undermine mutual struggle to work through confusing matters, communicative difficulties, and circumvent material constraints.

Benign striving enhances the generous presumption that others do harbor the best of intentions, unless or until proven wrong. When cast under favorable circumstance, attributional justifications are usually modest, understated, or inconspicuously identified. Finally, progressive attributions invite or encourage cross-checking, revision, or alteration without threats to the integrity of strong ties or binding commitments. Regressively slanted attributions, in contrast, are associated with the proliferation of petty disagreements and simple misunderstandings between opposing rivals. Attributed emphasis placed on separate (individual) over integrative (collective) responsibility often leads to less-than-optimum outcomes. Contentious individuals rarely see eye to eye, try often to take advantage of weakness or vulnerability, fail to grasp another's point of view, regress, guard what will be devalued, and confuse contexts—all of which reproduce conditions under which things just never seem to click.

DEFENSIVENESS

A world without risk or threat would require no need for any defensive reactions. An unassailable sense of personal identity would be impervious to actual or perceived slight, discredit, or denigration on the part of other people. The ultimate threat, of course, is not the uncertainty but the inevitability of death. Acquired knowledge of one's mortality may be envisioned as the final annihilation of all connections with other living things or as the irreversible decline of the person. The brute fact is that human existence cannot be sustained in isolation from other life forms. The terror of death, the sheer constancy of the threat of personal disruption and upheaval must be denied, buried, or covered up in the manner of a convincing illusion, a vital lie, one that is sufficiently compelling to enable one to live convincingly before others. The constancy of the threat of death becomes intolerable without symbols to shield and protect one from the darkness.

Terror management theory posits that defensive tactics serve to rationalize or deflect attention away from anything that is life threatening (Greenberg et al. 2000). Death-related anxieties activate direct psychological defenses to minimize the immediate threat (proximal defense) and then trigger signals, signs, and symbols as layers of metaphoric protection derived from one's cultural worldview (distal defense). Morality salience involves an implicit source of terror that activates anxiety-buffering mechanisms to dampen a disquieting sense of fear, panic, or alarm. Awareness of one's ultimate demise raises the possibility of cultural estrangement and ultimate rejection as an outcast from dominant social values and prevailing beliefs (Cozzarelli and Karafa 1998).

In a risk society, new sites of social apprehension, anxiety, and worry emerge from financial, environmental, nuclear, medical, and military threats. Moral panic arises when unresolved violations and transgressions coalesce into "hot potatoes" to be mishandled, botched, and fumbled by dumfounded authority figures (Ungar 2001). Moral outrage affords a defensive way to distance oneself from massive societal assaults on core personal values. Reactive and regressive social maneuvers include harsh character assessments of outsiders viewed as threat objects, a defiant stance of righteous indignation, vocal support for ostracizing and punishing deviant thinkers, and moral cleansing by reaffirming sacred values and privileged loyalties (Tetlock et al. 2000).

It is little wonder that people respond best to those who validate, without challenge, their own unique standards of what is valuable as an explanation for human existence, as a mystical promise of literal or symbolic immortality in a dangerous and precarious world (Greenberg et al. 2000). Threatened individuals may choose, as a communal defense, to immerse themselves in social activities designed to protect loyal members from errors and distortions associated with a "juxtaposition of awareness of inevitable mortality with the instinct for self-preservation" (Arndt and Greenberg 1999, 1332). The main implication is that human beings use a litany of words and gestures to shield or protect themselves from the light (disclosure), as well as from the dark (concealment), aspects of mortality. Stylized deflections can distance and detach frightened persons from the shared realization of any sense of "immediate threat" (mortality salience) via civic engagement in cultural activities in which the final threat can be delayed, postponed, and recast into a less-troubling vision at work in a more remote or distant future.

Defensive explanatory styles often follow a general operating principle. Personal misdeeds are discussed with great reluctance—unless, of course, they pertain to someone else. Mundane conversations can be easily manipulated or exploited to conceal or minimize unsavory aspects of personal history as applied in selective self-serving exercises, blotting out, ignoring, or erasing unwelcoming facts. Documented tactics include denying, delaying, deflecting, or minimizing personal responsibility for what goes wrong; justifying one's actions as being less harmful than they appear; indulging in special pleading; appealing to mitigating circumstance; using large doses of the passive voice; never apologizing except for trivia; omitting whatever is unflattering or uncongenial; manipulating facts; and admitting nothing except for minor mistakes on rare occasion.

Specific defensive tactics may be used to reestablish positive features of personal identity, remove negative social typifications, deny or refuse to admit what is obvious to others, or seek to dissociate or distance oneself from unwelcome implications through vain efforts at self-justification or endless excuse. Defensive explanatory styles relate to matters of personal violation and social transgression of current rules, norms, or expectations. Those who construe themselves as rivals, adversaries, or competitors are prone to mention their own misdeeds in guarded, watered-down, or elliptical terms. There is so much rationalization, special pleading, and self-justification coupled with an accusatory form of emotive reactivity at work among those who disagree or misunderstand their own complicity or duplicity for the very sorts of unwelcome outcomes for which they are, by definition, partially responsible.

Defensive use of language has been linked to a host of troublesome interpersonal factors. In the absence of clear-cut answers to complex procedural or substantive matters, some people are prone to attribute defensiveness to themselves and others in ways that badly miss the mark. Defensive styles thrive on deceptive or manipulative tactics. When success is presumed to reside within a self-serving person and failure is assumed to reside without, the basic conditions are satisfied for a state of defensiveness to emerge from a heightened sense of external provocation. On a larger scale, chronic emotional defensiveness links to distress, denial, hostility, withdrawal from intimacy, and vulnerability to illness (Elliott and Richards 1999). When external threat is clearly visible, personal aspirations, goals, or concerns (self-preservation) are seemingly in jeopardy (Gray and McNaughton 1996). Moreover, defensive tactics surface to minimize damage from threatened social identities. Central themes include denying (It didn't happen); reframing (It wasn't so bad); dissociating (It wasn't me); justifying (It was legitimate); excusing (I couldn't help it); conceding (I take responsibility); and pledging (It won't happen again) (Schutz 1998). Similar is the tendency for threatened individuals to conform even more rigidly to their distinctive idiomatic linguistic styles and thereby enhance their expressive singularity or idiosyncrasy (Vaes and Wicklund 2002).

Well-functioning adults reportedly apply a variety of defensive styles that vary as a function of the magnitude of threat and the ratio of aggressive and affectionate urges that one rapidly activates. An integrative analysis of a large body of relevant studies analyzed by Juni (1998–1999) underscores the salience of five defensive mechanisms. An accent on general aggressiveness results in unconscious effort to turn against another, thereby transforming an implicit sense of being threatened back into the countermove of making an additional threat. In intellectualized and rationalized responses, impending threat may be neutralized or dampened by triggering a general, abstract response to ameliorate stress. An intropunitive tactic turns unconscious reactions back on the self. Internalized threat produces psychic stability in moderation but guilt and depression when used to excess. A fourth alternative occurs in quick reversals in the tone of affect where new or opposing emotions arise to counter threat, as in repression and denial. Finally, projection, blame, or countertransference involve attributional shifts in the source of one's difficulties to others to alleviate anxiety arising from the construal of malicious intent. Usually, one experiences the arousal of defense as disturbing affect, fear, guilt, or threat as occasion for modification or distortion of thoughts or feelings.

Defensive distancing reveals an ambivalent mixture of sympathy and distress; discomfort arises from the fear that grave misfortunes suffered by others could befall oneself. Immediate responses to external threat dispose some people toward short-term thinking, even if such choices entail a greater long-term cost. Collective threats may be based on realistic conditions, symbolic material, anxiety, or negative stereotyping (Stephan, Dias-Loving, and Duran 2000). One relevant study examined individuals across the life span who had confronted lingering threats to their well-being. A meta-interpretation of major themes led to a formal theoretical concept of opportunity linked with courage defined as a dynamic phenomenon rendered salient in the presence of threat. The capacity to show courage (overcome resistance) under threatening circumstance develops slowly, as does effort to accept reality fully; it involves dealing with problems and issues in a discerning manner; and it engages movement beyond existing struggles in a progressive rather than regressive direction so that one can make contributions, help others, promote hope, and foster an abiding sense of personal integrity (Finfgeld 1999). Personal accommodation reportedly inhibits the likelihood of defensive reactance to threatening or menacing behaviors (Finkel and Campbell 2001).

Defensive maneuvers may register at implicit or explicit levels of cognitive appraisal, value orientation, and contested identity. Obviously, agreeable activity and psychological defensiveness are inversely correlated. Respondents who agree most readily underscore the absence of provocation, the mutual ability to stay calm and relaxed, the shared willingness to take things in stride, and, perhaps most important, the sufficient ability and resilient skill to maintain a disarming and nonthreatening manner. Moreover, solid agreements provide added psychic protection against the unwelcome imposition of threat and provide a buffer to soften tensions and minimize needless bickering, futile wrangling, or mindless dispute. In general, agreeable participants are neither weak nor defenseless but rather able, strong, generative, and resourceful in the face of tension, strife, and strain. Thin defenses are associated with animated conversations that preserve and nurture an abiding sense of safety and security. Personal defensiveness and strong verbal disagreement are closely interrelated, as characterizations drawn from the Wisconsin study make clear:

> S/O engage in bitter conversations where verbal and alcohol abuse leave
> a defensive and resentful scar; S thinks that O is judgmental, critical, and

reacts angrily, which sets off S's own defensive anger, and they end up in a match where S often ends up walking out of the room.

S/O compete for relational control—each one pulling a bit too hard; a lot of the problem is S's perception of O; S thinks O uses guilt strategies that unconsciously play on S's sense of worth—this puts S on the defensive, and S tends to snap at O in response; conversations start out as simple reminders: "Did you feed the bird?" "Don't forget about the steaks defrosting in the sink." "If you don't take the shirts out of the dryer right away, they'll need to be ironed." Hence, S often finds herself disagreeing with O just to have an opinion.

S/O engage in a holy war; when either one is crabby and says something snotty or short, the other quickly becomes defensive, and then there are two crabby people; for some reason, S gets into a certain mood and pushes all of O's buttons even more to make her feel crazy; S does not know why she practices this kind of torture, but she thinks it is a kind of a game.

S/O do not share much in common; S thinks that O tries to force opinions on S and that it makes S feel she has to defend herself; it also makes her feel uncomfortable; S/O impose their own spin on disputed subjects— they never just seem to let it rest; they interrupt a lot, too; there is often yelling or signs of frustration, such as stamping one's foot or fiddling with an object or slamming a door or drawer; S thinks that O has strong and unwavering opinions and views others from a narrow perspective—it is a constant struggle to redirect the conversation.

Personal disagreements provide symbolic indications of classic defensive behavior. There is widespread reliance on anxiety-differing tactics to cover or mask unmistakable signs of rejection or a steadfast sense of dismissive intolerance of significant others. Extreme tendencies seem to be stronger, on balance, than moderating and compensatory factors. Defensive styles mitigate against collective acknowledgment of personal flaws and failures and justify exaggerated estimates of other people's complicity for their own social flaws and failures. Hence, such reactive tendencies take the place of proactive initiatives. As the quality or climate of face-to-face interaction becomes more unpleasant, even distasteful, many respondents take refuge not in direct confrontation but rather passive aggressive indulgence in an opposite urge to withdraw or maximize emotional distance. The cycles of inflation and deflation are subject to repetition to the point of routine habituation and mutual reinforcement. It does not require a great deal of effort for one defensive person to provoke or arouse protective reactions in others.

Perhaps recent psychological literature is too sharply focused on certain highly selective personality traits of defensive individuals and insufficiently sensitive to collective defensiveness, which is more a by-product of systemic risk and threat than a narrow reflection of deficient character traits. Strong disagreements, unlike weaker variations, are relational to the core. Therefore, it is appropriate to construe defensive maneuvers and tactics as being collaborative and reciprocal in abstract design and practical execution. Collective defensiveness is much easier to acquire than to ameliorate later. It is quite unusual to find any transcript evidence of subsequent triumphs over prior acts of mutual defensiveness once the climate becomes toxic.

Although it might be too strong to claim that "once defensive, always defensive" in some global or totalizing sense, salient references frequently underscore a chronic or protracted history of relational violation, transgression, and defensiveness, one that becomes deeply ingrained and pervasively habituated rather than composed of single episodes that rise and fall quickly back into a more fulfilling or mutually satisfying routine. Although some aggressive rivals become enamored with the power to pick, bicker, probe, tease, needle, crab, or never relent, most offended parties profess not to enjoy any part of the process or the end product. Listed in the following are clear cases in which common misuse or abuse of a conventional speaking idiom is a major cause and aversive consequence of massive entrapment, bewilderment, and confusion. Defensive tactics often arise over serious misunderstandings that are not subject to resolution:

S/O talk in circles; there is a gap between what is said and what is meant; because talks involve intense emotional material, both persons are very defensive; they refuse to admit doing something wrong, and they purposely hurt each other with words just to get back; there is also a certain misunderstanding that comes from silence; S will not talk out of fear of a negative response, and O will not talk out of an obvious fear of expressing his emotions—this has all led to an awkward relationship and a painful breakup for both parties.

S/O have misunderstandings that usually center on feelings of jealousy, trust, or disappointment—each time the accused party becomes defensive; they stir up the past and bring up issues that are totally irrelevant to the current argument; typically, one rants and raves and accuses, whereas the other sulks and takes it all in.

S/O start to talk, but when either one tries to express an opposing point of view, the other one becomes defensive, and accusations start flying all indiscriminately.

S/O recently moved in together, and they have been finding it difficult to express themselves; many times when S feels that she is simply reminding O of something, O feels that S is nagging—the result is a lot of mutual criticizing, also name-calling, shouting, crying, tension, and defensiveness; it is scary that such trivial matters destroy a relationship—

what becomes even more difficult is that when the fight has blown over, it can never be discussed peacefully.

S/O misinterpret what each one has to say; they often take one another literally; when O questions S's motives, S becomes defensive and justifies what she does while he, in turn, belittles her statements; she begins to say things that she knows will bother him, because he has no regard for the grief he gives her; she is often frustrated from saying what she believes is true and important to someone who sees it as nothing; they feel as if they cannot speak to each other for a while after they fail to reach middle ground.

The social construction of chronic misunderstanding reflects an uneven mix of simple disagreements and complex misinterpretations. Unlike the acquisition of singular disagreements concerning one thing or another, a condition of mutual misunderstanding may go unrecognized or undetected in the manner of some deep, dark secret sense of discomfort or misapprehension. Here the contested aspects of personal identity are confronted not so much in a linear, serial order, but rather by a growing aggregate or mass of unfinished discursive business that is replete with ambiguity, uncertainty, or confusion about what transpires and what should be done about it. Such misunderstood aspects of personal identity are based on a hidden confluence of faulty assumptions, failed expectations, misattributions, and a dysphoric sense of falling short of the mark, missing the big prize, or not living up to some dramatic or erotic ultimate standard of consideration. When matters of truth telling are taken for granted, misdirected, or shortchanged, the aggregate of unresolved misunderstandings may take on a life of its own. In literal and figurative terms, the severity of mutual misunderstanding is a powerful measure of the scope of mismeasure and a perplexing source of discredit, disqualification, or devaluation (Mortensen 1999).

Personal accounts document a basic paradox about defensive communication. In most cases, a great deal of face-to-face interaction may yield very little in the way of distinctive communicative value or assigned worth. The mechanical, automatic, subconscious, and unintentional features of personal conduct can become powerful but in ways that deflate, neutralize, or discredit the search for meaning, import, or significance. Sometimes the pace of interaction appears to be lethargic, passive, shallow, or inert. At other times, interaction rapidly metamorphoses into an intense, noisy commotion. Frantic activity rarely diminishes defensive display. Personal accounts document cycles of escalation in protective cover-ups, duplicity, protest, and denial of personal culpability.

Clearly, defensive tactics are often designed to disperse an impending sense of risk, threat, or danger. In this way, defensiveness entails the displacement of idealized, self-enhancing features of personal identity. Favorable responses are likely to follow observed acts of validating prior standards of what is considered valuable or worthy about a given person or selective domain of shared activity. Unfavorable responses are likely to follow from observed acts of invalidating, rejecting, or dismissing prior considerations of what one considers credible or meaningful. It is important to recognize how powerfully key matters of personal identity both shape and in turn are shaped by the larger potential to form working agreements and tacit understandings of who and what is at stake. The association between contested social identity and escalated personal defensiveness is clearly indicated by the frequency of mention across the four main conditions (table 4.1). The main pattern is striking. Out of 85 mentions of defensive states or acts of defensiveness, excluding disclaimers, 82 occur in social settings in a climate of disagreement or misunderstanding is prevalent.

Virtually all expressions and accusations of defensiveness take place in close quarters where participants disagree and misunderstand one another. Few expressions or accusations of defensiveness occur when people agree or understand each other well. Moreover, the component parts of relevant statements can be broken down, inspected, and reassembled into schemes and models that shed further light on unfavorable circumstance in which someone begins to feel defensive or acts defensively in respect to something or someone else. Of critical interest are profiles of speaking subjects who are engaged with threat, resistance, or opposition of one kind or another. These episodes may be reconstructed into collective profiles based on three broad types of consideration: personal characteristics, traits, and stylistic characterizations of those who are viewed as a source of defensive activation; personal reactions of those who see themselves as targets of defensive-activating tactics; and depictions of unwelcome or problematic behavior.

In the a/u conditions, people are rarely characterized in defensive terms. The few who qualify are linked with implicit prohibitions against defense-evoking initiatives—such as attacking, name-calling, insulting, being sarcastic, and mocking—and with explicit practice of speaking in a moderate tone of voice; dealing with arguments calmly and not taking them too personally; trying to understand rather than reacting defensively; making sure others get to express things freely; causing others no need to become defensive; learn-

Table 4.1.   Defense and Defensiveness

	Agreement	Disagreement	Understanding	Misunderstanding
Defense and defensiveness	0	49	3	33
Disclaimers of defensiveness	5	0	3	0

ing to talk things out, rather than waiting and eventually blowing up or running away; remaining flexible; working hard to overcome barriers; compromising opposing viewpoints; validating behavior (one's own and others'); following established rules; feeling free and allowing others to feel free, to vent differences; staying focused; taking interest in others; remaining open to change; sharing secrets; and seeking advice.

In the d/u conditions, people are most likely to be characterized in defensive terms. Those who qualify are construed as putting down others to make themselves look good; using hostility to provoke defensive reactions; preying on the weakness of others; manipulating or threatening others; failing to see others' points of view; representing for others a source of anger, pain, sorrow, or tears; commanding others to do things that they do not want to do while insinuating that the viewpoints of others are wrong; articulating one's view and leaving without allowing the other any time to respond; engaging in loud, defensive talk; speaking *at* but not *to* others; avoiding issues that never go away and are never resolved; refusing to talk about anything real; expressing harsh prejudices until someone gets angry and defensive and tells the other where to go; putting another on the defensive by playing on a depleted sense of self-worth; giving advice to one who gets defensive and letting the cycle start all over; giving the impression that one is always right while refusing to listen to others' points of view; promoting mutual defensiveness and shared unwillingness to be wrong about anything; and picking on others who feel on edge or defensive over crude and vulgar remarks.

Conflict encounters between those who react defensively are cyclical, repetitive, and reciprocated by means of automatic triggers and sensory activation of ingrained habits and strong compulsions. Although personal defense does not necessarily lead to clear displays of interpersonal defensiveness, the linkage is nonetheless very strong. People who are most easily threatened are also the ones who are most at risk of taking refuge in defensive tactics. One compelling image finds people in close relations covering up and glossing over critical considerations with layers and layers of information assembled as a thick form of character armor. The decision to fill the air with excessive, nonstop talk may lead to the same end as would withdrawal into protracted silence—namely, emotional deadness.

Using language as a defense mechanism is likely to drain energy and repress spontaneous emotions that keep people from feeling fully alive in the present tense. Escalating patterns are reactivated to construct thick defenses against even brief displays of slight, grievance, and opposition that may not constitute an intentional threat to subvert or undermine another person's social identity. Intolerance of what is foreign or alien to one's experience is consumptive of time, energy, and effort that must be diverted from life-affirming pleasures to conservative and protective aims with negative overtones. What seems to be lacking or deficient is a base of discriminating sensibilities that tolerates slippage and imprecision in the attentiveness, concentration, and responsiveness of other people to one's expressive acts.

PERFORMANCE DEFECTS

Struggle, strife, and strain in matters of contested personal and social identity are not settled solely on behavioral considerations alone. What transpires is subject to selective and strategic forms of scrutiny and revision that cannot be predicted or anticipated in advance. By one standard or another, someone or something either measures up or fails to measure up to the observed scrutiny of someone else. Skill defects in personal competence have been linked with restrictive or restrained patterns of social development: lack of adaptation, observation; learning deficiency, as trained incapacity, learned helplessness; absence of opportunity to learn or perform; lack of models for imitation, motivation; psychosocial disadvantage; unskilled manner, style; unknown critical steps in performance of an interactive sequence; emotional arousal or flooding prevents acquisition, for example, anxiety, phobia, and hot anger; and poor impulse control (Gresham and Elliott 1989).

The study of performance defects aims at accounting for the things people do well but also the larger things that hold them back and keep them from fully functioning with each other from one situation to another. At issue is how defective or deficient performances are taken into scaled account and then figured into the larger equation. Complaints concerning conversation can be readily managed under conditions of working agreement and mutual understanding, but such potentially troublesome matters are not so easily regulated, it turns out, when a climate of disagreement and misunderstanding prevails. Individuals who lack sufficient skills for social success are constrained by a dual burden. Defective ability leads to erroneous conclusions and unfortunate choices. In addition, functional incompetence interferes with the ability to realize what is lacking. Hence, the inability to do well is accompanied by the metacognitive inability to know just how poorly one is performing higher-order tasks (Kruger and Dunning 1999).

The litany of reconstructed themes reveals that mentions of discontent and dissatisfaction almost never occur within the context of favorable, moderating, or compromising modes of linguistic interchange where there is a strong sense of common ground and sustained purpose. In contrast, nine out of ten references to social defects in the Wisconsin study refer to difficulties associated with performance defects that occur in unfavorable conditions with tendencies toward separation, opposition, and polarization. In the d/m conditions, twenty types of performance defects can be identified. The participants in question do not talk or stop talking; provoke, offend, threaten; devalue or discredit; engage in meaningless or futile efforts; constrain others from talking; abuse, misuse, violate, neglect; distort other peoples' intent; ignore, avoid, withdrawal; criticize others; adapt a deficient or inadequate style; become unable or unwilling to address problems, issues, or concerns; talk excessively; fail to listen; hide, disguise, mask; avoid eye contact; show lack of patience; say what others do not want to hear; misinform or lack sense and reason; drop issues unresolved; and fake, pretend, or deceive someone else.

Specifically, the central themes in these performance defects coalesce into larger clusters of association. Provocative acts offend, threaten, or coerce one party or another. Inflationary acts inflate, enlarge, exaggerate, overstate, or dramatize personal difficulties. Deprecating acts deflate, discredit, devalue, or disqualify the contribution of others. Distorting acts distract, deceive, mislead, mask, pretend, and fake. Frustrating acts aggravate, irritate, agitate, annoy, exasperate, or confuse. Inattentive/unresponsive acts neutralize or dismiss the meaning, import, or significance of the claims and contributions of other people. Avoiding/withdrawing acts promote emotional distance, detachment, separation, or disengagement. Taken together, these subversive tactics help explain why there is such great potential for faulty choices and bad decisions that lead to unwelcome or adverse consequences.

COLLUSION/MYSTIFICATION

Personal identity, whether stable or unsettled, is simultaneously resilient in the face of opposition and vulnerable to manipulation. As a consequence, close relations often prove much easier to get into than to get out of intact. Life *is* messy. People *are* complicated. Entanglements *do* proliferate. At times, causes *are* confused with reasons for undesirable or unwelcome outcomes. Moreover, the law of unintended consequences is alive and well. People do not always achieve what they want, need, desire, or deserve from others. Social comparisons shed light on talk concerning troubles and foibles, but so often the respondents are trying to figure things out by first trying to figure out *how* to figure things out. There is, in other words, a muddle, a double quandary. Some things make perfect sense, or at least ordinary sense, whereas other things make no sense at all. It takes a concerted effort to make sense of things, even those things that do not make any sense to anyone else.

Personal accounts do not always reveal deep secrets. Just because people are socially competent does not mean they will be compatible. Although it is important to acknowledge the diversity of things that people say and do to make things better, it is also necessary to recognize the magnitude of things that people do to make things worse, whether by design or inadvertently. The majority of accounts contain explicit explanation for what makes things better or keeps them from becoming any worse. Intimate partners often have little knowledge of how or why things go astray or head into the wrong direction or why they themselves lose emotional intensity or simply run out of things to try while dealing with complex issues and unresolved problems that do not seem to go away. Much of the explanation lies in the collective toil from all that goes wrong, whether by design or accident.

Sometimes the use or misuse of ordinary language leads to extraordinary outcomes. Particularly striking are the hypnotic and mesmerizing qualities of conversation that cast a magic spell on participants and observers alike. It is possible, after all, to engage in elaborate and complex modes of communicative activity that confuse rather than clarify, and mystify rather than enlighten, the respective participants. Questions involving personal identity may be covered up or buried over in collusive arrangements that preserve major disparities and critical discrepancies between what transpires and what is left out or added to subsequent recollections. In the aftermath, conventional discourse may become collusive in unilateral or reciprocal effort to gloss over undesirable aspects of what transpires or to magnify the welcome features of jointly determined outcomes.

Personal identities become collusive insofar as the respective parties agree to act as if they agree or understand far more than they actually do. The utopian illusion of complete consensus may safeguard and protect idealized versions of what is at stake. Moreover, it is tempting to assume that one's own personality is apparent to others, even during brief encounters with strangers. The illusion of transparency is based on biased assessments of others' ability and skill to read or monitor one's emotional states (Gilovich, Savitsky, and Medvec 1998). Less well acknowledged is that collusive striving may also work in the opposite direction, namely, to accentuate the negative and ignore the positive in hindsight bias. People may have a vested interest in dramatic reconstructions that idealize the sheer magnitude of gain, support, and empathy that is afforded or dwell on magnified versions of the depth of loss, devaluation, or deprivation to one person or another. When things go smoothly and turn out well, collusive idealization may serve to dramatize the magnitude of achievement and omit reference to stress or strain in the larger process.

In an early statement, Laing (1969) underscores the playful but risky tension between "genuine" confirmation and mutual desire for "authentic" disclosure, which is compromised by a gap or discrepancy whereby the contending parties, caught between trust and mistrust, confidence and despair, settle for counterfeit acts of confirmation on the basis of fantasy and pretense. Both parties must play the collusive game, even if they are not completely aware of the magnitude of deception and betrayal that is felt just beneath the surface. Collective willingness to engage in false confirmation of idealized maneuvers sets the ground for mutual evasion of truth or reason.

Finding someone to endorse false, inflated notions of oneself gives surface appearance a semblance of reality (113).

The allure of other people's virtues may strengthen the sense of initial attraction and create feelings of optimism and hope that bely or cover up recognition of frailties, weaknesses, or vulnerabilities. Romantic partners may seek to dispel the tension between emotionally generous aspirations and inevitable discovery of weaknesses and shortcomings by clinging to wish fulfillment and positive illusion, despite evidence to the contrary, mainly, signs of negativity and conflict. A false illusion of communication may form because unrecognized or unacknowledged feelings of closeness imply assumed symmetry and similarity and because defensive reactions may serve as buffers against disclosure of troubling insights into divergent thoughts and strange feelings.

Shared idealization of personal virtues and mutual discovery of faults may work together but at a great price. Collusive identity relies on highly idealized conceptions of partners' attributes and exaggerated estimates of control or influence, as well as a good measure of unrealistic optimism. Respondents who agree to agree about everything may be at risk, not only of constructing idealized illusions, but also of confronting disturbing truths and unpleasant realities that are neither a source of comfort nor a reassurance. Oddly, unqualified confidence in the ability and willingness of bonded partners to achieve higher levels of shared agreement and mutual understanding may help to promote a constructive climate but one that interferes with shared effort to acquire greater tolerance of harsh truth or disquieting evidence to the contrary.

Conversely, when things spin out of control or fall apart and cascade downward in a negative spiral, collusive denigration may be used to invert the direction of causal explanation to produce a one-sided focus on things that go astray. Narrative reconstructions enable people to play havoc with the "facts" and replace them with elements of fantasy and illusion as a matter of whim. Reciprocal collusion relies on theatrical play, deceitful discourse, allusiveness, and oscillation between multiple layers of reference and ambiguous personal boundaries. What is reality-tested is the good sense to separate fact from fiction, to know the difference, and to act accordingly.

5

Argumentation and Advocacy

There is no ultimate reality lying behind or beneath ordinary experience to which we turn intellectually as the court of last appeal. All meanings are born within the human world of the everyday, and have to return there to be tested.

—William Barret, *The Illusion of Technique*

Claiming to know ordinarily occurs against a backdrop of doubt and the possibility of disagreement and gets part of its meaning from the contrast, and from the possibilities for argument. Doubting is itself a kind of epistemic achievement; not a simple absence of belief, but a position within a framework of belief.

—John Lyne, "Knowledge and Performance in Argument"

The possibility of reasoning is a strong source of hope and confidence in a world darkened by horrible deeds. . . . Even when we find something immediately upsetting or annoying, we are free to question that response and ask whether it is an appropriate reaction or whether we should really be guided by it. We can reason about the right way of perceiving and treating other people, other cultures, other claims, and examine different grounds for respect and tolerance. We can also reason about our mistakes and try to learn not to repeat them.

—Amartya Sen, "East and West"

Applied social knowledge of appraisal, value, and identity come together, as implicit substrata, to define, inform, and enrich or to discredit, deplete, and degrade the credibility of public arguments. What informs speaker and auditor is, by definition, persuasive in one sense or another. The exchange of factual information without appeal to reasoned explanation is virtually worthless, if not totally useless, in validating or disconfirming the strength of personal arguments. Practical logic is indispensable for crafting plausible propositions, pro and con, that address the sufficiency of the status quo from multiple vantage points. An invitation to argue affords open opportunity to debate or dispute a range of contestable claims or propositions that may be subject to all manner of refutation by all the available means of persuasion. Argumentative disputes activate strategic social dissension between competing systems of personal logic in persuasive applications toward specific ends or goals.

PERSONAL LOGIC

Some people argue better than others. The ability to argue well has a number of intangible benefits, whereas the inability to argue well has sobering implications. Heated public controversies are subject to all manner of chicanery, manipulation, calculation, seduction, exploitation, violation, and entanglement in a discursive web of confusion, contradiction, conundrum, and paradox. Faulty modes of argumentation often go nowhere, and weak arguments over trivial matters settle nothing or merely waste time. Some advocates do not know where to begin, how to precede, or when to stop. Ineffective arguments register as points of discredit, devaluation, and disqualification of contentious social issues.

The work of Walton (1998) locates public argument in plausible social evaluations cast against functional warranted standards of whether affordable truth claims serve to enable or disable the enlightened goals of rational discourse. The object of public debate is to present strong reasons for one's valued conclusions and to question the arguments advanced by the other side. Multiple exchanges of reason-giving claims reveal comparative strength and weakness of alternative means to certain consensual ends. The limits of reason and rationality must be explored against a backdrop of strategic striving and tactical advantage based on passion, emotion, and vested interest. The best argument does not always prevail or win the day. Disputed social relevance is taken into account when specious arguments are irrelevant, go on tangents, or make useless points that weaken or undermine the main goal, which is to make sound decisions based on strong evidence for a course of action taken as being more prudent than plausible alternatives.

Elaborated arguments are generated, subject to challenge one at a time, and then rearranged into preferred categories and clusters in which assertive statements are advanced in support of others. Each claim requires at least one premise that leads, through a well-reasoned principle, to a sound conclusion. In the Toulmin (1964) model, data consist of all facts given to support, affirm, and justify a specific claim. Solid reasoning affords the necessary explanation in the form of a warrant presented as a rationale that applies to a specific case in point. Major propositions have varying degrees of persuasive force, as indicated by the interjection of a qualifier, such as "ordinarily" or "virtually without exception." Challenged warrants may require added backing, particularly during periods of claim refutation. Finally, appeal to a reservation makes reference to stipulated conditions or excluded circumstances. Debate formats vary from monologues, with one speaker on one side (pro) addressing a speaker on the other side (con), to more interactive forms in which the greatest number of participants enter into the larger process of civic deliberation.

REASONING TOGETHER

A critical consideration entails considerable interest in what makes argumentative situations qualify as being dialectical in tenor, texture, or tone. The core word *dialectical* has a wide range of meanings: as a struggle of opposed forces (in the Hegelian and Marxist senses), as a social exchange based on logical sequences of question and answer, as a test of the credibility of propounded views, and as a concerted deliberation to determine whether the standpoint of a protagonist is defensible against the critical reactions of an antagonist. These stipulated conditions presuppose that personal engagements in debate, dispute, and deliberation entail hard work and prove difficult to sustain at a high level of personal achievement or shared accomplishment. Skillful deliberations about reasons for linking data to conclusion require education, training, and practice perfected by repetition and habituation. Human reason qualifies as being objective only if it can be certified as being valid, irrespective of the point of view in which it is embedded. In a rational agent model, the wider the circle of application, the greater the force of a valid claim to unrestricted, abstract, or generalized status.

Strong advocates are motivated tacticians whose strategic choices and tactical maneuvers must remain sensitive to relevant information, logical consideration, social context, and a long-term goal. Effective reasoning leads to sound conclusions in disputed situations where both assertive practice and responsive interpretation count as being useful, productive, or fulfilling. Conversely, faulty modes of practical reasoning lead to low-quality deliberation under conditions in which both practice and interpretation serve as strategic indicators of linguistic misuse or misguided logic that involves abuse or neglect of sense, reason, or rationality. Inexplicable premises or implausible reasons undermine shared effort to understand the full magnitude of what is missing, does not follow, or leads nowhere in particular.

People give reasons for claims. Some claims are more compelling than others. Likewise, some people are more compelling in making well-reasoned claims than are others. What registers as being "intuitively obvious" to one advocate is not necessarily the case for any other advocate. Moreover, elements that fit for one person may not fit for anyone else. What is clear, relevant, or coherent to one source may be unclear, irrelevant, and incoherent to anyone else. Ultimately, what one party claims is grist for another person's disclaimer through the powers of refutation, rebuttal, or rejoinder without fixed formulae. False claims, logical failures, and weak arguments also figure into the larger equation, particularly in disputes, debates, and deliberations that have no beginning or end in sight. Argumentative disputes prove futile where there is no point in arguing about anything anymore.

It is possible, after all, to become quite saturated with the sheer force of compelling arguments, collective judgments, and overpowering verdicts. No wonder there is so much heated debate concerning the issue of whether human beings act as rational agents or more easily succumb to the appeal of relevance, hedonism, and mere whim. One side provides evidence that people reason poorly. Another side provides evidence that people reason well. Sometimes strong advocates reason well and badly too. Applied logical standards can vary greatly from one moment to the next. Everyday reasoning incorporates a mixture of formal, logical, and conceptual appeals blended with informal, emotional, and intuitive appeals. Individual reasoning, therefore, alternates between analytic appraisals, as those that are deliberate, controlled, tactical, and effortful, and heuristic appraisals, as those that are automatic, rapid, effortless, and reliant on biased judgment and flawed assumptions. Consequently, engaged advocates are likely to vacillate between elaborated, sophisticated, or advanced arguments and crude or superficial arguments based on vivid memories, passionate conviction, and rapid judgment.

It is neither obvious nor certain how to reconcile acts of sound reasoning mixed with episodes of erroneous reasoning based on fallacies, miscues, and poor decisions (Klaczynski and Robinson 2000). Moreover, relevant standards of critical cognitive assessment must take into account many disputed claims about difficult questions involving performance error, illogical distraction, and irrational reaction when human reasoning competence deviates from logical normative principles. Unfortunately, steadfast advocates cannot always be counted on to exercise due care and good sense in evaluating alternative worldviews and personal theories. Faulty argument occurs when rational agents are prone to explain and justify too much and to define and describe too little.

When competing arguments entail the appearance of irreconcilable personal differences, there may be no basis for choosing among them; hence, the potential for a sound verdict is rendered null and void. Public conceptions of human reasoning may be clear and optimistic according to logical standards for solving problems, or they may be subject to hidden biases in human judgment that proliferate rapidly for no good cause or reason.

Flawed reasoning qualifies as an intrinsic feature of dispute and debate across diverse reasoning tasks (Todorov 1997).

CONSTRUCTIVE ARGUMENT

The case for constructive argument derives from the generative and productive capacity of ordinary language itself (Zulick 1997). Salient subject matter qualifies as being at once innovative, infinite, and inexhaustible. When effectively applied by strong advocates who are both competent and credible, reasoned controversy produces generative and constructive themes linked by informal practical logic with supporting material in endless variation. Unfortunately, critical features of constructive argument and informal logic are often difficult to access and implement, much less to sustain in a clear and cogent manner.

Constructive argument provides an effective means to improve the strength of relational ties by keeping disputes interesting and by expanding the domains of personal agreement or mutual understanding. The likelihood of achieving positive outcomes depends largely on whether strong advocates are in a favorable position to test each other's ideas rather than test their personal deficiencies. Implicit requirements include a requisite base of resources, abilities, and skills sufficient to treat other advocates as equals, find common ground, and exploit attitudinal similarity in each other's evolved perspectives and worldly outlooks. Constructive arguments foster cooperative and congenial outcomes that are usually missing in far more competitive and aggressive disputes.

The weakest link in argumentation theory is the concept of practical reason itself. What counts as a premise or fact for warranted conclusions can be difficult to sort out, particularly during the early stages of inquiry when members impose their own definitions on unsettled matters in diverse ways that allow virtually everything to count as data. Faulty premises can be difficult to reconsider, even when they lead to unwelcome or adverse outcomes, perhaps as a consequence of false pride or defensive refusal to question them thoroughly. The implicative features of human reasoning, as Scheff (1990) claims, must leave some aspects of (content and form) unrecognized, unarticulated, or else missing. It is not always easy to draw the fine line between contesting an argument and attacking an opposed advocate as being defective rather than mistaken.

What counts as a reasonable argument cannot, even in principle, be settled through sterile disputes with one-sided appeal to relativism or perspectivism pitted against much broader types of universal or global applications of malleable logical systems. Notions of reason taken from idealized forms of civic deliberation rest on the illusion that universal standards of argumentative validity are possible in principle (Cheshier 1997). The complex notion of "communicative rationality" espoused by Habermas (1979, 1984) qualifies as a case of prototypic speculation that cannot be settled on solid empirical grounds one way or another. The basic premise here is that whatever counts as reasonable discourse is settled by good arguments. So far, so good.

Habermas advocates an idealized, almost utopian, conception of collective social judgment that is well grounded in a late-modernistic interpretation of the intrinsic requirements of applied language use in daily life. Hence, the force of better argument presumably carries the day through the successful application of uncoerced warranted consensus based on normative commitments and informed by the lofty embodiments of an idealized speech community. The basic presupposition is that strong advocates who engage in well-reasoned arguments and sound conclusions are somehow compelled to take such grand, expansive metaphors into enlightened account. Unfortunately, Habermas underestimates the passionate, aesthetic, and evocative underpinnings of normative judgments in a badly inflated account of reasoned discourse that surely qualifies as a paradoxically irrational overestimation of civic rationality.

An unreasonable defense of the so-called universal power of human reason unfortunately raises far more puzzling questions than it resolves. Habermas is reluctant to humble himself and admit the obvious. One, the localized power of communicative reason among speaking subjects may be neutralized, subverted, or overturned insofar as opposing advocates decide to pursue their own individual array of self-interests and vested personal concerns to the exclusion of others' logical appeals. Specifically, what is construed to be in one's best interest, when scaled against risk assessment of short-term investment and scaled measure of immediate return, may overwhelm the clarifying power of factual matters in contentious public deliberations. In addition, the mindless pursuit of self-interest, when combined with irrational outbursts of self-indignant protestation, may effectively neutralize the plausibility of rendering articulate, compelling, or sophisticated appeal for all human beings to "come reason together" about pressing communal concerns in a contested public sphere.

What is subject to the unified voice of human reason is, by definition, also subject to the countervailing force of illogical, unreasonable, or senseless responses to the collective expression of vital personal concerns. Reasoned appeals, invocations, or supplications to the transcendental power of a universal audience, however well intended, merely ensure a measure of personal access to a plurality of engaged people who strive to suspend premature judgment and find consensual resolution of conflicting claims and counterclaims in a given public marketplace. In effect, the best of human intentions cannot provide surefire protection or firm assurance against any unwelcome imposition of unreasonable or careless appeals by others toward scarce facts in order to support weak warrants for unwarranted conclusions based on false premises or faulty reasoning. The ultimate rational ideal of "all good persons speaking well" is subject to all matter of compromised convictions and expedient alternatives that seem to be intrinsic features of the reality of everyday life.

Those who pursue precise and exacting standards of reason or practical logic cannot be so effectively isolated, segmented, or sequestered in the co-presence of others who use inexact and imprecise logic to project an aura of unreasonable or irrational contentions. Moreover, the possibility of reaching certain consensus concerning what qualifies as the most convincing argument does not mean that the unity of reason will prevail over the fragmentation of reason. Protracted social conflicts are known to produce deep-seated disagreements and profound misunderstandings on a massive scale that is so pervasive or severe that discordant rankings of competing social values offer no binding categorical imperatives to guide them toward preferred or optimal solutions.

Manageable arguments that register on the surface of public opinion may still mask, confuse, or disguise deeper irreconcilable issues for which logical principles and factual descriptions are at odds. Intractable conflicts do not lend themselves to the presumption of common access to a universally applicable set of evaluative social standards. When uncertain forces and factors rule, the best argument cannot be found (Pellizzoni 2001). Wishing does not make it so. The critical issue, as it turns out, is not, as Habermas so mistakenly supposed, the subordination of coercive forces into the wider search for ideal or optimum conditions for civic deliberation. It is rather the sheer magnitude of personal tolerance of the collective struggle to incorporate or integrate any illogical, irrational, or unreasonable tactics into the larger deliberative process so that consensual achievements can be based on rational and reasonable standards of logical appraisal.

What qualifies as irrational behavior is, in fact, virtually anything or everything that may go astray or turn out wrong. What is construed by one advocate as being irrational or senseless may range in scale from sheer trivia to a supreme or final test of some ultimate consideration. Advocates who fail to satisfy the demands of reason make their presence felt nonetheless, even without good reason or without making any good sense of disputed matters. Irrational advocates do not behave as if they understand that there are some things that they do not understand about themselves. They are prone to take their own resentments and frustrations out on other people. When irrational advocates do not have their way, they are prone to generate hostility and anger toward other people; they are not apt to think about what they are doing before they do it; or they get so caught up in intense struggle over aversive emotional states that they lose touch with the appeal of common sense.

People who rely on irrational or unreasonable appeals often seem to think more about how their own misleading actions will affect themselves than about how they will adversely affect others. One should not underestimate the deft skills of irrational people to use acts of miscommunication and problematic talk to their advantage. Clever advocates know how to turn the tables, change the subject, or shift focus to something that does not portray them in harsh light. Mindless, repetitive, or habituated indulgence in irrational or unreasonable outbursts can take a tremendous toll on the reasoning efforts of other people.

Of course, it is difficult to deal with people who can give no rationale for their bewildering, senseless, or confusing actions. A reasonable observer may realize when others seem to have no clue, rhythm, reason, or rationale for the bizarre behavior that they may willingly display before others. Some appear to be out of control. Others seem to be lost, confused, or aimless. Still others seem to be unable to make sense of their own actions, much less the reasoned striving of anyone else. Personal preoccupation ranks at the very top of the list of disturbing signs and distressful symptoms. Human conflict can be exceedingly draining or exhausting when others are allowed to rant and rave or manage to talk nonstop, engage in self-indulgent, monologic excuses to babble endlessly about themselves, their petty complaints, criticisms, compulsions, obsessions, and the like. Some prefer to think out loud and repeat themselves without making any sense. Another common heuristic entails excessive emotional outbursts at little things, magnified, blown out of proportion, often in grandiose presentation. Fabricated debate can be so easy to fake.

Melodrama is an easy way to extricate one from a tight spot. Some resort to duplicitous tactics and double standards, such as "Do as I say, not as I do"; "You must listen to me, but I don't have to listen to you"; "I can set unobtainable standards, and there is nothing you can do to meet them"; "If I ask your opinion and you do not give me the exact reply that I seek, I will surely be upset, maybe even a little crazy"; "Since I know better than you do, your reasons do not count, because they mean nothing to me"; "Sometimes you cannot reason with me, no matter what"; "Sometimes I prefer to live in a bizarre world in which other people do not make any sense, but of course I am just fine"; "My sour mood swings and nasty disposition give other people massive headaches, but that is no concern of mine"; "I mouth my words with attitude, ulterior motives, hidden agendas, and suppressed hostility to make sure struggling conversations go nowhere." It can be disconcerting and disquieting to talk with someone who will take every word you say, pull it apart, twist it around, and throw picky details back in your face with no regard for your feelings one way or another. At times, the sheer emotional exhaustion and severe degree of relational deterioration can become an intolerable burden until the final verdict is rendered—it all becomes unbearable at the end. In question is the power of reason to overcome irrational outbursts and promote compelling justification for validity claims.

Although few would deny the presumptive possibility of discovering universally shared features of reason in public controversy, hardly any critic would be so bold as to specify in advance what constitutes or qualifies as a universal consideration at work on a local public scene. Unfortunately, Habermas adds density, obscurity, and confusion to the issue of civic deliberation while rendering a blurred distinction between facts and norms in contested modes of social advocacy. As his idealized social agents would have it, the search for valid truth claims presupposes far too much about a person's performative and interpretive capability at a critical or pressing moment. Ideal advocates behave exactly as they are supposed to act in the production and reception of polite civil discourse. What is critical is precisely all that Habermas cheerfully takes for granted about the chaotic features at work in a strongly contested human community. It is not self-evident how human beings should try to winnow and sift, distinguish between truth and error, by calmly, rationally, and securely struggling with competing truth claims on public display.

All this envisioned false decorum, politeness, civility, deference, and demeanor are naively expected to unfold in a resplendent and purified domain of secular glory, untainted by cheap strategies or unwarranted coercive tactics. Nor is it clear how members of an idealized speech community would work together to sort facts from fiction, fabrication, and falsification. If prevailing norms were so pervasive, inescapable, and obligatory, then perhaps sincere, respected, and articulate advocates of contested claims and counterclaims would have little or no choice but to set aside their petty interests, as well as covert vested interests, and wrap themselves in the bliss or euphoria of consensus so purely formed.

At issue is whether the best and the brightest of advocates are ever so favorably positioned to engage in freewheeling debate based on coercion-free speech that leads to normative consensus. It is a stretch to reconcile the local production of dynamic systems of pluralistic transaction with the sheer density of abstraction required to envision collective respect for diversity and pluralism transformed into a monistic universal (Frank 1998). It also requires what Crook (1998) calls a "great weight of theoretical baggage" (523) simply to dissolve all principles of form and substance into performance considerations. Linguistic aspirations, even with the best of intentions, interpretations, and informed conclusions, do not ascend to a quasi-transcendent sphere that subjects all modes of secular friction and earthly strife to meta-analytic reflection of philosophers who would be king.

What matters in everyday argument could not possibly measure up to such stringent stipulations about uncoerced consensus whereby social advocates willingly agree to the truth of warranted assertion and inclusive critical judgments spun from collective adherence to the so-called universal requirements of mundane language put to good use by spectacularly well-behaved and well-mannered citizens who speak well in a manner fit for all occasions. Idealized notions may severely limit a given speaker's intentions to make interpretive or understandable offers and to have them accepted by congenial listeners in a collective embrace of solidarity and cohesion. Habermas prefers to indulge in a purification strategy based on prototypic reconstructions of the rough-and-tumble tensions of daily life by interpreting the concept of mutual understanding as an intrinsic quality of civil language. To the contrary, entangled linguistic activities are not intrinsically bound to produce successful civic deliberations but rather serve as microstrategies and short-term tactics that operate as basic forms of applied social knowledge that is constrained by all the vested interests of users and observers of public controversy. Calculative styles, strategies, and tactical maneuvers resist transparent purification because they are grounded in manipulative mechanisms of adaptation, appeasement, and accommodation that are wholly contingent on a speaker's anticipations rather than on one's tight control of the reactions of those who are recipients.

Insulated notions of communicative rationality presuppose that opposing advocates have no vested interests, hidden agendas, or ulterior motives other than arriving at consensus on the basis that the best arguments prevail in the end. Appeals to strategic, coercive, or manipulative activity based on a calculus of utility lead only to unresolved theoretical problems and intractable communicative difficulties, which in turn leave congenial advocates in social dilemmas based on rationality and strategy in which appeal to reason and validity is pitted, sometimes unwittingly, against utility or cost-benefit calculations. It is, after all, one thing to pledge allegiance to reason and reasonableness unencumbered by daily burdens in the courageous truth-seeking efforts of an idealized speech community. It is quite another to seek to displace practical or applied logic from the rationalizing processes at work in the caldron of strategic human encounters. Rationalization triumphs over reason precisely in those public deliberations where adherents are not required to justify, much less exonerate, their own actions before others.

It is difficult to accept the rationalistic presumption that sensible people are capable, much less willing, to distinguish between discourse based on reason from what is masked to cover coercive tactics. Under the guise of reasonableness, political advocates may posture, justify actions in double-talk, and indulge in the inflated language of propaganda, both as a means to exploit uncritical and collective, mass-induced thinking and as a disguise of hidden agendas that work well for manipulative purposes, however vulnerable to suspicion and mistrust. It makes little sense to legislate coercive manipulation out of the larger equation of human advocacy, whether on grounds of intellectual piety, moral indignation, or insufficient adherence to some rarefied or utopian notion of transcendent reasoning.

Dismissive tactics whose aim is to segregate the encompassing power of substantial communicative reasoning from the calculating application of strategic interest only serves to cause one to badly miss the crucial point. For without the very potential for cogent expression of coercive intent and strategic manipulation in calculative tactics, the very notion of persuasive human language would hardly qualify as power in the ordinary sense of the term. Where there is no provision for the possibility or necessity of linguistic coercion, there can be no way to express or respond to the imposition of threat, risk, violation, violence, or threat of annihilation from external sources or unknown points of origin. So unless a cheerful, romantic theorist is prepared to subordinate but also insulate ordinary citizens from the pervasive impact of coercive possibilities—including linguistic and physical violence—the grand vision self-destructs and implodes from its own idealized but fatally untenable assumptions.

Daily arguments often serve to resist or undermine any idealized form of social purification. In a sobering rejoinder, Kaufman (1999) points out that users of conventional language do not necessarily operate according to such idealized obligations; that in all acts of speaking, the participants are not shown, even as a congenial disposition, to raise validity claims so that they can be redeemed; and that the most problematic feature is the insistence that good arguments win the day because of some all-inclusive evolutionary tendency for something like rationality to operate in the human world. Unfortunately, critical discussion is cut off without full explanation of how the universality of validity claims may be acquired by acting in such good faith. Although a robust conception of enlightened language use implies certain legitimating practices, it does not follow that legitimatized efforts, and hence a communicative rationality, have sweeping universal implications. Suspect language may just as well disavow claims to legitimacy as to certify them. Since arguers are free to imagine their own version of a universal audience, there are as many rational standards as there is the number of advocates who care about which arguments stick or fall short of the mark. Sometimes strident advocates eventually discover that they are addressing an audience of one.

ARGUMENTATIVENESS

An argumentative person is one who takes stands on numerous controversial issues and engages in multiple verbal attacks of the alternative standards advocated by other people. The confrontational style is striking: assertive, forceful, dynamic, and aggressive. Personal styles of argumentativeness and defensiveness come together in the routine misuse and abuse of ordinary language. Some people thrive by trying to look good by making others look bad. Offensive styles of presentation employ tactics of dominating or derogating of others. Personal attacks serve to establish a desired image of superiority by downward comparison. Sarcasm thrives as irony, used as a front that reveals, paradoxically, what it apparently conceals (Anolli, Ciceri, and Infantino 2002). Ironic statements create the impression of a sharp mind at work, show tough standards of evaluation, criticize the questioner, control the topic, shift away from anything that interferes with the impression of being in charge, and also move toward whatever perpetrates the illusion of sitting on a self-appointed throne as an object of admiration and endless praise (Schutz 1999). Conversely, as the magnitude of verbal aggression goes down, the more assertively other people can speak on their own behalf, of their own best interests, and for the welfare of others. Verbal aggression destroys further opportunity for more inclusive participation and thrives on subversive tactics directed not only at all the suspect arguments but on important features of the personal integrity of the active participants themselves.

Abusive language threatens as it sanctions the implementation and enforcement of "double standards." The exchange of emotionally charged pairings of words and gestures—particularly, relations to anger, disgust, and contempt—reflect minute physiological changes that dampen and reduce both the capacity and the willingness of advocates to generate new information or explore alternative perspectives instead of exclusive reliance on unwelcome or unhelpful behavior that reinvokes and reactivates deeply ingrained urges to fight or flight (Gorsevski 1998). Hurt feelings emerge from isolated acts or protracted episodes of relational discredit, devaluation, and distress and produce a surplus of negative affect, anxiety mixed with hostility, and enough adverse repercussions to go around.

Personal resources and social skills required to engage in well-reasoned argument provide critical measures of communicative competence and interpersonal compatibility. The main finding may be taken as a reaffirmation for a time-honored civic principle—skill in argument is inversely related to the magnitude of defensiveness and argumentativeness. Those who know how to reason well together are the least likely to promote or cultivate a rigid or inflexible argumentative attitude. Those who are not so skilled are prone to rely on distinctive styles of expression that others are likely to view in terms of four stable attributes: closed-mindedness and stubbornness, and a tendency to use argument for argument's sake as well as participate in heavy score keeping concerning who is right and wrong on issues of opposition, rivalry, and polarization. Argumentativeness, verbal aggression, and personal boundary violations are linked with contested social climates where strong disagreements and mutual misunderstandings are produced with no resolution in sight. From the d/m section, common narrative themes underscore the magnitude of difficulties encountered during contentious disputes:

Argument for argument's sake: S/O are confused and angry—whatever issue one wants to talk about, the other takes the other side; there is much argument just for argument's sake; it is nerve-wracking because personal logic seems to fly out the window; S/O cannot express themselves without appealing to false assumptions from flawed and faulty conversations taking over—they voice their own views without listening, and both argue points down to nothing; S/O started to argue more and more for unknown reasons; nothing was resolved, and now they do not even talk anymore; S/O find that each one tries to get the best of the other; it is hard to talk because it seems that whenever they do talk, they get into another argument and one more heated debate; S/O provoke each other just for the sake of argument—a lot of energy is directed at proving the other wrong; they often say things that end up irritating one another—they say things they do not mean and resent later on; simple conversation ends up in bigger disputes; S/O have so much emotional baggage from years of emotional torment that they find it difficult to talk about anything else besides the weather; S/O find it is hard to come to a consensus because each one sees the issue from such a different perspective; their arguments do not seem to influence one another; rather, they become ineffective and do not make much sense to anyone; each one tries to influence the other with what seems to be perfectly logical and correct arguments, but they both fail—it turns into a battle of wills and neither one ends up really changing the other's view; S/O defend their positions no matter what—debates continue until one person is ready to snap; in the end, they know they did not change their minds about anything; S/O disagree about virtually everything—they rip on one another and become defensive about petty arguments—they have started to avoid each other because each one knows there will be conflict no matter what either one says.

Stubborn: S/O argue hard, often, and stubbornly—they have little tolerance for each other, and they clash in varied ways about different beliefs over different things; S/O are stubborn, refuse to listen, and display judgmental attitudes and defensiveness whereby one person refuses to talk or they both raise their voices and one or the other walks away angry; S/O are very stubborn, and it is hard for either to back down; S/O never agree about issues—they raise voices about something petty or unimportant and then verbally attack each other—two stubborn people have serious disagreements because they do not understand one another, so they perpetuate arguments and disputes without end; S/O find out that stubbornness and sarcasm make it difficult to reach any type of binding agreements—there is a lot of bragging, name dropping, ranting loudly, or explosions; S/O are stubborn—they do not like to change their own minds about anything; they focus on their own thoughts and feelings rather than listen; they engage in talking over and ignoring one another, yelling, blaming, and crying; it is a mess—what starts out as a simple task turns out to be a major deal; S/O are stubborn people who share nothing in common; card games give rise to petty fights about little mistakes; the level of anger depends on how much one party watches his mouth, but when the other has been pushed to the limit, he blows up—they say things to get a rise out of one another.

Closed-minded: S/O have closed their minds to one another—often a defensive stance comes into the picture at which time daily interaction becomes intense and negotiation is suddenly out of the question; S/O rarely agree about anything—they have little in common; neither one is willing to listen to the other's opinion; each one is closed-minded, constantly interrupts, criticizes, or invalidates whatever the other has to say; criticism abounds, even on neutral subjects; there are shouting matches over something minor; each one is a total loss when it comes to dealing with the other; S/O are closed-minded and not open to each other's feelings, particularly if different from their own; S/O think their own way is the only way—neither one is willing to see the other's view as being worthy—one gets upset that the other is closed-minded, obstinate, will not listen—it becomes hard to discuss things when one person has no original thoughts, remains closed-minded, and refuses to listen; S/O will argue about anything—S thinks O throws out opinions as if they were laws; he takes too much for granted, and he hides behind facts that can be easily manipulated; it sure feels good to beat him at his own game; S/O often take the opposite view—each one seems closed-minded and makes rash statements; S/O advance arguments from only one side of the equation—hence, episodes of disagreement lead each one to be even more closed-minded than before.

Who's right/who's wrong: S/O take a different stand just for the sake of further argument; it gets to the point that it turns into another heated confrontation and they start attacking one another; they fight it out with each one striving to prove the other wrong—a constant battle; S/O fight no matter what—as if it were some sort of power struggle over the most insignificant topics—second place is not good enough—win or leave; S/O are contestants in a game—both are much alike, competitive, combative, and critical; fights leave each one feeling horrible—one angers the other because of the need to be right about everything—they spend countless hours in personal disagreement over even the simplest of things; S/O take turns, but neither one really listens; each one is planning what to say next just to reinforce a view—pretty soon there are two people talking in circles; neither one realizes how much breath each one is wasting; when they talk, each has a closed mind, and each one believes that his or her own opinion is the right one; S/O argue, become defensive, and fight over virtually anything; no matter how slight or trivial—it is only when personal argument dissolves into personal attacks and character assassination that they wonder whether proving their point really matters that much—they realize that proving that they are right is not worth the pain that it can cause to each other.

In general, questionable arguments are degraded or devalued insofar as the major issues become polarized, contentious, and quarrelsome. Extreme arguments begin to outweigh the forces of moderation, accommodation, and compromise. Assumptions vary, attention wanders, and mindless venting of alleged grievances serve as handy substitutes for reasoning and substantiating. Advocates get stuck in first-person perspectives with nothing to choose among them. They confuse trivial matters with consequential concerns. Interaction is one-sided, disruptive, or chaotic. Quibbles, complaints, and jabbing fill the air. People talk in circles, and continuing motion rules.

When argument occurs for the sake of argument, the basic instigating conditions are easier to turn on and much more difficult to turn off. There is a self-perpetuating and self-fulfilling quality to the erratic cycles and irregular trajectories of aggressive and confrontational advocacy that eventually evolve into ingrained habits and even deeper provocations. The distinction between constructive and destructive argument is rendered meaningless or moot when arguments are ripped asunder as fast as they can be advanced. Logic is expendable. Conclusions are deferred. It is not necessary to believe a word said by anyone who is on the scene. So argument becomes pervasive, a way of life, a mindless contest without end. Irrationality acquires momentum as a subversive force, reactivated in matters of interpretation, lexicon, and conflicting styles of claim presentation.

Some staunch advocates are obviously stubborn and dig in their heels. Intolerance abounds. There may be an underlying compulsion to appear as being all-knowing or always in the right. Resistance mounts to backing down, giving in, or seeming weak in the eyes of others. Harsh judgment mingles freely with cognitive lapses into a reactive stance of inflexibility, rigidity, and becoming stuck in first-person perspectives that preclude appeal to second- and third-person perspectives. Closed-minded or rigid advocates need not view consensual reasoning as a common goal. At times, the only universal audience is the one who talks and talks while no one else listens or responds. What counts is winning, or at least not appearing to be the one who is in the wrong. Provocations, score keeping, and button-pushing tactics ensure that everyone will become all riled up long before they settle down.

Interpersonal disagreements proliferate easily among opposing advocates who are intent on proving who is right and who is wrong. Truth claims not only fall short of the mark but also manage to distort, disrupt, or disable the goal of promoting improved discourse and sustained dialogue. Personal explanations are short-circuited when opinion is confused with authority. It is rare to find mention of qualifiers, backing, or reservations to temper wild or extravagant claims. What seems intuitively to be obvious to one advocate may fail to register that way to anyone else. Eventually, endless quarrels and countless disputes take their toll until a state of argumentative exhaustion settles upon the beleaguered rivals. Cooperative outcomes recede. In extreme cases, intractable matters cluster around the appearance of irreconcilable differences that are strongly associated with weakened relational ties. Concern about the supremacy of argument takes precedence over the integrity of the argumentative process. Serial arguments activate or trigger conflict episodes that capture the sense of argument and aggression taken almost as a way of life. The subjugating capacities entailed in the repetition of

unresolved argument can overwhelm or preclude shared attempts to fulfill
their emancipative possibilities.

RESOLVABILITY

The resolution of everyday argument is a major consideration. After all, argument for the sake of argument will carry one only so far in daily life. Likewise, strong arguments may not suffice, and winning verdicts may not be
worth the cost. Even skillful strategies and tactics do not necessarily ensure
favorable social outcomes, improve relationships, or make the world a better place. Argument is singular. The subject is general. Argument making
therefore involves a collective process. The consequences, whether short
term or long term, may be construed in progressive and constructive, or regressive and subversive, terms. By these definitions, the resolution of important personal differences is cast as a possibility or promise but not a necessary outcome of contested civic deliberations. The tension between
strategic tactic and felt sense of dialectical obligation may remain unsettled
or find eventual resolution under terms acceptable to everyone. So much depends on whether people can agree with each other about specific details
and understand one another in respect to general principles of reason in
controversy. By these standards, successful resolution of pressing personal
issues constitutes a high-order achievement.

Reconstructed accounts of everyday argument are worthy of serious consideration. Although it is important not to confuse the intrinsic features of
original events with subsequently reconstructed accounts, the practical logic,
rich vocabulary, and thematic content of each reconstruction can be subject
to rigorous and precise documentation of what matters most and what stands
out with the benefit of hindsight. At stake are the intrinsic features of public
arguments that converge or diverge over time. The intuitive presumption of
convergent or divergent tendencies is also subject to tests of verification as
sources of mutual understanding, mutual misunderstanding, miscommunication, or failures in sense making. Not only did participants in the Wisconsin study make these sorts of distinctions, but they also figured heavily in
personal accounts of favorable results and unwelcome outcomes.

The first task is to track the frequency of mention of three key concepts—
debate, fight, argue—across the four main conditions. These kinship terms
cut deeply into the meaning and significance of arguments, disputes, and
verbal wrangling (table 5.1).

Several generalizations warrant consideration. Arguments, obviously, are
far from randomly distributed. Almost 80 percent of all references to "argue,"
"argument," or "argumentative" states occur in d/m conditions. Likewise, almost 80 percent of all references to "fights" or "fighting" also occur in d/m

Table 5.1.   Debate, Fight, Argue: Frequency of Mention

	Agreement	Disagreement	Understanding	Misunderstanding
Debate	9	22	8	4
Fight	16	64	12	40
Argue	13	68	17	15
Total	38	154	37	59

conditions. Mentions of "debate" or "debating" are much less frequently in evidence but are still skewed in the same direction. Overall, almost three out of four references to the three key search terms occur in d/m conditions. The implication is that it may be a mistake to construct theories of argumentation and advocacy by focusing exclusively on the defining features of the constituent components. Everyday arguments do not emerge in hermeneutically sealed spheres of discourse or dialogue called by any other name. Static conceptions severely underestimate the fluidity of movement from one phase of shared activity to another—from frivolous debate to mindless dispute, from innocent assertion to harmful altercation, from petty bickering to savage contention, from trivial spat to shocking feud, from minor quarrel to major clash, or from faintly reasonable to outrageously irrational modes of assertion and response.

When people engage in arguments, they also become involved in lots of other things, too. Sometimes these "other things" may be of little consequence, but oftentimes they matter far more than the sequencing of arguments. Nothing is gained by ignoring the sheer magnitude of forces and factors that determine the ebb and flow of contested claims and counterclaims. The dynamic, multifaceted, and contextual features of human performance are critical, collectively if not individually, for all manner of definition, direction, and adversarial outcome. Nor is anything gained by ignoring the contingent foundations of argumentation and advocacy or, even worse, by giving in to the urge to take refuge in abstracted and rarefied models that collapse all possibilities into single theoretic formulations that by definition cannot possibly apply to all of the people all of the time, despite unfounded pretensions of unproven universal applicability.

An alternative is to permit respondents the space or room to specify the magnitude of substantive movement as well as the density of incorporated materials from the stance of their perspectives on one another. Each member constructs a composite picture simply by using words and describing gestures that specify the meaning or type of debate, fight, or argument in question; the type of presentational styles adapted by each member; and the central themes and underlying concerns that have the greatest salience or importance to the participants themselves. Each composite picture can also be examined for purposes of social comparison and then further organized into broader types, clusters, and scopes of shared activity. In this way, the anatomy of argument can be examined in inclusive global terms without sacrificing sensitivity to matters of context and circumstance.

There is little similarity between the argument structures that emerge under conditions of personal agreement and mutual understanding and those that arise under conditions of personal disagreement and mutual misunderstanding. Argument-making activity in the a/u condition is consistently described as being constructive, productive, and egalitarian in tenor and tone. Over a third of references describe the total absence of argument in relational matters. This can be read as a reciprocal prohibition, mutual effort never to argue, or mutual pullback at the slightest hint of argument emerging on the scene. Affirmative references describe skill in argument as being sufficient, sophisticated, and usually well-matched:

S/O argue from positions of assertiveness; at the end, there is no clear answer but two very well-argued sides.

S/O know each other so well that when they argue, they soon realize each other's points, so the dispute does not last for long.

S/O hardly ever argue; when they do, they make up rather quickly because they cannot go without the other person for very long.

S/O love to argue—they pick each other's brains to get at the heart of a point.

S/O agree about most things on a general scale, but they both love to argue small details just for the sake of arguing and the competition it generates.

In contrast, arguments that proliferate under conditions of disagreement are often construed in terms of dissension, acrimony, and substantive disarray:

S/O disagree with each other on so many issues that they can hardly argue any more—it seems useless.

S/O begin to argue more and more about less and less.

S/O always fight or argue about something—it must be some type of competitiveness, but it seems they will argue about the most trivial things.

S/O are together, and S thinks O will do something wrong, and O continues to argue because it pisses S and everyone else off.

S/O end up arguing about something that they should not discuss anyway—their only agreement is to stop talking about sensitive things that they will just argue about anyway.

S/O argue, then O stares off silent and S looks around, now and then smiling at the stupidity of the argument, shaking her head; when they disagree, O faces away from S (in despair), and S will shake her head in disgust until she decides to end the argument.

S/O argue all the time about everyday issues in the news and political views; S often finds himself arguing against O just to prove him wrong.

S/O talk and S usually argues with O because they do not have any patience.

S/O often disagree about issues they are indifferent about but happen to argue because S may see it one way and O may see it another, yet they do not really care about the issue in question.

S/O talk, but S thinks it is pointless to argue with O because he believes that he is the center of the universe and the only things in life are hockey and women.

S/O have talked through the years, and they have learned to accept one another's views, but they still frequently argue about the littlest things— such as if one needs to go to mass every week or if it is acceptable to live with someone before one gets married.

S/O argue with each other, become hostile, and accomplish nothing.

Contested matters of argument and advocacy are more settled, grounded, organized, progressive, and conciliatory in social conditions where advocates understand themselves, each other, and both the form and substance of what is at stake:

S/O do not argue in any disagreement over issues—they just listen to the other's opinion and find out why the other feels the way he does.

S/O rarely argue with one another because they both know how the other is going to react in any situation.

S/O find on the surface that they mock, argue, and disagree constantly, but on a higher level they know it is okay to have different viewpoints and still understand each other.

S/O can count on one hand the number of times that they have argued over the past two years of friendship—if they do argue at all, it only takes a few minutes for them to discuss and work things out.

S/O rarely argue about a certain issue, because they both fear losing each other.

Finally, the climate of argument in contested social settings where a litany of misunderstandings prevail virtually duplicates the tenor and tone of disagreeable negotiations:

S/O find there are not many situations in which they do not argue.

S/O argue about semantics rather than the overall meaning of conversation.

S/O will not let minor details go because neither one wants to acknowledge that the other has a point.

S/O do not disagree or argue very much, but they still do not understand each other well; even when they do argue, one would try to discuss matters calmly and the other would raise his voice and become defensive.

S/O are good friends who love each other, but they still argue a lot.

S/O don't argue all that much, but when they do, nothing really seems to get resolved.

S/O both feel as though they have all the correct answers, so when the other tries to make a comment, they always contradict each other and argue each other's points.

S/O can argue over something as simple as a movie or as complex as how worthless O thinks life is—he can't understand why anyone would want to live past tomorrow.

The central finding is striking. Arguments are not usually frequent, conspicuous, prolonged, or damaging in interpersonal relations where a climate of agreement and understanding prevails. Conversely, arguments are frequent, troublesome, problematic, and destructive features of interpersonal relations when a climate of disagreement and misunderstanding prevails. The full magnitude of difference occurs at two broad levels of explanation. The first may be attributable to high levels of competence and compatibility that sustain the quality of interaction in the a/u conditions. The second is a reflection of the much lower levels of competence and compatibility that typify the retrograde quality of so much interaction that takes place in the d/m conditions. An added consideration is the multiplicity of defects and deficiencies that keep people from achieving improved skill and knowledgeable participation in matters of argument and argumentation in the d/m conditions. In effect, the means required to produce a working base of binding agreements and mutual understandings overlap with the conditions that are associated with aspirations toward excellence in matters of argument and advocacy.

Relevant evidence shows up in the cognitive appraisals used by many respondents to frame and evaluate their own communicative, relational, and argumentative skills. Success draws attention to strength, whereas failure underscores weakness. By examining all claims about argumentative skills and disputed consequences, it is possible for one to reconstruct the defining features of those broad types of shared actions that appear to make a noticeable difference in the overall quality of what transpires. In addition, the composite picture facilitates greater understanding of the leading question of resolvability. The likelihood of successful resolution remains as dependent on dialogic skills as on argument-making ability per se.

In the construction of personal agreement and shared understanding, there is emphasis on a broad assortment of mutual abilities when both parties argue well; argue assertively; express ideas clearly; discuss issues seriously; make strong arguments; hold strong, forceful positions; stand up for personal beliefs; state opposing positions just so all possibilities can come to light; build on one another's ideas rather than refute just for the sake of argument; and determine where views separate, discuss the divergence, and find a common assumption that leads to different conclusions. Likewise, a strong emphasis on constructive argument is indicated in multiple references to validation of each other's positions; tolerance of flaws, shortcomings, and weaknesses in one another; and mutual willingness to talk about everything together.

There is a surplus of positive affect associated with mutual engagement in debate, argument, or civil dispute, typified as being fun, enjoyable, kind, or loving. Often, there is also a strong prohibition against attacking the other; getting defensive; fighting, mocking, name-calling, putting down, hurting feelings, insults, or using harsh words; holding one's tongue; avoiding or stopping a conversation that may get out of hand; engaging in excessive or extended arguments or, in some cases, any arguments or quarrels at all; and not feeling the need to have to argue one's case, prove a point, or defend oneself at any time. In a few cases, there are anomalous references that go against the grain: reluctance to argue out of fear of losing each other as a friend; shared willingness to engage in raging arguments that focus on offensive behaviors; make opposing arguments but not actually resolving anything while still making each other think, take a new perspective, and rethink one's own position; or argue until the truth hurts but not as much as it would hurt coming from someone else.

Resolvability of personal differences is a major theme. Respondents referenced a shared willingness to address a matter at the time it becomes bothersome so that they do not build up hostility and regret the outcome later; realize each other's points, so dispute does not last long; explore issues until complete agreement is reached; talk things through; usually wind up justifying each other's ideas; reach a compromise that does not belittle anyone; stay flexible; trust, enjoy, talk, and argue to get through things; complete business together so that everyone can celebrate; agree on solutions for problems in their lives; make up rather quickly after arguments; make sure by the end of conversation that each party's ideas and beliefs are clear to everyone else.

In the construction of personal disagreements and multiple modes of shared misunderstanding, there is emphasis on a broad assortment of individual rather than mutual abilities. Respondents, in effect, are likely to focus on self-enhancing intentions, interpretations, and inferences. A worst-case scenario occurs among those who care only about the right to vent and make a point. Others are content to make sure every opposing argument is ripped asunder. Often, there are so many disagreements about so many issues that serial arguments are repeated with such frequency that it seems useless. Matters that are no big deal to one party may be huge issues to the other party. There is a mechanical, repetitive, and cyclical quality to futile exchanges in which sticky issues are rehashed without rhyme or reason. Often, the arguments seem to be in control of the participants rather than the reverse. Some are utterly baffled or bewildered by conditions that arouse automatic, defensive, and reactive tendencies (mystification). However, some advocates are willing to take the other side of a contested issue simply to argue or provoke havoc. Some prefer to change the subject, blow off questions, crack a joke, take refuge in small talk, get off the track, refuse to budge, and the like. Some arguments appear to come out of nowhere, suddenly, unexpectedly. Some parties acquire an aversion to argument; still others persist in futile efforts until they reach a point of emotional exhaustion.

Power struggles can become battles about who is right or wrong. Some parties provoke or antagonize simply to rile another. One is wary of falling into a little trap and waiting for that one hostile comment or harsh criticism, undeserved and unwelcome, that invites retaliation. Win at any cost, through manipulation or any means available. Others clash out of sheer force of habit or polarize into a state of total opposition. One fight leads to another—the contentious parties become "angrier and angrier" until neither one can take it anymore. Everything may be up for grabs when neither party allows the other to get away with anything. Fights persist, no matter how trivial, when agonistic rituals provide one the chance to show the other up. However, an important qualification is in order. Although it takes two to fight, that does not mean that both parties are driven by the same urge. Sometimes, one party wants to fight with one who dreads the thought, responds in a reserved way, and tries not to react to the other's defensive and aggressive manner, fearing his or her wrath and seeing no point in another painful fight. It takes an adroit person to avoid one who is intent on aggressive confrontation no matter what the cost. The issue does not have to be important or have intrinsic significance. In fact, fights over foolish matters are widespread and common.

Ignorance causes disagreements to escalate into personal attacks because fights can sustain themselves on interest-based aspirations. Some people play games in which one party disagrees about issues to which both are quite indifferent and will argue endlessly merely to have the final word. Threats and ultimatums are not persuasive because they tend to make rivals dig in their heels, take extreme stands, and refuse to give in or make concessions no matter what. When power is a crucial issue, some antagonists try to outdo each other by insulting and demeaning the other party. Fighting about anything or everything seems to bring out the worst in everyone concerned. Others remain baffled because nothing ever is resolved.

Not surprisingly, there is a toxic surplus of negative affect associated with debate, argument, and dispute where rivals are described as being smug;

short; not very nice; intolerant; stubborn; militant; manipulative; calculating; demeaning; pig-headed; nitpicking; sarcastic; or intent on making others look stupid, foolish, or incompetent. Errors in attribution reflect the notion that it seems to be the other person's fault or problem. Conversation may begin rationally until one party blames others for what's wrong with himself or herself—there usually is a great deal of yelling and swearing, and little is accomplished. In some cases, the negative slant induces feelings of frustration and despair in private realizations that there was no need for argument in the first place.

Dialogic skills are often construed as being defective or deficient. At the top of the list are references to misinterpretation, miscommunication, poor communication, misconstrual of meanings, failure to listen, refusal to say anything—it would be pointless, ignoring questions, lying, pretending, ignoring, complaining, letting logic fly out the window, throwing out opinions like they are laws, snapping easily, hiding behind facts, yelling and screaming, coming on strong, getting the upper hand, belittling, attributing hidden motives, arguing matters down to nothing, making ridiculous accusations, and knowing what buttons to push to upset the other person. Many polarized arguments are cut off or aborted quickly in no-win situations. Respondents refer to an assortment of dismissive tactics: dropping the subject; refusing to react; blowing up; giving up, blocking the other; hanging up the phone; leaving any unfinished topics, feeling confused and angry; short-circuiting discussion before it can start; stomping out; leaving the scene; winning or leaving; cutting off chances for future interaction; stonewalling; stopping talking altogether; dissolving a relationship; or refusing to see the other ever again.

The potential for resolution is diminished for those who argue frequently without solutions; rarely settle disputes because neither party wants to be wrong or admit the other may be right; decide it is not worth the time or energy; argue about nothing and leave with a tension headache, wishing it had never begun; become sick of seeing each other; refuse to speak for days, weeks, or months; or refuse to be the first to try to reach the other after heated arguments. In some cases, respondents argue about touchy subjects but still shake hands and forget their differences. The battered and bruised often conclude that communication is not effective and even pointless at times.

6

Agreement and Positivity

An account of well-being or welfare should inform us about the ways in which an individual can be made both better and worse off; we want to know, in a general way, what accounts for enhancement and diminution of an individual.

—Mark Bernstein, "Well-Being"

When people observe their own behavior to try to discern what others think of them, their theories about themselves and about social life are important in determining what they see. To the extent that these theories are correct, then their understandings of how others generally view them are also correct.

—David A. Kenny, *Interpersonal Perception*

Constructive human relations flourish when goal-seeking participants are able and willing to secure a broad base of working agreements with one another. It is a mistake to view the completion of daily tasks, projects, habits, and routines as those conducted in a dull, dry, droning, or dispassionate manner. Personal agreements are not achieved, it turns out, in the manner of a bean-counting exercise. To the contrary, strong emotions are implicated across a broad spectrum of specific effects and protracted long-term outcomes. Mutual constructions of working agreement often evoke strong positive sentiments (love, joy, and happiness), whereas the mutual construction of complex working disagreement often arouses an equally salient range of negative sensibilities (anger, fear, and sadness) in response. In performance terms, the active sense of doing well yields to elation and eagerness while the sense of doing poorly gives way to movement into sadness and depression or, in cases of avoidance, to anxiety and fear (Carver 2004).

Social interactants who score highest on scales of agreeableness are often viewed as being moderate, tender-minded, sensitive, cooperative, and disposed to praise others rather than simply to praise themselves (Olson and Evans 1999). A personal style of agreeableness and warmth is also associated with trait measures of a strong interpersonal orientation (Hurley 1998). As a rule, explicit displays of personal warmth register on the brighter and lighter side of relational entanglements (Andersen and Guerrero 1998). A congenial stance of acceptance, agreeableness, assertiveness, and warmth fosters more lenient ratings of others (Hurley 1998). Persons often equate an agreeable manner with appreciative, kind, and generous responsiveness toward others (Sneed, McGrae, and Funder 1998). An agreeable manner also may portend less routine conflict but with more emotional distress when it does occur than is true of less agreeable counterparts (Suls, Martin, and David 1998).

The link between personal agreeableness and the potential for consensual agreement is robust. In a cyclical equation, persons who agree readily seek individuals who also agree easily, and, thereby, each one acquires a tacit base of constructive expectations and a more refined means to reproduce or renew favored circumstances. In contrast, individuals who score the highest on scales of disagreeableness appear to others as being pompous, conceited, egocentric, competitive, antagonistic, skeptical, overcritical, or distrustful toward rivals. A sense of agreeableness, along with a sense of extroversion and conscientiousness, qualifies as a stable personality trait. An agreeable disposition can be identified from a wide number of verbal and nonverbal cues; it correlates well with actual behavior; and it reveals substantial generalizability across diverse cultures (Quereshi 2000). Global indicators of personal agreeableness have been linked to an enduring sense of assertiveness, life satisfaction, and conscientiousness sustained over a life span (Lounsbury et al. 1999).

Agreeableness has considerable significance because of its close affinity with the reproduction of favorable impressions, pleasant responses, rankings of liking, and common willingness to submit or yield to the controlling influence of another person (Williams and Munick 1995). Social inconsistency in agreeable-relevant behavior does occur, of course, when people confront demands and rewards that go against deeply ingrained or habituated strivings. Another countervailing influence stems from the simple fact that cordial and congenial styles of self-presentation can be faked or feigned, despite the risks of appearing too compliant or overly cheerful. It does not require a clever or adroit person to project a contrived sense of sincerity, concern, or regard for the welfare of other people. Strategic acts of feigned sincerity constitute the heady stuff of which all manner of folly, nonsense, and chicanery can be used as a clever disguise or convincing illusion transformed by the use of word manipulation into a deceptive or magical pose of pretense, artifice, or fabrication. A false sense of amicability and ingratiation, together with strong self-enhancing and social desirability pressures, can be troublesome as a result of the value or currency accorded to politeness, friendliness, compliance, and tolerance in daily life.

Convergent constructions achieved between agreeable people acquire a strong, affirmative, and positive slant in emotional texture and affective overtone. There is a close connection between predictable adherence to demanding standards of agreement-making activity and personal engagement in the coproduction of a strong surplus of positive, affirmative, and constructive signs. Moreover, personal styles viewed as those compatible and comprehendible facilitate the greatest margin of opportunity for solidified agreements to be reproduced, replicated, or simulated on a systemic basis. Personal commitments to informal, causal, or platonic relations allow the respective parties to maintain an independent style of personal conduct where each one strives to preserve a state of autonomy regardless of how others may react or respond in return. Closer personal bonds, in contrast, require more sensitive interplay among bonded members who regard themselves less as individuals and more as a larger, pluralistic collective (Agnew et al. 1998). In effect, it takes only minimum levels of interdependence (A and B_1) to arrive at a simple point of agreement concerning a specific topic. Likewise, it requires moderate levels of interdependence (A and B_2) to produce a complex base of agreements that apply from one situation to another (cross-situational consistency). Finally, it takes refined and sustained levels of interdependence (A and B_3) to construct a core of working agreements that remain in place over extensive time frames.

Simple human agreements are predicated on a single point of reference to a particular point of consensus (Is X seen the same way by others?). Complex agreements, according to Kenny (1994), require a degree of consensus plus a presumption of assumed reciprocity (Do A and B view X similarly?). Fully elaborated agreements depend not only on the first two levels of scale and complexity but also on the larger interplay between small-scale and large-scale schemes of social comparison. An even finer set of distinctions—the magnitude of similar and different features of relational history—are construed in relation to identical and unique attributes of shared circumstance: assimilation (Do A and B view X alike?); uniqueness (Do A and B view X idiosyncratically?); target accuracy (Do A and B view X correctly or accurately from one situation to the next?); meta-accuracy (Do A and B know how one another view X?); and realization (Do A and B realize how they know they view X?).

As baseline levels of shared agreement move from simple to complex status or to fully elaborated status, the sheer number, complexity, and scope of appraisal standards are likely to increase in difficulty, scale, and scope as a result. For these reasons, people differ in what they are capable of and willing to agree about, as do the shared circumstances in which such mutual discoveries can be reaffirmed, disconfirmed, or discarded. Those who deal effectively with complex subject matter are best able to form well-organized social conceptions, integrate inconsistent information, adapt multiple perspectives, and act skillfully in difficult social situations (Burleson and Denton 1997). The capacity to underscore positive events with others is associated with constructive attitudes, beliefs, moods, and an enhanced sense of well-being; active, constructive response enhances secondary benefits—for example, intimacy and satisfaction (Gable et al. 2004).

Signs of personal affection and binding relational agreement often blend, fuse, and merge when each member feels valued, cared, assured, and appreciated in the course of daily life. Attraction and attachment generate greater motivation for direct access to selected persons who are accorded preferential, selective, and deferential treatment as major sources of protection and security. Personal agreeableness also serves as an effective antidote to strong anger or suppressed hostility. Amicable human relations tend to flourish when domains of consensus entail critical obligations: shared responsibility, flexible boundaries, congruent interpretations, and the meaning of friendship tested through good times and bad times. Enduring affiliations produce modest gains in consensus in cases in which personal meaning systems are openly shared (Kenny 1994). Relationship quality is enhanced insofar as the magnitude of consensual agreement increases with the length of relationship (Kurtz and Sherker 2003).

What actually transpires across diverse public settings may be difficult to separate from more idealized versions of what should, might, or could take place. Ideal standards load onto personal assessments of warmth (loyalty) and vitality (passion) in relational considerations (Fletcher et al. 1999). Individuals who invest heavily in stable, committed, and secure relationships often view their own feelings of love, commitment, and satisfaction as increasing over long periods far more than the actual degree of change that has taken place (Sprecher 1999). Insofar as intimates are motivated to construe their current relationships in affectionate terms, they tend to recall having a lower level of love and care in the past than they currently enjoy (Knee 1998).

Idealized personal appraisals may be subject to significant alternation, selective reflection, and reciprocated inflation upon subsequent reflection. A study by Murray, Holmes, and Griffin (1996) revealed that those partners who inaccurately idealized one another construed their relationships in distorted ways that, in reality, mirrored their own grand illusions. Some intimates take comfort in making deliberately misleading estimates that give false credence to a utopian vision of a love supreme. Few romantic parties, however, seek a purified love that can be specified or spelled out in unconditional terms—one that is better than all the rest, usually for a maze of inexplicable causes and unknown reasons. Selective inattention to a partner's negative attributes often enables greater focus on positive qualities, traits, and behavior. Alternative tactics acknowledge the negative features of another's behavior but downplay their importance or dilute their meaning by linking them back into the larger construal of the person's greater strengths.

Using a basic emotional vocabulary designed by Hazan and Shaver (1987; Shaver et al. 1987), the Wisconsin study identified three broad dimensions of positive reference in the four hundred accounts of consensual agreement, against a standard of frequency of mention. Resulting is a subset of positive emotional displays taken from the following list of relevant terms:

Love: adoration, affection, love, fondness, liking, attraction, caring, tenderness, compassion, arousal, sentimentality, desire, lust, passion, infatuation, longing

Joy: amusement, bliss, cheerfulness, gaiety, glee, jolliness, joviality, joy, delight, enjoyment, gladness, happiness, jubilation, elation, satisfaction, ecstasy, euphoria, enthusiasm, zeal, zest, excitement, thrill, exhilaration, contentment, pleasure, pride, triumph, eagerness, hope, optimism, enthrallment, rapture, relief

Surprise: amazement, surprise, and astonishment.

Results showed that seven terms occurred with the greatest frequency of mention: *like, love, care, enjoy, happy, excite*, and *cheerful* (table 6.1).

Likewise, the rich surplus of positive emotional display reveals extensive reliance on several major thematic clusters of free association. Moreover, relevant sentences contain multiple references to supportive social conditions based on themes of affiliation, solidarity, and cohesion between affectionate partners. In effect, agreeable and amicable persons promote personal attraction, recognition of intent, accurate perspective taking, credible identity, similar interests, core values, and quality of interaction. Personal statements vary widely across several clusters of free association.

Table 6.1. Surplus of Positive Affect

	Agreement	Disagreement	Understanding	Misunderstanding
Like	106	17	40	10
Love	61	37	64	20
Care	43	12	59	12
Enjoy	80	12	30	11
Happy	32	23	36	23
Excite	20	2	10	3
Cheerful	11	10	11	2
Total	353	113	250	81

PERSONAL ATTRACTION

Likeable Agreement

S/O like to encourage each other.

S/O like to pick up on the good stuff right away, if there is some.

S/O like the same music, movies, fancy dinners, watch plays, and hang out.

S/O like to poke fun at other friends and have fun doing it—sometimes it is great fun to gang up on people.

S/O like to spend time together; they seem to agree about everything.

S/O like karate, pool, tennis, basketball, lifting, and believing in God.

S/O share qualities of kindness and generosity, like the same sports, share similar views, and love to joke around and act crazy and goofy.

S/O can tell each other everything; other people tell them that they are so much alike that other people cannot tell them apart.

S/O like making agreements because it is like a support system, building up confidence within each other; when they do disagree, they are like lawyers trying to prove a point and get the other's approval.

S/O help each other, give positive reinforcement, look at the world in a similar way, like the same music, enjoy exercise, and love piano—it is clear that they agree about most everything.

S/O are so alike that it is almost scary; they work as a team when talking with other people; they play off each other, love to joke around, and be sarcastic; S/O are always up for anything; S draws the line in the exact same place that O does.

Enjoyable Agreement

S/O enjoy everything together because they have the same interests and deep personal concerns.

S/O enjoy hearing what the other one has to say—they both ask as many questions as possible.

S/O enjoy a close friendship where neither one is motivated by what can be gained from the other.

S/O enjoy ways that they can give to each other—it makes for healthy and enjoyable relations.

S/O enjoy making fun—each one antagonizes the other, laughing and joking all the time.

S/O enjoy the same things, stay pretty calm, and do not let little things bother them.

S/O enjoy sitting in the sun, as well as playing games just for fun, with no competition, such as pool.

S/O enjoy teasing or making fun without offending anyone or hurting anyone's feelings.

S/O enjoy sharing inside jokes, sitting, talking about nothing, and laughing.

Everyday agreements do not occur in a social vacuum. What is striking is how the slant of active personal voices, blended social identities, and engaging subject matter appear so life affirming. There is provision for reaffirmation and renewal of strong ties between kindred spirits. Convergent social transactions are attractive because they are often so generous, expansive, inclusive, pervasive, and forgiving as microsteering mechanisms for all manner of consequential public performances. Supportive conditions of attraction, liking, and enjoyment coincide with broad tolerance and mutual preference for conditions of proximity, immediacy, and reciprocity.

Likeable and enjoyable acts or prolonged episodes of valued social encounter depend on the cumulative informational value of moods, beliefs, and attitudes used as framing devices over rapid decisions to start or stop working on a plan, objective, or goal (Hirt et al. 1999). There is a playful spirit that features more than enough laughter, joking, kidding, and banter to go around. Personal identity rests on general relational consideration but is unsettled in respect to specific details. Strong measures of civility and taste often rest on little more than chitchat over simple topics: rumor, weather, clothes, books, music, fashion, fad diets, television, e-mail, Internet, lottery, cyberspace, or culture wars. Small-scale social agreements form into larger patterns and social trajectories that transcend the place of origin. Large-scale agreements fall into place on the basis of the strength of close relational ties. In a word, consensual agreements are an important source of social capital and afford considerable psychic protection against the corrosive efforts of wear and tear, stress and strain.

RECOGNITION OF INTENT

Mutual recognition of personal intent matters greatly in the acquisition maintenance, regulation, and preservation of social and personal relationships.

S/O can think each other's thoughts.

S/O finish each other's sentences.

S/O think alike on most issues.

S/O always seem to see things eye to eye.

S/O swear that they can read each other's mind.

S/O can tell each other's next move and every thought.

S/O give positive and constructive feedback without hesitation.

S/O act like the two of them are just like one single person.

S/O can tell just by looking whether the other person is happy or sad.
S/O know exactly what each other is thinking—S can read O's expressions
    or gestures like a book.

It is not always possible to determine what other people want or intend by
observing the distinctive way in which they express themselves across a diverse range of public situations. Personal intentions matter but not in any
simple-minded or self-evident manner. Speech acts provide a basic means
for reaching out to take one's lived circumstance into collective account on
the basis of self-reflection and selective reframing. An intentional orientation
is therefore at once interpretive, inventive, fabricated, and contrived. Human
interactions are permeated with a pervasive sense of purpose, striving, and
intentionality, which in turn gives rise to specific intentions directed toward
the immediate fulfillment of strategic goals, plans, and objectives. Emergent
intentions activate persistent and enduring strivings to move from uncompleted, partially completed, and then fully completed activities (Marsh,
Hicks, and Bink 1998). The limits of intentional strivings coincide with what
is foreseeable and with the ability to bring about a specified outcome
(Thompson, Armstrong, and Thomas 1998).

Intentional interpretations generate bias, slant, and skew in the larger
process of social inquiry. There is open provision for varying departures
from a state of emotional neutrality. The more you interpret something in
particular, the more you must invest in what you see, and by so doing, you
forfeit the claim to be indifferent, impartial, or neutral. Conversely, the less
you interpret of what transpires around you, the more you will move back
toward the moderating effects associated with an stance of neutrality, indifference, or detachment. Hence, there may be such a thing as "too much" interpretation of small change (exaggeration), just as there is a possibility of
"too little" interpretation of one thing or another (understatement). There is
a broad tendency to overestimate the transparency of one's objectives in the
eyes of others. The converse is to overestimate the transparency of others'
responses.

There is no surefire way to read another's mind. Intentional acts produce
intended and unintended consequences. Moreover, what someone actually
intends may not be obvious to anyone else. Intended meanings of observed
behavior can be revealed or covered up. Sometimes we do not have direct
access to our own intentions, much less the unspoken intentions of others.
Moreover, there is nothing to prevent the presumption that one knows why
others act the way they do, even if the hunch is wrong or out of place. What
we make of others' aims and purposes may not be taken for granted as being correct, with no or little effort at reality checking along the way. Mind
reading, the ability to read others' thoughts and feelings, is notoriously difficult to assess. In general, personal sensitivity to others' intentions reportedly

improves slowly as a function of the degree of acquaintance, situational knowledge, and adaptive style (Thomas and Garth 2003).

On a larger scale, social practices may change so dramatically over extensive periods that the bonded participants can no longer trace current conditions backward, toward a distinct point of origin. In effect, it is as easy to misread personal conduct as to construe accurately complex events in line with what others recognize as the intention behind a given course of action. At the center of an agreement-making activity is the generative and sustained ability to identify others' unstated urges, often without a word being spoken. An intuitive grasp of what is made explicit or left as implied is something to be achieved through hard work and concerted effort rather than something merely presumed or inherited as a special gift, trait, or attribute.

There are good reasons why people should be open to alternative and divergent readings of their personal conduct before others. Intentions may operate on the periphery of conscious awareness. Also, other people do things for complex reasons—some are unintended, mishandled, or garbled. Hence, there is much value in tolerating what goes wrong as a means to make it right. Moreover, the risk and cost of misreading others' intentions varies greatly over short time frames. It is not always easy to separate one's ability to make good sense of specific modes of action from the larger capacity to understand other persons as separate, distinct, and complete entities. From this perspective, momentary lapses or minor miscalculations may not mean a thing.

Sometimes misconstrued actions are subject to revision or subsequent alteration, or certain frames of reference may be disputed or reclaimed along the way. There is simply no assurance that those who are stuck in faulty ways of making sense of relational intent will be able to work their way out. Those who lose touch with the subtle and delicate intentions of others may construe future interaction as being bothersome and burdensome. Intentional accuracy is a positively related indicator of satisfaction in nondistressed marriages but not in distressed marriages with a greater number of negative intentions that appear due more to ill will than poor skills (Burleson and Denton 1997).

COMMONALITY OF PERSPECTIVE

S/O take delight in the discovery of common ground that feels precious and delicate.

S/O find that what either one says is usually on par with what the other is thinking at the time.

S/O stay up all night talking about goals, dreams, plans . . . the list goes on forever.

S/O share love, sympathy, and mutual willingness to take each other's perspective.

S/O sit for hours and analyze life together, partly because their views are
the same.

S/O discuss a wide range of topics based on the same types of thoughts,
views, and ideals.

S/O remain affable and drop issues if either one doesn't comprehend the
other's perspective.

S/O have the same perspective on personal issues—they know each
other's unspoken feelings.

S/O are able to maintain similar perspectives about difficult situations from
the past.

S/O share keen scientific perspectives—their eyes light up when they
know the answer.

S/O have common interests and similar personalities and like to listen to
each other gab.

S/O have common assumptions, similar interests, and comparable ways of
looking at things.

S/O have the most in common out of all the people that they interact with
on a daily basis.

Perspective-taking ability is particularly decisive. Shifts from a first-person
perspective to a second- and third-person perspective are useful as a sensible means of fostering greater emotional responsiveness, sensitivity to enhancing attributions, reduced negativity, one-sided blame, and amelioration
of the inclination to indulge in destructive cycles. Interactants who get stuck
in first-person perspectives react on the basis of short-term interest. They
must forego, therefore, the option of transforming assessable motivation toward collective, rather than individual, orientations and benefiting from
prosocial preferences, priorities, and enhancing rather than blameful attributions.

Rigid persons who lack adequate perspective-taking ability may compensate by striving to confirm their own grandiosity before others, often
amid futile efforts to satisfy exaggerated assessments of personal worth
and dramatic styles of public persona. The need for affirmation, idealization, and grandiosity often dismantles multiple perspective-taking ability
and, as a substitute, gives rise to controlling impulses, devalued relationships, and premature abandonment of cherished dreams, goals, and aspirations. The inability to understand the multiple, shifting, and alternative
perspectives of others fosters greater belief that social relationships are
secondary considerations of personal importance (Corcoran and Mallinckrodt 2000).

COMPLEMENTARY IDENTITIES

S/O have a great time together and balance each other out.
S/O are very different, but still they complement each other so well.
S/O are a lot more alike than even they realize sometimes.
S/O are very much alike; many people call them inseparable.

Interpersonal agreements are protective of mutual issues, preferred activities, and critical concerns. Agreement-making activities conserve possibilities of active gain or prevention of further loss. Mutual exchange of resources, abilities, and skills effectively reproduces a critical component of constructive change. Distinctive interactive patterns, once proven to be efficacious and socially accountable, help to clarify, cohere, repair, and restore enduring personal identities established through hard work and concerted effort over long periods. Cohesive individuals search for unity and quickly form unified impressions that facilitate subsequent expressions of affirmation and solidarity or dissolve instead into an opposing state of dissension or divisiveness. Hence, there is little need for reliance on a stance of argumentativeness or defensiveness because the interactive process appears to be tempered and evenhanded. There are few complaints about performance defects, deficiencies, or dysfunctions. To the contrary, there is consensus, which serves to emphasize, highlight, and underscore the considerable pleasures associated with the strategic benefits of making the dialogical process work to the advantage of each member and making solid agreements that measure up to demanding standards of mutual scrutiny.

SIMILARITY OF INTEREST

S/O like to sit, smoke cigarettes, and play video games all day long.
S/O share interests—tennis, skiing, running, reading, shopping, eating, relaxing.
S/O share the little things in life—grilling out, reading *Mad* magazine, and just goofing around.
S/O have each other's best interests and personal welfare in mind at all times.
S/O share whatever makes everything else in life seem easier—then other interests seem to fall into place.
S/O have mutual interests, and they talk about mutually agreeable ideas.
S/O share interests—they sit talking about nothing, just laughing.
S/O take genuine interest in each other—they are always open to change.
S/O have common assumptions, similar interests, and fluid conversations.

S/O consider one another's best interests in everything they say and do.
S/O share and know everything there is to know about each other.
S/O share intimate feelings and similar interests about everything.

The act of sharing mutual interests enhances the pleasure of spending time together. There is a presumption that it is easier to interact about similar interests than about divergent ones. What interests a person is not simply a measure of relevance or salience. It is also the standard by which to determine what brings certain individuals close together and drives others apart. Case studies on agreement show evidence of a strong similarity bias at work. The notion that opposites attract receives little support here. It may be difficult to say what it is that makes something appear similar to something else. The comparison may be assumed, taken for granted, or merely ill-defined—an invitation to fill in the blank.

There is a strong degree of personal satisfaction in making things fit in a coherent, pleasing, and well-grounded manner. It is not surprising, therefore, to find people who accentuate or even exaggerate the magnitude of presumed similarity to suit their own purposes—generally to enhance esteem, satisfaction, status, or sense of well-being. Simple, linear, serial agreements and shared interests serve as catalysts for communication. There may be no better reason for spending time together than for the rediscovery of mutual interests and both compatible and comparable ways of looking at the world. Solid working agreements are held in high regard. Feelings of oneness are a source of amazement and delight. Cohesion is a source of pleasure. A spirit of joy and delight leads to exuberant expressions of solidarity and strong praise over the affinity of close bonds.

COMPATIBILITY OF VALUE

S/O place a great deal of value on the goodness of people.
S/O share values—that is why they express themselves so positively.
S/O value what each one says because they are a lot like one another.
S/O share bonds that create similar values—they sit and talk for hours.
S/O value each other, so they don't let conflicts tear them apart.
S/O find core values match up, and they respect each other's experiences.

It is easier to foster a climate of working agreements when personal value systems are closely integrated and mutually accessible. Hence, it can be difficult to sustain a congenial atmosphere when the personal value systems in question do not match up well. Personal engagement in two-way translation of terms and active interpretation of intentions can be taxing. The enduring process is easier when interpersonal agreements arise from compatible value orientations. When individual valuations match up well, routine encounters are likely to flow smoothly and help to form a stronger bond. There is no need for total or unconditional agreement on every major issue. Social consensus need not be all-encompassing for the respective parties to talk freely about core personal issues without worrying about being contradicted or questioned.

When cognitive appraisals, value orientations, and personal identities mesh well, face-to-face interaction becomes less filled with monologues and shifts instead to mutual dialogue based on strong levels of cognitive interdependence and mutual application of egalitarian principles. Amicable and congenial respondents are flexible and tolerant of risk and change. A resolute spirit of adjustment and accommodation enables each party to make the best of the situation and not let petty mistakes or miscalculations stand in the way. Some respondents speak of working hard to talk things through and also refer to concentrated efforts to make sure everyone understands what transpires along the way. There is ample opportunity to review what remains unclear as well as adroit skill in knowing how much to explain and when to leave well enough alone. Moreover, there are numerous references among agreeable respondents both to the relief of not having to spell everything out in detail and the willingness to go back over troubling issues as much as necessary from one perspective to another. Some give credit to the unique modes of language that are employed in distinctive ways. Other persons place stress on matters of affection—empathy, positive regard, social support, or reciprocated matters of trust and respect. Still others appeal to the sheer strength or salience of the bond, as with soul mates.

QUALITY OF INTERACTION

Constructive conditions of love, care, and happiness do not easily arise, nor are they effortlessly sustained. Some positive emotions may be readily feigned or faked, but strong and passionate affections qualify as scarce resources. Abiding senses of power, affection, and involvement are critical dimensions of personal definitions of productive and enriching modes of social encounters. It is instructive, therefore, to study the informal logic, lexicon, and narrative themes that accompany rewarding and satisfying types and modes of shared constructions that are simultaneously deemed worthy of emulation as ideal or optimum models of congenial performance.

Agreeable relational achievements may enhance or diminish the severity of standards used to gauge what qualifies as a likable or enjoyable element of efficacious social performance. Desirability commingles with intensity and expansive conceptions of unfulfilled potential. Expressive styles remain sensitive to subtle cues, especially in picking up the slightest nonverbal change or subtle shift in mood or attitude. Agreeable forms of mutual adaptation work to counteract short-term effects of stress and strain on mood negativity rather than contribute to it. Also relevant is shared willingness to transform signs of negativity into signs of positivity (e.g., liability into asset). Enhanced accommodative tendencies also diminish the risk of negative reciprocity. Personal responsiveness facilitates a greater measure of understanding by capturing and validating the reactions of other people as both being accepted and highly valued. Affectionate social judgments have a self-enhancing, inflationary slant or skew. Individuals are prone to construe their own relations, when compared with other types, to look as good as possible. Illusionary superiority is equated with inflated judgments of relational quality at the expense of accuracy. Collusive agreement, taken to the extreme, may have tyrannical overtones—agree or else.

Loving Agreement

S/O believe in things so dear yet so inexplicable—like true love.

S/O listen at all times, keep an open mind, and show unconditional love.

S/O love to see each other light up when they talk about ideas.

S/O share basic views—religion, family, school, love, sex, marriage, and friends.

S/O have talked about everything—politics, morals, love for Madison, and fun and pain.

S/O love to in-line skate, work out at the gym, and do the same things.

S/O find that comfort shown out of love is easier than being confronted for some other reason.

S/O can make passionate love or share their troubles for nearly three hours at a time.

S/O can always reach a satisfying compromise—they have mutual trust, love, and a strong commitment to one another.

S/O find when they interact, there is nothing but a spirit of love between them.

S/O comfort each other, and both react in a very caring and loving manner.

S/O share unconditional love, devotion, and mutual willingness to help in any way possible without asking why.

S/O share a strong bond—if either one is in trouble, the other will always be there to express love despite everything—unconditional love is important to them every day.

S/O get along no matter what, and they always seem to talk about agreeable ideas because they love each other so much.

S/O love to talk about their favorite times together, and it makes them appreciate how much they have in common and how much they have to look forward to—they respond to each other so energetically because they both are such passionate people.

S/O love each other so much—they can talk about everything: men, cooking, catty women, politics, money, health, future goals, morals, sex, and the weather.

S/O find that walking into the apartment is like coming home; they are able to catch up quickly; conversation begins with their own concerns and expands to include other relations, past and present; when the phone rings, neither one will answer if they are actively talking—if one is thirsty, the other will bring a drink; likewise, if necessary, one will change a disc, pack a bowl (referring to smoking marijuana), or tie a shoe; there is a mutual feeling of utmost respect and care that has grown steadily over the course of the last eight years.

Whereas comparative social distinctions between like and dislike provide mostly weaker indicators of the magnitude of mutual attraction, comparative distinctions between love and hate are much stronger indicators of the sheer magnitude of mutual attraction. In the agreement section, there are no mentions of anyone hating anyone else or anything in particular. There is, in other words, virtually no provision or allowances for strong forms of negativity to surface, escalate, or become ingrained. References to objects of dislike and disgust are far and few between. However, convergent ability to accentuate the positive is not taken as a license to ignore the negative. Instead, unwelcome signs may be deflected, displaced, or covered up with layers of constructive affirmation, confirmation, and validation.

A surplus of strong, positive, and constructive affection is conducive to greater shared appreciation of the great value afforded by a supportive and communicative atmosphere where broad levels of shared agreement and explicit domains of mutual understanding lead to higher order achievements and shared accomplishments. On the other hand, the alignment, juxtaposition, and trajectories of highly integrated love styles also matter a great deal. Committed couples, for example, who share similar love styles slowly enhance the overall quality, depth, scope, and range of shared agreement and mutual understanding (Hahn and Blass 1997). Relevant gender differences are as follows: erotic, romantic, passionate love is construed as being socially desirable in men but socially undesirable in women; playful, ludic love is taken as being socially desirable in men but socially undesirable in women; and selfless, agape love is viewed by women as being socially desirable for women but socially undesirable in men (Davies 2001). Such tentative sets of gender-related observations are consistent with a presumption of men's permissive, instrumental outlooks. The search for love and intimacy is risky, of course, in matters of vulnerability, loss of individuality, and exposed faults used as objects of manipulation, calculation, betrayal, neglect, or abandonment. For the majority of men and women alike, however, the promise far outweighs the hazards. Intimate exchange enables caring partners to feel alive, fresh, vital, loved, cared for, listened to, and revered in return.

On the affirmative side, expansive domains of human opportunity abound: one loves to agree; one agrees to love; and one loves to agree and agrees to love at the same time. What is at stake is the dynamic interplay of living subjects who interact about loving subjects in a tender and sensitive manner. Loving agreements are manifest in common striving for states of proximity, physical closeness, playfulness, and mutual touching. There is ample provision for extensive collaboration, support, intimate topics, secret codes, and improvised idioms where much is grasped with a tacit, intuitive, and unspoken sense of commitment to the preservation of shared history mutual circumstance.

Maintenance strategies in affectionate personal relationships accentuate multiple expressions of cheer, optimism, warmth, openness, assurance, and affirmation. Enjoyable matters encompass an enduring sense of appreciation, assurance, accessibility, and commitment as judged by a sense of congruence, endurance, tolerance, and perseverance. There is an enriching sense of closeness; deep affection; mutual responsiveness; strong expressive styles; shared commitment; and abiding sense of solidarity, cohesion, and openness. Mutual capacity for intimacy, passion, and commitment promotes an expansive sense of bondedness, closeness, connectedness, passion, and fidelity.

Caring Agreement

S/O care very much about the well-being of one another.

S/O feel a sense of security knowing the other will care to hear one's own problems.

S/O get along so well and agree on many issues because they both have a caring nature.

S/O care about each other's well-being—it makes their friendship very strong.

S/O listen with attentive, caring, empathetic eyes and direct focus on one another.

S/O care about each other, and they both want the very best for one another.

S/O know how to comfort each other—they are extremely caring and supportive.

S/O hear each other, and their reactions are caring, understanding, and motherly.

S/O let each other know they care with words or actions (gifts, surprise visits, etc.).

Certain aesthetic features of multiple verbal references to diverse expressions of love, concern, and care are remarkably similar in thematic texture and tone. There is a pervasive, all-embracing spirit at work in the proliferation of unspoken signs of reassurance or admiration. The sights and sounds resemble a communal celebration. It is one thing to be imbued with an abiding sense of love, care, and concern for the welfare of a specific person. It is another thing to be imbued with an abiding sense of love, care, and concern for the expressive and receptive valuation accorded to each member in a collective expression of cohesion and solidarity. The two streams of mutual regard may work together to produce even stronger, more fully amplified and codetermined support for affection-laden activity between intimates and the discourse of intimacy that is sustained between them.

There is also a strong sense of secure attachment and mutual acceptance for the sake of the living subjects and the intangible subject matter they may seek to secure or sustain. One may love to talk about love to the one who is the object of love. Some prefer love and care directed toward other persons or other living things. Mutual displays taken from an attractive lexicon of comfort, care, concern, cheerfulness, confidence, commitment, and closeness all serve to support and sustain mutual capacity for spontaneous intimacy and sustained passion. In the a/u conditions, the prevailing styles revolve mainly around themes of companionship, playfulness, and, to a lesser extent, selfless regard. People who care about themselves help people to care about each other. There is pleasure in the shared construction of a living text. Participants know where and when to draw the line.

Happy Agreement

S/O know what makes each other happy.

S/O know each other well and can make each other happy or angry with equal ease.

S/O share a strong sense of give-and-take—they have a great system of finding ways to keep them both happy.

S/O talk about the very things that make each of them sad, happy, mad, or anything else—they often blurt things out and interrupt each other also.

S/O are open and honest with each other, knowing that each will accept and understand anything that the other has to say; whether it be a helping hand in a job search or sending the other a small gift in the mail, they both work to help each other succeed and be happy.

Happiness is recognizable: a pleasant spirit, a spontaneous manner, a positive contagion that is at once expansive, reinforcing, and wholly or partially reciprocated, with lots of smiling, interest, excitement, and joy seen as active, energetic, and preferential striving that can be displayed or revealed before significant others. Measures of happiness are not easily calculated in terms of a zero-sum game, where the more for you, the less for me; and the happier you get, the sadder it makes me feel. To the contrary, public displays of mutual happiness fit better into a positive-sum equation where the more for you, the more for me, and the more for you, me, us, and the others, too (second, third parties). A spirit of happiness and joy is an antidote to hostility in conflict situations with potential for cruelty.

Leading conceptions of personal happiness cluster around appraisals of positive emotion; life satisfaction; absence of negative displays or signs of distress; depth considerations, such as one's purpose in life; and collective value, concern, achievement, and pleasure. Moreover, men and women depend on use of similar resources, abilities, and skills in the pursuit of happiness (Aldous and Ganey 1999). A seventeen-nation study of happiness in marriages found moderate consistency across diverse cultures in the association between spousal satisfaction over cohabitation or unmarried status in an equation that applies equally to men and women in judgments of personal well-being and global happiness (Stack and Eshleman 1998).

The experience of joy signals that success has been achieved, or progress made, toward a valued goal. Happiness, in contrast, reveals a deeper sense of well-being, pleasant moods, renewed sense of positive experiences in the course of daily events, and personal maintenance of optimum levels of goal achievement across multiple domains and different spheres of human encounter. Global happiness and life satisfaction are closely linked (Lu 1999). In longitudinal studies, happiness is shown to be moderately stable (short term); sensitive to diversity; and acquired or diminished in transient, short-lived gradations (McIntosh and Martin 1997). The construct of personal happiness, therefore, is sensitive to transitions and shifts in lived circumstance, good and bad, particularly for major events and dramatic scenarios cast in recent life consequences. Goal beliefs and life events shape the larger malleability of peoples' judgments of their own happiness relative to their assessments of the personal happiness of those around them.

Exciting Agreement

S/O vocabulary consists of slang and jargon mixed with excitement and laughter.

S/O are very talkative and use expressive body language whenever they get excited.

S/O get along well and get excited about each opportunity to talk with each other.

S/O react well, listen carefully, and love to see the other light up when talking.

S/O express excitement with joyful reactions to each other's names, embraces, pats on the back, and handshakes.

S/O conversations are quite intense—it's not only the words that are used but also the many nonverbal gestures, eye contact, touching, hugging— there's a lot of excitement; hours can go by making plans.

S/O do not judge each other—they love to talk about anything, serious, frivolous, or just things neither would discuss with anyone else.

Multiple expressions of interest and excitement provide indirect indicators of personal involvement in basic relational concerns. Exciting conversations can continue for hours, or forever, without end. No one runs out of things to say. There is excitement about the opportunity to talk, to hear, to see each member seem happy, to react joyfully and in a spirit of good cheer. Interest and pleasure go together as vital determinants of a strong relational bond. The flow is easy and natural. Energy fills the air. There is mutual satisfaction and mutual expression of personal feelings of great happiness and joy. Give-and-take is fair, equitable, sufficient, and satisfying at the same time.

Cheerful Agreement

S/O know that it helps to have someone along the way to cheer one on.

S/O listen when things go wrong; they offer advice and cheer one another up.

S/O are there in hard times to offer support or cheer the other up.

Solid working agreements are attractive because so much is required to achieve them. It is not always easy or effortless to produce or reproduce the requisite conditions for their complex elaboration. Personal attraction is likable and enjoyable to the degree that strategic intentions can be identified, key perspectives are held in common, relational identities are accepted more than contested, shared interests prevail, core values mesh, and amicable participants learn how to get in synch and remain closely aligned.

Affectionate respondents use a wide range of strategies and tactics to work through chronic communicative difficulties and address problematic concerns. Where firm and fluid agreements prevail, delicate matters involving implications of personal weaknesses, deficiencies, shortcomings, and vulnerabilities are treated with sensitivity, concern, and care. Persons who invest heavily in affectionate relations do not often take advantage of weakness and limitation but take such constraining considerations into special account. Instead of giving in to the urge to push someone else's buttons, it ostensibly is better to leave well enough alone. As a rule, respondents find it useful to know each other's limitations—soft spots—and devise specialized tactics or subroutines to circumvent or work around what cannot be addressed in conventional terms. In

such settings, there is less reason to get defensive as a means to ward off potential threat. Irrational or irritating actions can be deflected, neutralized, or dif-
fused as a means of bringing comfort or relief. Respondents speak of soothing
troubled feelings. Support is discovered in the transition from crisis to routine.
Likewise, they allow expressions of divergence and dissensus to recede or
fade into the background of conscious awareness and personal concern.

Basic issues may be repeatedly tested and retested. There is usually a
heavy investment in strategic mutual strivings toward significant meanings
that are explored freely and in great depth and detail. The pursuit of a secure
sense of solidarity and cohesion is often balanced with unspoken sensitivity
to personal boundaries and broad tolerance of tacit knowledge over what to
exclude, avoid, or dismiss from active dialogical consideration. Moreover,
those who share the deepest and strongest bonds also benefit from the gradual expansion of inclusive agreements and broad consensus that pertain to
all facets of social life, including productive relations with second and third
parties.

Some affectionate members claim to agree about every thought and feeling that they share together. Other respondents take pleasure in sharing feelings of intimate comfort, maximizing time spent together, enhancing the
quality of interaction, or exploring complex subjects without limit in a spirit
of personal freedom balanced against ingrained standards of personal accountability. A few congenial respondents make sweeping claims: they
know everything about each other; they always come to full agreement; they
achieve strong agreements without condition, reservation, or stipulation;
they agree no matter what because they allow each other to speak so freely;
they agree about everything in general but like to argue small details; they
are open to the point where they do not have to worry about what the other
party will think because they will agree in any case; and they speak their
minds but never pressure each other to go one way or another. In short, a
spirit of faith and fidelity in solid human connections transcends reason and
logic as an aesthetic explanation for generative agreement-making activity
that facilitates the preservation of close, intimate bonds.

7

Disagreement and Negativity

Jack can see
that he sees
what Jill can't see
and that Jill can't see Jill can't see it
Jack can see that he sees
what Jill can't see
but Jack can't see
that Jill can't see it
Jack tries to get Jill to see
that Jack can see
what Jack can't see
that Jill can't see that Jill can't see it
Jack sees
there is something Jill can't see
and Jack sees
that Jill can't see she can't see it
Although Jack can see Jill can't see she can't see it
he can't see that he can't see it himself.

—Ronald D. Laing, *Knots*

An acerbic tone poem captures the spirit of a wide spectrum of troubling personal disagreements and dense linguistic entanglements that have great potential to unfold, sometimes without reason or without any end in sight. Strong advocates are likely to become ego involved in complex, difficult, or problematic matters, and suddenly they are at risk for greater entrapment in misdirected or misguided social exchanges that implicate what Laing (1970) has well characterized as "knots, tangles, fankies, *impasses*, disjunctions,

139

whirligogs, and binds" (57). Common linguistic difficulties are likely to multiply in unfavorable, unstable, or unsettled social conditions. An initial base
of common references may facilitate the acquisition of affirmative constructions (common ground) or otherwise may work conversely to undermine
preliminary sense-making efforts and transform shared endeavors into
strained disputes concerning core matters of definition, classification, and
explanation.

Sometimes what starts out as a simple point of disagreement between opposing advocates may well end up as being nothing more than a single point
of discordant social reference. At other times, what starts out as a single point
of routine disagreement may lead into a complex of much more deeply implicated disagreements and a blunt forewarning of sobering things to come.
Serious disagreements, nonetheless, pose important questions, puzzles, and
issues that may not be easy to resolve, much less decipher. Moreover, serious unresolved disagreements or prolonged relational disputes may be difficult to decode or disentangle, particularly when key issues are badly conflated or unduly constrained by a maze of unspoken disagreements that go
unacknowledged or undetected in a routinized, habituated, or mindless
manner.

Personal negativity is a potent force in human encounters. We know that
conspicuous signs of manifest negativity are a leading indicator of a general
personal disposition to discredit or devalue others in a mindless, abusive, or
insensitive manner. Strong negativity, when taken personally, is painful to
endure in large doses. It hurts, after all, to be repeatedly or chronically subjected to relentless or unrelieved censorship, criticism, castigation, or condemnation before other people. Salient considerations of a negative general
personal disposition include a general state of unhappiness; life dissatisfaction; low self-esteem; mild depression; rigid, inflexible, or maladaptive styles
of routine interaction; negative behavioral response; discredited social reputation; and damaged self-image (Furr and Funder 1998). However, shared capacity to anticipate specific points of disagreement (over turn taking or sudden shifts in systemic organization) provides a strategic and tactical measure
of possible conversion of potential trouble spots into reconstructed frames of
reference or projected frames of restorative action in which repair and cor-
rection mingle with offers or requests to forestall risk and threat.

Personal disagreements are nearly as varied and diverse as the wide spectrum of engaged individuals who participate in their collaborative construction (or misconstruction). In global terms, three clusters of free association
seem to best account for strategic designs of intense social disputes or protracted modes of verbal strife and communal discord. Critical terms are derived from selective and strategic focus on numerous application of various
social constraints, limits, and boundaries of personal tolerance and collective
forbearance. A second cluster consists of secondary associations that func-

tion mainly to demarcate or circumscribe the magnitude, scope, or severity of an antagonistic or adversarial encounter. Relevant cases will be examined along a continuum ranging from simple or trivial matters all the way up the scale of measure to encumbered, burdensome, or complicated social strategies at work in strictly oppositional terms. A third type is based on the degree of resolution of disputed matters. The boundary lines of demarcation between the scope of simple disagreement and the magnitude of complex disagreements are seldom subject to total or final resolution. The strength of resistance to persuasion may be weighted against the willingness to give in, yield, and submit to the veracity or salience of alternative means to achieve uncertain common ends.

PERSONAL DISAFFECTION

One way to deal with intensely disputed or contested modes of social confrontation is to act as if the observable subjects or actions in question did not really exist. Personal avoidance occurs when respondents lack the ability or willingness to subject implicit, unspoken tensions to explicit forms of recognition, acknowledgment, or disclosure. The magnitude of what is left implicit or as yet unspoken can matter a great deal to one person or another. Individual reservations may arise from a sense of caution or hesitation acquired from the impact of prior sequences of direct interaction construed as being somehow ineffective, faulty, or incomplete. Regressive efforts often serve to magnify the scope, scale, or significance of all the messy unfinished business. At the center of the human drama is the core issue of how mutually accessible individuals are able and willing to move in or out of varying states, degrees, or gradations of difficulty and perplexity with one another. Covert markers of personal relevance and shared meaning are fully implicated in how well or badly individuals may treat one another in the course of real-life encounters.

Where serious disagreements turn sharply negative, personal avoidance begins in earnest. One party may be willing to act in a rather two-faced fashion to avoid a sticky situation in which someone attempts to confront and reveal what someone else strives actively to conceal or cover up. Central themes include avoiding mention not only of personal problems with no solutions in sight but also the "bad stuff" that arises during adverse, ugly, or unpleasant times. It may get to the point where there is less and less to say about more and more intensely disputed or contested personal issues than ever before. Unfavorable prospects may well lead one party to avoid a task, topic, situation, or direct contact with the offending party. A rule of thumb is to avoid all civil disputations, particularly the most intense, severe, or prolonged cases in point. Avoidance of anything but a simple communicative act may appear to be socially desirable. Success is measured against a stringent standard. People who cannot get along are the very ones who are most inclined to avoid any future contact.

Acts of inaction and inertia follow a course of least resistance. A stance of indecisiveness takes less effort than one of avoidance. When in doubt, do nothing. Inertia has a certain appeal. Ignore what is bothersome. Postpone. Delay. Defer. Wait and see. Do not start anything. Ignore what the other says or does because it will lead to nothing but more trouble later on. Let attention wander. Stay unfocused. Act aimlessly. Try not to argue. Overlook unwelcome ideas. Drop touchy topics right away. No use explaining. Provide only minimal or noncommittal reactions to substantive or procedural issues. Tune out when there is no chance to cope. Ignore abusive actions in the faint hope they will simply go away. Neither disagreeable party may believe what the other is saying anyway.

Severely agitated parties can go for incredibly long periods of time without talking to one another, without so much as a single word or gesture. Everything else is absorbed, or reorganized, into protracted states of mutual silence. Put out the bare minimum. Go through the motions. Expect nothing in return. Multiple pathways of avoidant inaction often lead to a disquieting sense of exhaustion or lack of motivation to talk about anything seriously ever again. An inert or unresponsive personal stance is typically equated with a lingering or haunting regard for what is lacking, absent, missing, or misplaced in the totalizing effects of confusing or confounding sense-making efforts. It is relatively easy to, without end, manufacture justifications, explanations, and rationalizations for inert and futile courses of shared action. A style of avoidance and inaction is akin, therefore, to a mood of resignation or passivity.

Denial and refusal go together in a similar manner. Both types of personal negation are far more labor intensive than the typical passive reactions of avoidance or inaction. Shared effort may be one-sided, particularly when one party brings up a subject only to have the other deny it in the manner of a curt dismissal. Conversely, one source may refuse to drop a chronically disputed matter just as intensely as another source strives to bring it up. Two-sided efforts occur where there is shared refusal to acknowledge the magnitude of what has gone wrong plus shared refusal to talk until things have settled down.

Some strong advocates hide true feelings and make others think that they share the same views when in fact they do not. Others defend their inert tendencies through acts of delay, deferral, or denial in which their words and deeds are inconsistent but in which the implicit, tacit contradictions go unacknowledged. Living in a state of disavowal involves minimal engagement in public acts without focused awareness under conditions in which awareness should be taken as a given, as obvious. Hence, denial negates action whenever one refuses to accept what transpires or takes place. Acts of inattention promote a stance of passivity, avoidance, and disavowal of real-life events for purposes of disowning unwanted features of self-presentation by distorting manipulated meanings in a given public sphere.

Acts of denial do not automatically pose great difficulty in ordinary or routine sense-making efforts. The denial of unpleasant truth may change rapidly, on a day-to-day basis. As a coping mechanism, the urge to minimize danger affords protection from the ill effects of disruptive forces, invasive events, or deteriorating personal relations. Acts of minimizing entail a measure of selective inattention to sensitive matters or the desire to ignore negative facts. Acts of verbal disavowal may be used to contradict any unwelcome inferences, implications, or false expectations. Unrealistic beliefs may transform apparent signs of communicative difficulties into acts of mutual misconstrual and underestimation of the true magnitude of risk or threat. Deteriorating social relations are vulnerable to continual unspoken denial of core problems, their gravity, or the slim possibility that anything can be done about them. When faced with a painful reality, couples who are out of touch with underlying relational issues are prone to trivialize the true significance of their communicative difficulties or dismiss them as being somehow inevitable—such as through fate or bad faith. By focusing on distractions, diversions, and withdrawing or by reducing daily interaction concerning troublesome grievances, some distressed spouses, for instance, may seek to displace problems, shift responsibility or blame, or simply be content to explain their troubles away.

Disclaims of disagreement can be laborious to confront because of the diverse features, attributes, and types of denial that parties invoke in response to the confusing and obscure manner in which they are manifest. Wholesale denial of claim and counterclaim often works to subvert or undermine the efficacy of shared appeals to communicative reasoning, particularly when the parties in question know full well that something is the case but nonetheless manage to perpetuate gross inconsistencies in thought, word, and deed. Steadfast refusal to accept contrary perspectives is indicative of a pervasive denial of the legitimacy of other people's standards.

As a reaction to the entangled "one among many" issues of personal and social identity, some distressed participants to chronic conflicts may seek escape or refuge in dualistic acts of perspective taking in which some points of view are ultimately privileged, elevated, as sovereign, at the expense of equally viable sources of interpretation that may be subject to strategic discredit or tactical devaluation of worth, meaning, significance, or consideration. What is left out of the larger systemic equation registers but only rapidly in the manner of a socially constructed blank spot or an erased trace settled with an unspoken urge to wipe the slate clean. Typically, this sleight of hand requires that, instead of multiple perspectives being considered simultaneously, some options are ruled out or presumed to be irrelevant at least or superfluous well in advance. Rarely, however, is there steadfast refusal or any unconditional prohibition on personal engagement in discordant disputes. Only two accounts out of four hundred reflect such an extreme approach:

> No one promotes disagreement in my life at this point; I'm not the type of person who looks for a fight; when others have a definite view of how something should be, it doesn't matter to me.
>
> I don't have any relations with anyone who disagrees with me; if I do disagree with someone, it's something petty and the argument is solved within a matter of minutes.

Personal constraints limit the magnitude of social opportunities. They may well restrict, narrow, rule out, and exclude certain types of substantive matters from active or concerted public deliberation. The imposition of tacit, unspoken restrictions, limitations, and prohibitions function as strategic mechanisms designed for regulative purposes. Personal strategies and adaptive tactics provide alternative ways to manage the flow of private information, guard against implications of failure in goal attainment, or ward off further risk and threat.

In general, when the cumulative magnitude of complexity and complication increases slowly over time, unstated questions and unspoken personal concerns about implicit or unspoken performance defects or skill deficiencies may become major issues, even when personal knowledge and social motivation are sufficient. Since cognitive activity *is* so very labor intensive, people are unlikely to devote a great deal of attention to bolstering unimportant attitudes or peripheral concerns. Misdirected efforts are linked with acts of denial, avoidance, and cover-ups. It is important, therefore, to know where salient personal boundary lines lie and to be in a collectively favorable position to calculate scaled risks associated with any alleged violation, transgression, or blunder.

Small Talk

Personal disagreements are extremely variable. Verbal disputes do not emerge in standard shapes and sizes. There is no single yardstick, weight, or measure to take into account the enormous diversity in frequency, duration, intensity, and persistence of use or application (or misapplication) in the social construction of complicated public argument. Each one has a distinctive set of features and attributes. What stands out is the magnitude of variation in theme, texture, and tone. Small-scale disagreements provide a useful starting point. There is something at once fascinating and frustrating about shared efforts to take simple matters in stride—one topic, issue, or problem at a time. Sometimes the scale of personal differences provides no cause or reason for concern. One person thinks, feels, says, or does things one way, whereas the next person thinks, feels, says, and does the same things but in a completely different way. There is one type of discontent, however, that is both common and vexing. It consists of personal engagement, even preoccupation, with small things however trivial or minute they may appear to someone else. From the smallest imaginable infraction may arise what appears to be nothing more than a trivial concern that will multiply, cluster, and congeal into a larger, unspoken stockpile of petty complaints concerning minor matters that receive only indirect, tacit recognition until the mutual misrecognition of personal differences starts to get out of hand.

Respondents refer to struggles over stupid things. The issue in question may be small, a dumb little thing, something ridiculous, petty, picky, insignificant, empty, or even pointless. Nothing substantial need be implicated. What matters most to one source may elicit a response of utter indifference on the part of any other source. Nothing is too small or too inconspicuous to ignore. Mere disagreements include "Yes, the furnace is set too high at 73" or "No, it is just right at 71"; "Yes, the sky is blue" or "No, it looks red"; "Yes, the weather report is on channel eight" or "No, it is on channel seven right now"; "Yes, it's going to rain" or "No, it is going to snow." Such trivial disagreements may come down to who took how many bottles of beer out of the cooler without putting any back.

Even if the subject matter in question is viewed as being trivial or actually not worth arguing about, those who are most prone to indulge in sustained modes of adversarial bargaining may argue anyway, even late into the night. Some profess not to be able to help themselves; others report being suckered or drawn into mindless debates about minor details. Petty bickering, slights, cuts, rips, slips, grudges, raised eyebrows, or edgy voices are all fair game. Nothing that registers as a meaningful act to anyone can be dismissed out of hand as a meaningless gesture by anyone else. Simple events may be cut up into thin slices, one or two seconds at a time. Hairsplitting may become the order of the day.

Small talk is not randomly distributed. It plays a strategic role in tentative matters of impression formation during the initial stages of relational development, and it is decisive during the later phases of badly eroded or deteriorated networks of close social and personal relations. The former equates mainly with safe, low-risk topics, and the latter with modes of resignation or withdrawal. On one level the emergence of small talk is valuable as a social lubricant. It provides safe, low-risk, ritualized mechanisms for people to become acquainted without undo stress or strain. Everyone can easily say *something* about virtually anything that may occur, at least in a shallow or superficial manner. Gossip and rumor provide added opportunity to express

fleeting or transitory opinions, attitudes, and beliefs that are innocuous and
nonthreatening and make no real difference in the end.

At issue is a larger pattern in which all the little things leave a trace or
residue that registers but not in any simple or additive manner. Sometimes
what seems trivial or inane at the moment of utterance may have unforeseen
effects that slowly become a collective weight or burden:

> S/O engage in small talk, but it soon leads to a much larger dispute—it
> could be anything from how to prepare potatoes to clashing views over
> abortion; they stay on guard because each one knows that the other
> might devalue what is said; they don't have much respect for one an-
> other, and they never seem to think what the other is saying is right or
> valid.

> S/O talk, but S thinks O keeps things bottled up inside; usually, it's the lit-
> tle things that add up to big things, and then he withdraws until she de-
> cides to drag the truth out; he feels that little things are no big deal and
> shouldn't be mentioned; if it is big enough to bug her, she thinks it's big
> enough to mention, but he refuses to discuss them nonetheless.

> S/O are never thinking the same thing or thinking the same way; because
> they can't agree about anything of real value, nor even how to converse
> in a mature fashion, conversation consists of small talk and nothing more.

> S/O get along well as long as they don't discuss any real issues; S often
> feels that O is looking for an argument; O will say something she knows
> that S does not believe; whether S ignores O or disagrees right away, O
> will continue to talk about it; S says things she knows will aggravate O;
> when O became a vegetarian, she began trying to make S feel guilty for
> eating meat; so S had a turkey sandwich one day, and O said, "That's so
> disgusting, eating an animal's flesh," and then she made a face; S smiled,
> finished her sandwich, and said, "This tastes great."

> S/O used to share deep thoughts and emotions, but they have grown so
> far apart that neither one thinks intimate exchanges are appropriate or
> appreciated by the other party; so they skim topics briefly, make small
> talk, but never truly talk anymore.

Small talk becomes a larger issue when repeat offenders are routinely construed as being shortsighted as they refuse to let little things go, become all
caught up with minutiae, devalue details, mismanage differences, quibble
over semantics, display impatience, or speak without thinking. What initially
is safe and manageable territory can deteriorate quickly. There is a striking
degree of mystery at work in such cases. Babble, babble, and babble without end. Participants who engage in small talk often appear to be utterly unaware of what happens to them. Petty arguments seem to come from
nowhere, often triggered by nothing obviously tangible or substantial. Words

and gestures cast a magic spell. Numbing, senseless banter has a certain hypnotic or seductive appeal. Minute matters can be seized and transformed into critical matters of truly mythical proportions.

Adversarial social relations become bewildering and baffling insofar as the agitated respondents can offer no good cause or reason for what unfolds. Misery arrives in small doses that can nonetheless add up slowly, almost invisibly, at the periphery of working thresholds of conscious awareness and personal control. Eventually, all the little things may have a collective impact that seems, upon reflection, to be badly inflated and may thus culminate in a climate or atmosphere of resignation and acquiescence. Mutual construction of invisible walls are real walls nonetheless to those who imagine their collective imposition.

Escalation

A much larger class of disputed social events unfold as serious or sustained disagreements that persist in selective, stipulated spheres of struggle, strife, and strain. Here is where the potential for trouble escalates to levels far more conspicuous than those of selected instances of small talk or idle chatter. Human relations evolve through the cultivation of selective and strategic spheres of social influence. At issue is the larger interplay of resources, capacities, and abilities cast against the cumulative weight of unspecified shortcoming, weaknesses, and vulnerabilities.

Certain critical qualifications are in order. Serious disagreements require at least a moderate degree of personal investment or ego involvement in contested matters. When people take things seriously, latitudes of acceptance narrow and latitudes of rejection broaden (Sereno and Mortensen 1969; Mortensen and Sereno 1970). In addition, the lines of demarcation separating the respective domains of acceptance and rejection also sharpen. Consequently, personal boundaries acquire clear definition, and levels of ambiguity and noncommitment decrease over the short term. When people know exactly where each other stands, there is a tendency to take sides, engage in adversarial bargaining, employ zero-sum logic, and pit one position or stance against another. Concerted effort is directed toward the common pursuit of a favorable collective verdict—namely, a declaration of who is right, who is wrong, what is true, and what is false.

Metaphorically, strong advocates employ selective language that at once calls attention to the full range of personal difference, ignores or discounts the importance of personal similarities, and invokes an either-or orientation by which one selectively and strategically assigns disproportionate credit to his or her own stand and discredits or discounts value to any alternative positions assumed by other people. The imagery is striking. Many become caught up in power struggles in which each party takes an opposing stand on a controversial topic and then becomes mired in clashing dualisms and conceptual imperatives. Participants appear to be knocking heads or are unable to see eye to eye. No one wants to back down or budge so much as an inch. Neutral reactions diminish. It is common for rivals to falsely claim that they have nothing in common. It is tempting to try to move one up and to put the other down. Polarization is common, and unresolved dualisms abound. Concessions are rare, and compromise is often precluded. Pride comes before the fall.

Personal disagreements promote considerable sensitivity to the press and play of the totalizing weight of individual similarities and differences. Sentences with references to a stockpile of exclusionary features and opposing attitudes are commonplace. In personal accounts devoid of mention or appeal to social similarities, or whatever is held in common, disaffected parties either construe a sweeping range of inhibiting relational considerations as being too great to overcome or else dismiss them as being unamenable to negotiation, much less resolution. On contested interpretive matters, a host of troublesome beliefs about things in general may be present. Many disputants are filled with appeals to disparate assumptions, desires, intentions, expectations, opinions, attitudes, beliefs, views, habits, routines, priorities, goals, interests, backgrounds, value systems, morals, outlooks, perspectives, lifestyles, and worldviews. There is also an absence of consensus concerning what is actually important, what life is about, how to deal with people, and what fundamental issues are not considered worthy of negotiation. Against the strain of claim pressed against counterclaim, strict advocates become rigid and inflexible, dig in their heels, and cling to ingrained or entrenched status positions. Often, the confusion and chaos resemble a game without end or means of clarification. People spin their wheels, so to speak, but it is to no avail.

S/O find the more they get to know one another, the easier it becomes to provoke intense disputes where each one struggles to keep core beliefs intact; routine arguments turn into a battle for respect.

S/O adapt opposite viewpoints about virtually everything; contradictions are common; S thinks O assumes everyone in the world is bad, and S sees everyone as good until proven otherwise; O is forever the pessimist—the world will never be on one's side; S is an optimist—so today was bad, tomorrow will be better; they have no common interests and often engage in debates just for the sake of debate.

S/O don't see eye to eye on anything; what involves a simple favor to one party becomes a sheer impossibility to the other party; petty bickering is common; because they feel so alien and they disagree about so much, talk easily becomes tedious and obnoxious; generally, issues are dropped out of sheer frustration because so many stem from hypocrisy—O will say one thing and then do another in a vicious cycle; now S tries to avoid conversations of substance and disagreements with no solutions—they just cause headaches.

S/O quibble and argue all the time, mostly over semantics; they will not let minor points go, because neither one will acknowledge the other one has a point; criticism is constant; O tells S to just keep her trap shut and look pretty because men find it attractive; S/O have such different styles that they hardly ever get along.

S/O share few of the same views; daily interactions are frequent but about as deep as a shotglass; they often talk about their lives together, but S disguises things because O is quick to judge what S says, and O speaks negative about their fundamental differences, which always seem to get in the way.

In these characterizations, discordant participants seek to control or exert further influence on one another's thoughts and actions but mostly without apparent success. The law of unintended consequences is clearly at work here. There is not only limited ability to shape the unfolding process but also insufficient resolve to identify alternative methods of constructive inquiry. Generally, active levels of resistance and inflexibility seem to be more powerful than what registers in the weaker and more compliant forms of inaction and withdrawal in the emergence of small talk and idle chatter. Moreover, there are also far more robust forms of discredit, disparagement, and devaluation at work in the social construction of serious disagreement and mutual misunderstanding.

Still unanswered, however, are the causes and reasons for the persistence in social activities that, for the most part, the parties know on the basis of self-reflection to cause trouble and disable shared efforts to achieve individual goals and fulfill common purposes. In effect, many do not know why they do what they do when things go wrong, but, they nonetheless still perpetuate and pursue the same unrealistic or unobtainable outcomes. The massive inability and shared unwillingness to talk about shared faults and failures serves to make matters worse. One thing seems certain: When one big thing goes wrong, lots of little things are sure to follow, as is revealed in the following excerpts, which relate to tension, irritation, and annoyance.

Tension

S/O talk, but they are silent a lot—when they talk, it is rather tense and brief.

S/O do not like each other—communication is very tense and very unnatural.

S/O seem to disagree about everything, and much tension and frustration ensue.

S/O used to talk, but it was so tense and unnatural that they don't have any direct contact anymore.

S/O don't see eye to eye—they end up in disagreements over any issues that might arise. S/O end up hurting one another, and this makes the apartment tense and unbearable.

S/O say things sometimes just to get a rise out of each other; right now the relationship is very tense—they barely talk to each other; whenever they do see one another; each one is waiting for the other person to make some kind of move.

Irritation

S/O seem to bring out personal differences just to irritate one another.

S/O talk, but S thinks that O is somewhat irritating, and S does not know why O's presence makes S feel so on edge.

S/O talk, but S thinks O says things for no apparent reason other than to irritate the hell out of S, who thinks O says things that degrade others.

S/O chose to close their system in order to avoid tension and irritation due to the fundamental differences that they cannot overcome.

Annoyance

S/O annoy the hell out of one another.

S/O talk, but S finds O irritating, yet S doesn't know why and it's an awful feeling to feel.

S/O take opposite stands on virtually everything—sometimes this gets very annoying.

S/O split up, and it becomes real annoying to S when people tell him that they see his ex-girlfriend around and that she is doing fine.

S/O talked but he wanted to be intimate and she wanted him to get lost so she found more ways to reject him by getting annoyed no matter what.

S/O talk, but S is insulted by the things that O does; S gets annoyed with things O says, so S replies in short answers or doesn't say a lot.

S/O find that talk often starts off on the wrong foot and that S gets annoyed and her anger shows (even when she tries to calm down).

S/O are complete opposites; O enjoyed doing things that S despised and S enjoyed things that O hated—it became annoying.

S/O talk, but S thinks that O goes too far with his joking a lot and then wonders why people get annoyed at him.

Tension is ubiquitous. Mild distress is associated with hesitation and indecision as well as reluctance and discomfort. Unspoken moods, offending manners, strong dislikes, taboo subjects, and codes of silence conspire to diminish the level of spontaneity and synchrony of talk concerning undesirable elements or unwelcome considerations and sometimes cause the pace of speaking and listening to grind to a halt. The accompanying silence can be awkward and typically signifies a mood of reticence and apprehension from the adverse effects of so many people feeling so ill at ease, at the very same time. Unrelieved and unspoken tension, stress, and strain often appear to register at the periphery of conscious awareness or personal control. Disruptive matters reportedly arouse the sort of private unpleasantness that is seldom discussed or addressed explicitly before others. Successful metacommunication is a rare occurrence. Moreover, turn taking is generally described as being irregular or disjunctive, and the atmosphere or linguistic climate may vary from depictions of mild but unrelieved friction, strife, and strain to something that is construed as being far more oppressive, unnatural, or even unbearable. Mounting tensions have considerable potential to unsettle and disable the participants and the larger generative process at the same time.

Linguistic tension persists as resistance to manifest strivings toward complex goal attainment. Often-mundane dialectical contradictions stand in the way. Mixed motives repel and attract at the same time. Even routine conflict episodes may well revolve around issues of autonomy directed toward or away from someone or something else. Likewise, conflicting imperatives convey competing strains between the urge to open up or close down; move closer or further apart; and become involved or remain detached from a person, place, or thing. Finally, at a pragmatic level, there may be lateral or reciprocal movement in aligned or misaligned directions, progressive construction or regressive destruction, and effective intervention or ineffective resolution. Dramatic movements may play out at implicit, tacit, and covert levels; have explicit, overt, literal meanings; and be mythical, symbolic, or transcendent in signification.

Tension does not lead inevitably to tense modes of face-to-face interaction. Spillovers of tension, stress, and strain occur in the shared production of chronic discord. Negative emotions acquire collective force when there is a direct transfer of mood, affect, or style of personal presentation from one public setting to any other public setting. Tension, stress, and strain accumulate inside and outside relational boundaries. Stressful work obligations provide occasions for further efforts at withdrawal in the face of shifting demands and variance in affective or cognitive overload from one day to the next. Tension, stress, and strain register in aversive attitudes and biased attributions of personal responsibility for conditions of irritation or agitation directed at source and subject matter alike. A few respondents in the Wisconsin study claim to be merely irritated at themselves, but most profess to be irritated or annoyed with the offensive antics of someone else. The central object of personal concern is shared engagement in a faulty process that in turn intersects with equally ineffective or futile methods of dealing with divisive topics, themes, and subjects. Hostile tactics based on button pushing and tacit provocations lead many adversarial bargainers to be on edge in what amounts to an agonistic game, a passive aggressive duel, with unspecified provision for score keeping, pestering, teasing, joking, one-up moves, and subtle put-downs.

Serial arguments promote resentment, discredit, offense, insult, and crazy habits. Feelings of irritation and annoyance usually signify some measure of escalation in the sheer magnitude or salience of collective discontent or personal ill will. Although signs of displeasure or dismay may be expressed directly, the underlying causes and reasons are rarely specified or appear to be remotely understood by the contending parties. Mild discomfort and nonspecific displeasure may be elusive, puzzling, and perplexing regardless of any sober reflection in the emotional aftermath. Serial arguing occurs in ordinary social exchanges relating to matters proving difficult to control though not necessarily harmful; especially, perceived resolution is associated with the strength of relational ties (Johnson and Roloff 2000).

Scaled measures of social constraint, small-scale discrepancy, dispute, and discordance contribute to episodes of tension, irritation, annoyance, and serial argument. Relevant attributions involve chronic episodes of mutual conflict based on a spirit of discordance, disaffection, antagonism, and discontent. In effect, disagreeable and divergent participants experience strong levels of misrecognized intent, misaligned perspective taking, contested identity claims, verbal abuse, verbal fighting, and problematic interactive circumstance

MISRECOGNITION OF INTENT

S/O talk and S will say something, but O won't acknowledge it or, worse, O will turn it around to mean something entirely different from what S intended; so S sits in front of O, tense and rigid, and frustration and anger are worked up until S walks away with a lot of anxiety.

S/O get on each other's case; what is really detrimental for their relationship is that S thinks that O doesn't take anything S says seriously, or O misinterprets S's intentions—because they don't understand each other, they really have no chance to cope with any disagreements they may have along the way.

S/O do not get along well at all—conversations are so surface with no meaning to them; it's so casual and boring, so S tries to act interested in what O says and does, and O seems totally uninterested in what S says and does but that's okay with S, who thinks O doesn't need to take the time to talk with S or be nice if O really doesn't mean it.

Signs of personal disaffection coupled with displays of denial, cover-up, or refusal leave minute traces of emotive residue behind. Upon reflection, personal inability or collective unwillingness to talk about faults and foibles often gives rise to even more tension, stress, and strain, which if left unresolved shift or change upward in intensity, duration, or salience. Small matters of irritation and annoyance qualify as low-threshold indicators of the total magnitude of discontent, divergence, or divisiveness at work in the larger situation. Equally important, what participants may experience as emotional agitation or aggravation may not be self-evident or obvious to anyone other than those who are directly and adversely affected.

Psychological discontent may go unrecognized by observers, or the distress may be barely detectable, if at all. Factors that operate on the fringes of conscious awareness are not transparent and therefore may be subject to selective inattention and mistaken identification. The mere existence of divisive sources of ambiguity and confusion may not be consequential. However, what does matter is how much cognitive distortion is attributable to a serious misreading of other people's aspirations, intentions, and goal-directed activity.

Individuals often disagree on several levels of abstraction at once: how to view certain things, how to view one another's view of these things, and how to reconcile signs of discrepancy and disparity in one another's view. Those who disagree routinely on several different levels of abstraction at once are also the most likely to misidentify, misinterpret, misconstrue, or misread the underlying, tacit aspirations, intentions, and strivings of other people. Unless the parties involved are able to come to terms with escalating episodes of friction, strife, and strain, the most aggravating and agitating qualities of discursive interchange may develop greater velocity or momentum over time. A sustained pattern of mutual misrecognition may unwittingly increase the level of mutual vulnerability to severe difficulties in perspective taking and perspective framing (and reframing).

DIVERGENT PERSPECTIVES

S/O are not really willing to look at each other's viewpoints; they are way too different in background, belief, and behavior.

S/O never agree about anything—O will state O's side, and S will state S's side, and then it begins all over again; O tells S her idea is wrong and why, and S tells O that her idea is wrong and why—it's okay because it's just stupid anyway.

S/O have interactions where controversy can go on forever without either
of them being able to say that one party understands the other one—
their perspectives are from opposite ends of the spectrum, and they often cannot reach a middle ground.

Limited perspective-taking ability is a decisive factor in the social construction of a broad spectrum of personal disagreements. Competent interactants demonstrate the capacity and willingness to adopt open-ended and
flexible frameworks of interpretation that shift readily from first- to second-
and third-person viewpoints—that is, *I, you,* and *we.* It is not always easy to
adapt multifaceted perspectives toward multiple subjects or subject matters.
Motivation strongly influences personal perception in direct relation to the
magnitude of effort required to distance oneself from one's own conception
of the situation and thereby assume the perceptual stance of others. Conflicting imperatives, irreconcilable antagonisms, conceptual opposition, and
strict polarities entail dynamic tension, stress, and strain relating to the magnitude of discrepancy and disparity in contested matters involving contradictory goals, priorities, aspirations, or motivations. Accommodative dilemmas arise in situations in which one person attempts to take the perspective
of another but is faced with an abusive party intent on enacting potentially
destructive behavior. Unrealistic gender beliefs, opinions, and attitudes are
important factors in the unspoken reflections of men and women about irreconcilable differences in respect to their relational needs (Fitzpatrick and
Sollie 1999).

CONTESTED IDENTITY

S/O talk, but S thinks O's insensitivities toward discussion of personal issues makes S want to block out the subject, too—their mutual inability
to see the other's point of view means that they never resolve anything.

There are few instances of reconstructed disagreements that may be
judged, at least on the surface, to function in strictly neutral, impersonal
terms. Disagreements rarely emerge from matters of indifference. What
makes "no difference" is subject to discredit, devaluation, or disqualification
from further consideration because, after all, it is really "nothing." Small-
scale conflicts, disputes, debates, and quarrels often coalesce or pivot
around observed differences that really do make a difference; hence, strictly
oppositional differences are the most likely to be difficult to reconcile. The
more the total magnitude of discrepancy and divergence is open to discussion or subject to further reconsideration or elaboration, the more likely the

advocates in question will effectively tip the balance between impersonal and personal considerations in favor of the latter; thus, they will slip into the use of slanted scripts that support an attractive illusion that everything may be now taken personally and that virtually nothing is left out of the transformed equation so that no detail is too small or insignificant to be dismissed as being irrelevant.

Exaggerated social conceptions based on divisiveness, discontent, and divergence begin to take an emotional toll on polarized advocates. Insofar as personal and social identities are called into question, the interpretive identifications are themselves thrown into an unsettled, chaotic state. It is not so much a matter of battered and bruised egos at stake but rather an unsettling process in which one's personal claims are subjected to equally personal disclaimers from the other side. Calling into question the veracity of another person's declarations (truth claims) may also take into account any defect or deficiency in the manner or style of personal presentation. Even so-called trivial disclaimers over contested subjects may convey or evoke a unsettling sense of displeasure with the stylistic mode of presentation or representation of advocates who take opposing stands on controversial issues. As a result, intense wrangling about questionable matters may eventually reflect negatively on the credibility of the person who holds steadfastly to a questionable issue, a problem, or pressing concern.

Frustrating Disagreement

Robust aversive stimulation often leads to frustration or acute distress. Unsatisfying situations involving the personal inability to escape the control of others prove troublesome when those who could resist or help instead pursue their strategic interests and thereby bypass public appeal to standards of communicative rationality or show no willingness to so much as lift a finger to make things better. A legacy of poor-quality interpretations or faulty performative actions also implicates routine exposure to harsh social outcomes that end the same way, namely, in a lack of social validation or confirmation of a segment of one's own identity.

Passive reactions to disabling scaled constraints in linguistic resourcefulness increase personal vulnerability to distress or renewed aggression by others (strangers). Stress and grievance go hand in hand. Violations and transgressions give rise to strategic countermoves and countervailing tactics—accusations or admonition directed toward the alleged offender. Congruent interplay among one person's interests, preferences, acquired abilities, and affordance is likely to promote and foster refinement and elaboration of joint activities that slowly increase the precision and consistency of interpersonal dealings in the course of daily life. Incongruent interplay among unbalanced alignments of interests, preferences, and abilities is likely to result and sustain a surplus of imprecise or crude indicators of disabled social endeavors.

> S/O know how to make the other upset, and they also enjoy getting the other frustrated because they know how and are willing at any time.
>
> S/O are lost because they cannot convey shared feelings very effectively; they react out of sheer frustration and rarely end conversation on a good note.
>
> S/O view one another as being completely incompetent; they don't even want to listen to what the other wants to say—it is frustrating—no one gives in and no one seems to care.
>
> S/O never let it rest—they interrupt a lot—there is often yelling or signs of frustration, such as stamping one's foot or fiddling with an object or slamming a door or drawer.
>
> S/O find talking puts them on edge; each one gets frustrated with the other because of a tendency to blow small things out of proportion.

Aggravation

> S/O talk in ways that make S want to say things that she knows will aggravate the other.
>
> S/O have conflicts that make S frightened at the thought of further aggravation.
>
> S/O can't get along—its not worth the aggravation.

Frustration, by definition, complicates sense-making activity by making it confusing or vexing for the parties to figure out what just transpired—that is, what happened quickly, rapidly, or suddenly, as an out-of-nowhere experience or as a blurring, blinding moment or momentary lapse of reason. Five leading indicators of interpersonal frustration are heavily concentrated in personal accounts of acute disagreement in the transcripts from the Wisconsin study (table 7.1). Clearly, manifest frustration discriminates no one. While not every small-scale dispute is occasion for aggravation, annoyance, irrita-

Table 7.1.   Frustration Measures

Term	Agreement	Disagreement	Understanding	Misunderstanding
Tension	2	12	1	4
Irritation	2	14	1	7
Annoyance	12	29	10	28
Frustration	10	47	14	48
Aggravation	3	8	2	1
Total	29	110	28	88

tion, frustration, and tension, most things that matter on a personal level register in terms of friction, strife, and strain.

Nothing is too small, minute, or trivial as an object of concerted consideration (or reconsideration). After all, two or more people may want two different things at once, or they may want the same indivisible thing at the same time. Some things are intangible, while other things are unobtainable. Still other types of things cannot be precisely or accurately calculated, measured, divided up, sorted out, evenly petitioned, parceled out, or cut in half. Sometimes people simply decide that a negotiated state of all or nothing is the only acceptable course. Hence, frustration is pervasive in settings in which the participants are quick to judge the situation and lack or lose the patience required to reach mutually satisfying outcomes. Thematically, the magnitude of frustration mounts quickly and decisively among those who lose hope, become tired, run out of energy, give up, or give in to one source of resistance or another.

Sometimes, freely talking about frustrating circumstances makes things better; at other times, talking about frustrating circumstances only makes things worse. Furthermore, the lower and upper thresholds of tolerance and forbearance are usually unknown, uncertain, or undecipherable. What frustrates the production and reception of expressive utterances is discovered in real-time constraints relating to alternative courses of action. Performance-based grumbling and complaining are diffuse, inclusive, and commonplace. Frequent mentions in the transcripts include unwelcome arguments; gaps and lapse of insight, or weak imagination; poor listening; lack of eye contact; mind-numbing monologues; barely concealed urges to escape, run away, or hide; and counterattacking or fighting back for the sheer pleasure of seeing someone else squirm and wiggle on the hook or be ripped apart, upset, insulted, degraded, or otherwise reduced in size, status, or prestige. In such cases, punitive and retaliative tactics abound, and petty power struggles become a way of life.

Manipulation and calculation are never far away. Questions are misdirected, and answers only disappoint or fall short of the mark. Contradictions stem from a slow pileup of tiny, small-scale divisions, a result of which is that little things get blown out of proportion, mostly from shortsighted pronouncements and imperial declarations. Weak spots are dissected and probed for the slightest advantage. Whatever aggravated participants may feel, think, say, or do adds to the possibilities for their being taken apart, turned upside down, and discarded or left in shambles. Acute frustration involves forsaken pursuits, broken dreams, discarded values, and conflicting preferences.

Angry Disagreement

S/O try to talk about touchy subjects, then one or the other will get angry, and they end up in a shouting match.

S/O talk, but they get angry because they hate arguing and they can't seem to stop it.

S/O never agree about anything—slowly O learns that the only reactions O is going to get from S are a toxic combination of anger and tears.

S/O talk, but O avoids talking about what S is talking about, and O is always exasperated and frustrated, sighs very heavily, and walks out leaving S very angry.

S/O try to talk, but S shuts O out with harsh, mean words that do not help O understand S's point of view.

S/O have short, hostile, or cold conversations; they are often angry about things that happened in the past that they have not confronted—because these implicit angry feelings are often left unspoken, their interactions are hostile and they often do not know why.

S/O have hurt each other in horrible ways—they let little things drive them apart; they have become infatuated with their anger and stubbornness.

S/O are complete opposites; talks usually turn into bitter fights; they both get defensive and jump to conclusions; they are hostile whenever they talk; they get angry very easily—they are never relaxed or comfortable, and they always have their guard up.

S/O find that sometimes O makes S so angry that S doesn't care to see O for days at a time—when they are together, they are always yelling or talking very loudly.

S/O become very angry with each other—the level of anger depends on how much S thinks that O is watching his mouth and how patient S is—they have crossed the line many times before.

S/O often get angry with each other; sometimes they go without speaking, and they just let things blow over until they've put the argument behind them.

Anger is expansive. Things happen. Certain subjects and certain topics lead to uncertain circumstance. After all, other people may not say or do what anyone else wants them to say or do. Persuasion is influential, but people strongly resist unwanted or unwelcome imposition of coercive, calculative, or manipulative intent in others. Resistance leads to persistence. Implicit anger in small doses risks inflation into large doses of explicit anger. Stubbornness and patronizing attitudes and condescending sentiments figure heavily in the fury and the fuss. Repeat offenders have crossed the line many times before.

Provocation infiltrates. Some become all riled, fly off the handle, lose control, and engage in a shouting match; they scream, yell, and refuse to calm down; they slam doors, knock out the television, break pictures, throw pots and pans; they speak with clinched fists or gritted teeth, claw, bite, and scratch; they are sure to kick, push, and shove for good measure; they smash up the place and tell somebody off. Secondary expressions of fury and verbal outrage exhibit a similar ethos. It pays to insist that one partner is completely right while another party is completely wrong. A slow, incremental pileup of little things can drive people apart. People say things they do not mean, jump too quickly to premature conclusions, and describe complex matters far too little and explain little matters far too much. Special pleading, after all, is everyone's favorite mind game for the obdurate reason that common appeal to mitigating circumstance can be dredged up by almost anyone, no matter how stupid, ignorant, or misinformed. It is often usually futile to try to refocus other people's states of inattentiveness just to redress past wrongs that cannot be verified one to another.

There is a moral to this story. By reasonable measure, public display of strong anger ranks among the most frequently experienced negative emotions, and it is typically associated with frustration stemming from failures in goal-relevant events. Outbursts of anger, by definition, are provocative, blameful, and coercive. Angry responses may be activated from an implicit sense of being treated unfairly, obsessional thinking, increased heart rate, and yelling or swearing in a faulty effort to control outbursts of verbal anger. Aversive affect-laden scripts are complicated by being interwoven into selective magnification of misdeeds, usually when another person is construed as being responsible for thwarting a major goal. Personal attacks do not require solid evidence and, even when provided, likely fall short of conventional standards of relevance, objectivity, and decorum.

VERBAL ABUSE

The usefulness of routine talk is subject to the regressive effects of countervailing social forces as a result of the often unintended short-term types of adverse outcomes associated with the misuse and abuse of ordinary language in severely contested public confrontations. The concept of verbal abuse presumes some prior misuse of words and gestures at someone else's expense. Ineffective or faulty use of words and gestures may invoke or provoke the shared acquisition of regressive or counterproductive linguistic conditions in which defects and deficiencies in sign relations serve to thwart, subvert, or undermine the perpetuation or reproduction of constructive, elaborated, or coherent ways of making sense together. Furthermore, careless or reckless acts of verbal misuse or physical abuse may well induce a major shift in the tenor and tone of shared deliberations over long periods of time. Repeated acts and protracted episodes may cross a major boundary into serious transgressions and major violations with underlying implications of hurt and harm.

When intangible forms of linguistic misuse or abuse lead to distress, misaligned responses to conflicting subjects are likely to be construed as being aversive and ineffectual in terms of short-term consequence. There is a close tie between personal judgments of verbal arguments escalating into acts of intimate violence; generally, intense verbal fights appear to provoke virtually all manner of partner violence known to people in many cities (Miller and Bukva 2001). Various measures show that psychological abuse occurs in the majority of bonded relationships that are also physically abusive (Follingstad and Dehart 2000). A good deal of emotional abuse is often thrown in the toxic mix for good measure (O'Hearn and Davis 1997). Moreover, verbal insult, jealous provocation, extreme accusation, and emotional intimidation are frequent precursors of physical violence among battered women (Neufeld, McNamara, and Ertl 1999). Human violence is overwhelmingly propagated by males. The sobering truth is that if human beings could eliminate, minimize, or reduce male violence, we could, as Barash (2002) notes, "pretty much get rid of violence altogether" (B7).

Satisfaction and pleasure in sexual relations appear to diminish for a considerable number of victims of physical abuse or sexual assault, often for long periods, suspended between fear and morbid arousal, anger, shame, and guilt; as well as risk of sexual dysfunction, posttraumatic stress symptoms, or clinical depression (van Berlo and Ensink 2000). To add psychological insult to physical injury, some women who are abused in intimate relations may deny, downplay, discount, or omit critical information before others. Tactics of minimization occur in a third of the cases of abused women's disclosure to friends and relatives (Dunham and Senn 2000). As documented widely by Yelsma (1996), deficit of affect, more than presence of negative affect, qualifies as a significant indicator of physical abuse in intimate relationships (Yelsma 1996).

Coercive actions can take the form of a direct threat of physical force or an indirect threat, in the form of verbal demands, commands, injunctions, orders, or ultimatums (do or die). In general, verbal coercion is the main form of sexual coercion by men and women in heterosexual relations. Relevant tactics are manipulative, calculative, argumentative, pretentious, or merely fanciful. Women subjected to violent sexual coercion show poor adjustment long afterward: deteriorating emotional tone; depression; low self-esteem; negative body image; and low-quality friendship, romantic interest, and love life (Zweig et al. 1999). Social support for abused women remains a potent predictor of emotional recovery, regained sense of self-regard, and reclaimed sense of trust and loyalty (Fry and Barker 2002).

Sexual harassment entails a coercive expression of sexual interest followed by some responsive indication, either in words, gestures, or suggestive silence, of a refusal to consent to such behavior and a subsequent repetition of unwanted, intrusive, or bothersome sexual messages (Wall 2001; Landau 2003). Prevalent sexual harassment in the workplace is directed toward females, who usually construe their perpetrators as predominantly male (Murphy, Driscoll, and Kelly 1999; Sbrage and O'Donohue 2000). Whereas males experience sexual harassment as annoying remarks that discredit or demean a personal sense of masculinity (Berdahl, Magley, and Waldo 1996), females commonly report more discomfort, greater security fears, and pervasive responses of other female victims (O'Hare and O'Donohue 1998; O'Sullivan, Byers, and Finkelman 1998; Rotundo, Nguyen, and Sackett 2001). Men's reports of workplace sexual harassment are rarely acknowledged and less frequently examined. However, men who fail to display "acceptable" masculine behavior are likely to be construed as "women" than as "real" men (Lee 2000). By implication, "wimpy" males need not apply (Stockdale 1998). In addition, comparative lack of gender-related power in an organizational hierarchy only magnifies the scale of power differential and, as a consequence, heightens female vulnerability to remarks with intent to demean.

Centrally implicated are sexist comments, offensive, sanction-free sexual advances, unwanted attention, risque comments, dominant nonverbal displays, dirty jokes, macho intimidations, offensive manners, wolf whistles, crude stereotypes, objectifying disclaimers, and aggressive efforts at coerced sexual compliance—either implicit promise of benefit or threat of punishment. To make matters worse, most female victims decide not to report coercive, degrading, and sexualized encounters, whether out of fear of reprisal, retaliation by perpetrators, or lack of belief that anything will be done about alleged grievance (Welsh and Gruber 1999). Furthermore, victims who take the direct, confrontational approach often place themselves at greater risk of psychological, emotional, and somatic symptoms.

Gender-related differences over conflicting definitions of "friendly" behavior may well promote rapid cultivation of discrepancy, disagreement, and misunderstanding of what constitutes an appropriate or acceptable standard of acceptable workplace actions. Where workplace communication is baffling, bewildering, or ambiguous, the confusing process is apt to be interpreted as harassing (Markert 1999). Mixed messages, in addition, may also preclude clear, cogent, or straightforward interpretation (Marczely 1999). Moreover, double standards confer greater discretionary power for dominant group members to allege, deflect, or transfer the central workplace focus onto suspect actions of marginal, subordinate, or peripheral group members, who bear the brunt of sexualized interaction with greater possibility of danger and damage than enjoyment or pleasure (Williams, Guiffre, and Dellinger 1999).

In general, men and women use one another as perpetrators and victims at roughly comparable levels of salience, intensity, and aversive effect; however, men see themselves more often as the objects of verbal coercion, whereas women are more likely to report threats of physical violence (Russell and Oswald 2001). Strong disagreements between distressed couples have great potential to escalate to a point at which the threat of violence is a real possibility, particularly when reactive alignments are marked by threatening episodes based on negative reciprocation, anger, contempt, and deprecating actions (Bradbury, Fincham, and Beach 2000). Although national survey research indicates that both men and women are likely to use violent tactics as a last resort, women impose the threat of physical force for self-defense and escape, whereas men employ violent means largely to impose greater control, punish, or gain attention (Hamberger et al. 1997).

Male domestic violence is often predicated on a foreboding sense of threatening intimacy or menacing communicative atmosphere. Coercive tactics escalate in unilateral acts of verbal aggression, repeated cycles of demand and withdrawal, unconstructive responses to destructive communication, and ineffective efforts in mutual problem solving (Feldman and Ridley 2000). Malicious verbal abuse leads to physical aggression more frequently than less severe forms of abusive behavior (Hamby and Sugerman 1999). Verbal aggression and the emotional aftermath both contribute to a climate of negativity, replete with harmful consequences, such as decreased relational quality and lack of well-being (Kenny and Acitelli 2001).

The miscommunication hypothesis documents the central role of poor-quality affectionate interaction in the preliminary stages of sexual coercion. Three basic thematic patterns emerge: men overestimate women's interest in sex; men discount women's refusals as being token or feeble; and women are reluctant to refuse directly unwanted sexual advances (McCaw and Senn 1998). Men and women disagree about the frequency of male-to-female violence in intimate relations. Women and men remember past encounters differently: women remember more vividly, but both genders selectively remember and tactically recall that they were right and the other was wrong (Armstrong et al. 2001). Abused women reportedly assign more weight to their aggressive partner's *positive* qualities, particularly when they construe their male counterparts as showing some care and concern about hurt and harm (Marshall, Weston, and Honeycutt 2000).

Across a broad spectrum of turbulent social encounters, intense verbal anger can be rapidly activated when defensive cognitive appraisals hold others disproportionally accountable or responsible for barriers or obstacles to goal-oriented achievement or shared accomplishment. Expressions of anger, hostility, jealousy, and hate seem to merge, fuse, flow, and congregate, particularly under conditions of disagreement and misunderstanding (table 7.2). Emotional flooding only makes matters worse. Extreme anger and verbal outbursts—slamming doors; saying nasty things; and acting out of malice, vengeance, or spite—might serve a hidden purpose associated with unrelenting control, dominance, or intimidating others. Nonetheless, verbally aggressive styles and generalized disagreeableness are maladaptive in the long

Table 7.2.   Anger, Hostility, Jealousy, and Hate

Term	Agreement	Disagreement	Understanding	Misunderstanding
Anger	20	52	15	53
Hostility	4	19	2	5
Jealousy	5	41	7	7
Hate	10	21	3	8
Total	39	133	27	73

run because provocation amplifies difficulties and hinders efforts to new, novel, or innovative forms of goal achievement (Martin et al. 1999).

The sheer magnitude of verbal anger increases in direct proportion to perceived unfairness in regard to outcomes versus process in matters of distributive or procedural justice. Moreover, attributions of blame mediate relations between angry feelings and subsequent construal of the provoker's intentions to injure, the justification for harm, and the magnitude of harm inflicted on unwilling subjects. The central theme is, anger is acquired from a critical assessment that provides a rough approximation of all that goes wrong.

Strong anger escalates when adversarial relations reach a critical limit—the participants cannot agree about anything that has binding force. Thus, verbal anger constitutes an intensified expression of resistance and revolt against the oppressive intentions of other people. Likewise, intense anger leads to emotional flooding relative to everything that has made matters worse or has else eluded reconsideration up to now. What annoys and aggravates is subjected to external forces and factors that register beyond one's control to alter one way or another. Anger culminates in bursts of outrage concerning flaws and failures in sense-making practice, particularly the ill effects of being subjected to dominating forces that impose constrained conditions that require submissiveness, obedience, and docility on the part of the many for the exclusive benefit of a select few.

Hostile Disagreements

S/O have conversations that consist of hostile silence punctuated by disgusted sighs.

S/O talk while S thinks that everything O says or does causes S to avoid O or be hostile.

S/O talk, but ordinary conversation is hostile and heavily laden with unspoken expectations—it often has a snowballing effect, making it difficult to get out unscathed.

S/O find that even civilized small talk usually results in veiled hostility to each other.

Respondents' accounts from the Wisconsin study contain considerable mention of hostility spelled out in toxic terms. Expressions of hostility are associated with several different types of anger, from mild to strong. One central strain entails a brooding, smoldering, slow-burning anger mixed with low-grade hostility and barely concealed resentment. Another major theme revolves around escalating episodes of anger, hostility, and resentment relative to observed actions seen as unfair or unjustified when some form of recognition and responsibility is expected, desired, or demanded but never forthcoming. In short, people are assumed to be the sources of their own public outbursts, but many observers fall into the classic trap of blaming their anger on others; in other words, they deny or cover up the possibility of their own angry responses, as well as their reactive and resentful energy, and attribute it all to that coming exclusively from others. The blind spot here is that it is easier to view the angry expressions of other people as the real source of social difficulty than it is to view one's own angry outbursts as the original source.

Hostility is an accompanying mood state and has either a dampening or an intensifying effect, depending on the magnitude of risk or threat imposed by unwelcome messages. Respondents outline several different types of free association: there is hostile silence and a lack of personal warmth but lots of cold responses; effects of some hostile acts persist in the absence of further provocation; and hostility often comingles with frustration over whatever has gone wrong, fallen short of the mark, been misguided, or fallen apart. Prolonged hostility can be exhausting and leave the adversely affected tired, grouchy, worn out, or totally spent from the sheer sense of futility and frustration. Invidious displays of hostility are mixed with strong anger, outrage, and violent intent, which make it difficult for entrapped subjects to escape unscathed. Protracted hostility, unrelenting and unrelieved, is neither subject to further negotiation nor amenable to further accommodation.

At a simple level, hostility is commonplace. Salient markers cluster and coalesce around impressions of cynicism, mistrust, and suspicion. Hostile individuals manufacture and fabricate interpersonal difficulties and abrasions that, long endured, increase vulnerability to physical illness, morbidity, and morality. The corrosive side effects of unrelenting hostility include greater potential for defensiveness, conflict, misattributions, miscalculations, and withdrawal (forced retreat) into protracted negative moods that heighten susceptibility to illness and deteriorated measures of personal well-being and diminished relational quality (Fiedler and Semin 1995). Salient markers include a durable disposition to criticize, undercut, strip down, turn off, disapprove, mind read, supply intentions, question motives, digress, go off on tangents, change subject, withdraw, disengage, lapse into silence, or fail to listen, observe, or care (one way or another); furthermore, such markers include steadfast discontent, restlessness, and low-grade irritation over trivia that has gone wrong or stood in someone's way. Complain, vent, bitch, rant, and rail through the day or during the night—woe is me. Endless is my sorrow. Little wonder anger mingles with disgust and contempt, annoyance, and aggravation.

Hostile persons use different, and often less adaptable, coping styles that foster stress-induced impairment of health or psychological well-being. Hostile personal traits include impatience, a strong drive, success orientation, and competitive temperament. An uneven mix of uncomfortable conditions, automatically primed aggressive thoughts and feelings, and motor-expressive activation combine, blend, and overlap in personal encounters in which low-threshold annoyances have additive or multiplicative effects that amplify and spread in escalation of ill will, bad feelings, or suppressed hostility. Aggravated and hostile individuals generate mutual conflict and mutual defensiveness and likely entrap or ensnare others into protracted difficulties that undermine or erode social support in a climate of unrelieved tension, stress, distress, mistrust, and suspicion.

Jealousy

> S/O are hot-blooded and loud, which makes control over emotions difficult because one always slams vicious personal attacks in the other's face; S thinks that O is spiteful and jealous and can't handle the fact that no one wants to be like her at all.

> S/O fight constantly; they are such opposites—S thinks O is jealous of S and O puts S down to make himself feel good—O gets hostile and usually aggravates S on purpose, just to prey on S's weaknesses.

> S/O have always been so competitive—S now feels uneasy telling O things because S believes that O is jealous of S's ex-boyfriend, because O has spent so much time cutting S and her ex-boyfriend down.

What is critical is not simply the cumulative weight of jealous experience but the way people express and interpret jealousy over time. Persons who react in constructive (rather than destructive) ways are more likely to maintain satisfying relations despite their jealous feelings, thoughts, and sentiments. Emotional reactions to infidelity shed light on the narrative construction (or reconstruction) of noxious events and strangely erotic and dramatic performances being acted out by those who no longer control their turbulent emotional life; in fact, their negotiated emotional undercurrents are in control of them. Infidelity in committed relations is threatening, dangerous, detrimental, and difficult to treat in therapy (Atkins, Jacobson, and Baucom 2001).

Sexual infidelity is often fueled by emotional infidelity, and the two toxic forces, when taken together, conjoin to make for destructive, even deadly consequences. Jealous ruminations center on unspoken suspicions of mistrust, possessiveness, surveillance, manipulation, threat, rivalry, derogation of competitors, active distancing, avoidance, denial, violence toward objects, and violent communication (Carson and Cupach 2000). A study of romantic attachment revealed significantly elevated levels of jealousy in men who were maritally violent and men who were nonviolent but unsatisfactorily married (Barnett and Lee 1997). Even suspected jealousy can have devastating consequences (Shackelford, LeBlanc, and Drass 2000).

Jealousy makes control over intense or complex emotions more difficult. Spite, bitterness, resentment, irritation, and aggravation combine to reveal personal weaknesses, shortcomings, vulnerabilities, faults, and failures in feeble or futile engagements at restorative modes of sense-making activity. As a consequence, people feel on edge, indignant, provocative, or vicious in matters of character assassination and personal attacks where the respective parties strive constantly to edge each other out. Jealous feelings in romantic relations surface in response to external competition and exclusionary personal boundaries as sources of great apprehension and uncertainty with great potential for hurt and harm as major relational transgressions. Jealousy often results in intense surveillance behavior, such as spying, checking up, keeping track, looking for telltale signs of trouble, and self-indulgence in clinging or desperate operations and maneuvers under covert operations, even if at great expense to one's own sense of dignity, worth, and self-esteem. Jealous feelings in love relationships are related negatively to member satisfaction. Sexual jealousy acquires social definition insofar as culture contributes to emotional response while institutional affiliations mediate the severity of expressed aggression in each highly charged atmosphere (Hupka and Bank 1996).

Jealousy may blend evocative features of anger, sadness, and fear. Perhaps it is not so surprising that forty-eight of sixty acts or episodes of reconstructed jealousy occurred in the d/m sections of the transcript. Likewise, forty-one of the forty-eight instances reportedly occurred during periods of relational disagreement. It is not clear from such closely fitting correlations whether disagreement fosters jealousy, whether jealousy is disagreeable, or whether some unspecified blend of mounting negativity comes with a sense of impending loss of someone or something that matters a great deal. Moreover, attributions of jealousy may be accusative or confessional. The obtained ratio is heavily slanted toward the former and away from the latter. An admission of jealousy is neither self-enhancing nor self-compensatory but rather an ugly acknowledgment or confession of a socially undesirable trait on the surface of public opinion but common and pervasive underneath.

Personal disclaimers abound, of course, precisely because they are so effortless and easy to produce. Furthermore, the jealous party may be demonized as being frivolous, mindless, dismissive, impatient, interruptive, or guilty of greater crimes—mainly variations of personal attack. Sometimes flirtatious behavior is innocent and useful as a way to break the ice among previously unacquainted persons. However, often what starts out as harmless or benign translates into heavy score keeping on all sides. Reciprocity is surely not far behind. Source A becomes jealous of relations between source B and source C, and then B and C catch on to A's antics and decide to return the favor so that everyone is jealous of everyone else at the same time.

The ambiguity and massive confusion surrounding jealous sentiments are evident in the all-purpose fact that virtually anyone or anything can serve as a signal or a sign of something deeper at stake. Petty resentment, arguments, bickering, and episodic fighting may offer sufficient justification for mutual silence or lateral refusal to acknowledge jealous sentiments over what grants credit to someone at the expense of someone else's loss. Moreover, occasions for jealous crosscurrents are imagined without end. The possibilities are truly endless. The steadfast inability to confront such disturbing or disquieting possibilities of sexual, aesthetic, or ethical violations may leave some beleaguered partner frozen or suspended, as in a state of paralysis over terrible secrets or unspoken lies.

Verbal Fights

Personal accounts in the transcript contain frequent and repeated mentions of hostile exchanges in which verbal use turns into verbal misuse and abuse.

> S/O are best friends who can turn into the worst of enemies; S/O have endured many violent fights, both physically and emotionally abusive, with inconsiderate, selfish feelings and harsh criticism over nearly everything, just to make the other feel bad; they can say awful things without actually realizing the actual degree of hurt that is caused, and then pretend afterward that nothing happened.
>
> S/O fight about anything and everything; they seem to thrive on conflict—they're so afraid of being cut off that they try to cram lots of stuff into a short period—in the end no one's mind is changed, and they both end up very frustrated.
>
> S/O were roommates who shared food together; one day S noticed that someone had used her stir-fry sauce—O was the only one who had rice for supper, so the next day S bluntly told her that she owed her a bottle of sauce, and it turned into a psycho–blown up fight—the fight was over something so small and dumb, but this sauce, at the same time, was sacred in their apartment; soon O turned cold and irrationally moved out—it seemed to build on both sides and suddenly blow all at once.

S/O could have fought World War III because they had such an adversarial style of interaction that always had to have a winner; S worked hard to avoid that type of interaction, but O seemed to thrive on it, subjecting everyone else to sharp condescension—finally, S had enough and joined the battle with relish; they looked for each other's vulnerabilities and exploited them—points of possible agreement were dismissed as useless; twisting each other's words became an art form—big points were to be gained from this tactic; taking offense at innocuous comments was an excuse to start another fight; being right was critical—even defending a position O knew was ridiculous to admitting she was wrong.

S/O have their fights and problems, but they have a very hard time facing and confronting the conflict; they don't deal with conflict in the same way; O does not fight and likes to be left alone, while S likes to fight in order to face it and get it over with—this makes it very hard for S/O to get their feelings about each other out in the open.

S/O can say anything, but unless they are careful and censor what they say, a fight follows and there is never a winner—it is amazing that they have not killed each other; they both try to reason with the other, but it never helps—they try to understand the other's viewpoint, but it's hard; they yell, roll their eyes, or make snide comments about what the other says, all of which usually evolves into an argument on lots of touchy subjects.

Instances of serious verbal fighting are heavily concentrated in the disagreement and misunderstanding sections, which account for 71 percent of all mentions across the four main conditions in the computer transcript. Conversely, less than a third of all reported instances of concerted verbal fighting occurred within the relatively safe confines of agreement and understanding. Moreover, isolated acts or protracted episodes of pronounced verbal fighting about personal disagreements account for 60 percent of all mentions across the four main conditions. While interpersonal disagreements, even the most serious, pressing, or passionate cases in point, do not necessarily escalate into more risky or dangerous fights, the odds of their doing so are rather strong. Furthermore, respondents engaged in sharply adversarial relations selectively track and monitor reconstructed instances of verbal fighting across a broad spectrum of antagonistic or competitive activities that vary widely in salience or intensity, ranging all the way from very weak to very strong. As a corollary, the sheer magnitude of psychological misuse or abuse is closely associated with severity of disagreement; slow or rapid movement from episodic to chronic status; degree of slant in the surplus of negative affect; use of punitive or degrading tactics; and mutual refusal to let small things go unnoticed, ignored, or unmentioned as sources of minor irritants, grievances, or complaints.

Acts of manipulation, calculation, intimidation, and threat will carry one only so far. A meaningless threat is a threat disarmed. Each one thinks and feels that someone else does not get it. Ignorance is costly. Above all else, each dismisses possible agreement as being useless, a waste of time. Those who always try to outdo each other are likely to end up in a vicious self-fulfilling cycle or prophecy whereby they mindlessly, ignorantly, habitually, or constantly try to outdo and outmaneuver one another. This linguistic game is over only when the game is truly over. Alas, the enemies are, as always, a expression of the magnitude of ignorance, stupidity, and sloth.

Mild, moderate, and intense fighting serve to magnify, in varying degrees, the routine misuse and chronic abuse of ordinary language, often at the expense of the shared pursuit of more useful, heuristic alternatives. In this equation, mild fighting qualifies as a mixed motive game played against the protective backdrop of a loosely enforced set of rules. Alleged violations are test cases for what will qualify as instances of dirty fighting. Some instances may start as little more than a stressful quibble or an ill-mannered quarrel. Serial disputes occur one at a time, usually in safe and secure settings with no one becoming bent out of shape. Usually, all that participants need to resolve such mundane issues is some semblance of tacit agreement to air personal differences in the manner of venting, ranting, or letting off steam. Clearly implicated are disputants who know full well that they are going to argue, fuss, feud, and wrangle over matters that matter, but only for a relatively brief period.

Episodic conflicts of low or moderate intensity are by far the easiest to take in stride. Petty fights, nonetheless, can turn into a constant battle of wits or wills in which risks are limited to bruised egos, false pride, and angry outburst but usually find quick recovery without visible scars or internal wounds. This is also a confusing and ambiguous verbal arena in which cooperative and competitive urges can be mutually expressed, often in creative or innovative ways that some rivals may find quite attractive or intoxicating. Nonetheless, only a plurality of strong advocates appears to thrive on endless rounds of dispute, debate, argument, conflict, and fighting, mutually construed as a way of life in which the operative discursive boundaries are reasonably well understood and participants agree to play aggressively but in accordance with the implicit but understood rules.

Far more hazardous are those instances of intense verbal fighting that register at moderate levels of duration, salience, or frequency of occurrence. Here playful fighting dissolves into mutual exploration of vexing issues, taboo topics, hidden agendas, pressing concerns, and active opposition concerning personal priorities, strength of attachments, and depth of relational commitments. Troubling circumstances give way to troubling talk about troubling circumstances. However, unresolved, problematic, or badly polarized sources of resistance and opposition are not so easy to deliberate, much less repair or work through successfully.

Sometimes, episodic considerations are transformed regressively or retroactively into chronic sources of distress or misery, and sometimes, about half of the time, they revert to milder episodes of lingering displeasure and smoldering discontent. Only rarely is anything so real yet so intangible and liable to be settled once and for all. Most severe are those strong or intense fights driven by an acquired but deeply ingrained sense of mutual antagonism and unrelieved animus. The sheer preponderance of intense negative affect is often troubling and also disquieting. Supposedly purely impersonal but seemingly irreconcilable personal differences are susceptible to regressive transformation into a hidden stockpile of unresolved matters with great potential for bitterness, cynicism, contempt, and disgust in the emotional aftermath.

When conventional language is the means of unrelenting personal attack, otherwise sensible and civil participants discover potential for volatile exchanges to unfold without reason or without restraint. Only rarely does volatile language cross the line into life-threatening acts or episodes of physical abuse or brutality with malice of forethought and unbridled hate.

Hate

S/O talk, but now S hates O and avoids communication as much as possible.

S/O broke up because S couldn't stand anyone on Earth worse than his ex-girlfriend, and S can't believe he wasted six months of his life with this schizophrenic, dual-personality, chemically imbalanced, possessive, domineering bitch; S can honestly say he wishes she did not exist.

S/O try to talk, but S hates even to begin to talk with O about anything because of the fact that they disagree about everything.

S/O usually only interact in the morning and at night, so its very casual surface information, boring, with no meaning at all; S thinks that O is very funny and lively but that she makes a lot of negative comments: "I hate it when . . ." or "It bugs me that . . ."; it gets hard to hear over and over.

S/O try to talk, but it is hard to really talk because they don't take the same views on the outside world and their talks always end up in arguments or in having one person hating the other one.

S/O talk, but S thinks that O always sees herself as being right and can't be wrong, even if she is completely wrong; S hates it when O does ridiculous things, and he doesn't mind telling her at all—O hates the fact that S always disagrees with her so forcefully, but S always tells his other friends what S is thinking without holding back.

S/O talk in ways that make O thinks S likes him, but she doesn't really like him and she hates it when men think she likes them when she doesn't like them at all.

Signs of disgust and contempt figure heavily in the social production of violence, malice, and bitter hatred. Contempt, shame, and humiliation seem to go hand in hand. Impulse and unthinking revulsion promote the durability of disgust and revulsion over aberrant sensibilities. It is a sad truth that some chronically miserable people stay in hateful relationships for inexplicable reasons, regardless of the magnitude of hidden damage or the eventual costs. Reciprocated hatred can take a tremendous toll on body, mind, and spirit. Relational partners may become entrapped in a living hell of their own making. Intimate relations may be pressed to the limit, the outer extreme, without a sufficient reserve of moderating factors to act as a safety net. Unfortunately, oppositional intimacy may entail a stance of malignant vindictiveness, whereby severe strife is acquired, manufactured, and fabricated from relentless and steadfast insistence on pressing one rigid and frozen claim against another, tit for tat, one right after another, often without let up, break, or relief.

A vicious cycle may emerge from the persistent application of radical defensive measures that leave relational members alienated yet idealized at the same time. Human relations illuminate character traits that in turn are subject to sharp focus and specificity of demands, commands, injunctions, instructions, declarations, and imperatives. What hurts, from a relational perspective, is the sheer magnitude of discrepancy between idealized image and concrete reality. When each partner seeks frantically to fulfill idealized aspects of personal identity, rigid structural conditions are set up where the confirmational needs of each member are bound to fail. Rage, spite, vindictiveness are not all that difficult to dredge up where friend and lover transform themselves into foe and enemy.

Problematic Circumstances

Insult

S/O insult each other in every possible way.

S/O always insult each other, usually in a humorous or joking way.

S/O know each other very well, and they know how to insult each other very well.

S/O have conversations that escalate into personal attacks; power is the crucial issue, and they constantly try to outdo each other in an argument by insulting and demeaning the other (his or her personality or otherwise).

S/O try to talk, but S thinks that O is so sure that he has everything figured out and that anyone with a different opinion must be an idiot—so, anyone who talks to him and doesn't share his views unavoidably feels defensive and insulted.

S/O talk, and O will tell S little things that are incredibly obvious, which S finds insulting, so S will make some snappy little answer or reply.

S/O talk, but S thinks that O usually tries to insult S if he doesn't like her answer—and if he does like it, he just shuts up.

Fear

S/O talk, but conversations all end up on an unhappy note; regardless of the cause of faulty communication, S tries to avoid O out of fear of another unpleasant conversation.

S/O talk, but S can't express herself freely—she fears rejection and therefore doesn't express herself enough.

S/O clash in ways that make S think that O has tremendous fear of things that don't mesh well with his scheme of life.

S/O discuss touchy issues, and both tend to become irrational; instead of trying to understand each other's viewpoint, they degrade one another's views; part of these reactions stem from fear, and others from feelings of rage and mistrust.

S/O argue, and O defends her ideals and feels the need to attack S's thoughts; S tries not to react to O's arguments, fearing her wrath and seeing no point in a fight; O, on the other hand, seems to thrive on opposing S.

What is so striking is how a disagreeable person who discusses disagreeable subjects may unwittingly weaken strong ties and strengthen weak ties to other people. The stronger the scale, scope, or magnitude of personal disagreement, the more that fear and apprehension are likely to be about complex matter of closeness and intimacy. Profound disagreements have considerable potential for the participants to distance themselves both linguistically (from their respective opposing stands on controversial issues) and emotionally, aesthetically, and spiritually (from each other).

Unspoken, invisible, and intangible forces and factors may inhibit, restrict, or preclude close and sensitive thoughts and feelings from coming to the surface of mutual observation. From this perspective, the social production of personal fear registers in the urge, striving, or aspiration to move away, change focus, redirect energy, withdraw, escape, or explore alternative spectrums of possibility. Thematically, a spirit of trepidation, fear, and loathing culminates in a greater measure of denied access (e.g., modes of escapism, xenophobia, indifference, alienation, malaise, shyness, emptiness, or isolation), missed opportunities for future interaction (e.g., missing out, failing, and disconnection), and bitter retreat into vicarious or imaginary modes of conversation for actual human encounters (e.g., secrets, dreams, fantasies, lies, illusions, withdrawal into factious worlds).

Logophobic fear links to failure to live up to the generalized expectations of other people, a dreadful and disquieting sense of private malaise—feeling disconnected, tacit, unspoken distress and discomfort regarding what others may feel, think, say, act, or do and inexpressive or noncommunicative styles of face-to-face interaction that demonstrate a greater spirit of intolerance, resistance, antipathy, and devaluation of expressive and responsive signs of freedom and spontaneity. Therefore, a climate of fear pervades troubling or disturbing social settings in which one construes signs of danger and risk as central features of the effective environment. What adds insult to injury are strong signs of disrespect too significant and decisive to ignore as abstract markers of injury, hurt, and harm perpetrated on unwilling or unwelcome subjects. Hence, primordial fear and trepidation relate to the sheer strength of aversive conditions.

Extreme fear may become inexpressible for the very fear of its effect. The meaning of an anticipated or expected performance of a speech act can have tremendous power "when one conforms because of fear, and when this becomes a matter of habit, that authenticity is at stake" (Markova 1997, 274). Entrapment opens itself, as Blum (1996) shows, to a foreboding sense of inescapability and entrapment that is deeper than physical confinement, suggesting restriction upon one's freedom to leave. A study of social constructions of "ought," "ideal," and "feared" sources of self-definition revealed that self-discrepancies and disparities were predictors of agitation and dejection; overall, self-discrepancies and disparities from feared selves predicted anxiety and guilt preempting the role of discrepancies from ought selves, whereas ideal and feared self-discrepancies and disparities both predicted depression and despair (Carver, Lawrence, and Scheier 1999).

Sadness

S/O talk while O performs "funny" little things on people she may not even know and makes them feel humiliated and worthless; personally, S finds this to be obnoxious, mean, degrading, and sad.

S/O have face-to-face communication that is almost always a disaster; conversations are always brief and tense; S dislikes arguments with O, so S mentally thinks how sad it is that they have become so different and that they cannot tolerate each other's presence.

S/O do not see eye to eye; they do not feel comfortable sharing personal things, and it is all very sad and very odd to S.

S/O have a sad situation; they're not soul sisters but rather eternal adversaries.

S/O have mostly one-way conversations; it is sad that O is a nice person
and means well, but she does not understand that she talks too much.

The emotional consequences of jointly produced negative outcomes are
severely tested in the absence of a supportive network of affirmative outcomes. Failure is instructive, however, if only in hindsight or in adding to
foresight. Disappointments involving broken dreams, lost hope, lack of desire, or unfulfilled promise serve as a bitter reminder of all that has been
lost, misplaced, discarded, abandoned, or forsaken. Anticipated disappointments often entail "what if" or "if only" counterfactual projections of personal performance that miss the target or fall short of the mark. Expectancy
violations may be few and far between, or they may acquire a density, a
thick critical mass of momentum, as in a cloud of doom. Unspoken implications of further entrapment in future interaction manage to promise to
perpetuate trials and tribulations as daily routine, a constant burden, as in
falling into an aimless or lost way of life. Abandoned optimism occurs when
people reduce their own personal estimates to minimize the likelihood of
performing worse than expected and to avoid unwelcome exposure to long
string of heartaches.

Aversive outcomes promote a residue of guilt and shame among a few respondents, but most participants reveal little concern, regret, or remorse
about things that turn out badly for other people who are in their midst. The
concept of shame represents a moral feeling of disconnection between persons and the most social of all distressful emotions because it is a key negative affect that amplifies the experience of boundary crossing, trespass, violation, offense, and moral failure. A framework for the analysis of shame-laden
transactions advanced by Crozier (1998) emphasizes the act of taking an
"other" perspective on the self, the recognition that one's actions give rise to
another's interpretations, even if he or she does not believe it to be justified,
and that the core is attributed, deflected, transferred, and projected back to
the self in question. Preoccupation with how one's behavior is regarded by
others serves only to reinforce the steadfast belief that one has botched things
up, missed the mark, or badly fallen short in the eyes of those who are most
concerned and, therefore, the ones most deeply affected by one's worst shortcomings.

There is a major anomaly, one utterly counterintuitive, in the personal lexicons used by respondents in the Wisconsin study to reconstruct central
themes and underlying dynamics of very difficult human encounters. One
might expect conscientious and careful mention of certain types of adverse
or inequitable outcomes spelled out in strikingly negative and unflattering
terms. However, one-word computer string searches of critical vocabulary

reveal virtually no mention of words that make reference to any sense of guilt, shame, or remorse about the adverse, unwelcome, and disquieting effects of daily encounters in which everything that could possibly go wrong does go wrong, sometimes in spite of the best of intentions. Slowly, rapidly, or all at once, so much of the constructive "stuff" comes tumbling down, with nothing to replace it. Nonetheless, the frequency of the word *guilt* is quite low across the four main conditions: agreement (3), disagreement (8), understanding (0), and misunderstanding (2). This means that the word *guilt* occurs seventeen times while the word *shame* occurs just two times in almost sixteen hundred accounts. While it may not be surprising to find virtually no mention of guilt and shame in a/u sections, the paucity of mention in the d/m section is baffling and inexplicable.

We are surveying a rich and varied linguistic landscape described in a database of almost four hundred thousand words, and yet the entire set is practically devoid of explicit acknowledgment of any feelings of guilt, shame, or remorse. Empty categories (no mentions) tell a troubling story. Out of eight hundred reconstructed personal accounts in the d/m section, there are no references to states of anguish, gloom, woe, melancholy, dismay, disappointment, displeasure, remorse, or alienation. In addition, there are few mentions of states of despair (2), regret (2), isolation (2), and neglect (1). What is so telling is the larger pattern of what is excluded from self-reflective reconsideration, sometimes described in the manner of what is forgotten or misplaced, at other times in multiple perspectives on individual and collective levels of activity where someone or something is left out of the larger equation. Selective blank spots are conspicuous by their absence. What is so striking is the enormous anonymity of those subjects who subject themselves and other people to all manner of ill will and unprovoked discontent and then, after the fact, leave out a critical consideration: regret. The majority of respondents admit to no second thoughts, no regrets, and no guilt or shame worthy of the name. False innocence covers a multiplicity of small sins and slippery linguistic misdemeanors.

Respondents cannot be justly accused of adopting amoral personal vocabularies because of all the solid evidence of moral fiber and ethical grounding in the respective value orientations of participants whose explicit and generous expressions of respect, honesty, trust, patience, and value integration were the order of the day. Admittedly, there is probably no good reason to expect considerable mention of guilt, shame, and remorse to occur in constructive social climates where agreements and understandings underscore credit rather than discredit, and credibility rather than incredibility. Where there is no harm, there can be no foul. By the same reasoning, however, it is neither obvious nor easy to explain the obdurate fact that virtually all the persons who engaged in serious disagreement and mutual misunderstanding profess no sense of guilt or shame about anything.

It is so incredulous to discover such a massive and overwhelming sense of failure, blunder, poor performance, mistake, miscalculation, misfortune, and adverse reaction, to say nothing of needless misery, pain, and suffering and yet find that the interactants are still not able to muster the courage to own up to a sense of personal responsibility for all that has gone wrong, all that is lost, and all that cannot be reclaimed. Distressful emotions are mentioned to the point of profusion but without any really solid accompanying mention of sorrow, sadness, concern, or remorse, much less guilt and shame. Nor is it clear how such vicious abuse of others can be dished out with such relish and impunity but without any accompanying admission of failure for thoughts, words, or deeds gone wrong. There is a passive sense of shame but not much admission of guilt in mentions of refusal or hesitation to confront the offending parties for the purpose of clearing the air.

QUALITY OF INTERACTION

Alienation and estrangement emerge as radical or extreme methods of dealing with impossible people or implausible tasks, obligations, burdens, unresolved issues, and emotional baggage sustained from prior interactions with poor-quality or meager results. Personal rejection plays a central role in one of the most aversive of human experiences. Strong aversive sensory activation arises in response to romantic rejection, isolation, abandonment, expulsion, ostracism, disavowal, repudiation, and shunning. Excommunication is not excluded as an extreme measure or case of last resort.

Hurtful Disagreement

S/O say awful, abusive things that are easy to be hurt by.

S/O do not want to face the truth of how much O has hurt S.

S/O talk, while S thinks O seems to thrive on hurting others.

S/O avoid the topic of X because O's opinion hurts S very much.

S/O find that S gets hurt feelings when O doesn't call S on the phone.

S/O got along great at first, but although S still finds O's life interesting, O never felt likewise for S, who feels very hurt and defeated.

S/O often let off steam about what they don't like about each other, and these things end up hurting each other's feelings and make the apartment tense and unbearable.

S/O talk, but S finds herself getting annoyed at things O says—S replies with short answers, or she doesn't say a lot, and S can tell that O feels hurt by this treatment—S feels guilty, and she makes an extra effort to be nice to O for a while, but sooner or later it starts all over again.

S/O are two intimate people who find that their own personal feelings are very different—so different that both people want to convince or change the other person to see things differently, but this doesn't work and all that results is more trouble because ultimately someone gets hurt or one person must compromise or give up to avoid further disagreements.

S/O have disagreements where S thinks O seems not to have a feel for when enough is enough—O is self-righteous and will keep antagonizing just to make herself feel better—this leads to hurt feelings and some grudges held in the future by others.

Respondents struggle to define the meaning of hurt and harm in their daily encounters with other people. Even the best dictionary is not much help. To do harm is to inflict hurt or injury on unwilling or resistant subjects. Usually there is a nominal stipulation that the acts in question must be intentional and the injury physically or otherwise deliberately sustained. Unfortunately, it is not clear what types of hurt and harm qualify as other than physically imposed. Human beings, after all, are physical beings who inhabit a material world. Matter and manna go together. Hence, it is superfluous to suppose that pain and misery may somehow transcend the physical or material conditions of the human world.

Verbal aggression is enacted through words and gestures to convey an impending sense of risk, threat, or rejection of others who are deemed expendable, undeserving, disadvantaged, defective, or inferior. Studies of relational hurt and harm document the elusive, intangible, pervasive, and inexplicable features of destructive or damaging actions. For self-serving reasons, intimates often depict themselves as acting in a prudent, understandable, and justified manner but describe relational partners as acting in irrational or inappropriate terms. Justifications are grounded in one-sided pleas of having no real intent to harm, as well as stylistic emphasis on each partner's own needs but to the detriment of the other partner's feelings (Schutz 1999). What counts as being worthy of discredit and devaluation is idiosyncratic and sensitive to situational cues indicating disapproval, rejection, or exclusion (Leary et al. 1998).

Such hurt feelings are diffuse, complex, turbulent, and peculiarly aversive. Many who seem to thrive on the use of punitive tactics for strategic gain discover that they are vulnerable to the same type of damage that they would inflict on others (Vangelisti and Crumley 1998). The exact mix of toxic sentiments appears to depend on whether the provocation is construed as being justified when anger ensues or unjustified when hurt occurs (Fine and Olson 1997). There is a strong, tense, pervasive sense of injury, hurt, and harm that resonates as a central theme in the majority of the reconstructed disagreements. Nine times in ten, respondents presumed they are the exclusive objects rather than the main sources of much acrimony.

In general, people are far more sensitive to the offenses of other people toward themselves than to the offenses that they perpetrate on other people. Part of the explanation is that not all causes are subject to definition and not all reasons are rendered fully explicable. After all, toxic emotions may be acquired without anyone being able to say how, what, or why such intense and salient modes of disaffection and disaffiliation are taking place. Furthermore, some forms of hurt and harm escape observation, so some must suffer in silence. Other types of linguistic harms may be disguised, denied, or faked. Moreover, no abiding sense of having been subjected to hurt or harm need not be visible to the naked eye. Nor need such a presumed condition have a precise point or origin, or a specific site or location. The one who really hurts feels the hurt all over. No bodily contour, region, or extremity is immune. Some forms of bodily hurt, acquired or derived from direct human encounter, occur in all regions, all at once, and at the same time.

The impact of coercive words and harsh gestures is cumulative, totalizing, and pervasive. Hence, it is not reasonable nor necessary to ask the offended, injured, or abused individuals to locate the precise point or place where it hurts most. Relevant entries in the transcripts underscore a multiplicity of slights, injuries, violations of sensibility, and major transgressions (of veracity or integrity) that border on the uncontrollable or the intolerable: a stream of awful, abusive things stated in menacing terms; refusal to face up to disquieting truths or disclose terrible lies; disavowal of serious intent or plead mitigating circumstances; acknowledgment that sometimes it helps to be indifferent, callous, to the needless pain and suffering of others; careless talk, cheap talk, disquieting talk—above all else, letting off steam and making things tense and unbearable.

There is a poignant form of hurt and harm that provides for an enormous amount of needless pain and suffering (see table 7.3). In question are social conditions in which the participants cannot, will not, or do not know how to talk about what troubles them about either the climate of interaction or the unwanted side effects. It hurts not to be able to talk about the hurt and harm endured during damaging or disabling encounters. It creates another layer of hurt and harm, the unspeakable or unspoken qualities of what is endured in silence and conveyed only by the silence, the vast domain of the unspoken,

Table 7.3.   Hurt and Harm

	Agreement	Disagreement	Understanding	Misunderstanding
Hurt	18	37	20	43
Harm	0	5	0	3
Total	18	42	20	46

the inexplicable. It is painful, obviously, to feel compelled to resort to demeaning, divisive, divergent, defective, or discrediting devices and tactics when one is unable to resolve disparities and discrepancies in respective viewpoints, beliefs, and attitudes about daily obligations, tasks, opportunities, and achievements. The respondents who are most inclined to call into question the aspirations and strivings of other people are also most prone to resort to extrapunitive transfer of blame, refuse to submit to the authority of other people, and harbor certain vulnerabilities and susceptibilities to temporary lapses into short periods of disorganization and maladaptation when most under duress. There is, however, considerable latitude of involvement, tolerance, and willingness to indulge in acts of denial, disruption, defensiveness imposed on unwilling subjects who feel the collective brunt of someone's discontent, distress, and discord.

Intense verbal fights multiply the sheer magnitude of opportunity for exploitation, manipulation, coercion, and abuse in public settings in which words and gestures serve as weapons and a potent means of personal defense for which the risks are high and the stakes quite real. Harsh, savage, unrelenting criticism or severe moral condemnation carries much of the brunt of dirty fighting when words and gestures serve as blunt instruments to enforce or impose a sense of payback, retribution, vengeance, sabotage, intimidation, betrayal, abandonment, slow torture, or threat of annihilation. Some speak of enduring the bitter sting of physical abuse aggravated by an inescapable maze of incorrigible means of abuse. Physical punishment fueled by a torrent of crushing and castigating forms of personal criticism add the force of one's tongue to the force of one's clinched fist and gritted teeth. Mere infliction of physical pain, by definition, may be far too much to suffer, let alone absorb the added infliction of the aversive force of words and gestures utilized as tokens of threat, risk, and danger in dramatic attacks on the integrity, veracity, or well-being of other people. Militants are left to take false refuge in invectives and epithets, ranting, wailing, and railing from dawn to dusk or long into the night.

8

Understanding and Convergence

The world should have a universal language. That would make it easier to understand when talking to someone, even if you sort of understood that language. It might give our world more of a sense of unity. We would probably not have as many wars if we were doing things alike in different countries. Despite everyone on Earth needing to learn to speak a new language, it would really benefit future generations.

—Eric Lewandowski, seventh grader,
Hamilton Middle School, Middleton, Wisconsin

We are always trying to understand the meanings that actions and utterances have in the inhabited world, the world of everyday life, the world in which we go about living our lives. This is the ground that lies before us, the quest for the meaning of our actions as situated beings. . . . our efforts to present, to articulate, to pronounce, or say what we think we understand are inseparable from our efforts to understand. . . . Understanding and speaking meaning are intertwined.

—Thomas A. Schwandt, "On Understanding Understanding"

The human body is ultimately inexhaustible and unknowable, because it is open to endless transformation and reconstruction.

—Ian Burkitt, "Bodies of Knowledge"

At issue in the analysis of human understanding is the constructive possibility of minimizing a condition of significant misunderstanding and achieving a state of genuine understanding with other people. We assume a dual risk of misunderstanding and of being misunderstood, particularly in those complex, confusing, or perplexing public deliberations in which it seems that little or nothing can be done to make much sense of what transpires. In effect, the pursuit of human understanding is subject to the possibility and the risk of human misunderstanding. There is no way around this humble admission. No other type of empirically grounded conception is worthy of consideration or defense in a dynamic social context. Personal misinterpretations often stem from misdirected or misguided beliefs that lead all too easily to the strong conviction that the ideas we signify by our words and gestures are, coincidentally, the same as others, as signified by the use of those same words and gestures.

The concept of human understanding is elusive. The question of what it means to achieve a state of genuine understanding with other people is not easily settled. Not surprisingly, it turns out that there are as many viable ways to define the larger question as there are alternative ways to search for satisfactory answers. The subject has been a perennial source of contentious wrangling and intractable controversy in Western philosophy. Furthermore, the key construct is one of those old-fashioned notions that simply cannot stand alone, much less as that disembodied from real-life conditions and settled merely as a utopian vision or a dramatic abstraction. One can place any number of adjectives in front of the key term or attach any number of stipulations behind it in a single declarative sentence and still not be justly charged with talking gibberish. Likewise, salient attributes may be specified in terms of potential, possible, or actualized conditions of human understanding. Here potential captures a sense of capacity, facility, or power to be in a position to recognize, grasp, or comprehend what transpires with someone or something in particular but only in the nominal sense of being able to better distinguish or differentiate the mere appearance of one thing from another. The concept of "actual" signifies achieved satisfaction for a person who satisfies a minimal requirement of shared activity that is realized as a specific case in point. The construct of "possible" designates further opportunity for sense-making activity, whether certain ends are fulfilled or left unfulfilled.

As a tentative presumption, it is useful to think of the acquisition of human understanding as an unfinished working project. Mutual achievements are potentially infinite and inexhaustible rather than fixed or final, without sufficient opportunity for revision or reinterpretation. Salient conditions are also subject to endless reevaluation and cross-checking, bounded by tradition and social context, and fashioned from irregular or cyclical movements rather than acquired in a strictly linear process or a bold leap from ignorance to truth. Hence, a personal interpretation that "hits the mark" is still a matter of how much and what specific aspects of shared activity come under greater cognitive control.

A healthy dose of skepticism is an effective antidote to any sweeping urge to make excessive or extravagant claims about the dynamics of human understanding about one thing or another. A celebrated skeptic, John Locke, was the first modern philosopher to sketch a systematic conception of human thought and in so doing crafted possibly the most famous essay on the possibilities for human understanding ever published in the history of Western philosophy, *An Essay Concerning Human Understanding* (1659). John Locke's prodigious treatise sets a high standard of scholarly achievement in a cautionary tale that is very much with us after more than three centuries of trenchant criticism and prolific commentary.

LOCKE'S PUZZLE

Caution precedes skepticism. John Locke believed that all human knowledge is grounded in physical sensation and culminates in conceptual matters of intellect and reason as the two essential requirements for the attainment of truth defined on a dramatic human scale. His modesty is revealed in a conservative presumption that substantial achievements in human understanding must fall short of grasping or comprehending all that exists, but his optimism is reflected in the conviction that human knowledge is sufficient for ordinary daily purposes and therefore worthy of careful scrutiny. The finitude of human understanding must ultimately reach the outer boundary of whatever remains as unknowable, inaccessible, or incomprehensible in material terms (Brown 1999; Lowe 2000; Stanford 1998).

A hint of skepticism registers not so much in Locke's persistent affirmation of faith in the real, objective features of earthly existence but rather in his firm denial that human beings could ever understand with certainty the essence of substances in a material world. The essential properties of the material world somehow elude our collective grasp (Crane 2003; Walmsley 2000). His deepest conviction was that all thoughts and feelings derive from human experience, either from the direct imprint of sensation or from secondary reflections about ideas already acquired. The powers of reflection and contemplation reside in working memory and persist over the life span. Locke, however, bypassed systematic consideration of representational problems associated with the continuity of memory and the conceptual distinction between true and false memories that occur across the life span. After all, imperfect and defective memories may be presumed to give way to equally imperfect reconstructions of some prior, first-order process (firsthand).

Unfortunately, Locke's conception of memory as the foundation of all viable mental content is difficult to sustain in light of the notorious cognitive difficulties associated with memory losses; gaps; blank spots; lapses; and all that is forgotten, distorted, or convoluted in the course of everyday life. The problem of mistaken memory must be taken seriously. Imperfect memory registers as divided attention; distraction; disruption; forgetfulness; failure to notice; misdirected action; momentary emotional overload; losing track of time; and confusion over names, times, and places (Wallace, Kass, and Stanny 2002). Personal effort to reclaim past events operates on a temporal pattern of abstract predicates (verbs and adjectives) for remote memories that do not preserve much contextual detail and are distanced, displaced, and detached from current events (Semin and Smith 1999). Mistaken estimates of change contribute to pervasive beliefs in the inevitable decay, decline, and deterioration of the social fabric (Eibach, Libby, and Gilovich 2003).

False, fragmented, or dissociated memory, including delayed recall, lapsed recall, and recovery from trauma, is subject to the fragmenting force of inaccurate, distorted, or fabricated sensory data rather than the gradual acquisition of a steady stream of alert consciousness that is neither broken nor discontinuous in matters of space, time, or location. Moreover, make-believe memories can contaminate what a person recalls, and false memories can be suggested or introjected outright into the thought processes of speaking subjects (Loftus 2003). The problem of reconstructed knowledge must remain open to the possibility of using memory to convert an irrational belief into a rational one or the other way around (Huemer 1999). Old, faint memories can be imposed on current recollections or anticipated future social encounters just as present and impending changes reflect and reorder ruminations and trace acknowledgments of the faint imprint of the distant past. Finally, there is no way to know for certain that acquired distortions, disruptions, and delusions of identity do not occur.

The notion of the human mind as a container filled to the brim with a sweeping conception of a fixed set of ideas only makes things worse because it muddles, confuses, and obscures a critical distinction. A penetrating essay by Clark (1998) stresses the "generative power" of the Lockean metaphors of mind as receptacle and of senses as "inlets" to an "otherwise insurmountable enclosure; an internalized psychic space, inhabited by constellations of atomic particles; and a presiding consciousness in the alternative guises of eye, candle, and workman" (246). Analogues to enlightened human understanding resemble "a closet wholly shut from light, with only some little opening left, to let in external visible Resemblances, or Ideas of Things without" (Locke 1659, 2.11.17). Ideas labor from work in darkness behind shuttered windows. Visually, a veil covers the face just as mystery envelops each outward gaze. These graphic iconic metaphors bear some resemblance to biblical images of the act of seeing through a glass darkly and Plato's haunting image of moving human shadows on the walls of an ancient cave.

Misguided beliefs concerning applied social norms and routine conventions in daily language use arise from a faulty conviction that the ideas, words, and references of speaking subjects may be perfectly aligned or correspond in the manner of a precise replica. Uncritical faith in the presumption of exact correspondence between words and things shared among speaking subjects leads to false confidence in the ease with which people believe themselves to successfully communicate with one another. The dogma of double conformity in human meaning systems thrives on mistaken assumptions about language use.

Locke's skepticism concerning other people's misguided beliefs in the sufficiency or efficacy of language use eventually turns back on itself. In a critical passage, he outlines a demanding standard for attaining successful acts of sense-making practice:

> Unless a Man's words excite the same *Ideas* in the Hearer, which he makes them stand for in speaking, he does not speak intelligibly. But whatever be the consequence of any Man's using of Words differently, either from their general Meaning, or the particular Sense of the Person to whom he addresses them, this is certain, their signification, in his use of them, is limited to his *Ideas*, and they can be Signs of nothing else. (3.2.8)

Dogmatic insistence on strict correspondence in the exact alignment of ideas, words, and things between expressive speaker and responsive hearer invokes a perfectionist standard that could not, even in principle, be satisfied under daily circumstance with real-time pressures, frictions, and constraints. So Locke, then, faults others for their uncritical presumptions of successful communication, without offering equally critical examination of the very presumptions he has tacitly accepted for the sweeping, inclusive, and dramatic claim that it is quite a serious mistake to assume that other people ordinarily understand each other. Fallible activities would all fail miserably if measured by a single infallible standard of evaluation, assessment, judgment, or appraisal.

Credible refutation of Locke's thesis abounds. In a trenchant statement, Schutz (1967) dismisses as simply absurd the very postulate that one person can observe the experience of another person so precisely or accurately over time. For the notion in question presupposes that the observer would have to duplicate the other's experience down to the smallest detail while living through another's experiences in the same order and giving each detail exactly the same degree of attention, focus, and consideration. Moreover, two separate but aligned streams of unfolding consciousness would have to coincide, which is tantamount to claiming that one person should have to *be* the other person:

> We are asserting neither that your lived experience remain in principle inaccessible to me nor that they are meaningless to me. Rather, the point is that the

meaning I give to your experiences cannot be precisely the same as the meaning you give to them when you proceed to interpret them. (Schutz 1967, 99)

There is irony in this. Imagine the plight of the towering figure of John Locke. He pours over a cherished manuscript for several years—polishing, revising, refining, and agonizing—over the enormous sweep of a dramatic theoretical statement that seeks to demonstrate, with as much precision, rigor, and clarity as possible, how the imprecise, nonrigorous, and ambiguous misuse of conventional language in daily life stems from mistaken beliefs and misguided assumptions.

Locke does not acknowledge the fundamental contradictions that stand in the way. If ordinary language is so badly flawed, then the same inclusive and sweeping claim holds for any philosophical treatise designed so painstakingly to establish exactly, precisely, or accurately how badly flawed and imprecise language really is. Moreover, Locke is at the utter mercy of what he takes as a suspect language to show how words and gestures often fail us, without necessary or sufficient recognition of how they must also be failing him. After all, a convincing demonstration cannot in principle emerge from such an imprecise medium, one that is not sufficiently accurate and compelling to be convincing to others.

A badly flawed language system can only be expected to produce the steady reproduction of badly flawed statements about the precise meaning of the implicit presumptions themselves. If it is separate and autonomous entities who measure their own distinctive presence in a human world, then the prevailing standards of measure must accommodate the possibility of mismeasure as well. Alas, dense appeal to a standard measure with or without mismeasure must fall short of what is required—namely, provision for the fallible possibility that anyone who would measure all things must surely mismeasure some things along the way.

AUTHENTIC DISCLOSURE

It would be difficult to identify a single twentieth-century philosopher who conceives of the greater search for human truth in terms more alien, obscure, and distant from the aesthetic tone of Locke's puzzle than what characterizes the dense work of Martin Heidegger. At issue are working premises for the subject of what would constitute a defensible conception of authentic understanding among speaking subjects. On this matter, Heidegger was too intelligent and gifted to allow himself to become bogged down in a pernicious maze of categorical distinctions based on such false dualisms as mind/body, internal/external, and self/other. Each living being, constituted as a separate, distinctive, and autonomous subject, is situated as a unified singularity rather than a loose assemblage of poorly joined or disjointed collection of parts. His early project, *Being and Time* (1962), may be described as an attempt to develop a systematic conception of what it is to be alive in the world, in a spirited, engaged, and meaningful way. Since the focus of his "I-World" model is an inquisitive, singular subject, Heidegger deserves credit for escaping the facile temptation to declare the sovereignty of language or culture or some other hopelessly reified abstraction of totality.

Strict methodological adherence to a radical vision of the individual as the irreducible, singular unit of critical analysis serves only to preempt consideration of an equally compelling type of alternative possibility. It seems contradictory to posit first an abstract view of individual autonomy, with each entity awash with creative possibilities, and then strip the living subject of strong communal aspirations and determined resolve to achieve a deep and abiding sense of solidarity and cohesion with other living beings. Surely it is a mistake to posit a notion of human beings caught up in the tedium of everyday life but somehow not equally under the sway of everyone else's tedium. Consequently, his tutorial about what it means to be alive in a world "alongside" other living beings is seriously flawed on two broad fronts at once. First, there is no critical consideration of what it means to interact with other living creatures like ourselves. Second, there is little appreciation of what it actually takes for speaking subjects to construct high-order social achievements in concert with other persons who are equally preoccupied with their own issues of authenticity or optimizing potential. As a meager substitute, there is a stark but brave portrayal of individuals struggling in stupefying isolation to find their own unique way in a messy and murky world depicted in sober tones as being lonely, grim, depressing, and sad. There is neither solace or recourse to shift the burden of meaning from the weight of individuals bearing their own burdens all by themselves to a communal enterprise in which the participants make meaning together and alone.

The brute fact is life itself. The foundations of human understanding are determined by the possibility of being alive in a world that is shared with other living creatures. In the master equation, life is defined and given always in a specific way of being present when something happens. Human understanding, therefore, acquires definition and direction in historical and temporal terms. We find ourselves being thrown into a prefabricated world that is infested with bias, prejudice, and vested interests. Thus, the quest for personal and collective understanding may be opened up or closed down, revealed or concealed, and uncovered or covered up from public view.

The main idea is clear. The wider search for human understanding is confronted as a problem in existence *in* the world. A hermeneutic conception of the world does not refer to the earth or a purely secular realm but rather to the personal course of creative endeavors that acquire a cumulative value "alongside" the innovative enterprises of other people. If our common problems can be solved at all, they must be resolved in the expressive and responsive relations that we all share with other living things. Personal existence affords an unspecified margin of social opportunity to endow or confer the world with meaning. Speaking subjects engage in a primordial confession of what registers, what counts, and what is worthy of treasure to cherish above all else.

A person may be construed as a performer of intentional acts bound by a unity of meaning. We assume a distinctive point of view insofar as we become intentionally directed toward the presence or absence of someone or something in particular. As we become increasingly aware (reflective) of what we take into active account, the more completely transparent is our experience of being alive in the world. Conversely, the less we are aware (nonreflexive) of what transpires, the more opaque is our experience of being alive in the world. However, a state of interpretive transparency is an ideal never fully realized. Life is not static. Events constantly change in irreversible directions. This means that we can never go back to what we were or jump forward to what we will be. The tacit, implicit, unspoken features of experience do not always translate into explicit, manifest form. Interpretive activity can only be understood in terms of what actually transpires. To ask what constitutes an interpretation is to inquire into the definition of one's own existence. Interpretation, then, is that which enables something to reveal itself for what it is. Acts of interpretation are specific, concrete, and tangible because they entail choices and decisions as distinct possibilities grasped in this way but not in any other way.

Heidegger uses the metaphor of light and darkness in a dialectical sense that stands in sharp contrast to Locke's vision of a dark veil. When we interpret something, the point of reference is manifest as an unfolding process of taking something from a state of darkness or hiddenness and bringing it to light. Truth-seeking exercises represent movement from darkness into light, from hiddenness into disclosedness, and from tacit into explicit domains of disclosure. In short, human interpretation involves a process of discovering something that matters as a object of concern and care. Heidegger describes the hidden as that which is not yet or no longer given to expression in the absolute present tense. Personal concerns may remain covert in the sense that they reside in mindless exercises that promote more idle talk and meaningless chatter. Personal interpretations may create tension between those things we grasp in their original and intuitively self-evident sense and those we grasp in only an indirect and nonreflexive manner. Each subject, therefore, is a source of mystery, a mix or blend of acts of concealing or revealing gradations of truth and error. One may be struck with wonder and awe that things really are what they are. In any case, we remain as sources of mystery and myth to ourselves and to others as well.

An act of interpretation is in every case specific, particular, and concrete. It is not a matter of interpreting things in general terms but rather "my" distinctive interpretation of "your" own unique response and so on. In every case, the one who interprets something afresh is the same person who creates or produces objects of concern and care. Acts of neglecting, renouncing, or leaving undone are not actual ways of showing concern but rather are defective ways of expressing lack of concern (indifference). Heidegger insists that when we care about something, we do not merely stick a label on an object or throw a net around a point of reference, but rather we "indwell" or "inhabit" something of relevance and significance. When something is encountered directly, the thing in question already has an involvement that we disclose in our unique understanding of the world. Instead of affording an internal or private activation of sensory experience, the world of interpretation signifies the totality of one's creative investments. In this way, the source of interpretation maintains its own stable identity through changes in personal experience and various ways of behaving across diverse, divergent, or divisive societal circumstance.

By implication, personal interpretation binds the interpreter to what is interpreted. It would not be inappropriate to speak of the binding force of interpretation, whether it calls into question a person, object, or thing. For Heidegger, acts of understanding involve the power to grasp one's own possibilities for being alive in a unique, distinctive, original way. Surface interpretations are embedded in prior understandings that emerge along a wider and more diffuse horizon of conscious awareness. Individuals understand one another insofar as the temporal horizons of their interpretive acts work to fuse, intersect, or overlap. It is worth noting that such a dynamic conceptualization transcends the simple correspondence theory of truth because the horizon is not a rigid frame but something that moves with and invites one to advance further. In the existential tradition, emphasis is on relations rather than self-contained considerations; duration rather than instantaneous insight; what is possible rather than what is merely assumed; and partial, finite discovery rather complete or absolute claims (Bennett 1999).

The notoriously difficult problem of human authenticity cannot possibly be settled in a stance of aloof detachment or disinterested speculation. There is no way to withdraw or turn ourselves into spectators or neutral observers of our daily tasks, because we are already fully immersed in the particular activities that we aspire to grasp and comprehend. It is possible, however, to fall into a state of diminished appreciation, a weak substitute, for wondrous appreciation of life as the ultimate source of all creative possibilities.

In the face of their bonded relationships with people, places, and things, human beings are afforded an unspecified measure of freedom—through feeling, thinking, and praxis—to determine the authenticity of their mortality, that is, their own existence as autonomous entities. The question of authentic existence is not a matter of following some grand formula or adhering faithfully to a timeless prescription. Neither is it to be confronted as a standard or criterion of goodness, sincerity, virtue, or success. Instead, it is a contested struggle to fulfill one's distinctive possibilities of being alive in a world of infinite variation, ceaseless motion, and constant change.

It is possible, of course, to go through the motions, fake it, cover up, or just pretend. One may fall into a degraded, discredited, or devalued state in which daily encounters reduce to the lowest common denominator. Heidegger employs hierarchical metaphors to outline routine social conditions under which some things are apprehended in an average way but remain insensitive to gradations of genuineness that never seem to get to the heart of the matter. It is not difficult for anyone to be caught in fleeting and transitory impressions in which everything is obscured, covered up, or passed off as familiar to everyone who is present when something happens. Evasiveness is inscribed as taking the easy out or following the path of least resistance. One may fall into a degraded state of numbness, inertia, and atrophy.

On one point, Heidegger and Lock share an infinity of spirits. When people are content simply to mouth their words, talking for the sake of talking or just filling the time of day, it is quite tempting to presume that successful communication is taking place, without misgiving, hesitation, or second thought. So perhaps people do ordinarily understand one another rather ordinarily. Everything may look as if it were genuinely understood, yet at the bottom it is not. Strategic ambiguity is the main culprit because it obscures recognition of what is covered up—a double concealment. Shallow talk—tempting and tranquillizing—involves a downward plunge into endless discursive entrapments and subversive relational entanglements. The sham of authenticity produces a state of turbulence. Boredom, anxiety, and psychic numbness lead the way to a state of the groundlessness of inauthentic disclosure. What is required to reverse the downward spiral are the courage and strength to accept the burden and the risk of rising above chatter and distraction to seize upon the power of words and gestures in one's own unique way.

EMPATHIC IDENTIFICATION

The fallacy of the supremacy of abstract thought over concrete praxis dies hard. Orthodox conceptions of human understanding unduly privilege thought over feeling, contemplation over action, often in dense and rarefied abstractions that cling stubbornly to tacit presumptions that resist revision, challenge, or reconsideration. Neither Locke nor Heidegger was able to call his own sweeping intellectual achievements into question on the very intractable issues that would have the greatest constructive consequences in the long run. Both philosophers relied on abstract claims that unduly privilege the conceptual base of human understanding relative to the erotic and sensual domains. In rhetorical terms, personal logos is privileged over ethos, and pathos is eliminated from the equation.

There is, obviously, a good measure of sensitivity required to distinguish between the expressive acts of a sender and the conceptual reactions of a receiver. Empathic resolve is predicated on a tacit presumption of emotive generosity. The experiential worlds of other people may be construed as being accessible and ascertainable through mutual engagement in empathic identification. Empathetic sentiment is more easily aroused in the case of people, places, and things about which one cares deeply. Conversely, emotional generosity is absent from situations in which people care little or nothing about what transpires. Sympathy registers in greater cognitive appreciation for the alternative perspectives of others and in affectionate empathy for the emotive displays of other people. Empathetic agents, as Pizarro (2000) claims, are most readily able to show an abiding sense of care and concern for the welfare of others, particularly in adverse social settings in which people suffer.

Resourceful individuals acquire a rich and deep language—clear concepts and elaborate ideas—that they employ in an economical manner across a broad spectrum of social settings. Salient abilities cluster around affective, cognitive, and behavioral spheres of attentiveness and responsiveness, as well as enhance capacity for multiple perspective taking, particularly the accurate identification of another's mood, motivation, or state of emotional arousal. Varied shades of meaning are invoked to capture fluid and delicate subtleties: fusion, melding, resonance, permeability, empathy, hospitality, affective contagion, affective sensitivity, transposition of self into other and other into self, and expanded capacity for identification with the nonhuman realm as an essential part of what it is to be human. Greatest emphasis is on domestic themes of civility, decency, restraint, and common sense, putting oneself in another's place, listening actively, paraphrasing, diminishing self-focus, seeking validation, and participating in compensatory role reversals.

Although empathy provides no assurance of one's ever reaching a state of genuine understanding with any other person, repeated empathetic failures surely undermine the potential for such valued accomplishments to occur and persist. It may be relatively easy to infer another's thoughts and feelings about rather straightforward matters, but it becomes more difficult when relational partners must struggle with discrepant attitudes, negative reactions, prolonged unhappiness, or lingering dissatisfaction (Simpson, Ickes, and Blackstone 1995). Specifically, it is one thing to identify with someone else's concerns, but it is quite another to imagine how you would feel if only you were in the other's position. Empathetic emotion evokes altruistic motives, while an act of imagining oneself in someone else's circumstance also arouses greater egocentric motivation and vicarious distress. Furthermore, the act of "feeling the way another feels" does not ensure that one will also understand the other's feelings.

Oddly, instances of empathic failure provide dramatic evidence for the core value of empathy as a decisive component in relational matters of high-quality functioning, competence, and compatibility. On the positive side, empathy is a precursor to mutual understanding but not in any uniform or predictable formula. The magnitude of linkage is strongest in congenial social settings in which empathetic sensitivity qualifies as a resource and is weakest in stressful social situations in which task-oriented considerations are paramount. Respondent accounts document a host of communal pleasures gained from mutually empathic modes of constructive social praxis. A state of empathetic understanding presumably facilitates a greater measure of responsiveness and sensitivity in perspective-taking matters, as well as greater likelihood of accurate and precise identification of other people's motivations, aspirations, or states of emotional arousal and physical activation. Various shades of negotiated meaning exhibit a rich array of semantic hues, textures, and overtones. Empathetic relations are tolerant of brief or sporadic acts or episodes of disagreement and misunderstanding that we take into account and place into a clearer or more coherent perspective. Mutual expansiveness thrives under conditions in which mutual support, care, and concern become commonplace. Empathic identification in respondent accounts often elicits a greater measure of sympathy, tenderness, and compassion in return.

Likable Understanding

S/O like to cheer each other up and bring a smile when the other's having a bad day.

S/O like to tell each other everything that is going on in the course of their lives.

S/O let each other know if they like or dislike the way things are going between them.

S/O like to talk about absolutely anything—they are comfortable with each other; they are very much alike and they react to things similarly.

S/O like to watch television, drink, gamble, play video games, talk about work, and talk about dating women—they understand every statement, even about difficult topics.

S/O like the same types of things, and they can talk about almost anything—this ability to talk about anything (no matter what) promotes greater interpersonal understanding.

S/O like to explain things, and that helps both express themselves or re-explain something that one didn't mean and wants to take back.

S/O once liked one another's company, but they've grown apart, maybe because of the long distance, and they wish things were like they once were.

S/O seem to have mutual understanding that transcends verbal interaction—S thinks that O knows all of S's likes and dislikes—maybe as a result of the fact that they grew up in the same neighborhood in Singapore.

S/O express their real feelings without being indirect—they try to express themselves clearly, honestly—their understanding is based on honesty, trust; genuine, clear, and true expression of desires and feelings; positive encouragement; and true liking of each other.

S/O have a high level of understanding that can be explained by the length of time they've known each other—S thinks that O understands S as well as S understands O, and S/O try to make each other feel better.

S/O have an understanding of each other that goes beyond that of a typical relationship; they discuss worldly issues—O likes to make sure that S knows what is going on—both of them would be willing to do anything for the other, at any time; it goes without saying.

Agreeable respondents like to agree in far more varied, diverse, expansive, and inclusive ways than the varied ways in which understanding subjects like to understand each other. Since personal attraction to achieved states of basic working agreement and conditions of mutual understanding are strongly correlated, optimum conditions are shown to occur when speaking subjects like to agree about lots of things and like to understand lots of things about each other. A central theme is that agreement plus understanding equals a condition of mutual realization. The major achievement may be acquired at low, moderate, or elaborated levels of shared endeavor. Thematically, similarities prevail over differences; likes prevail over dislikes; convergent movements prevail over divergent movements; and progressive actions overcome acts of misdefinition and misdirection.

Partially reciprocated displays of mutual attraction toward source and subject increase the likelihood of acquiring strong social bonds aligned with a provisional and tentative sense of common ground. Mutual empathy is not, thereby, necessarily ensured, but favorable conditions are certainly rendered more accessible in the mutual pursuit of desired outcomes. Enhanced perspective taking facilitates accuracy motivation and accuracy identification of salient personal boundaries. Personal horizons fuse, intersect, and penetrate prior boundary conditions, neutralize constraints, and renew a greater sense of openness to alternative perspectives.

Strong empathy is a critical personal resource and a protective buffer against temporary lapses into conditions of empathic failure and egocentric preoccupation. Finally, there is little mention of friction, strife, and strain in personal accounts of reciprocated acts of empathy, concern, and care. Strongly empathetic participants become deeply involved in the events of daily life and thereby offer renewed opportunity for one to put things into perspective; discuss almost anything in a fresh, spontaneous way; support expressive initiatives and responsive tendencies; maintain quality relations; and appreciate prospects for renewed acquaintance. Variations in themes of fidelity, accountability, and loyalty are cited in the transcript as the main fringe benefits.

Loving Understanding

S/O have had tough times together, and sometimes they have fought like cats and dogs, but when all is said and done, S/O have the ability to share things and understand each other so well; they see wonderful things in each other because S/O share a deep sense of unconditional love; they are able to say even negative or potentially hurtful things and still find some sense of mutual understanding—no matter what is said, they can find a way to relate to one another's perspective; knowing that they understand each other so well is what makes a big difference in their lives.

S/O find oftentimes that it seems as though a word, a sentence fragment, even a touch expresses what it might take hours to explain to any other— the deep love they have for each other means they strive to maintain harmony; both assume the other has the best of intentions and is given all the chance in the world to clarify, before jumping to conclusions—the outcome is a feeling of warmth and harmony.

S/O understand each other very well; they often share the same moods: joy, happiness, humor; sad, angry, calm; somehow they seem to know how to act when one acts one way and the other acts much differently; as a result of mutual effort and naturally clicking, S/O coexist very well; what it takes most is genuine caring and friendly love for the other.

What is so remarkable about the language of love is the bewildering number of sites where it can be found once again—as rediscovered, reclaimed, and reconstructed in a spirit of wonder and awe. The force of energy, heat, and light extends, resonates, and transforms in the manner of an aura.

Caring Understanding

S/O care deeply for each other; they are considerate of each other's feelings and adjust quickly to accommodate each other's needs; they feel comfortable and they don't feel the need to put up a front; they are able to express a wide range of emotions and constantly know what to expect of each other, and count on each other in times of need.

S/O engage in a great deal of give-and-take; they can speak freely without becoming defensive because it is a given that they really trust each other's judgment; they are so comfortable that they can say virtually anything; because they respect each other's advice, they don't take criticism personally or negatively; there is a great amount of care and thinking that goes on within each party; no one attacks the other, and they take into account how what they say will affect the other.

S/O know that each other's actions and words will always go together; they discuss their feelings openly and without ridicule; they talk about personal issues and receive support and encouragement; they treat each other with respect and dignity at all times; they are flexible and caring about each other's wishes; they express their real feelings without being indirect or pretend; they are honest and try to express themselves clearly.

S/O are different people, but the magnitude of difference actually brings them together; they rarely get into fights, because they know each other so well—not to mention that S has known O since birth, so S has seen O through it all and knows O inside out, which makes it all the more easy to understand; they express their true selves and hold nothing back; whether they agree or disagree about something, they understand each other's moods and when to leave things alone; they listen deeply and treasure advice; when they go out and things get messed up or go wrong, it is not a big deal because they both know that they really care about one another—their friendship will endure because through good and bad times they manage to understand how each one thinks and feels.

S/O get along great, think alike, and enjoy similar things; they connect on the same level; they often talk on the phone and sometimes visit each other, but no matter how much time has passed, they always catch up quickly; they enjoy each other's company very much; they understand exactly what the other is saying; they care greatly for each other and remain very close; they are the best friends in the world; they rarely get into arguments; they have a deep understanding of each other—they do not know what they would ever do without each other.

S/O come to a mutual understanding by compromising; there is mutual give-and-take; they talk, listen, and do not interrupt until the other is finished—strong understanding helps them think and learn from the other; their understanding also helps them settle differences in a respectable manner; they know how to comfort each other when there is something wrong; they know what and how the other feels, and they can reflect on one another's feelings; they care about how the other feels, and they don't say

anything that will make the other upset; interactions involve a lot of love
and understanding; they talk mainly about things in their daily lives; they
do almost everything together.

Love is elusive. Some love others for themselves, whereas others offer love
to remedy their own deficiencies. Intimacy, passion, and commitment inter-
mingle. Personal variations promote the welfare of the loved one, high regard, dependence in time of need, mutual understanding, emotional support, intimate conversation, and optimal value of the loved one in one's own
life. Signs of intimacy engender tender feelings of closeness, warmth, connectedness, and close bonds. Passion promotes personal drives and common strivings for romance, physical attraction, sexual consummation, and intense longing for secure attachments.

Personal commitment entails short-term decisions but also long-term consequences of resolve to maintain a spirit of love, tenderness, and concern.
Different combinations of loving features and caring attributes generate wide
variation in love styles. Personal accounts of affectionate understanding underscore the critical priority assigned to truly interdependent expressions of
love, care, and intimacy. Benefits of loving commitments arise in a creative
manner with all the necessary support, approval, and stimulation required
by the loved one to reach maximum fulfillment.

Sexual preference and gender orientation are powerful indicators of one's
social status. For both sexes, partner support and comparative strain are
closely linked to broad measures of personal well-being, though a reserve of
supportive buffers against detrimental short-term strains may work somewhat better for women than for men (Reevy and Maslach 2001; Walen and
Lachman 2000). Closely related is tentative evidence that, on average,
women may be somewhat more likely than men to value supportive skills
and use person-specific language when seeking to comfort a distressed partner (Samter 2002). The magnitude of reported sexual differences is often
small, possibly due in part to societal stereotypes that mask a deeper consensus concerning what counts as a supportive message or condition, the
importance of comfort, and gender preferences in support-seeking behavior
(Burleson and Gilstrap 2002). Strength of commitment among heterosexual
and homosexual couples is moderately related to relational satisfaction; the
range of alternatives in sexual relations; investments in personal resources;
and sufficient time, energy, and depth of involvement (Sacher and Fine
1996). As relational commitments increase slowly in salience, relevance, or
inclusiveness, unilateral and mutual attributions of blame and accusation diminish in turn (Mills and Malley-Morrison 1998).

Mutual expressions of love, care, and concern matter greatly as strong, intense, robust emotions and as strong, intense, and robust types of bonding
mechanisms. Loving understandings are construed as high-level achieve-

ments rather than simply as desirable or favorable end states. It takes a great deal of hard work and dedication at an individual level, and equally demanding effort at a collective level, to acquire and establish a strong sense of mutuality, accountability, and responsibility. There is in intimate relationships a strong sense of partly reciprocated senses of warmth, immediacy, and tender virtues of compassion and dedication.

The litany of minor themes resemble a diverse repertoire of linguistic resources that foster and promote expressions of affection and also generate favorable conditions for mutual exploration of elaborated expressions of fidelity, cohesion, and solidarity. Finally, fluid interactions seem to encourage a greater measure of expressive freedom; alternative perspective taking; skillful coping strategies; effective problem-solving efforts; and more refined levels of metacognitive accuracy in identifying the prevailing states of mood, affect, attitude, and belief among speaking subjects.

Enjoyable Understanding

S/O enjoy their daily interactions because each one is designed to promote the greatest level of interpersonal understanding possible.

S/O enjoy talking a lot—even for a telephone conversation, they'll go on forever.

S/O enjoy each other's company; there is a lot of physical contact, touching, comfort.

S/O are there if possible to console and make the other feel better—a lot of time is spent just talking or enjoying each other's company; O is someone whom S has a great deal of respect for and trust in, and its comforting to know that O wouldn't betray S or cause S to lose that trust and respect that S has for O.

S/O do not always agree, but if they do disagree, they understand why thoughts and feelings differ, and they respect personal differences— O may know exactly how S responds or feels in certain situations without S explaining it to O.

S/O talk about their futures, plans in life, lack of plans, current relationships, past relationships, and families and their effects on S/O; sometimes they talk about nothing and instead just spend time with one another, walking O's dog in the woods or watching television—S/O seem to enjoy these times as much as those spent in deep conversation.

S/O can enjoy almost any social activity together, and both can believe what the other person says is true—that kind of confidence and support goes a long way in this world, and knowing they understand each other makes a big difference in their lives.

S/O lead common lifestyles, enjoy the same things, and they can look at each other and understand each thing that is said and done.

Enjoyable understandings are great intensifiers of mutual affiliation and positive-sum power relations. Notice how enjoyable references encompass keen appreciation and enhanced regard for high-quality interaction, mutual investment in acts of derived pleasure for each other's company, and value of time spent together. Also salient are key markers of interest and excitement: talking a lot; talking about anything or everything; talking in depth and in detail; talking passionately; and all the while showing restraint over personal differences, interpersonal difficulties, and unfavorable social circumstances.

SYNCHRONY AND ALIGNMENT

One good measure of personal competence and interpersonal compatibility is the degree of synchrony and alignment in the integrative styles of varied personal conduct. Those who stay in synch and remain closely aligned are in a most favorable position to integrate and unify the particulars of what they say and do into a larger coherent narrative. There is some measure of consistency in how finely tuned relationships evolve over time. Respondents are flexible and tolerant of risk and change.

A spirit of accommodation and compromise enables each participant to make the best of the current situation and not let petty miscues, mistakes, or miscalculations stand in the way. Respondents speak of working hard to talk things through and of concentrated effort to make sure everyone understands what transpires at each step along the way. There is ample opportunity to revisit what remains unclear, as well as skill in knowing how much to explain and when to leave well enough alone. Notice multiple references to confidence in not having to spell out everything in detail and the willingness to go back over troubling issues as much as necessary. Some give credit to the unique modes of language they employ. Others stress matters of affection—empathy, positive regard, social support, or reciprocated matters of trust and respect. Still others appeal to the sheer strength or salience of the bond, as with soul mates or a spirit of unrequited love. Also relevant are frequent references to an underlying sense of safety and security in relational terms. It is not simply a matter of being unafraid to speak out but also a willingness to reveal almost anything about oneself. Equally important is the broad tendency for distinctive styles of daily interaction to become increasingly similar over time.

Equitable opportunity to participate in the give-and-take and back-and-forth movements of conversation is a fundamental precondition for the reproduction of constructive human encounters. Skillful turn-taking organization facilitates routine achievement and constitutes an enabling mechanism for spoken interchange (Schegloff 2000). Moreover, speaking turns are valued discursive resources as well as potential liabilities for matters of influence, persuasion, and personal control of current social outcomes. Coordination of turn taking requires considerable fine-tune adjustment and accommodation to acts of intrusive cross-talk, disengaged and lapsed talking, as well as reengaged actions at speaking transitions (Szymanski 1999). Cross-talk often leads to a degree of asymmetrical turn taking when engaged participants do not share the same stylistic markers or they are at odds over privileged constructions of context and interpretive priorities that result in misinterpretation, accidental miscommunication, or failure of communication.

Asymmetry is a common feature in turn-taking modes of conversation. Disruptions undermine coherence in the form of emotional upheaval, charged outbursts, and surplus of negative affect. Much depends on perceived asymmetry in positive or negative slant or uneven distribution of scarce power resources. On balance, inequities in matters of power, affection, and involvement are all manifestations with periodic and chronic measures of asymmetry in the alignment of current social classifications and cultural categorizations (Mummendey et al. 2000; Georgesen and Harris 2000). Such results hold for two asymmetrical sources of dependency: task dependency (short term, goal oriented) and evaluation dependency (assessment of one's performance) for jointly produced social outcomes (Stevens and Fiske 2000).

ACCURACY MOTIVATION

Understanding other people requires considerable sensitivity to matters of accuracy and veracity as construed through performance-based standards of cognitive appraisal, value orientation, and identity formation. The accuracy standard has been idealized whenever truth is pursued as a cultural ideal. We are enjoined to enhance the truth that will set us free. Fortunately, treasured truth is not simply motivated nor easily determined. Brown and Dutton (1995a, 1995b) provide a preliminary note of caution: people do not vigorously seek accurate self-knowledge; people do not typically possess accurate self-knowledge; and people are better served by activating views of themselves that are slightly more positive than realistic. Nonetheless, accurate self-knowledge is necessary. People strive to hold reasonably accurate views of themselves, as construed through direct contact with the expressive aspirations and interpretive responses of other people, whether encountered in face-to-face or mediated settings. Moreover, personal relationships require a heightened understanding of each member's view of relevant traits, prevailing moods, and broad-based consensus sufficient to preserve a spirit of harmony and cohesion (Gill and Swann 2004).

Accuracy-motivated persons rely on systematic and elaborated decisions, engage in extensive critique and revised interpretation, consider alternative ways to enhance goal achievement, and preserve strong desires for cognitive confidence or comprehensive understanding. Personal confidence in private deliberation and careful decision making is an important determinant of persuasion and self-validation (Petty, Brinol, and Tormala 2002). Moreover, accuracy motivation decreases one's susceptibility to extraneous information and one's stereotyping of other people while increasing one's scrutiny of relevant information and one's deliberate cognitive resource allocation. In relational matters, engaged individuals' measures of interpersonal sensitivity are related to accurate judgments of friends' measures of interpersonal sensitivity (Carney and Harrigan 2003). Likewise, there are complex, delicate, and subtle distinctions between the expressive sensitivity of a sender and the receptive sensitivity of any given receiver (Snodgrass, Hecht, and Ploutz-Snyder 1998).

Accuracy motivation is complicated by difficult confidence considerations. It is well known that most people are inclined to be far more influenced, altered, or persuaded by an eyewitness who is certain about what has just transpired (Memon, Hope, and Bull 2003). In studies of eyewitness accounts, confidence–accuracy calibration entails confidence in some estimated probability of being correct as weighted against the objective probability of being correct (i.e., in identification response). In general, confidence–accuracy calibration is poorer when decisions are difficult or when problems are demanding. Conversely, confidence and accuracy are better when eyewitness accounts involve a large number of observations, permit gradual movement from basic tasks to complex tasks, and stress positive rather than negative outcomes (i.e., recognize rather than reject) (Weber and Brewer 2004).

Accuracy motivation reinforces the presumption that the human world is predictable, coherent, and controllable. Knowledgeable people acquire more stable attitudes and critical core beliefs that are resilient yet resistant to change. Interpersonal verification may hinge on implicit preferences for affiliation-laden cues (liking, attraction, or positive feedback) or for more competence-laden cues (accuracy, precision, or inclusive goodness-of-fit between one source and another) (Bosson and Swann 1999). Personal attributions may be assigned to causality or reasons for discrepancies and disparities in interpretation and performance—that is, standards of correctness, reference values, ideals ("shoulds"), faith, hope (for better times ahead), or relief (from things getting any worse, falling apart, or deteriorating further) (Duval and Lalwani 1999).

Broadly based, explicitly defined, and rapidly activated social skills and ingrained personal abilities reportedly enhance speed of performance and accuracy in the completion of joint tasks, solutions, and end states (Roberts and Stankov 1999). Intrinsic motivation comports with an emphasis on helping others and generating feedback that signifies competence. Moreover, intrinsic goals depend on the tentative, immediate, and contingent reactions of other people. In effect, extrinsic goals are typically activated as a strategic means to some further end. Conversely, intrinsic aspirations relating matters of self-acceptance, affiliation, communal feelings, and physical health are predictive of higher levels of well-being, broadly conceived, and less frequent physical symptoms (Kasser and Ryan 1993). Intrinsic motivation is multifaceted. It entails selective engagement in social activity for no apparent cause, rhyme, or reason other than what a person seeks to fulfill. The number of practical reasons for all practical purposes is unlimited. A personal calculus of reward and cost is reality tested as events that strengthen resolve and events that weaken further effort to some end (Reiss 2004). Reciprocal elements of cooperation and competition may lead to higher levels of intrinsic motivation (Tauer and Harackiewicz 2004). When satisfied, enduring personal strivings for competence, autonomy, and relatedness yield to enhanced self-motivation and well-being; when thwarted, they promote diminished motivation and well-being (Ryan and Deci 2000). In general terms, intrinsic pursuits are congruent with growth and actualizing efforts that are likely to satisfy basic psychological needs.

Social agents who promote pragmatic accuracy appear to facilitate the achievement of relationship-specific interaction goals (Gill and Swann 2004). Recall of prior encounters, in support of social control or needs for autonomy as desired end states, blend with current interpretations of others' motivations in the formation of expectations concerning how enjoyable and interesting a social activity is likely to be. Cognitive appraisals of others' extrinsic motivations lead to expectations of diminished enjoyment and less positive affect, whereas subsequent disconformation of others' extrinsic motivation reverses the slant of expectation in favor of more psychological relatedness and positive affect. A state of progressive understanding enables engaged partners to predict forthcoming reactions accurately, adapt to unexpected responses, and thereby increase the likelihood of achieving successful outcomes. However, overestimates of accurate relational predictions fit closely with evidence of overconfidence, which can be based more on the richness of accessible cues of intimacy impressions than on accuracy and can thus produce an illusionary feeling of knowing one's partner (Swann and Gill 1997).

One way to assign credit and discredit for jointly produced life events is to subject selected and strategic aspects of individual performance to the collective standard of others' judgments. Our ability to judge others, as well as to be judged by others in return, may depend on how much direct or mediated contact we have with them; individual differences in interpersonal accuracy might be a consequence of the fact that some people are objectively less predictable or controllable, not only by themselves, but also by other people. Accuracy measures may confound the distinction between the capacity to understand or be understood and the right to understand or be understood on some global scale where vested interests and hidden agendas threaten to obscure or blur the larger distinction between those who are capable or incapable of speaking truthfully about the full measure of their participation in the linguistic construction of consensual reality in daily life.

Happy Understanding

S/O find that just hearing each other's voice makes the other one happy.

S/O share the same moods often: joy, happiness, humor, sadness, anger, and calm.

S/O can tell, just by facial expression, whether the other's scared, lonely, or happy.

S/O can sense when each other is happy, sad, depressed, or hiding a true feeling.

S/O feel happy and content—their responses to each other are so encouraging—they talk about their opinions and hear one another out.

S/O understand each other better than anyone else that they know. They have known each other since birth, grew up together, and always stood behind each other when either one had a conflict with anyone else. If something bothers one, it will bother the other too—they know each other's tendencies very well; they always have fun together and know when it's time to be serious, sad, or happy or to cheer up each other.

Exciting Understanding

S/O are excited for one another—S thinks that O understands everything; they sometimes get so excited that they break into the middle of one another's sentences.

S/O share a room and spend a lot of time just talking—they wait their turn to talk but usually don't interrupt or change the subject at inappropriate times—without S telling O, O can read when S's upset, mad, excited, and so forth, and S usually can read O too—they still talk to their other friends a lot, but they understand S/O like S/O understand each other.

S/O enjoy each other's company—they have a common understanding of each other, but they never know what to expect next—they get along better because of this—it makes their relationship seem more exciting.

S/O find it so exciting—they look at each other in amazement about what has happened in the short time they've known each other—when they talk, they don't have to say much—when S feels safe with someone and can trust that person to help, then S knows there is a strong interpersonal understanding at work in the relationship.

S/O find it is exciting to have someone listen to what the other is saying and to be interested and able to respond intelligently—S finds herself listening enthusiastically to O.

S/O can tell from the excitement they saw in one another's face that both of them would bring up subjects that were intensely interesting.

Cheerful Understanding

S/O can both cheer each other up when feeling down.

S/O are always there for each other—their wonderful hugs say a million words without saying a single word—S thinks O can sense when things aren't the best, and O can cheer S up easily—just hearing O's loving voice calms S down, and S knows that O needs S too.

S/O are friends—O always seems to know when something is bothering S, and O is always there for S to talk to, which is great—O understands S's feelings, and S knows exactly what to say to cheer S up, and O feels the same way about S—they obviously have a special friendship.

Cheerfulness is an antidote to sadness. Gracious respondents express admiration and praise toward those relational partners who are able and willing to cheer up others from low spirits or depressing periods. Such individuals seem to know what to say and do to cheer up a disgruntled but much valued person. Numerous references are made to special friendships in which the participants can each evaluate a nonideal situation, stand by one another, and act accordingly. Some profess being able and willing to make relational partners cheerful—no matter what may come or go. Sharing fun, laughter, and gaiety makes things easier. The central theme is that the worst is over and tomorrow will be a better day. There is much happiness with each opportunity to be together. Some respondents claim to harbor the exact same views about how to live a happy, healthy, and good life together. Happiness also resonates in partners' reactions to one another's choices, priorities, and preferences. Understanding what makes a significant other feel real good is an added source of joy and bliss. A friendly and happy atmosphere can make all the difference in the world. Furthermore, there is little or no evidence of feigned happiness, with some parties deciding to "fake it" and act disingenuously when they are not glad about what transpires. Perceptive observers can tell whether a highly valued person is scared, lonely, happy, or glad. Others can sense when either partner is happy, sad, or depressed so that there is no reason to hide true feelings or settle to just pretend.

At a reflective level, interdependent parties take delight in the heuristic application of specific personalized knowledge of what makes each member happy or sad. Genuine human understanding is instantiated in applied forms of social knowledge that reflect evocative and emotive tributes to the core. There is ample provision for the social construction of mutually sustained states of joy and happiness when things go well and genuine sadness when they go badly. In this sense, a happy state or set of conditions is not conceived so much in terms of a peak experience or a purely enhanced, singular emotion but rather a rich blend of strategic and somewhat automated sensitivities to favorable circumstances and, accordingly, to the mix of persons, topics, or situations that make other people happy, sad, or irritated and how to deal with a plurality of other people during complicated, rapidly blended, and exciting mutual recognition of optimum fulfillment.

MEMBER SATISFACTION

Member satisfaction registers in reciprocated explanations for the acquisition of high levels of stability, consistency, and continuity in relational history. Evidence reflects the catalytic meshing of personal styles, background life experiences, personality traits, and environmental conditions that arise during early stages of relational history (Johnson, Bush, and Mitchell 1998). Evolution into a synchronized and closely aligned set of collaborative habits, routines, and stylistic manners of deference and demeanor appear to promote long-term consistency and continuity in relational definition and direction, provided, of course, that major structural or systemic shifts, alternations, or disruptive changes do not occur.

It turns out that democratic and egalitarian relations are much easier to envision or idealize than they are to acquire, regulate, or sustain in the uncertain course of daily life. Contemporary marriages are notoriously unequal and continue to be the norm in American society, even among those who endorse the principle of marital equality as a cherished ideal. Equity theorists assume that individuals strive to maximize relational outcomes, accept mechanisms for equitable distribution of rewards and sanctions, reward others for egalitarian responses, threaten others for inequitable consideration, and endure stress in direct relation to the other's responses to shifts into unwelcome inequitable alignments (Larson, Hammond, and Harper 1998).

Strong bonds facilitate attachment, security, cooperation, compliance, and high-order achievements, whereas weak bonds foster uncooperative, divisive, and problematic behavior. Close ties encourage relational convergence toward more similar coping styles and incremental gains in member satisfaction. Moreover, equitable relations involve acts of sharing and caring that intersect and overlap in ways designed to limit unbridled selfishness and indiscriminate altruism (Wagstaff 1998). Closely related is solid evidence that marital satisfaction is positively related to reliance on constructive problem-solving strategies, mainly negotiation and compromise, and negatively related to the use of negative problem-solving methods, mostly coercion, withdrawal, and avoidance (Bowman 1990). Couples who are less accurate in anticipating each other's responses diverge in their respective conceptions of intimacy (Heller and Wood 1998). Generally speaking, open and explicit problem-solving tactics are associated with individual satisfaction with jointly produced outcome. In effect, personal satisfaction is a mutual achievement, a reward for the ability to sustain a high level of interdependence with others (Bradbury, Fincham, and Beach 2000).

9

Misunderstanding and Divergence

Every understanding; every interpretation involves misinterpretation. Understanding and interpretation are not coterminous, but they are intrinsically interrelated.

—Agnes Heller, *Can Modernity Survive?*

Communication is always a risky task . . . the borderline between communicative and non-communicative intentionality in speakers is a territory full of mystery and self-deception.

—Herman Parret, *Pretending to Communicate*

Thrust into an existence incomprehensible, unjustified, and possibly absurd, we grasp at fleeting sensory tendrils, like hot puffs of steam in the night, attempting to catch and retain some clues as to our own essence— an essence that ultimately eludes us.

—Peter Jamison, "Human and Ultimate Consciousness"

Perhaps understanding is never anything more than the illusion of understanding.

—Laurence De Looze, "To Understand
Perfectly Is to Misunderstand Completely"

The use of ordinary language cannot be isolated from the adverse effects of any misuse or abuse of common idioms along the way. In situations in which there is tension between effective use and ineffective misuse of applied social knowledge, one may recognize ineffectual use of ordinary language from signs of inadequacy, or from the inability of the source of a given signifier (expressive act) to capture the multiplicity of the signified object (observed act), and metaphoricity, the semantic surplus of the signifier over its referent (Tang 1999). Here the construct of discursive inadequacy entails partial failure of expressed initiatives (signifiers) to capture the multiplicity of references associated with the signified object, whereas the construct of metaphoricity involves the magnitude of semantic surplus of the signifier over its signified sphere of reference. The implication is this: in shared acts of sensory activation, we see more than we can say about what we see; we hear more than what we can say about what we hear; and we can say fewer things about what we feel than what we actually feel. Hence, we are not at the mercy of our common idiom so much as we are at an unspecified margin of opportunity for engaged or detached forms of social praxis to leave us better or worse off.

Personal awareness of defective and deficient use of common words and gestures need not be a reason for giving up hope in the efficacy of writing and speaking as a basic resource of literate human understanding. Mundane subject matter may be presumed or severely contested in collective struggle as the implicit basis for unspoken thoughts and feelings and for individual and collective consciousness in general. Narrative disclosures and discursive concealments surface in miscalculations that register along the general lines of "I saw A—I approached A but to my surprise it wasn't A at all. I must, therefore, be mistaken" (Kenaan 1999, 3).

In human affairs, no one is infallible. Hence, the margin of difference between success and failure is, by definition, a matter of a "more or less" rather than an "all or nothing" sphere of social outcome. In the moment-by-moment sequences of imprecise translation and slippage in interpretation, Grace (1987) shows why it becomes virtually impossible to discuss detailed subject matter with anyone who has not been aware of the existence of a particular subject (qua subject). Since the rules of conventional language use are not identical from one speaker to another, each language has a unique potential for reality construction, as each subtends a different set of potential realities.

Skilled speakers are the best prepared to engage in acts of mutual influence when the ground rules of situated knowledge are clearly specified or well known in advance. Routine interactions take place insofar as the parties in question are able to rely on a stable tradition of prior interaction for tacit guidance and implicit direction in deciding what to do in the present or in the future. However, when dealing with unusual, unexpected, or uncertain types of social circumstance, there may be a greater measure of difficulty in coping with embedded issues of complexity and complication concerning intended choices and unintended consequences. Specific substantive problems may accumulate, one after another, without an equal number of viable solutions in sight. One thing is clear, however. It is easier to verify whether individuals agree or disagree than to figure out whether they really understand one another and, if so, to what extent and in which way. As a rule, people have the greatest difficulty in reconstructing complex but fast-paced encounters where misinterpretations and misunderstandings are produced and reproduced on a systemic basis.

Serious public disagreements are often simply self-evident—observable and demonstrable—whereas the emergence of complex misunderstandings between speaking subjects may well operate below the surface of conscious awareness and beyond anyone's current grasp. Serious misinterpretations usually extend beyond the scope of simple disagreements. It is not just a matter of whether the ratio of differences and divergences outweigh those involving similarities and convergences. Something far deeper applies. The discovery of sustained disagreement provides renewed opportunity to work through personal problems and relational difficulties and to move on to better things. Serious misunderstandings, in contrast, require greater labor-intensive effort to reconcile the coexistence of incompatible, paradoxical, or contradictory ways of making sense of people, places, and things. Consequently, routine acts of miscommunication or problematic talk may well reflect a surplus of surface disagreements, deep-seated misunderstandings, or an uneven combination of both types of linguistic confusion.

It makes little sense to express vague abstractions in a distinctive social idiom that others will not be able to grasp or comprehend in their own ways or in their own terms. Therefore, we undertake conventional discursive practices with a minimal presumption of some likelihood of success. In civil discourse, there is at least an implicit duty or obligation to construe actions in light of their intended aims. This makes the search for meaning a pragmatic as well as a semantic and syntactic enterprise. The dynamic process unfolds directly at the level of one's utterance and indirectly by one's working out implicit meanings, particularly when the latter markedly differ from the former.

The fallible or probabilistic aspects of such common personal expectancies and social anticipations are often overlooked. The task of mutual comprehension requires explicit interpretation, whereas grasping involves a more intuitive sense of how to work through the underlying inferences and implications. Failure to grasp and comprehend the multiple purposes of negotiated social action will likely lead to a kind of collective misunderstanding (indirect, elusive) that differs significantly from the mistakes and miscalculations associated with misguided or ineffective application of practical logic or informal reasoning.

Mismatched interpretations occur when the criterion of coherence is at odds with the principle of relevance. Acts of mutual misrepresentation, in contrast, presuppose that some speaker has conveyed or evoked false information (Fraser 1994). Whether a specific frame of information qualifies as being "false" depends on verification of suspect information and commitment to the informative falsity that a given person believes to be true. Intentional misrepresentations (e.g., exaggeration, flattering, and lying) mingle with unintended and unforeseen misrepresentations (even though the speaker does not mean to mislead but does so) due to the vagaries, ambiguities, and confusions in the mix of personal styles. False information registers as part of a larger flow of explicit messages, but some aspects register in tacit, indirect, and implicit modes of sense-making praxis.

BOUNDARY AMBIGUITY

In the study of face-to-face interaction, it is important to know several things: where the personal boundary lines are; how they are shaped, implicated, or merely presumed; and what functions they serve, either to enable or disable collective participation in the shared pursuit of individual intentions, plans, strategies, tactics, functions, and goals. Likewise, repeated, habitual, or ingrained acts of misreading, misconstruing, or misinterpreting multiple sets of relevant claims and conflicted considerations may be associated with a derived or acquired sense of some small-scale infraction, violation, or transgression taking place. The acquisition of stable but fluid personal boundary conditions acquires definition and direction with the attribution, ascription, or imposition of an unspoken array of inferences and implications. Hence, concerted personal effort to maintain current boundary conditions cannot be separated from the larger possibility or necessity of dissolving them later on. Presumably, the expressive freedom of each party is constrained by the interpretive slant of every other party.

Tilly (2004) stresses the importance of distinguishing between the internal boundary conditions of engaged social agents (performance structure) and the external boundary conditions with outsiders (social structure). Personal boundaries are subject to negotiation over constraints and opportunities that operate within an open system. These small-scale enactments produce microlevel domains for mutual exploration and open up or close down, include salient subject matter or exclude implausible subject matter, and assign preference and priority to the fulfillment of certain end states at the expense of a larger array of potential alternatives. On a macrolevel, personal boundaries are subject to indirect negotiation over the participants' association with second and third parties, institutional affiliations, and diffuse cultural influences. As Tilly (2004) notes, "Social boundaries interrupt, divide, circumscribe, or segregate distributions of population or activity within social fields. Such fields certainly include spatial distributions of populations or activity, but they also include temporal distributions and webs of interpersonal connection" (214). At stake are causal mechanisms of boundary change, mechanisms constitutive of boundary change, and consequential mechanisms of desired ends.

At issue are the sorts of small-scale violations and large-scale transgressions that occur in contested public settings in which shared, collaborative goals are difficult to achieve. As a rule, the higher the level of friction, stress, and strain, the greater the potential for closely scrutinized forms of collaborative activity to come sharply into play. Generally, simplistic, repetitive, or low-risk routines, activities, and daily tasks are far less demanding and, therefore, much less vulnerable to critical reassessment or shared reappraisal. Across a broad spectrum of sense-making activities, any ineffectual, misguided, or poorly executed message designs, strategies, and tactics may evoke any number of slights, mistakes, miscalculations, or transgressions that diminish the quality of interpretive performance. Closely related is the wider tendency for disturbing, insensitive, or offensive actions to produce a chain of harsh or negative reactions, often with adverse or unwelcome social consequences. Of central interest is the dynamic tension in unsettled or encumbered social situations in which the dividing lines are subject to contested definition or alteration in relation to what each participant expects, wants, or needs from anyone else.

Interpersonal boundaries may be subject to negotiation, regulation, and blurring of the lines. Opposing tensions register in alternative construals relating to whether to remain apart or join together. Some things fit well together. Other things do not fit at all. Still others sometimes fit together one way or another but only for short periods. A shared sense of ambiguity or uncertainty provides an added margin of opportunity for successful renegotiation of interpersonal boundaries as they shift from one type or sphere of shared activity to another type of collaborative endeavor.

Ambiguous or indistinct clues emerge when a person is confronted by an array of unknown, uncertain, unfamiliar, or incongruent modes of personal conduct. Mutual negotiation involving ambiguous social conditions may strengthen or weaken shared resolve to come to terms with negative, aversive, or intolerable conditions. Likewise, a pervasive mood of emotional turmoil may contribute to a climate of confusing, conflicting, and contradictory markers of ambivalence, misdirection, and mystification. Mutual failure to acquire, maintain, alter, and transform the prevailing personal boundaries surely qualifies as a major predictor of member dissatisfaction, relational deterioration, and intimate disillusion. Likewise, a toxic combination of physical aggression and verbal conflict greatly increases the likelihood of relational deterioration specified as "till discord do us part" (Demaris 2000).

Angry Misunderstanding

The anatomy of angry misunderstanding is compellingly instructive. Direct personal encounters can be broken into component parts (minimum thought units) and reconstructed in richly clustered and deeply elaborated forms to reveal an array of implicit, unspoken conditions shaped often by unfavorable or unwelcome relational circumstances. Relevant instances are grouped around two broad types of aversive or antagonistic confrontation. For one type, the term *lateral* refers to a case of one-party anger, whereas the term *mutual* refers to the alignment of a two-party anger in the other type. Admittedly, there is overlap as well as fuzzy boundary lines between these two key constructs, but the distinction is still useful as a nominal device to separate contentious points of origin and their immediate associations and short-term consequences. Most conspicuous is a dynamic interplay between multiple clusters of anger salience:

lateral: one party thinks the other party is stern, strict, almost always angry, outwardly bitter, and often very upset.

mutual: each party belittles the other party—they jump all over one another and down each other's throats over trivial and unimportant things—the result is anger, frustration, and unnecessary episodes of mutual contention.

mutual: S/O find it hard to determine if either one is hurt or angry by the other party; they often hold back from telling each other what they feel because they both don't know how the other will react out of fear of causing greater damage.

mutual: S/O used to get so angry that now they don't want to talk about anything anymore.

mutual: S/O nag, talk gets heated, and they often end up in a five-minute screaming match involving everything they don't like about each other, and they stay angry for at least a day or two.

mutual: S/O clash—they want what's best for each other, but they never can get to the point of showing it; they hate the fighting and pain but they can't get past it; the saddest part is knowing that so much anger and pain can stem from overpowering love, which itself is frightening and sickening—they fall into the same old patterns every time they see each other.

Anger salience interacts with certain types of anger styles mixed with distorted versions of contested aspects and features of direct personal presentation and interpersonal representation:

mutual: one party gets nervous over trivial things, frets, nags, and shows temper; both parties' speaking styles make one another angry—it is strange that they have been living together since birth and, as young adults, are still annoyed at one another's speaking style—it's not getting worse, but the problem is always there.

lateral: one party displays anger by his face, loud voice, choice of words, creased forehead, and clenched jaw.

mutual: one party can almost always tell if something is bothering the other party—she'll be real clumsy in what she says and how she speaks—if she is angry she'll speak in a cold, uncaring tone; the other party reacts mostly in silence—if he is angry, he doesn't talk either; S/O listen but don't understand what the other says, and neither one cares enough to seem interested enough to ask any more questions.

mutual: S/O get along fine, but there are times where S will say something and suddenly, much to her surprise, O will get angry, yell, and stomp off—fortunately, she comes around shortly and they make up; such interaction is hard to explain because neither party seems to know what really happens—somehow one person says the wrong thing, and the other gets very upset and hurt and starts to engage in a personal attack; S/O don't do much talking until one is ready to apologize for flying off the handle, but the messy situations never get resolved.

mutual: S/O don't understand what is required to make either one feel better—when he tries to help her with the kind of advice he would want from other people, she seems to get frustrated and angry at him so he ends up feeling even worse than before.

Not surprisingly, a toxic mix of strong anger and volatile styles of personal presentation and representation are linked with a maze of misconstrued and miscalculated messages that often unfold in several ways and on several levels at once:

mutual: it is rare that either party has a clue as to what the other person is talking about—one yells, screams, and gets angry while the other party (laid back) reacts with confusion—this only causes more anger on her part, so basically, every time they talk, they fight.

mutual: S/O don't always know when each one is playing around or being serious, and they don't understand why either one can get so angry and why they can't realize when the other is serious or not—this often results in severe arguments, which are later disregarded by both of them.

mutual: S/O have serious misunderstandings because they don't always state what they want clearly, but each one still expects the other party to understand what is being said anyway; they leave brief and shallow interactions and go into their separate rooms, where each one gets angry about what the *other* misunderstood; they are also sarcastic with each other, and they find that sarcasm conveys hostility and anger but it doesn't really get either one's message across; it also makes the other person defensive and unwilling to listen; they often expect each other to understand just from nonverbal cues what each one is feeling—such as slamming things around, turning the music up, or ignoring one another.

Those participants who rely on repeated outbursts of strong anger are most likely the same persons who amplify suppressed anger over the magnitude of explicit anger and suppressed hostility that does not seem to go away.

> *mutual*: S/O do not understand each other, and they don't communicate very well at all; if they could only talk to each other, they would have a better relationship—as it is now, they don't—she won't tell him what is wrong, and, if anything, she will get upset about something, and instead of telling him she just won't talk to him, and this in turn makes him very angry because she won't speak to him and he has no idea what he did— then he ends up leaving her alone until she gets over it—they don't talk about anything, and they don't really solve anything that really matters to either party; they don't yell at each other, but they just don't understand how the other party really feels, and they don't know how to be open with each other so they both end up not knowing how the other is feeling or thinking at all.

Although it takes only one party to be mad or become angry, it takes two or more social agents to become entangled or embroiled in the mutual misconstruction of intemperate, baffling, or mystifying modes of protracted misunderstanding. In simplest terms, the social construction of mutual misunderstanding makes people angry more often than for two other types of negativity, namely, scaled variations of fear or sadness. In general, the intensity or salience of anger relates to the scale or magnitude of serious misunderstanding, whether defined in episodic or chronic terms.

The salience of anger can be volatile, unpredictable, and often jarring. Some antagonists escalate quickly upward or rapidly downward on a broad sliding scale of anger intensity. Other types eschew hot outbursts in favor of less heated but more simmering and smoldering displays of disdain or disgust that register mostly beneath the surface or at the periphery of conscious awareness—at times disguised from facial view and at other times spilling over explicitly from internalized or suppressed behavioral form. Thus, some hold anger in and walk away, whereas others struggle to keep angry rejoinders in check or under control. Still others make little or no effort to disguise or conceal strong or intense aversive stimulation but rather use mounting, rising levels of anger as explicit motivation to confront others by whatever means they deem necessary.

The very fear of anger also enters in, either in giving rise to volatile aspirations or as a means to close threatening things down. Sometimes angry confrontations make things better; at other times, angry confrontations make things worse. As a generalization, the slow, gradual buildup of tacit signs of mounting anger usually gives rise to threatening or aggressive escalations that in turn have sharply downward directional consequences, with collaborative conditions becoming much worse before there is added incentive to make them any better. The aversive presence of too much "bad stuff" has great potential to overwhelm shaky or unstable social conditions with too little "good stuff" in conflicted situations so unduly constrained by scarce coping resources, low relational maintenance abilities, or deficient social skills.

Strong, flashing anger often stems from a strange but uneven mix of linguistic factors coupled with habitual and mechanical forces at work. The sound of the voice, for example, acquires maximum definition in dramatic and elaborately stylized outbursts: becoming choked up; feeling ready to cry; adapting a stern, strict tone of voice with evocative overtones of disgust and insult; displaying bitterness; or deciding mindlessly to rant, rave, accuse, blame, argue, curse, swear, scream, belittle, deceive, badger, bicker, complain, nag, rag, slam, or stomp off. There is often as much intense struggle to keep things in as there is acute verbal struggle to let them out. Visceral respondents are often caught up in the emotional confusion and turmoil of having to cope with multiple and contradictory types of personal sense-making systems that generate and regulate the magnitude of linguistic conflict and severe clash relating to irreconcilable categorical imperatives. The most visceral expressions are replete with seemingly endless rounds of imperatives, demands, claims, injunctions, and impositions, to say nothing of the subversive friction associated with countervailing forces of resistance and restraint of another's coercive, abusive, or malicious tactics.

The key linguistic features are often easy to spot. Conundrums, contradictions, and confusions can prove to be most formidable and thereby resist concerted effort to resolve personal issues with a mutually satisfying solution. Resignation, withdrawal, and passive abandonment are common and often decisive in protracted linguistic predicaments with no technical solution in sight. Whether sensitive, delicate, or touchy subjects are dropped quickly or begrudgingly, the short-term consequences are much the same. There is also much intuitive, interpretive guesswork. Participants readily assume that they cannot tell if the other party is really angry; they have trouble reading one another's feelings; they hold back from making any explicit mention of anger on grounds that they do not know, and they fear the uncertain reactions of other parties; they cannot move past the suffering and the pain; they are unsuccessful in mutual efforts to construct alternative ways or methods of jointly making sense together; they rely on message constructions that have long since outlived their intrinsic utilities, yet the unbending and unyielding antagonists cling to them in spite of evidence to the contrary; they complain endlessly about messages not getting across or their otherwise being screwed up; and they often settle for superficial communication, defective skills application, pseudocommunication, idle chatter, and small talk as cheap substitutes for the real thing.

INAUTHENTIC DISCLOSURE

It would be a serious mistake to downplay the relevance or impact of salient personal disagreements, particularly when coupled with enduring or intrinsic elements of misinterpretation, miscommunication, and misunderstanding, in affectionate social settings in which positive sentiments prevail—namely, a surplus of reciprocated expressions of love, care, and concern. When multiple expressions of affection and appreciation commingle with scaled disagreements and mutual misunderstandings, there is often a struggle involving personal identity, and vexing questions arise about the disturbing implications of authentic disclosures:

S/O love each other very much, but they have endless misunderstandings anyway; somehow, the meanings of words and gestures get all twisted around; they take jokes the wrong way, and sometimes they must labor greatly to explain things even in a very simple way.

S/O have yet to figure out how the other person thinks; S has a hard time talking with O without offending her in some way; they both share good intentions, but they view things in very different ways—things that are no big deal to O are usually huge issues to S; they are good friends and they love to spend time together, but they argue a lot, and routine interactions are often difficult because they both have to spend much of the time trying to word things in ways that don't offend the other.

S/O love and care for each other, but they still stumble around trying not to hurt each other; they get into big misunderstandings over small issues that could be avoided if they would explain themselves better.

S/O love each other a lot, but somehow they both will do things with good intentions, and the other sees it in a totally different light; they say things while meaning well, but the other party will take it the wrong way—S does not understand O's logic, and O does not understand S's logic.

Multiple expressions of love, care, concern, and misunderstanding, taken together, clearly demonstrate that personal failure to achieve high standards of sense-making practice need not automatically produce a strong surplus of negative displays, particularly if basic precautions remain in sharp focus. Certainly, minor misunderstandings can still be upsetting, even if a surplus of positive affect is in place. Little things get in the way. Words get twisted around. Intentions are misconstrued. Speech acts are taken in the wrong way. Despite the best of intentions, misinterpreted signals and signs require labor-intensive effort to explain or cross-check against an alternative standard of cognitive appraisal. Mutual efforts to try even harder to figure things out do not always make a difference. Themes of love, concern, and care may be eroded, weakened, or diluted by a hidden legacy of disagreement or by the magnitude of mutual misunderstanding that must be endured.

Central themes register in a collective sense of the utter insufficiency of multiple expressions of love, care, and concern to offset the countervailing effects of unresolved disagreements conflated with a legacy of chronic misunderstandings. Some intimates discuss such reciprocated love in spite of discord and dissension. Here affectionate exchanges make disagreement or misunderstanding somewhat easier to handle. Participants speak openly and freely, but complex or entangled feelings and sensibilities are hurt; resentments build; and shared efforts to explain difficult social situations may be seen as futile. Moreover, the magnitude of love, respect, and care may be insufficient for parties to get through to each other or to understand how each other really works.

Quite poignant are fragile attempts by disillusioned parties to convince each other that love is still there despite the scale of disagreement or the magnitude of things taken in the wrong way. Some fumble around in the dark trying not to hurt or harm each other. Mutual efforts to discuss relational issues and pressing concerns just go in circles. In the manner of a faint whisper, some intimates offer assuring reminders that they *do* in fact love each other, despite weak communication and the strong tug of disconnection, as the only way to keep them going from day to day. Likewise, loving, affectionate intentions are apt to be construed in a different light, one that prevents or forestalls mutual attainment of multiple personal goals. Finally, the magnitude of shared love may be insufficient to move past all the fighting, pain, silence, contention, troubled relation, unbridled malice, or unmitigated hate.

There is a somewhat stronger version of abiding love in which a legacy of mutual misunderstandings are preserved in spite of whatever may stand in their way. Mutual expressions of faith in unfinished possibilities manage to reaffirm prospects that, in fact, the worst is over and things are bound to get better soon. Distressed intimates proclaim that big misunderstandings involving small issues could be avoided if only the partners could explain themselves better. Others affirm the presence of enough love to heal, or at least compensate for, the toxic or aversive effects of troublesome questions, tough challenges, or major threats. Simply because intimates fail to agree or come to understand pressing or problematic concerns, it does not follow that abiding love dissolves or troublesome things are beyond repair. The sufficiency of love, respect, and care can withstand the sheer weight of countervailing forces for those with the courage and foresight to steer the course.

Frustrating Misunderstanding

As the following excerpts from the Wisconsin study transcripts reveal, prevailing levels of salience frustration closely match the salience of angry outburst whenever mixed with a great deal of suppressed hostility:

lateral: S/O talk, but the way O tries to describe things is so abstract that S doesn't even know where to begin in order to ask questions to have her explain what she means; when this keeps reoccurring time after time, the sheer magnitude of misunderstandings get worse, and there is really no use in trying to understand—such a high level of misunderstanding can get a person so frustrated during disturbing episodes when there are no words to describe what you believe or feel at that particular moment.

lateral: S/O misunderstand each other all the time—when S tells O to meet S somewhere, O ends up going somewhere else—she is a hard person to rely on because she is either late or doesn't show up at all—it would frustrate O if S would bring any of this up to her, so S just keeps it all inside—this is one type of problem in interaction that will never go away, and it will never be solved.

mutual: S/O love each other, but bad moods that mean quietness to one party are taken by the other party to mean something is wrong—they compete in games where they are at odds and disagree about everything—it is frustrating for S to endure.

mutual: S/O talk in a frustrating way—they are constantly trying to make sure they don't say the wrong thing as not to cause offense; it's almost always a fake interaction because they keep such a close watch on what they say—the reason is that they constantly misinterpret what the other person means; they are always on guard, and both try hard to stay neutral; they do not say too much, because that causes misunderstanding and unhappiness, so they only talk about things that do not relate to themselves, because they usually misunderstand and this ends up causing even more offense.

mutual: S/O don't know if the other feels the same way about important subjects, because their own fragile relationship is filled with mutual misunderstanding; they are constantly engaged in a constant state of clarification—conversations are marked by references as "No, I didn't mean that . . ." or "I say that because . . ." and both parties use such tactics; their ideas aren't all that different, but they don't get their own thoughts expressed clearly—it seems as though there is more frustration because one or the other does not understand or comprehend what is said and they must spend more time trying to clarify themselves.

mutual: S/O don't know why there seems to be something that prevents them from getting on the same wavelength—it makes it hard and quite frustrating when you are always getting asked what you mean and you don't know how to respond.

mutual: S/O find it is most frustrating at times because they get into these full-blown arguments about how things are said—she wishes she could see things how they are meant to be seen—she tends to read into things a lot more than he does—she always thinks there is a hidden agenda in what he is saying when, in reality, he has no hidden agenda—chalk it up to mutual immaturity.

mutual: S/O don't understand each other's point of view or why they feel the way they do; because S/O don't understand how each other feels, they don't listen and generally don't respond to each other at all; they try to avoid each other and they both get frustrated, which in turn leads to further arguments and greater fear that they will get into more fights—in effect, it is less stressful not to talk at all because it prevents further episodes of frustration, conflict, and arguments.

Some misdirected efforts in sense-making practice are instantiated as little more than vain exercises in syntactic, semantic, and pragmatic futility in routine language use. Frustration arises as resistance to the fulfillment of distinctive personal aspirations and collective strivings. It occurs up and down the scale of complexity and elaboration and registers freely in the flow of discursive process—desire, intention, interpretation, strategy, tactic, or goal fulfillment. The more trivial the objective, the less severe the friction, strife, and strain. Unlike many other "hot" affective measures of negativity, frustration is, in a nominal sense, the common burden of everyone. It is relatively uncommon for one participant to experience all the frustration while another participant is alleged to experience none of it.

Frustration has contagious and expansive consequences insofar as it can be said that what blocks or thwarts one member's sense-making efforts also blocks or thwarts other's strained effort to attain certain desirable ends. States of frustration, commotion, and turmoil make it more difficult to achieve particular outcomes: to make sense of things; to afford coherent explanations for questionable acts; to render clear, fluent, spoken actions that can be reasonably interpreted by a reasonable observer; to acquire generative vocabulary and compelling logic for the pursuit of shared objectives; and to transform limits and constraints into renewed opportunity for mutual exploration of alternative options.

The central theme is that the larger systemic process does not work well. The participants, often for inexplicable reasons, do not work well together. Someone or something always stands in the way. Confrontational conversations, in extreme cases, are aborted quickly among those with long, embellished memories of prior failure and little patience for repeats of "bad" performances. A dense, abstract vocabulary is deadly, as Locke would have it, for disengaged listeners. From the standpoint of task orientation, some do not know where to begin, how to proceed, what to do, or how to settle things in the end. In unfavorable circumstances, even small-scale, so-called harmless or innocent layers of misunderstanding may resist successful scanning. However, microlevel serialized misunderstandings, repeated often enough over an extended period, acquire added emotional weight and thereby resist all efforts to make things better. Others are easily discouraged by ineffective effort to explain (or reexplain) baffling, confounding matters, and they simply give up and walk away without a clue but with a discomforting sense of defeat. Still others describe their mutual frustrations as justifications for weakened faith or diminished hope that unresolved matters, somehow, will ever be successfully addressed. In dialectical terms, common small-scale disagreements and simple misunderstandings are generally quite tolerable or innocuous. What causes the greatest amount of psychological damage entails the subversive interplay between small-scale misunderstandings (speech acts) and the larger-scale influences stemming from repeated failures to understand other participants' systems of understanding. When we misunderstand the goal-directed behavior of other people, we may also misunderstand other people's ways of understanding.

In relational terms, a self-defeating metanarrative discourse is usually self-justifying and self-exonerating in tenor, texture, and tone. A common lament is that belabored talk is difficult: Strain not to say the wrong thing. Stop reading into things too much. Strive not to offend. Heuristic shortcuts are no real substitute for systemic processing of what transpires: Stay on guard. Some feel compelled to engage in constant clarification, cross-checking, and much back and fill. Eventually, a wide succession of painful stalemates, impasses, and blockages strengthens the unspoken, often sickening sense of communication breaking down. A hidden agenda, real or imagined, offers too little comfort or solace in the end. The full measure of what goes wrong or simply falls apart may be well beyond measure or beyond the participants' power to control or overcome. In the final analysis, interactive or communicative failure cannot be accurately reduced to discrete matters of language, personality, relational types, or social structure but rather to the fragile dynamic of the entire system itself.

EMPATHETIC FAILURE

Serious human misunderstandings occur when too many important social considerations are missing from the larger equation. Sensitive interactants may notice what is absent, missing, or left out, and subsequently take any critical omissions into active account. Thematically, in the reconstructed accounts of personal misunderstanding, there are no mentions of tenderness, adoration, sentiment, arousal, lust, passion, infatuation, longing, amusement, bliss, gaiety, glee, jolly, jovial, joy, delight, jubilation, ecstasy, euphoria, enthusiasm, zeal, zest, exhilaration, pleasure, pride, triumph, optimism, enthrallment, amazement, or astonishment and virtually no mention of compassion, desire, cheer, gladness, satisfaction, thrill, contentment, eagerness, relief, or surprise.

Empathetic failures undermine and discourage the free interchange of emotional vocabularies and thereby have considerable potential to weaken or impoverish levels of emotional support for sustained endeavors and collaborative pursuits, particularly those that serve to reintroduce a great deal of emotional baggage from prior sequences or protracted successions of faulty or ineffective encounter. Markers of emotional impoverishment register in serious or protracted misunderstandings with a strong surplus of negative affect. Although the participants in the Wisconsin study do not often use the word *empathy* in their accounts, they do employ a minidictionary of critical terms that refer to aversive emotions mixed with cognitive misapprehension. Relevant instances cluster around alleged deficits or deficiencies in applied social knowledge.

Failure to implement important relational skills leads to changes not fully understood by one member or another in a viable speech community. A succession of inaccurate human understandings on a small scale, when unabated, contribute to a climate in which widespread presumptions of enduring misunderstanding acquire lives of their own. Persons who become utterly convinced that they are stuck with a partner who fails to grasp and comprehend, validate, and understand important relational concerns, personal sensitivities, and intimate feelings may be vulnerable to diminished member satisfaction, less hope of future happiness, and reduced level of affectionate interchange (Sanford 1998). Specifically, men report greater willingness to frighten their domestic partners than do women, who report greater willingness to reciprocate verbalized threats of physical abuse out of a self-protective or defensive motive (Barnett and Lee 1997).

Sexual Harassment

Misinterpreted, unwelcome, or unwanted acts of intimate touching, particularly in poor-quality or weak social relations, are conducive to the emergence of suppressed hostility or accusation of sexual harassment in public work settings. Acts of physical contact can be interpreted in many conflicting, contradictory, and confounded ways: arousing, provocative, intrusive, or invasive. In organization settings, coworkers may have to walk a fine line between low-risk, appropriate, and deferential displays of interest, affection, and sexual strivings versus high-risk, inappropriate, and volatile consideration of implicit boundary lines and their explicitly intrusive and disruptive modes of boundary crossing, violation, and transgression (Lee and Guerrero 2001). Broad-based societal evidence indicates that female workers are often somewhat more likely to view intrusive behavior as inappropriate or sexually harassing than are men (Hendrix, Rueb, and Steel 1998). Questionable behavior includes bold and assertive acts based on sexually explicit jokes; stares, glances, or looking the person in question up or down; unwanted and unwelcome acts of physical touching or crude comments about someone else's figure, build, or dress; and repeated requests to get together, go out, and party. Men who strive to assume dominant social positions in work settings are most likely to be interpreted in terms of sexual harassment (Murphy, Driscoll, and Kelly 1999). Unreasonable interference is closely associated with perceived or construed personal intent to intimidate or offend (Sbrage and O'Donahue 2000). Relational intrusion implies unwanted, unwelcome, or unwarranted striving, pursuit, or invasion of someone else's sense of privacy.

Indifference

S/O usually miss much of what is said and done.

S/O have babble sessions where they just tune each other out.

S/O don't seem interested, nor do they make any effort to understand each other.

S/O find that it's not worth the energy it takes to even try to interact with each other.

S/O find themselves unwilling to make any effort to reach out to one another.

S/O speak different languages, so there is no use in trying to understand.

S/O just talk in a nonchalant way, and they could really care less.

S/O are not responsive, because they don't have feelings for each other.

Inattentiveness

S/O just ignore each other, avoid eye contact, say nothing, and never seem to get along.

S/O tune each other out because they want to say what the other doesn't want to hear.

S/O are preoccupied for reasons that keep each of them from ever really understanding one another.

S/O never pay full attention—they both find it virtually impossible to get through to each other.

S/O are so easily distracted, and neither one pays full attention to what is being said or done.

S/O have irreconcilable misunderstandings that are being entirely ignored.

Inexpressivity

S/O refuse to offer feedback.

S/O are never sure how to express themselves.

S/O are afraid to express their true feelings—they are left in awkward silence.

S/O can't express real feelings, out of fear of misunderstanding or rejection.

S/O find that there are no words to express or represent their true feelings.

S/O pass each other on the stairs, say nothing, and get no response every time.

S/O do not open up, so they end up not knowing what the other is thinking.

Inconsiderateness

S/O don't understand each other well enough to be considerate of the actual feelings of one another.

S/O say things without taking into consideration how the other person will feel about what transpires.

S/O put words in each other's mouths without understanding a single thing that they both try to say.

S/O see uneasiness rise too high, and they both take leave to their mutual relief.

Impatience

S/O are in too much of a hurry to pay close attention.

S/O are quick to take things the wrong way.

S/O do not allow one another time to explain anything fully.

S/O lose patience, interrupt, and want only their own feelings to be expressed.

S/O lose patience, are easily distracted, and usually jump to the wrong conclusions.

S/O are very impatient and they often grate on each other.

S/O are always on the go and never slow down, with no chance to process talk.

S/O rattle off what they want to say as fast as possible, and both of them are always rushed up.

S/O try each other's patience—truthful answers and lies mean the same thing.

Insensitivity

S/O brush off whatever the other one says, without hearing a word.

S/O find it useless to discuss personal feelings with someone who doesn't reciprocate.

S/O read into each other's verbal statements the very things they fear most about themselves.

S/O give each other uneasy feelings and act as if they could care less.

S/O are never sure what to say or how to express themselves to each other.

Annoying Misunderstanding

S/O might push a joke too far or nag too much but still think it is done in a friendly way when in fact it is annoying or hurtful.

S/O talk, but S finds it's much like talking to a door knob—you have to turn it just right in order for it to click and for the door to open; repeating things over and over gets rather annoying.

S/O get along, but they snap easily with each other; S thinks O is short-tempered and defensive with what S says—even if S is only being sarcastic and joking; O only sees the sarcastic side and often takes offense, and S gets annoyed by her short, snappy temper and gets mad; they completely misunderstand one another, and each one thinks the other one is completely unreasonable.

S/O talk, but S thinks that O gets on his nerves so bad he can't even stand to be around him; O keeps repeating stupid little things over and over until it just annoys the hell out of S, who does not see eye to eye with anything that O says or does.

S/O feel for some reason that they should get along, but they don't; O says something that S agrees with, but the whole conversation is not natural, and O will think that S was offended (when she wasn't) and then apologize, which annoys S and makes her antsy—they don't talk that much, just sort of irrelevant, frivolous things.

S/O try to talk, but S just doesn't understand the things O does or says; she thinks people will only like her if she does things for them; some things she does really annoys S because she will do almost anything for others, even if she hates it.

Jealous Misunderstanding

Severe disagreements concerning protracted issues of sexual jealousy often lead to more extreme misunderstandings involving tacit presumptions or explicit claims of infidelity among intimates. Troubled gender relations related to escalating disagreement in matters of sexual rivalry are complicated by the sheer magnitude of misunderstanding. Suspicions of sexual infidelity are rife with troublesome implications: diversion of potential reproductive resources, disturbing allegation of relational inequities, lack of commitment, or prevalence of betrayal. Emotional upset across many cultures is greater among men, who react to sexual infidelity, than among women, who become more upset over emotional infidelity (Shackelford, LeBlanc, and Drass

2000). Modest gender differences have also been linked with sexual orientation. Men appear to find male–female sexual infidelity most upsetting, whereas women are more likely to find male–male sexual infidelity most upsetting (Wiederman and LaMar 1998). Romantic jealousy is also associated with emotional upheaval and cognitive turbulence based on narrative themes of vengefulness, sadness, and fear (Sharpsteen and Kirkpatrick 1997). Secondary associations cluster around conflicted mood states: helplessness, shock, nausea, repulsion, humiliation, despair, or mere relief.

The intended meanings of relational displays of strong, passionate affection are vulnerable to false causal attributions. The three magic words ("I love you") may be construed at multiple levels of semantic association: implications and inferences, favorable or unfavorable; literal interpretation, taken at face value or dismissed as empty promise; and transliteral or heavily symbolic representation. Disagreeable individuals reveal more unpredictability, uncertainty, and variability than agreeable ones, who rely on frequent use of negative declarations and dominating responses (Wallace et al. 1999). Questionable impositions may also evoke or convey a diffuse sense of hidden motives, seductive ploys, or expectancy violations. Deception, deceit, and duplicity add sensual density and erotic mystery to the intoxicating mix of jealousy and envy.

ASYMMETRY AND MISALIGNMENT

Asymmetrical arrangements emerge from imbalanced resources, defective ability, or disproportionate commitments to the process of interaction itself. Typically, one party seeks greater involvement whereas another party desires diminished participation. When anger is highly salient but one-sided, there is often considerable effort to suppress hostile outbursts; deny aggressive sentiment; and withhold, withdraw, or curtail threatening or volatile exchanges. Mutual contentions, however, are more problematic and sometimes intensely disquieting. A heightened risk of symmetrical escalation serves only to upset equilibrium further and keep things out of balance. Exaggerations and small-scale inflation of unresolved grievances figure heavily in destabilizing or disorienting disputes, but more serious episodic imbalances are indicative of a collective failure to know what to do or how to proceed. Chronic instability, in contrast, gives way to persistent failure or fatalistic despair. When the interactive system seems to be pervasively flawed, there is temptation to abandon or avoid direct contact altogether.

Asymmetrical insight occurs when people judge their knowledge of other people to be far greater than they do other people's knowledge of them. Thematically, one source assumes, "You don't know me, but I know you. Hence, you are apt to misinterpret my behavior or misconstrue my character or motives." If this estimated imbalance in assumed interpretive accuracy is merely presumed rather than actually tested, then there is no reason to entertain the notion that others are viewing us more clearly and reasonably than we do ourselves (Pronin et al. 2001). This social illusion helps one explain how people can exhibit remarkable ignorance, delusion, or emotional blindness about themselves before others.

Confused individuals are prone to acknowledge not only a defeatist mentality but also a massive degree of uncertainty regarding basic causes or good reasons for troubling or deteriorating relational outcomes. Extreme conditions are progressively difficult to modify or appease. A legacy of serious misunderstanding, when coupled with intense disagreement, leave some beleaguered participants with a sense of futility or confusion concerning what goes wrong, what causes repetitive or unresolved tensions, what conditions make things worse, and what can be done to make things better. The downward spiral seems to shape or control the most troubled participants far more severely than what the antagonists are able to shape or control the process in return. Thematically, socially undesirable admissions surface: no one has a clue; no one knows what is really happening; no one realizes why things turn out badly; or no one can stop the same destructive patterns from repeatedly occurring. Conversely, the most discontented parties seem to be mystified, baffled, or unable to get past the heartache and the pain.

Some patterns of asymmetry and misalignment promote the emergence of syntactical irregularities and chaotic transitions in speaking and listening. Participants transform ordered sequences of deliberation into disordered pairings in turn taking or serious imbalances in total speaking time. Other configurations accentuate semantic misalignment, slippage, flooding, or stonewalling. Still other interactive imbalances are purely pragmatic in nature. Sometimes the very tactics that work well for one party come at the expense of another party. Although syntactic, semantic, and pragmatic disjunctions tend to coalesce, intractable problems in assigned meaning and valuation surface most frequently over longer time frames.

Semantic slippage is magnified under conditions of divergent meaning and generate systems in which a surplus of negative affect prevails. What means something of great importance to one party may fail to mean anything to anyone else. Relating to diverse meaning systems is a critical consideration both in direct measures of the quality of personal relations and in the cumulative productivity of interaction. Asymmetry and misalignment in semantic considerations accentuate irregularities in valuations and ascriptions of what counts in all that matters. Empathetic failures abound when conflicted participants construct too many constraints relative to the magnitude of opportunities for mutual exploration or shared inquiry into pressing issues or unresolved concerns.

Chronic states of indifference, inattentiveness, inexpressivity, inconsiderateness, impatience, and insensitivity are all deflationary mechanisms that diminish the meaningfulness of what transpires. Potential sources of renewal and reassurance are then easily discounted, devalued, and discredited in advance. Moreover, petty irritations and annoyances undermine semantic coherence by way of scale distortion, distraction, and disruption that operate at lower thresholds of social discrimination and interpersonal sensitivity. Disaffection and misunderstanding also reduce factors and forces of meaning and connection to their lowest common denominators. If the meaningfulness of everyday life is occasion for communal celebration, the deconstruction of the meaningfulness of everyday life is occasion for resignation and retreat.

MEMBER DISSATISFACTION

Serious problems in social and personal relationships qualify as a significant cause of personal stress, distress, or unhappiness (Holmes 2000). The most compelling evidence occurs in romantic or marital settings. Shortly after marriage, a monotonic decline in spousal satisfaction occurs over long time spans, sometimes over two decades or more (Huston and Vangelisti 1991). Small-scale complaining and grumbling sustained mainly in relation to trivial or minor matters may give rise to equally small-scale countermoves of trivial or minor denials. A successful and happy marriage, for instance, may be slowly but surely subject to regressive transformation into a dissolved state of union. Endless cycles of cross-complaints turn into regressive cycles of demand and withdrawal. Inaccurate inferences accumulate under conditions of threat in close relationships in which members are somehow rendered insecure about their future. Dissatisfied persons may not be able to shield themselves from some unpleasant truth of their partners' aversive feelings and thought and thus develop low thresholds of differential sensitivity that suggests a vigilant readiness to see and respond against further negative expression by either partner.

Technical literature provides reasonably accurate measures of individual discontent by simply asking subjects if they are satisfied with the quality of their relational investments, commitments, and returns. Unfortunately, the most crucial issues usually occur at a relational or systemic level where misconstrued, misdirected, or misguided efforts in sense-making practice are clearly the most decisive determinants of relational deterioration, decay, or dissolution. The most conspicuous fact is one that is often neglected or totally ignored when related individuals are asked if they are satisfied or not. What matters is not so much the sheer magnitude of discontent but rather the severity of underlying difficulties in making clear and coherent sense of what transpires. Collective dissatisfaction therefore constitutes an active expression and sober reflection over the maze of procedural or substantive matters that are poorly understood, badly misunderstood, or not understood in any real sense at all.

Worrying Misunderstanding

S/O don't really talk about personal problems; O avoids any "heavy" confrontation, while S feels a need to let her emotions out and let her feelings go—these two methods of dealing with things can lead to conflict; they have different tones and different voices, which lead both to interpret things in the wrong way; S thinks that O likes to worry out loud too much, so S gets sick of words that have anything to do with trivial worries that come out of O's mouth—an unspoken sense of frustration and annoyance may lead S to not be sensitive to O's worries and concerns.

S/O shared a brief, intimate relationship that only lasted a month; O couldn't understand S's values, and S/O held opposing goals; he wasn't perceptive to her feelings, and he said she worried too much about him—they had nothing in common except for the fact that they didn't understand the other.

Intersecting chains of sensation, feeling, and rumination may become weighty or burdensome, possibly in part as a result to the profusion of negative affect and defective means to control its aversive consequences. Uncertain outcomes figure heavily in introspective problem solving that leads nowhere or remains aimless. It can be quite draining to feel compelled to invest heavily in weighing up all relevant factors and forces that could possibly make a difference one way or another. Obviously, a certain degree of fatalism may be at work below the surface of public apprehension. Nonetheless, protracted worry offers a means of escape from current pressures to perform at a level that may not be feasible to achieve or sustain.

Worry defeats sharp definition, clarity of focus, and depth of concentration. Likewise, chronic worry degrades nonverbal measures of coherence and verbal fluency as well. Those who are most inclined to worry out loud are also most likely to be construed as an emotional burden to others in times of discomfort, discontent, and distress. Insensitivity to the worries of others is itself a mild form of social accusation by neglect. On the other hand, telling someone else not to "worry so much" may well lead them to worry even more. Unrelieved worry and concern about the quality of interaction, or the communicative value of what transpires, center all too often on matters of diminished or failed expectations—that is, how another will react adversely to an unexpected admission of discomfort or mild distress.

Fearful Misunderstanding

S/O talk while S feels anger, frustration, and fear of repercussions for voicing any opinion; O wants to control S's actions, and S feels that O isn't listening to what S has to say and that O will only tell S that O is right and S is wrong no matter what.

S/O are not quite in sync with the styles of one another; they look at the world differently; they are from different racial groups, and that causes differing viewpoints, beliefs, values, language, and cultural norms; he talks about gangs, murdered friends, family members in jail, and problems in U.S. society; he has trouble understanding that she is going through a very rough time herself; they have trouble expressing themselves and are unsure of how the other feels, and they don't honestly say how they are feeling, or they fear they may be rejected or let down.

S/O talk while S thinks O is a very closed person, and S has a hard time understanding her because S is an open, flamboyant person; O is quite moody, which makes S feel like she can't say anything wrong or she will be upset; O can be short with S, even when she hasn't done anything wrong, and this causes unwanted tension; S often tries to make small talk and carry on conversations because O's silence makes S nervous, and S doesn't want to make mistakes in what she says for fear O will get mad.

Linguistic environments are multifaceted and multivalenced. Rapid detection of signs of fear is contingent on the rapid recognition of facial expressions displayed in the presence of external threat and varies as a function of personal assessments of severity, risk, and magnitude of danger. Extreme fear is, in a sense, a composite response to what a person dreads to lose the most—a soul mate, lover, or friend over signs of social rejection, betrayal, disgrace, condemnation, or abandonment. Fear of rejection is shown to inhibit open discussion concerning romantic interests. Systematic miscommunication between affectionate partners occurs when there is great reluctance to talk about the status of relational ties and avoidance of clear and direct expression of underlying intentions or motivations. Individuals may be torn between a desire for greater intimacy and their concealed concerns about the risk of rejection or exclusion (Vorauer et al. 2003).

Fear of communication is closely associated with aversive anticipation of destructive or disabling consequences. Extreme forms of anticipatory fearfulness are a critical factor in disabling some of the potential for communication before the events in question even begin. Heavily implicated are widespread and intensely aroused urges to withdraw, run away, hide, shrink, disappear, become immobilized, or remain inconspicuous. By this conservative standard, solitude is the only solace. Self-protective urges quickly take over during fearful episodes of miscommunication and retrospective communication over fearful consequences.

The language of fear underscores the power of appeasement and deference to higher-status persons, as well as the lateral exchange among equals of verbal accounts of fearful events, by asking others for comfort, support, or help. Shared alleviation of personal fear is rendered through a generous display of reassurance as an anecdote to imagined or real exposure to threat and danger from external sources. From an interactive standpoint, there is fear for further contact with those presumed to harbor risk, threat, or danger. There is also a far more robust level of fear of interaction deteriorating, falling apart, proving inadequate, or becoming a mere waste of time. One may fear rejection from people who shy away, and no one explains why. Fear of the inability to express oneself effectively is linked with people who get angry when things are taken in the wrong way. Specifically, there are subordinate fears of being misread or of true meanings being lost in the shuffle. Unspoken fears rarely make spoken fears go away. Apprehensive fear is useful, therefore, to prepare an individual for fight or flight, to confront or avoid, the presence of appraised risk, threat, and danger from other people. Disabling anxiety, trepidation, panic, and alarm are not so useful, however, because they often lead to extreme appraisals that may be exaggerated, overgeneralized, or disproportionate to what actually transpires.

Sad Misunderstanding

S/O found that their relationship grew wonderfully, with an equal balance of mental and physical intimacy; they would interact endlessly, and it seemed that their desire to know everything about each other had no limit; over time, however, S slowly came to realize there were disparities between what O was telling him and her actual mental state; he found that he could no longer trust what she was telling him because he started to notice slipups and now and again see a glimpse of her real self, which sadly enough was a very depressed and frightened woman; after she made her first suicide attempt, he was literally stunned because he didn't understand why she had tried such a thing; later he learned that she had numerous problems at home, including physical and psychological abuse; in effect, she always wore a beautiful mask telling the world there were no problems, but inside she was self-destructing; instead of the intimacy he thought they had, there was really a wall she built around herself for some amount of protection; even though he was honest and caring as he could be, she couldn't open up; in retrospect, he could see several points where their communication failed; she was attempting to give him small signs about her depression, but because of his inexperience he didn't interpret them correctly; as a result, she closed herself off even more and left him in the dark; he guessed that he wasn't assertive enough to ask her if anything was wrong; even when you have the illusion that you understand someone, you must probe further, hoping to breach the wall of defenses; after therapy, she turned her life around, and they still keep in touch.

While fear disables the potential for genuine human understanding, sadness reflects both fear and misunderstanding all mixed together. Misunderstanding states of fear and fearing conditions of further misunderstanding fit closely together. In this equation, unlike so many static taxonomies of negative human affect, the concept of sadness is not a separate compartment that keeps track of all unwelcome consequences of prior faulty interaction. At the risk of oversimplification, states of severe disagreement and conditions of chronic misunderstanding most often make people angry, and unrelieved anger then gives rise to even greater fear of threatening outbursts and, in addition, a greater measure of sadness relating to the joint magnitude of fear and anger. Conversely, if verbalized anger, whether by imposition of aggression, threat, or abuse, can be brought under a great measure of personal control, the intensity of fear is likely to subside, and the magnitude of sadness diminishes rather quickly.

Difficulties in self-expression and interpersonal reception rank high on the chart of occasions for sadness and sorrow to be prolonged. Sadness undermines accurate judgments of others. Persons render social evaluations that are slanted in the direction of their current affective states or transient moods. Hence, negative reactions distort rapid recognition of another's changing moods as well as global conceptions of other people (Ambady and Gray 2002). Moreover, repetitive episodes of mutual clash, clamor, and conflict have a way of wearing thin. Also, sometimes sadness registers not so much as a deeply felt lament over low-quality interaction, mutual misinterpretation, or painful disconnection but rather in the demise of once-promising conditions, favorable circumstances, and first-rate treatment; such treatment was once so full of promise yet somehow taken for granted and then gradually subjected to mild forms of abuse or neglect until what was once considered precious, privileged, sacred, or treasured was allowed to deteriorate and spiral all the way downward in steep descent to an unspeakable sense of loss that can no longer be renewed or reclaimed. Unrelieved sadness, however, remains suspended somewhere between the fringes of anger and disgust on one hand and surprise and fear on the other. Melancholic emotions, sadness, grief, and depression are primarily grounded in social interaction marked by an imposed or induced sense of shared exposure to unwelcome or otherwise undesirable outcomes. Ultimate sadness is simply unspeakable.

Hurtful Misunderstanding

S/O approached each other while S was walking down the streets of New York when he felt like doing a good deed; he saw a blind woman who was trying to cross the street; as he approached her, he saw she was carrying some heavy bags; when he got over to her and asked if she needed help, she started to yell at him; she rattled off the claim that she was not helpless—that being blind doesn't make her incapable of doing what others do; she said she was able to do a lot more things better than what seeing people do and that we seeing people would be smart to take some lessons from the blind; when he tried to explain to her that he approached her to help her carry her things and he would have done it for anyone, regardless of whether or not that person were blind, she just laughed and said, "Well, then, why don't you go help somebody else and leave me alone"; he realized afterward that his intentions were completely misconstrued because she carried with her the stigma that she was inferior to those who see; he really couldn't defend himself, because he lacked knowledge of how she would feel—he also feels there is a societal stereotype that lingers in the city—whenever someone approaches you, you automatically assume that intentions must be malicious—it was just an unintentional misunderstanding that unfortunately hurt him as well as the lady.

S/O don't listen fully, they interrupt, and they think that they know what's going to be said before the other finishes speaking; each one thinks the other is out to cause hurt and harm—it is hard to have mutual understanding with all the mutual misinterpretation and the fact that problems never get solved in any way.

S/O stumble about trying not to hurt each other's feelings; they get into minor episodes of misunderstanding over small issues that could be easily avoided if they would only explain themselves better, listen better, and ask questions when unclear.

S/O feelings get hurt because neither one wants to stay around much any more—they jump at each other over little things as an indirect way of saying that one has been hurt by inattention and neglect.

Words and gestures have great potential for hurt and harm when one takes them personally and adversely at the same time. Here the search for cause or reason is largely superfluous. Few claim to know what leads to adverse outcomes. What matters is the margin for discredit, disqualification, or devaluation of the participants themselves. Some things are taken the wrong way. Other matters are inverted so that what was intended by one party to be positive or constructive is misidentified or misconstrued as negative or destructive by another party. Still others are assigned to persons who seem to be oblivious to the harsh implications of their careless or reckless statements.

Few acknowledge they are hurt rather easily, either from the residue of prior relations or from the harsh effects of current improprieties or indiscretions. Far more frequent are proclamations of innocence or refusal to admit any explicit sense of having done anything wrong. Anticipated fear of harmful consequences is an occupational hazard of close relations. Those who feel that they are under constant scrutiny rank among the most vulnerable. Misconstrued intentions are not necessarily injurious, except when perceived as deliberate attempts to take advantage, pull rank, go one up, or put another down. Most often, encumbered and burdensome residues of toxic emotion are difficult to articulate and easy to misread or be cast in a harsh light.

Spoken discourse provides a rich lexicon for inflicting a sense of hurt and harm on others. Verbal aggression entails verbal discrimination unleashed either in explicit personal attacks or in implicit, subversive efforts to undermine other people's character, dignity, or integrity. Of course, it is quite critical for acts of bearing false witness to be couched or phrased in accusatory and adversarial terms (Graumann 1998). The linguistic generation of hurt and harm is shown to be "as acute and aversive as the physical pain of bodily injury, and it sometimes lasts for longer" (Leary et al. 1998, 1225). Furthermore, invisible wounds and symbolic injuries are strongly linked with negative message evaluations (Vangelisti and Crumley 1998) and hurt feelings construed as signs of relational devaluation (Leary et al. 1998).

Violations and transgressions qualify as offensive maneuvers. What qualifies are signs of activation of abusive cues that indicate dissociation, disapproval, derogation, betrayal, rejection, revenge, or moral exclusion, which in turn give rise to general distress, disarray, and discomfort; plus reactivation cues indicating discomfort or distress stemming from largely unspoken types of hurtful sources of neglect or avoidance in response to the infliction of aversive consequences on unwelcome or unwilling subjects. The degree or magnitude of hurt and harm may have nominal or decisive impact on the tenor or tone of subsequent personal encounters.

Motives for hurting others are neither clear nor obvious. The mere presumption of disagreement or misunderstanding is neither a necessary nor sufficient condition for the imposition of needless pain and suffering. However, ascriptions of deliberate intent are usually enough to spell trouble. Although some measure of discursively imposed hurt and harm may be assigned to accidental, inadvertent, or unanticipated shifts in mood, attitude, or temperament (insecurity, defensiveness, apprehension), much more of the broad spectrum of variation is solidly linked to abuse or misuse as a defensive mechanism against the participants' getting hurt themselves. Provocative tactics qualify as a linguistic defense or disguise against imagined or projected damage.

Emotional responses to romantic breakups provide a composite sense of pain according to the type of love involved, the gender, and the coping strategy. Passionate love affairs are dissolved with great anguish, more so for clingy partners, who suffer most; for those with insecure love styles; and for men, who were less likely to feel a sense of joy or relief after dissolution than were women (Choo and Levine 1996). Blameworthy actions are scaled against evaluative standards of intent to harm, avoidability of a breach of good conduct, and offense severity with judgments of intention and magnitude of injury typically viewed as the major consideration of whether to forgive and forget (Boon and Sulsky 1997). When social actors overestimate the magnitude of their blunders, miscues, or public failures, they are likely to focus exclusively on their misfortunes, ignore situational factors that moderate observer impressions, and develop exaggerated fears of how severely they will be judged (Savitsky, Epley, and Gilovich 2001).

Although hurt feelings may arise from a seemingly endless variety of negative events, there is usually an underlying sense of personal discredit or relational devaluation at work, along with heightened sensitivity to rejection, indifference, disregard, or exclusion. It is not clear whether familiarity intensifies hurt feelings on grounds that aversive acts of devaluation are more serious in significant relations or whether harmful actions are modified in intimate relations as a buffer against hurt and harm (Snapp and Leary 2001; Vangelisti 1994). It is well documented, however, that strength of commitment is decisive as a moderator of the hidden desire for retaliation (Johnson, Caughlin, and Huston 1999). In general, hurt feelings are magnified in dark personal moods, stressful events, and drawing closer to an intimate partner (Murray et al. 2003).

Alas, the law of unintended consequences may exacerbate confounding tendencies or operate counterproductively in misguided, albeit well-intended, reparative efforts to keep others from further hurt or harm that somehow still end in one saying or doing the wrong thing. Scaled measures of hurt and harm register often in distancing movements with unspecified strivings for retaliation in the manner of justified payback. Consequently, the sheer magnitude of pain or discomfort may be initially greater than any salutary efforts to make amends. Moreover, respondents who suffer most from harmed or battered sensibilities may feel better about themselves just by making others feel worse. Put-downs, for example, are relatively effortless to construct and easy to impose as a convenient or expedient tactic to avoid being too close to other people or merely to avoid further exposure to more noxious psychological pinpricks inflicted by others upon them.

Inoculation motives also enter into the larger equation. Persons in caring relations often try to hide, conceal, or mask unpleasant truths about pressing or urgent matters that they think will only render added hurt, but acts of benevolent protection through the use of double concealments usually lead to more hurt themselves. Clearly, silent repression of undeclared disagreements and misunderstanding relating to implicit pain and sorrow may become more harmful than the unarticulated or unclaimed pain itself. Particularly troublesome is the irksome sense that hurt is inevitable when troubled participants are unable to forego retribution, make claims for restitution, or quell desire to exact reappraisal. Such empathetic failures may be quite painful, but the emotively dense recollection of troublesome events may serve to increase the magnitude of shared pain in mutual reflection of shared hurt from somewhat inexplicable or irreconcilable viewpoints.

There is something quite poignant and particularly painful about the kinds of emotional wounds and injuries that are unexpected, ongoing, and unresolved. Interactive tensions become chronically painful as interactants feel the subversive, aversive effects of increased fatigue, greater isolation, or total alienation and estrangement (Mortensen and Ayres 1994). Those who feel badly hurt are prone to respond through acts of acquiescence—yielding and displaying signs of vulnerability—whereas those who feel somewhat less hurt are more likely to respond by dismissing or discounting the importance of scaled measure of hurt and harm (Vangelisti and Crumley 1998).

In extreme cases, often repeated or highly protracted acts of verbal outrage may give way to murderous urges that stop just short of physical violence. The focal point of paramount importance in the social construction of symbolic aggression is the unremitting frustration of life's problems and concerns. Symbolic battles place interactants and observers alike at risk. Severely strained discursive practices are ultimately depleting and draining. Protracted confrontation may leave participants without sufficient personal resources to contend with the full magnitude of symbolized discontent that arises between them. Thematically, there is an escalating sense of risk and urgency concerning the impending consequences of a sustained breach of trust and care. In severe cases, a war of words may culminate in acts of physical assault. Here the sheer volatility of the linguistic environment serves both as cause and justification for multiple lines of physical coercion.

10

Repair Mechanisms

The person who seeks help through the healing word suffers not from an impersonal illness, such as an inflamed appendix, but from a distinctively personal perplexity.

—Thomas Szasz, "The Healing Word"

If we recognize the value in mediating hurt and restoring parties to a right relationship with each other, then the adversarial system should be one of our last choices. Enduring solutions and positive outcomes will far more likely occur in a non-adversarial environment. Thus, attempts to generate a "restorative" milieu have been explored to try to address this conundrum.

—Rick Sarre, "Justice as Restoration"

Disapproval must be communicated; harmful consequences must be discussed with those who have inflicted them and those who have suffered them.

—John Braithwaite, "Repentance Rituals and Restorative Justice"

Forgiveness is more than a moral matter; it is an interpersonal process that represents a possible response to wounds or injustices encountered in a relational context. How a person conceptualizes and experiences relationships, particularly more personal and intense relationships, should influence the process of reconciling a relationship disrupted by unjustly induced pain.

—Charles A. Romig and C. J. Veenstra,
"Forgiveness and Psychosocial Development"

If we want to make the world a better place, we must be prepared to construct less violent means of cohabitation and communication.

—C. David Mortensen and C. Ayres, "Symbolic Violence"

Even simple acts of miscommunication, conflict, and problematic talk can
readily reproduce the basic conditions required for disquieting or distressing
social outcomes to unfold on a larger temporal scale. The ill effects that cu-
mulate from chronic repetition of faulty human encounters do not simply
disappear because the original toxic conditions have since been eclipsed, resolved, or allowed to run their course. As a consequence, protracted arguments, disputes, conflicts, and fights defeat strong advocates long before
they are able to complete urgent, unfinished, or unresolved business and acquire renewed opportunity to get on to better things.

Unfulfilled social expectations, failed sense-making efforts, and aversive
social exchange outcomes can take a cumulative toll, with the total magnitude
of damage, deterioration, and dissolution working to undermine much of
what already has been usefully achieved. Mutual destruction of productive
human encounters often comes at a severe cost—as intangible and invisible
damage that may not be subject to repair, restoration, or reclamation. Personal accusations of alleged unfairness or wrongdoing are subject to strategic
manipulation and tactical response. Concerted academic efforts to produce
broad-based classifications of salient repair mechanisms vary greatly in terms
of general categories and specific subtypes, ranging anywhere from three to
well over a hundred options (Benoit and Drew 1997). It may be neither easy
nor effortless to categorize what transpires when things go terribly wrong or
badly astray.

Repair mechanisms are designed to open up greater insight and promote
better understanding of troubled or taxing aspects of social encounter. Restorative acts involve strategic decisions of overlooking, leveling, averaging, discounting, minimizing, or ignoring the adverse effects of multiple slights, complaints, and criticisms taken together with a corresponding release of anger,
resentment, and dampened or tempered control of retaliatory or vindictive
urges. It may take determined effort to replace antagonistic or malevolent
countertactics with a more integrated and realistic view that transforms, in-
verts, reinterprets, or recalibrates both good (desirable) and bad (undesirable)
aspects of social encounter. Negative restoration entails the pent-up release of
disaffected thought, feeling, and action. Positive restoration involves a deliberative effort to forestall, delay, or prevent the perpetration of offensive violations or major transgressions.

Repair mechanisms produce strategic measures and tactical indications of
the quality of communicative activity that has taken place. Three main sub-
sets of restorative effort can be identified across the domains of agreement,
disagreement, understanding, and misunderstanding. The first cluster of

cognitive reappraisals places far less emphasis on the search for corrective or remedial strivings and far more on the progressive realignment of the prevailing standards of social explanation themselves. Implicit repair mechanisms may operate at the fringes or lower thresholds of social cognition. Compensatory social exchanges provide considerable allowance for rhetorical appeal and ploy: personal excuse, rationalized self-exoneration, vain appeals to mitigating circumstance, defensive claims of accidental damage, denial of bad intent, or special pleading—as in a temporary cognitive impairment. The second cluster of reparative devices places far less emphasis on mutual reactions to clashing standards of individual reinterpretation and far more on the common pursuit of corrective courses of remedial action. Included are diverse mentions of spoken confession, modest concession, volitional compensation, face maintenance, reputation building, and reformulated action plans. A spirit of mutual accommodation promotes the discovery of worthy pursuits and common strivings conceptualized as the unencumbered pursuit of high ideals. The third cluster of reflective associations is more difficult to clearly specify, presumably because of the sheer density of unspoken cues that give rise to the main types of silence that precede, and the major sorts of silence that follow, each spoken utterance and each audible sign of contrition, regret, or remorse. Public silence speaks volumes, and the sheer depth of what can be experienced in the solitude of discursive silence is simply too immense for reliable calculation. Although discursive silence is rarely included in reparative taxonomic schemes, the pivotal subject nonetheless acquires critical importance in the emotional aftermath of cumulative social distress. In reflection, contrite persons can decide to mull over what goes wrong and to identify what can be recovered as something that feels fresh or new.

EXCUSE

Remedial tactics and compensatory strategies are not often used as a "one at a time" method of resolution; rather, they unfold in complex sets, blends, crossovers, and thick composite descriptions that resist precise conventional description. Conceptual and intellectual quandaries can also give rise to erratic variations and misdirected acts of rationalization and dismissive explanation, whereas emotional blind spots can just as easily lead to affective distortion, denial, and avoidance of troublesome matters that remain as yet undefined, as inexplicable, confusing, or mystifying. A passionate outpouring of clever rhetorical excuses—often covered with inflated justification, rationalization, or tortured explanation—may be used to reinvent core relational definitions, realign the scope or the scale of prevailing social boundaries, or shift directions as a compensatory means of

restoring preferred personal identities or more favored modes of social accommodation.

Underneath the surface of explicit denials of harmful intent are subtle indications of tacit strivings and unspoken urges to dilute or diminish the
scope of personal responsibility for unwelcome or adverse outcomes. Personal excuses shift common focus and shared attention away from the actual
causes and viable reasons for problematic events or unwelcome news.
Causal substitutions, deletions, omissions, and defensive responses are designed to protect the offender's sense of esteem, integrity, or ultimate worth.
Excuses provide low-risk methods of coping with misguided intentions,
faulty performances, disappointing outcomes, and negative implications that
sometimes make the respective parties feel better but only after the fact (Linden 1993). However, individual excuses for organizational outcomes are reportedly more beneficial when blended with personal explanation rather
than self-justification (Shaw, Wild, and Colquitt 2003).

As communicative devices, a litany of personal excuses often imposes an
implicit sense of obligation by the offended person to quell, encapsulate, or
suppress strong hostility, resentment, or heated anger toward those who
stand most directly accused. Personal excuses that work well defer the risk
of angry outbursts until the offender is given a chance to explain. Excuses
that function poorly qualify as unique ploys in which an offensive act is presumed but in which complete personal responsibility for the social act is not.
In the manner of a cheap trick, a rapid slight of hand, the focus of conflict
shifts away from the benign intentions of the offender to the disabling influences of other participants. Work by Schlenker, Pontari, and Christopher
(2001) underscores certain risks of excuse makers being regarded as deceptive, duplicitous, self-absorbed, or ineffectual, particularly when credibility is
low (e.g., failure to receive corroboration), when goodwill is low (e.g.,
blame failure on others), and when long-term disengagement occurs (e.g.,
postponed or failed effort to correct personal deficiency).

Personal excuses cross into uncharted territory where half-hearted justifications are assembled as distracting invocations and where offenders may
accept some small measure of responsibility for aversive or degraded social
outcomes. Gestures of pardon and apology also figure in as minor themes
based on hints, probes, and forays into multiple efforts to exempt some of
the full severity of harsh judgments by recasting offensive actions as atypical,
unusual, or not really a valid representation of what the offender may have
actually intended at the time.

Moral control requires perpetrators to regard themselves as causal agents
for harmful outcomes. Therefore, moral excuse may lead to strategic disengagement, which operates through evaluative justification where hurt and
harm are reconstructed as intended for the service of some redemptive purpose; through sanitizing descriptions by way of euphemisms and convoluted

terminology, such as minimizing or disclaiming, to make a breach of conduct look more acceptable, respectable, or benign; and through exonerating comparisons with more flagrant transgressions (Bandura 2001). Accused persons are likely, moreover, to reconstruct events in self-enhancing ways consistent with their desired images of themselves (Bahrick, Hall, and Berger 1996), even if long-term impressions work to distort recollection of what transpires as a means of justifying their current relational statuses (Karney and Frye 2002).

Those who stand accused of unfairness or wrongdoing may choose to indulge in dramatic acts of special pleading or excuse making to distance themselves from the stigma of poor performance, unfavorable circumstance, or harsh competitive situations. Denials of any wrongdoing appeal to unknown or uncertain factors; involuntary causes, conditions, and consequences of mistakes, mishaps, or miscalculations; claims of lack of power to foresee or forestall misfortune; and being forced to do what one would otherwise not say or do, as when one is under pressure, threat, or duress from external sources.

EXONERATION

Personal exoneration requires insight, empathy, and sensitivity toward those offenders who inflict needless pain and suffering on others. The process of justification also requires diminished insistence to hold the alleged offenders as solely responsible for their disquieting or disturbing actions. It is not always easy or effortless to acquire even a tentative consensus about the magnitude of violations or transgressions in question, much less to offer clear signs of contrition concerning damage or harm already imposed. Personal accounts of what goes wrong must necessarily address embedded matters of fault, failure, blame, and reproach in mitigative tactics aimed at midcourse corrections of downward spirals. Tactics of exoneration may enable offenders to maintain a positive image, minimize significant problems, and avoid retaliation (Knaus 2001). Exoneration theory posits that persons who are subject to blame and criticism may be inclined to deflect or divert attention away from acknowledged responsibility by pointing fingers, rationalizing, denying, stonewalling, filling the air with empty words, engaging in ad hominem arguments, and using other means of distorting reality.

What is not clear is how a given set of scaled offenses, violations, and transgressions may qualify as being worthy of remedial compensation. Indirect social influences revolve mainly around subtle or vague acts of hinting, humor, hugging, symbolic gestures, tacit overtures, unspoken assurances, tokens, gifts, poetic cards, or flattering remarks. Explicit social influences, in contrast, entail stronger emphasis on reconstructive modes of verbal dialogue punctuated by acts of pardon, apology, and forgiveness. Instead of a one-way transmission of reparative effort, relevant literature supports the importance of intensive dialectical engagement in a difficult and arduous process whereby all parties strive to work closely together through difficult, disturbing, or troubling matters and thereby acquire greater desire and motivation to restore favorable conditions in the foreseeable future.

Mitigative tactics also function to moderate extreme reactive tendencies and cancel out the influence of undesirable character traits. An appeal to mitigation, where successful, works to ameliorate or minimize others' hurt feelings (Hodgins, Liebeskind, and Schwartz 1996). The central decision is whether to risk direct exposure to the unknown hazards of direct confrontation or rely instead on passive methods of withdrawal and avoidance. Public acknowledgment of wrongdoing or social unfairness may well require a great deal of mutual sensitivity and reparative effort to neutralize well-established but highly disruptive feelings, thoughts, and disabling action tendencies. Redefinition of status differences, personal disparities, and marked discrepancies may foster or promote acts of, acceptance centered on greater resolve and increased tolerance of uncomfortable circumstance; selective discounting, deflation, or dilution of unfavorable relational outcomes; or open acknowledgment to facilitate better cooperation and discover the shared means to repair or restore close bonds (Harris 1997). The purpose of emotional mitigation is often to blunt the force or magnitude of mutual antagonisms in corrective interchange designed to restore equilibrium or at least save face.

Cognitive appraisals of injustice, unfairness, or wrongdoing may entail clever or devious "recalculations" and tacit "refinements" to downsize the scale or scope of offensive allegations in question. Acts of "shaving" and "leveling" occur by faint appeal to extenuating circumstances, including the often unrecognized distress of the offender. Affective distance from emotional injuries, real or imagined, may be contingent on repeated use of upward social comparisons (e.g., far worse things occur to other people) or selective indulgence in downward social comparisons (e.g., it couldn't have been all that bad). Finally, if the injured party is presumed to have deserved it, had it coming, or was merely looking for big trouble, then any alleged suffering can be recast as being somewhat warranted; hence, empathy toward the guilty party is rendered null and void. Moreover, the pursuit of making amends is one useful way to mitigate lingering feelings of guilt or shame. If there is no reason to identify with one's victim, then acts of misuse, abuse, or wrongdoing are, in effect, barely subject to reflective reappraisal. Conversely, a strong desire to make amends can be transformed into an all-inclusive moral imperative or ethical injunction—if anything can be done to restore a sense of fairness or equity in human relations, it must be done (Miceli and Castelfranchi 1998).

REFORMULATION

Acts of personal reformation require considerable reciprocal adjustment and continuous mutual accommodation, whereby troubling social affairs can be brought into sharp focus, made sense of, and then discussed from convergent viewpoints adopted by a plurality of participants (Grossen and Apotheloz 1996). Reformulated modes of social inquiry require broad tolerance of cross-checking over prior but faulty interactions that still stand in the way. Since each speaking turn modifies the significance of the preceding speaking turn, shared acts of modification, accommodation, and corrective procedure need not precede willy-nilly but rather stay on course until verbal mentions of trouble, discord, and psychic misery have all received a fair hearing, sufficient at least to vent and air unresolved grievances until a sense of relief is achieved.

Discovery of the means of settling accounts between competing advocates is the price to be paid for admission into the fray. Personal decisions to withhold relational complaints and minor irritations are indicative of a person's confidence in the ability to achieve confrontational goals; when personal expectations are relatively low, there is often greater reluctance to voice complaints or air grievances (Makoul and Roloff 1998).

Individual acts of social reframing facilitate gradual reformation of the interpretive features of faulty or ineffectual spheres of social performance. Personal acts of relational reframing entail active recognition of any salient indications of psychological distance, discomfort, and distress. The ability to reframe pressing or problematic circumstance opens up an added way to diminish the severity of destructive effects and thereby reduce estimates of others' responsibility for alleged infractions. Acts of reframing occur each time a victim ceases being resentful and stops making negative judgments toward a transgressor.

Restoration of damaged human relations requires considered abstinence from the countervailing forces of vengeance and retribution, both of which thrive on jealousy and refusal to forgive or reconsider collective enforcement of punitive verdicts. Likewise, pressing or problematic spheres of communicative difficulties may also be subject to selective and strategic recasting, whereby extreme interpretive frames—consisting of excessive features of dualism, absolute thinking, and polarized societal labels—are revised to appear somewhat more normal, mundane, or ordinary. Harsh personal assessments may be diluted, downgraded, or distanced in tacit pockets of agreement and unspoken understanding to deny or else disavow any previously held contentions. Definition slides into redefinition in the manner of calming things down, easing tensions, or making the best of a bad situation.

Indirect speech acts provide a useful alternative to an imperial or demanding style of social inquiry. Instead of engaging in a dreary litany of harsh directives, commands, or demands imposed on other persons, some assertive, forceful speakers may soften a harsh or abrasive tone by means of indirect appeals to milder inferences and warmer implications. A modest request substitutes for a harsh demand. A subdued warning dampens a rising sense of alarm. Verbal threats based on hints and innuendo minimize the risk of direct confrontation. Although acts of affirmation and acceptance are enacted explicitly, directly, and quickly, countervailing signs of rejection, disapproval, and disaffiliation are just as easily deferred, delayed, muted, or mixed with faint praise. Defensive silence thrives on acts of withholding, omitting, or concealing shared recognition of critical, competitive, or contemptuous urges. However, volatile acts taken as unforgiven and unforgivable violations of core human values may well delay or even prevent and forestall mutual expression of conciliatory gestures toward the possibilities of constructive transformation.

In the emotional aftermath of intense conflict, some offended parties decide to indulge in stark fantasies of revenge and retaliation interspersed with benign wishes for reparation or reconciliation. When close social and personal relations are ripped up or torn apart from all the cumulative conflict, antagonism, and animus, any lateral, one-way effort at relational restoration will be at risk of being dismissed or ignored as incredulous or totally absurd. When cooperative movements are not matched by any conciliatory gestures in return, an asymmetrical alignment is set up in the manner of a stalemate, which can be complex and painful to withstand for very long. To overcome the pain of breach, what matters most decisively is sufficient shared recognition of unfinished relational business that stands in the way of further constructive or progressive effort. Personal acts of unconditional resolution or restoration require strong collective resolve to explore issues of offense or violation with common focus on the recovery of mutual loss. The intangible "healing" power in the retelling of distressful life narratives includes greater insight into choices and possibilities for added inspiration or greater liberation from what would hold one back.

Key measures of relational quality are closely linked to a generous and congenial spirit of accommodation, willingness to sacrifice, and motivation to preserve conflicted or entangled social ties. Members of tightly bonded social and personal relations are likely to adopt long-term outlooks and show uncommon willingness to overlook small-scale elements of hurt and harm as a means to maximize the likelihood of preserving and conserving large-scale collaborative endeavors. A strong collective orientation promotes greater willingness to engage in beneficial endeavors with relational partners, even at a cost to oneself. As motivation to avoid direct contact with offenders recedes, the groundwork is established for diminished resolve to seek revenge or retribution.

Defensive storytelling is a telling case in point. Insofar as persons find minor violations or major transgressions rather threatening, they may be inclined to take some sting out of the discursive features of risk and threat. Since a strong surplus of negative responses may severely undermine an acquired sense of closeness and connection with significant others, the sheer severity of negativity is not infinitely tolerable. Signs of fault, futility, and failure may be restructured in restorative forums of collective scrutiny aimed at transforming negative attributes and thus diluting or reducing their potential to subvert or threaten mutual expression of positive conviction, commitment, coordination, and concern. When partners work together to diminish feelings of insecurity, weakness, and vulnerability, acts of charitable reconstruction are better able to correct severe imbalances in negative sentiments and become subject to redress or greater reapportionment.

Progressive reintegration of positive and negative personal attributes may facilitate a collective search for a better inclusive goodness of fit in relational matters, a unified conception, a holistic stance in which the meaning of individual faults and collective failures are recast into an uplifting spirit of benevolence and virtue. Defusing the magnitude of destructive impulses is crucial as a preliminary preparation for a renewal of shared hope, belief, or faith in better things to come. The offended person facilitates the process of restructuring by adopting a softer style that presses for mutual recognition of personal culpability for aversive or antagonistic actions. The case for revision is established by recasting ignored positive virtues through stylistic embellishment and compensatory commendation of praiseworthy qualities. To enhance the integrity of retelling once sad stories with a renewed happy spin, those who see themselves as victims may defuse a sense of risk and threat by constructing explanations that accent the positive or refute accusations of shortcomings and liabilities of the offenders. The credibility of an apology or pardon coincides with the scale of increased sympathy for the offender.

RECONCILIATION

Acts of reconciliation require a period of healing and recovery so that a tradition of endless quarrels, fights, disputes, and petty bickering can be settled, opposition weakened, acquiescence granted to unpleasantness, and resolution of conflicting viewpoint rendered somehow compatible or consistent (Pankhurst 1999). Substantive reconciliations take opposing valuations and reform them into something new and more worthy of emulation (Hickins 1998). A spirit of personal reconciliation reflects an abiding sense of cohesion and solidarity with kindred spirits (Irani and Funk 1998).

In a broad sense, all verbal efforts to address disturbing social questions about unacknowledged sources of hurt and harm are confessional in nature or at least have cathartic features. Unfortunately, the term *confession* is severely conflated with theological and psychological notions that are somewhat incongruent with each other. Confessions by believers of faith in an almighty deity do not unfold in the same scope or on the same scale as confessions of wrongdoing before one's fellow human beings. Still, whether under the presumption of divine intervention (supplication) or a secular sense of apology (pardon), some pervasive humane issues seem to cross over from the lofty domain of the sacred to the mundane sector of the secular and the profane. After all, acts of penitence and contrition may be couched in sacred or secular terms. Across both sweeping social domains, themes of guilt and innocence, responsibility versus refused accountability, are played out in a bewildering, contested, confluence of good causes or senseless reasons for the unwelcome imposition of intentional hurt or accidental harm.

The day of reckoning for unjustified acts of hurt and harm may be formalized around rituals of apology or pardon to validate the injured parties feelings, intuitions, perceptions, and sensibilities. An apology may lead to reconciliation, but a formal apology may not be required for acts of forgiveness to occur. The decision to forgive or pardon is something that an injured party can do privately, without any involvement, knowledge, or acknowledgment by the offender. Implicit pardons, therefore, do not necessarily result in explicit reconciliation, unless offended members receive assurance that they will not be hurt again. The offending parties who refuse to discuss degraded or discredited relational matters may preempt the basic wisp of trust required to move away from a preemptive stalemate or injunctive impasse (Fow 1996).

When compared with the use of excuse, justification, and denial, spoken apology appears to be the most effective in minimizing stressful episodes of interpersonal conflict (Metts 1994; Takaku 2001). Verbal apologies often convey a sense that a transgressor has felt guilty and suffered; therefore, part of the emotional cost has been acknowledged and accepted. Despite the difficulty of owning up to serious violations of relational sensibilities, the victim is less likely to blame or punish in return. Severe trust violations, however, are often difficult to repair, particularly when apologies for lack of competence do not successfully restore misgivings about the offender's integrity (Kim et al. 2004). Relational commitment is subject to severe tests where there is a fear of losing a partner (McCullough, Worthington, and Rachal 1997), a lack of attractive alternatives (Rusbult, Martz, and Agnew 1998), or a lack of affection, which makes it harder to frame transgressions in the best possible light (Roloff, Soule, and Carey 2001).

The refusal to forgive can also be hazardous to one's health and well-being. An unforgiving person may refuse to forgive by clinging to a cold emotion, implicating hidden resentment, bitterness, even hatred, along with lingering retaliatory motivation (Worthington and Wade 1999). Similarly, feelings of righteous indignation are linked to strong motivations to seek revenge or see harm come to the perpetrator (McCullough 2000). Personal reflections about real transgressions may accentuate unforgiving ways, such as rehearsing the offense or harboring a grudge, or may emphasize forgiving mechanisms, such as empathy with the propensity to grant acceptance. Unforgiving responses have been associated with higher elevations in systolic and diastolic blood pressure, longer recovery time from physiological stress (Berry and Worthington 2001), and diminished closeness (McCullough, Worthington, and Rachal 1997). A study by Maltby and Day (2004) suggests that a neurotic defensive style constitutes a significant barrier to genuine forgiveness in core matters of interpersonal conflict. Furthermore, instantaneous forgiveness for harmful transgressions may not stand the test of time required to produce significant prosocial change from revenge to benevolence (McCullough, Fincham, and Tsang 2003).

Acts of forgiveness entail valued decisions to forego retribution for hurtful conduct and relinquish claims for restitution. Forgiveness in committed relations facilitates a spirit of recovery, hastens the demise of invisible wounds, and prepares the afflicted parties for a greater measure of renewal and regeneration (Montiel 2000). Individuals are most likely to forgive and forget in bonded relations that are characterized by closeness, commitment, satisfaction, and empathy for their offenders (McCullough 2000). One critical precondition entails a willingness to subdue anger, rage, or malice, and thereby defeat lingering desires to exact reprisal or compensation. Equally critical is sufficient reflective engagement to uncover one's own psychological defenses; confront disquieting anger; realize the impact of adverse outcomes; submit to the larger possibility of a change of heart; and demonstrate willingness to reframe an offender's injurious conduct by transforming troublesome events into a more inclusive, integrated, and constructive framework spelled out in cohesive gestures and communal conciliations.

The act of letting go of bitterness and hate may be simply straightforward or excruciatingly prolonged, depending on whether the process of restoration is complete or incomplete and whether all things in question are presumed to be worthy of forgiveness. Studies of reconciliation after marital separation, for instance, demonstrate the hazards implicit in vain attempts to rescue close bonds from threatening or troubled collaborative circumstances in which nothing is ever settled and virtually everything is in jeopardy.

While spoken acts of forgiveness may be a precursor or consequence of a renewed spirit of relational reconciliation, the willingness to pardon or forgive seems to be necessary for true reconciliation to occur (Enright and North 1998). Nonetheless, laudatory accounts of the transforming power of pardon, apology, and forgiveness fail to recognize that to forsake retribution an offended party may face a greater measure of transgressor compliance but also may be accompanied by a sense of indebtedness, obligation, or guilt over the unstated implications of receiving an unsolicited gift. For without the transgressors feeling genuine remorse over harms ensued, inequity distress may be low among those who feel no responsibility for their unjust acts.

Acts of hollow forgiveness involve an outward display of contrition without an inward conviction; conversely, an act of expedient or silent forgiveness entails inward acknowledgment without an outward manifestation (Baumeister, Exline, and Sommer 1999). An act of fake forgiveness represents the possible abandonment of true or intrinsic forgiveness when conscious choices lead offended individuals to give up legitimate claims to retaliation and substitute conciliatory responses (Zechmeister and Romero 2002). Passage of time is a strategic aspect of genuine forgiveness. Reductions in avoidance or revenge, as well as increased benevolence, not only take time but also require a passage of time for major transgressions to be overcome with greater forbearance toward the perpetrator (McCullough, Fincham, and Tsang 2003). Intrinsic forgiveness, under optimum conditions, confers strength, healing, and well-being to the perpetrator and renewed commitment to the restoration of intimate relations (Karremans, Van Lange, and Ouwerkerk 2003). The process of forgiveness culminates in the power to overcome anger, antagonism, and animus (Boleyn-Fitzgerald 2002).

Salutary social outcomes associated with contrite acts of pardon, apology, or forgiveness include uplifting affective experience (joy and relief) combined with a renewed desire or sense of obligation not to hurt another person again (Gassin 1998). Relief from the disabling effects of hurt and harm affords an added measure of opportunity to regain trust, reconcile, diminish guilt, and achieve closure for disturbing or painful events. Morally relevant affective consequences include a deeper sense of empathy for injured persons, subtraction of negative elements, and purposive addition of positive features (Freedman 1998). Invisible wounds recede as offender and victim undertake a difficult task to take the well-being of each party into full account. Optimistic and generous narratives rely on the transforming power of bad things being turned into good things.

UNSPOKEN RESTORATION

The technical literature on face or image restoration may be justly faulted on two fronts. First, the captivating notion of sacrificial forgiveness is elevated to a purified position of sovereignty and ultimate privilege and then treated as a master category in the conceptualization of conflict resolution and peacemaking typologies. Any brave soul who would follow each one of the twenty separate soul-searching stages of one charitable model to help people forgive (Enright and North 1998) would surely qualify for sainthood at the end. Although it is necessary to give the usefulness of forgiveness its proper due, no good cause is served by constructing puritanical, romantic, or sentimental versions of what is required or what is actually at stake. Second, there is insufficient recognition of the enormous heuristic power of finding solace and refuge in the protective aura of dialogical silence, the unspoken and unspeakable depth of entangled social circumstances.

Sound permeates exteriors and penetrates interiors, whereas discursive silence punctuates the ebb and flow of verbal sequences and implied social meanings. Participants and observers alike may take in the sound and the silence in direct proportion to their capacity and willingness to defer the production of talk for an unspecified period. The sheer density of silence is a muted expression of the cumulative burdens of all that is left unsaid. One who cannot tolerate a wide open space for public silence is not apt to thrive on the routine production of talk. Those who make no provision for talk leave no room for silence either. Offended persons who feel great antagonism may simply refuse to forgive or pardon a major transgression on grounds that it is neither necessary nor justified. Most offended parties, however, discover that even a small measure of silence provides comfort and solace from the harsh effects of careless, abusive, or reckless talk.

The power of unspoken gestures may be sustained through silencing mechanisms to elicit passive conformity. Verbal maneuvers of trivialization (Clair 1998), neutralization (Deetz 1992), pseudocommunication (Mortensen 1997), and noncommunicative silence (Jaworski 1993) are tactical devices to silence, subvert, or disable in advance subordinated voices of protest against oppressive social forces. The courage to break through oppressive silence requires not only a renewed search for names for silenced events but also explicit validation so nameless harmful social activities do not remain unseeable or unsayable (Cockburn 1991).

Participants who must struggle with a cyclical proliferation of strong disagreements and serious misunderstandings are often compulsive and obsessive about talking things out and, at the same time, impatient and intolerant of considered personal decisions to remain silent but vigilant. In such troubled social settings, the protagonists may be inclined to spew forth a torrent of words and gestures designed to make things better while only succeeding in making them even worse. Exclusive reliance on verbal cures for primordial wounds serves unwittingly to perpetuate extreme and uneven imbalances in the synthesis of sound, sense, and silence. To be fair, excessive silence by one party is no antidote for loquacity by any other party.

When confronted with chronic episodes of verbal misuse or the greater threat of physical abuse, the decision to remain silent appears to have a number of salutary benefits. The most obvious is that one party, at least temporarily, does not reproduce or perpetuate a series of intrusive acts of verbal coercion by other people. Even brief deferral of retaliatory or defensive talk provides a moment to calm down and think things through more carefully before speaking. Most accounts of physical coercion are preceded by sustained verbal outbursts that taint, taunt, and tempt acts of vengeful reciprocation. Finally, whenever severely agitated antagonists insist on unleashing a torrent of verbal abuse on unwelcome or resistant subjects, the choice of offensive words, insulting gestures, and their toxic effects cannot be taken back. Once the damage is done, the damage *is* done. So the real question is whether there is anything left to be reclaimed.

Stonewalling provides a poignant case in point. It occurs, for good reason, almost exclusively in chronic personal disagreements and serious mutual misunderstandings about which frequent quarrels, disputes, semantic quibbles, put-downs, slights, picks, and digs can become the order of the day. Tactical aspects of stonewalling implicate far more than simplified and stereotypic notions of antagonists who walk out of the room, refuse to make amends, and never speak again. To the contrary, decisions to withhold subversive speech occur during contested episodes of verbal wrangling and nonverbal disputation. Unlike other domains of discursive relevance, individual justifications for stonewalling rarely revolve around a single theme or master trope. To appreciate the rich texture of the diverse explanatory lexicons at work with regard to repair mechanisms, it is useful to examine unspoken frictions that register on a moment-by-moment basis.

Silence neutralizes the flow of disturbing talk in thin slices and small durations. Most common are fleeting choices to stop talking, but there are many subtle variations on the general theme. Say almost nothing. Clam up. Let others babble. Hush up and keep quiet. Ignore false allegations that might be viewed as self-incriminating. Skim topics briefly. Refuse to confront urgent or pressing issues. Leave things as they are. Do not pay attention. Let attention wander. Do not listen or maintain eye contact. Pretend not to have a clue. Stay passive. Refuse to talk until the worst is over. If all else fails, stop trying. Overlook things. Pretend not to notice. Refuse to open up but be quick to close down. Back off quickly. Don't put up a fuss. Keep things bottled up inside. Hesitate. Be cautious. Minimize time for interaction. Keep it short. Don't let anything get too deep. Tone things down. Give one-sentence answers. Don't ask questions. Refuse to elaborate. Pretend nothing goes wrong. Rarely ask for input. Adapt a muted slant. Hold back. Refuse to listen—indifference is the safest way out. Keep conversation as short as possible. Never address serious concerns in a direct or straightforward way. Rely instead on subtle hints, unspoken cues, and hope that things do not get any worse than they already are. Act like nothing is wrong. Withdraw into your own little world. It will not make a difference in the end. If all else fails, hang up the phone, walk out the door, and leave the scene. At all costs, push others away. Shut things down and walk away.

Grow apart. Do not look back. Stay away at all costs. Sometimes unspeakable relations are the only way to go.

Composite silence in distorted, disrupted, and disgruntled accounts of personal disagreement and mutual misunderstanding are neither a necessary nor a sufficient condition for reparative success. Most intangible pain, suffering, injury, and psychic misery unfolds when people choose to disagree vigorously and badly misunderstand each other at the same time. In effect, there is far too much to repair or restore, and excessive reliance on tactical silence is a mere palliative, nothing more. Linguistic constructions of episodic and chronic episodes of misconstruction and miscommunication are subversive in subtle ways that can make it difficult to define, acknowledge, work through, and resolve on terms acceptable to each witness. Conversely, consensual dialectical tensions between modes of speaking and listening are less problematic and, hence, less necessary to reframe, repair, reform, or restore.

Respondent accounts document the social application of an ingenious set of silent tactics to quell verbal outbursts and thereby minimize further damage to contested subjects or deteriorated subject matter. Some stop talking to provide temporary relief from the endless proliferation of verbal entanglements and escalating spirals of reactive negativity. Others seem to be more adroit in the clever manipulation of hot, sensitive, or touchy subjects: change the topic; shift the tone; pretend not to hear unwanted speech; or simply refuse to address vindictive allegations or relational vulnerabilities, limitations, and shortcomings that are much too painful to confront directly. Still others find solace in the refusal to perpetuate a litany of false accusations or one-sided blame.

Detached subjects are likely to cling stubbornly to a variation of what Kierkegaard (1962) describes as a state or condition of *shutupness*. More passive use of tactical silence may be utilized in the service of aspirations toward withdrawal, avoidance, or suspension of degraded or discredited activities. Protracted silence occurs most often in deeply troubled relations where everything has fallen apart and there is nothing more to say, or nothing more can be said, to make any difference in the end. A state of sustained or protracted silence may involve periodic or permanent disavowal or dissolution of relational ties. What follows are clusters of representative themes taken together with diverse sentiments about what has gone wrong and what, if anything, can still be done to make things right.

Stop Talking

S/O stopped talking because one party would always bring the other party down—so now they are not even friends anymore.

S/O caused so much deep sadness that they stopped talking altogether.

Hang Up Phone

S/O leave phone conflicts unresolved because either party will just quickly hang up on the other party for no apparent cause or reason.

S/O talk, but when they have had enough crap, they hang up the phone.

S/O avoided discussion of painful issues—so one party had enough of it and suddenly hung up the phone and never called back.

S/O like to unload on each other over the phone; they say exactly what and how they feel, and then either one will quickly hang up phone.

Mum

S/O are rendered speechless, dumbfounded.

S/O tell each other over and over again to keep "your own trap shut."

S/O respond to arguments in the exact same way—they both rely on the silent treatment.

S/O used to talk about everything, but recently they decided not to talk to one another at all.

S/O explode at each other, and then they both pretend that nothing happened, until the next big trauma hits.

Change Subject

S/O try to change hot topics as quickly as possible.

S/O will not bring up certain things, whereby the discussion is over before it can even start.

Remain Unspoken

S/O know some things are better left unsaid.

S/O have engaged in many violent fights, and then after each one they both pretend that nothing really happened.

S/O grumble and gripe—if one gets an honor, the other won't talk for almost a month.

S/O avoid touchy topics with hurtful outcomes and charged consequences.

S/O blow small things all out of proportion, then both parties feel the intense need to avoid or minimize even casual interaction.

S/O dance around touchy subjects, so they must infer what is meant by what is left unsaid.

S/O get upset, ignore each other, and refuse to listen but rather tune each other out.

S/O look out in space or try to change the subject as soon as possible.

Unspoken Refusals

S/O refuse to deal with any serious controversy; they prefer to just exist in their own way and leave it at that.

S/O never talk about major problems and unresolved concerns, which makes the climate of discussion that much more disagreeable.

S/O talk so harshly—S feels uncomfortable, threatened, a cornered animal who refuses to talk.

S/O misunderstand each other due to lack of communication and refusal to say anything about it.

S/O harbor deep personal resentments—they don't speak during meals over their unresolvable differences.

S/O keep things bottled up inside, withdraw, and have to drag the truth out of each other later.

S/O shut each other out, put up a wall, and refuse to listen to what the other says.

S/O know, due to faulty communication, that much remains unsaid, way too much.

S/O never discuss their bitter fights or their silent spells in the emotional aftermath.

S/O kept things inside and usually didn't work them out.

S/O find interaction turns into a battle of wills, and neither ends up changing anything.

S/O talk about trivial things but do not respond much to what each one really has to say.

Chilling Effects

S/O talk only about trivia, and they disagree constantly in an icy, cold, tense atmosphere.

S/O are hostile, cold, brief, without mention of anything much in depth, and they don't even know why.

S/O are angry about things from the past they haven't confronted once.

S/O leave angry feelings unspoken, give dirty looks, avoid eye contact, and slam doors.

S/O don't say anything, turn up music, and drown out what the other is saying.

S/O don't talk about anything, and so they can't really solve anything.

Shutupness

S/O both say "shut up" as the only way they each know how to be quiet and leave one another all alone.

S/O have short, snappy tempers, take offense quickly, and either one will tell the other to "shut up."

S/O find there is a lot of times where either one just gives up and shuts his mouth.

S/O have too much baggage after years of torment to talk, except about the weather.

S/O eventually gave up broaching new topics—they now go about their own routines.

S/O find that it doesn't bother them if they don't talk at all during the course of the day.

S/O talk, so surface, no meaning; they seem to push away and not say anything.

S/O sometimes make each other so angry that they don't care to talk for days at a time.

S/O find small talk consists of "shut up" or "I don't care."

S/O cut each other off; both use a nasty voice to simply say "shut up."

Withdrawal/Resignation

S/O initiate shallow talk, give short replies, and then stop trying.

S/O make countless efforts to see eye to eye, then they just give up.

S/O construct a void from a pervasive sense of not listening to what each one had to say.

S/O usually did not manage to say anything real, but when they did, it was pointless anyway.

S/O drift apart into a limbo where many things go unsaid, many others go unnoticed.

S/O walk out often—they no longer want to waste time trying to figure each other out.

S/O don't feel they are getting anywhere, so they don't bother anymore.

S/O find that emptiness and shallowness mean that separation is imminent.

S/O conclude that there is simply nothing there and that there is nothing left.

S/O never seem to get feelings across—that's why they don't see each other anymore.

S/O hold back from telling true feelings because they don't know how each will react.

S/O dodge questions, avoid controversy, guard talk, and then slowly stop making effort.

S/O seriously misunderstood, and now avoid, each other and refuse to give each other the time of day.

S/O find that hurt feelings lead both parties to avoid direct interaction altogether just to avoid more pain.

S/O find that once they cut off all direct contact, it can be very difficult to restart.

S/O have learned not to talk about their own opinions because they just cause more problems.

S/O talk, but it is bullshit, so uneasiness rises, and leaving the scene is a relief.

S/O realize it's a lost cause, shake their heads, and give up.

S/O are just polite enough to get by.

Suspend/Avoid

S/O believe that if you ignore problems, they will go away.

S/O can go for weeks without speaking—neither one wants to give in or get back in touch.

S/O find things get so bad that they have to avoid conversation at all cost.

S/O avoid daily conversation as much as they can because it is really no fun at all.

S/O get so tired of dodging the truth, fooling around, that they don't want to talk anymore.

S/O find that avoiding anything by simple communication can be highly desirable.

S/O blame, yell, throw television remote, freak out, walk out, wait days, and then work it out.

Shunning

S/O live together, but currently they are not speaking to each other.

S/O can go for long periods without talking and then, only briefly in small talk.

S/O have periods of not speaking for a month over something small, trivial, or stupid.

S/O fight, end up in a yelling fiasco, and there is no interaction for days at a time.

S/O talk only under duress—there have been long spans where they wouldn't speak for months at a time.

S/O know much work needs to be done before they can interact again.

S/O think it's a sad situation—they are not soul sisters but rather eternal adversaries.

S/O have had so many sharp disagreements that they have gone several years without speaking once.

Exit Tactics

S/O don't interact—when one walks in the room, the other walks out.

S/O start out with civil talk, soon they both get annoyed, and one or the other will run of out the room in sheer frustration.

S/O slam doors, walk out of the room, without ever offering even a hint of explanation.

S/O become angry, get in a match, and end up walking out of the room over bad attitudes.

S/O walk away from heated conversations because they usually are so charged with intense emotion.

S/O allowed small conflict to build up—all blew up at once—they have never talked since.

S/O both want the last word—they end up slamming doors, driving off, or locking doors.

S/O fight, yell, accuse, make demands, and then they both storm out of the room.

S/O say something, then suddenly, to their surprise, one gets angry, yells, and stomps off.

S/O hardly talk because they fear the other will leave right away.

S/O can't stand even brief disagreements; either one will just get up and leave.

A litany of chronic disagreements and serious misunderstandings in close human relations are likely to promote, foster, preserve, and maintain a contentious atmosphere punctuated with awkward and misaligned silence and insufficient opportunity to give it a rest or just be quiet. After all, a stream of incessant talk leaves little room for silence as a counterpoint of relief, renewal, and redirection. Serious imbalances in the ebb and flow of sound, sense, and silence give rise to any number of conundrums, contradictions, and quandaries. It is not all that unusual for rigid and inflexible persons to talk and gesture their way into a stance of fixed or static positions from which one party does virtually all of the talking and the other party does virtually all of the listening. When the submissive member does attempt to say something, words are brushed aside, dismissed, ignored, or ruled out. Talk on the offensive side appears largely to be impatient, frantic, hectic, and demanding. Oddly, what little face-to-face interaction does occur is a mere symbolic cover-up for private ruminations and tacit realizations rendered mute as having no distinct expressive or communicative value. Ruled out is the very possibility for mutual discovery and recognition that one member cannot grasp the adverse effects of his or her own behavior on others nor see what others can see, hear, touch, and move but never say.

An aura of uncomfortable silence, hesitation, reticence, and apprehension can contribute greatly to a muted but tense social atmosphere of shallow and superficial silence where participants are at a loss for words with nothing to say about much of anything that transpires. Silent discomfort is unnerving as well as annoying. It is not just a matter of avoiding risky subjects or hot and heavy subjects that seems to bring one party down. Sometimes saying nothing is better than sounding stupid. If garbled talking leads nowhere or falls short of the mark, no one can win, and depression and sadness may enter into a decision to forfeit opportunity for further talk. Where talking can be painful, silence can be construed as a painkiller. Any sudden urge to unload pent-up talk must be suppressed, even at the cost of smoldering, simmering hostility.

The nostalgic notion of silence as absence or lacuna is patently false because it takes hard work, considerable focus, and concerted cognitive effort to be silent and to *stay* silent in noisy social settings with strong conformity demands for everyone to say something, anything; to then say something in return; and to keep the conversation going. To stay absolutely mum is to leave problems, concerns, and pressing issues unspoken, as domains of tacit knowledge both untested and uninformed by mutual and multiple tests of verbal confirmation, verification, or replication.

In the relevant transcript accounts, there are many droning references to guarded talk, watching what one says, refusing to speak out or having to keep one's own mouth shut, withdrawing into unsettled lapses of total silence, a source of mere presence, and much redundant and mindless use of the silent treatment. It becomes easier and easier for the disconnected and the disaffiliated to sit in a room, stare into space, and not say a single word no matter what. Some claim to be speechless, dumfounded, or unable to speak out or address what transpires. Vacuous and vacant styles of expression and response aim for inertia or status, a linguistic vacuum inscribed only as a feeble unspoken protest. Sometimes, even short answers are too much to ask.

Chilling effects emanate from disgruntled or protracted spirals of personal negativity with a distinct edge, an undercurrent of tension that never goes completely away. Participants who seek emotional distance are usually described as being aloof, remote, frozen, and cold, and they often prefer to talk mostly in grunts and sighs as a symbolic protest that further talk is futile and empty, a void stripped of conviction and credibility. Mumbling or mouthing words barely speak for themselves. Personal strivings to maintain a detached stance of withdrawal and resignation do not require much more than shallow, disjointed talk consisting of short replies, lulls, breaks, and dodged questions. The effort to talk is presumed to be a waste of time, pointless, and not worth the effort. Even so, it would not change a thing: Slowly stop making effort. No good can come of it. Better to crawl into a shell. Stay in limbo.

Shunning is not uncommon or lacking in redeeming value. In fact, when all else fails, a protective code of silence may be rigidly enforced as a protest or defense of last resort. In other terms, some forms of shunning may be self-imposed as a strict refusal to say anything at all, not as a matter of expediency, but rather one of principle. Anger, sadness, and fear each play a part in the larger unspoken equation. Anger may be driven underground by means of suppressive or repressive tactics. Likewise, intense sadness may be endured in total solitude. Finally, unspoken fears may arise in disquieting but nameless, uncertain, or unknown factors and thus become an intolerable encumbrance in someone else's life. Some participants manage to struggle with what they cannot define or articulate—what lingers as inexplicable or strange bodily discomfort without a clue as to cause, rhyme, or reason. Unarticulated concerns often cluster around underlying implications of anticipated or imagined forms of direct antagonistic or divisive social encounters. Here one central theme stands out—fear of not being able to make sense of one's experience while in the presence of others.

Silent dress rehearsals may indicate tacit and anxious effort to wait for the right time and place to bear witness to some as yet unspoken aspects of one's lived circumstance before others. Of course, one may wait in total silence for something to happen that never does. In this sense silence is literally without end. Here one waits in silence for the fulfillment of unspecified potentials never realized in manifest form. Shunning, therefore, covers a multitude of petty sins and minor infractions along with lingering feelings of shame, guilt, or remorse relating to the inability of some persons to live with the way things are rather than insist on the way they should be—in the manner of an unspoken communal fraud. Here a vow to shun must do double duty. Enforced silence may neutralize, subvert, repress, thwart, or destroy some measure of expressive freedom or interpretive response of someone else.

Uncomfortable silence is often a sign of troubling things to come. Particularly striking is the telling effect of protracted or entrenched silence as an unspoken gesture of a diminished sense of weakened intentions, resignation, withdrawal, and retreat. Where disagreement and entangled silence coalesce, relief matters often far more than does restitution. Withdrawal into the depths of the unspeakable and the unspoken may well have confessional significance. Say no more. It is no use. Why make matters worse? There is no hope. Fate is no longer within our grasp. There is no way to avoid all manner of contention, disagreement, disagreeableness, drawn-out disputes, mutual mystification, inarticulate sources of pain and suffering, recycled blame, frustration, or offense. The massive influence of endless disjunctions, discredit, and disqualification can take your breath away, leave you speechless, flabbergasted, with nothing to say. Many hidden truths may be kept in secret. Destructive silence resembles a state of paralysis, one subverted, sandbagged, or disabled—regardless of reason, sense, or further risk of danger and detriment.

SILENCE AS SANCTUARY

Within the production of discourse and dialogue, there must be some room for each participant to move fluidly from one state or mood to any other. As one starts to speak, silence is broken. As one ceases to speak, silence is restored. The desire for silence is complete only when one lives or inhabits the auditory silence in the manner of an embrace, a source of primordial relief from prevailing social pressures to fill the air with groundless or meaningless talk. When one feels inarticulate, as in the case of a loss for words, silence provides an alternative to the frustration of not being able to speak clearly, fluently, or distinctively. Provisional lapses into silence and inattention afford momentary escape from the confluence of sights, sounds, and signals of everyday realities that are around. An appropriate conclusion is that silence is a valuable personal resource. It allows any language user to conceal or hide given facts or segments of private discourse within the wider context of what transpires. What one shields in the silence is as open as the nature of the type of world one inhabits. Silent preparation, mental dress rehearsals, may indicate effort to wait for the right time and the right place to bear witness to some as yet unspoken aspects of one's lived circumstances.

Participants employ two different profiles of sound and silence discrimination. Major narrative themes demonstrate that the organization of silence in the d/m sections is rarely comfortable, supportive, or reassuring. Instead, stressed and uptight participants struggle and strive to use tactical silence as a small-scale reparative mechanism but to no avail, for two main reasons. First, far too much damage, pain, and injury have usually occurred from a tradition of disagreement and misunderstanding for any preferred alignment of sound and silence to make much difference in the end. Here, silence is a necessary but not sufficient source of corrective for reparative issues. Second, far less damage, pain, and injury usually occur from a tradition of agreement and understanding so that fewer unspoken reparations are required. In effect, consensus silence has less work to do. Consequently, the compositional features of sound, sense, and silence work together much better during convergent movements, both by comparison with mentions in the d/m sections and by intrinsic features associated with strong personal achievement and social accomplishment in the a/u sections. Thematically, uncomfortable, icy, cold silence is reproduced, replicated, and reformulated in divisive settings almost as a matter of whim, often on a daily basis. Chronic episodes of disagreeableness, misunderstanding, and misaligned turn taking are symptomatic of adverse conditions only partially amenable to shared reparative efforts.

By contrast, the mix of agreeableness, understanding, and silence/sound patterns are far less symptomatic and far more indicative of constructive connections with sufficient silence for each participant to gain in the end. Based on one-word search procedures (silence/silent) in the a/u sections, it is clear that amenable participants are usually clear about what transpires in silence and what the organization of silence expresses in return. Consensual respondents underscore several major themes. Most frequently mentioned are a series of consistently applied exclusionary considerations. Great pleasure is evident in reciprocal claims of no uncomfortable silence, no disturbing unspoken acts or episodes, and no intolerance of silence in what transpires.

The restorative value of silence, quietude, and the unspoken domains registers in patterns of direct contact and deep engagement that are relaxed, silent, and easy to take because the participants feel comfortable just hanging out together. Where there is no damage, there is nothing to repair. Some respondents greatly enjoy the opportunity for silence in conversation because they like to think about things carefully that they do want to talk about and have nothing to say until they have a chance to think things through. Some respondents are so comfortable with intimacy that they are willing to invest time and effort to reach the point that they can go for indefinite long periods without thinking twice about talking and not feel awkward at all. Some profess strong faith in the renewal of viable human encounters where direct communication always takes place whether the participants are talking or not. Some intimates may want very much to remain silent but will talk freely if someone else feels it necessary. The vitality of silent periods is tested when participants can speak their minds at any time to keep differences of opinion from turning into futile debates.

Constructive silence helps people reconcile differences of opinion and reach effective compromise. Even the occasional urge to fight is neutralized with lots of silence, such that neither party says anything and both are willing to drop contested issues. Furthermore, the depth of mutual understanding is a crucial factor in the acquisition of fluid, clear, and coherent turn-taking signals. There is also frequent mention of individuals who are able to speak in calm and reassuring voices and allow others to share thoughts and feelings without someone else cutting into something. When moments of silence do occur, those participants are usually not anxious to fill the silence with words. Some profess to know each other so well that they feel they know intuitively when to speak or remain silent and fully present for each other. Under ideal conditions, the participants are never short of words and gestures, and each can always talk about various matters; yet even during silent periods, they manage to understand each other so well.

Uncomfortable silence is often accompanied by greater difficulties in making sense of what transpires. Conversely, comfortable silence is often accompanied by relatively fewer difficulties in making sense of what transpires.

Constructive expansive silence protects against unwelcome imposition of verbal injury, hurt, or harm. It also promotes greater resilience and efficacy insofar as it prepares for further scrutiny of whatever harm may be incurred along the way. Silence is sufficient. Silence is compelling. Silence, therefore, is an important source of renewal, rediscovery, and redirection in resilient human encounters.

Insofar as the boundaries of discursive silence by one source may facilitate or promote a greater range of expressive freedom by any other, the tension between the unspoken and the spoken is apt to dissolve. Conversely, as the discursive silence of one makes it more difficult for other social actors to express themselves freely, the strain between the unspoken and the spoken resurfaces. In acts of appeasement, the sequences of punctuated silence are tolerated and sustained within a larger framework of an unfolding, incomplete, and unfinished dialogue. Individuals adopt styles of personal presentation that make it more or less difficult to facilitate the transition from spoken acts to unspoken urges. Consequently, acts of appeasement require a fluid and flexible stance of adaptive interaction, a process analogous to breathing deeply in and out but also akin to a mutually sustained urge to go with rather than against the flow of what transpires. Maximum expressive freedom is often accompanied by minimum interpretive resistance. Matters of personal efficacy, status, prestige, credibility, and power are not given or taken as being self-evident but rather represent valuations to be reconstructed and renegotiated in future encounters.

In the final analysis, silence may offer a sense of human sanctuary, but this condition is rare and precious. Nonetheless, there is an encompassing sphere of silence in which the ideal culminates in the real and whatever is then brought to light. For once, there is no tension between individual intent and unforeseen circumstance. Through shared struggle to integrate, the ordinary is transformed into the extraordinary. Individual aspirations and communal obligations come together, fuse, congeal, and coalesce in a spirit of restoration and renewal.

Under optimal conditions, the participants in question are in a position to maintain a healthy level of coherent interchange that permits each one to feel safe and secure. This most significant type of communicative achievement reaches a point of culmination where individual light can become a common source of collective enlightenment. What is felt, thought, said, and done reinforces the presumption that this *is* the best of all possible worlds. Nothing that is expressed is found wanting—no sense of unfulfillment, deprivation, or deficit. For once again, if even for a short time, all is right with a world revealed in translucent terms. Here, the respective parties are free from the usual clatter, noise, din, friction, strife, and strain of everyday life just long enough to make each one yearn for things to be exactly as they are.

The human world is once again discovered as a sanctuary, our early home. An inclusive sense of spiritual silence invokes renewed faith in human possibilities to overcome whatever would resist or hold one source or another back. The human world, once again, is transformed, spontaneous, fresh, and new. The risk of slippage and miscommunication is taken in stride, and free speech and interpretive responses flourish. In this manner, human beings constitute the ultimate resources to enable themselves not only to survive but to prosper socially without losing a sense of wonder and awe. In the primordial sense, silence always has the last word.

References

Agnew, C. R., P. A. M. Van Lange, C. E. Rusbult, and C. A. Langston. 1998. Cognitive interdependence: Commitment and the mental representation of close relationships. *Journal of Personality and Social Psychology* 74:939–55.

Ahmed, S. 1996. Beyond humanism and postmodernism: Theorizing a feminist practice. *Hypatia* 11:71–94.

Airenti, G., B. C. Bara, and M. Colombetti. 1993. Failures, exploitations, and deceits in communication. *Journal of Pragmatics* 20:303–26.

Aldous, J., and R. F. Ganey. 1999. Family life and the pursuit of happiness: The influence of gender and race. *Journal of Family Issues* 20:155–80.

Alicke, M. D. 2000. Culpable control and the psychology of blame. *Psychological Bulletin* 126:556–74.

Ambady, N., and H. M. Gray. 2002. On being sad and mistaken: Mood effects on the accuracy of thin-slice judgments. *Journal of Personality and Social Psychology* 83:947–61.

Amirkhan, J. H. 1998. Attributions as predictors of coping and distress. *Personality and Social Psychology Bulletin* 24:1006–18.

Andersen, P. A., and L. K. Guerrero. 1998. Principles of communication and emotion in social interaction. In *Handbook of communication and emotion*, ed. P. A. Andersen and L. K. Guerrero, 49–96. San Diego, CA: Academic Press.

Anderson, C. J. 2003. The psychology of doing nothing: Forms of decision avoidance result from reason and emotion. *Psychological Bulletin* 120:139–68.

Anderson, R. L., and C. D. Mortensen. 1967. Logic and marketplace argumentation. *Quarterly Journal of Speech* 53:143–51.

Anolli, A., R. Ciceri, and M. G. Infantino. 2002. Behind dark glasses: Irony as a strategy for indirect communication. *Genetic, Social, and General Psychology Monographs* 128:1–21.

Aporal, X. B., and C. E. Rusbult. 1998. Standing in my partner's shoes: Partner perspective taking and reactions to accommodative dilemmas. *Personality and Social Psychology Bulletin* 24:927–48.

Archer, M. S. 2000. *Being human: The problem of agency*. New York: Cambridge University Press.

Armstrong, T. G., G. Heideman, K. J. Corcoran, B. Fisher, K. L. Medina, and J. Schafer. 2001. Disagreement about the occurrence of male-to-male female intimate partner violence: A qualitative study. *Family and Community Health* 24:55–75.

Arndt, J., and J. Greenberg. 1999. The effects of a self-esteem boost and mortality salience on responses to boost relevant and irrelevant worldview threats. *Personality and Social Psychology Bulletin* 25:1331–41.

Arnston, P. H., C. D. Mortensen, and M. W. Lustig. 1980. Predispositions toward verbal behavior in task-oriented interaction. *Human Communication Research* 6:239–52.

Atkins, D. C., N. S. Jacobson, and D. H. Baucom. 2001. Understanding infidelity: Correlates in a national random sample. *Journal of Family Psychology* 15:735–49.

Aune, R. K., S. Metts, and A. S. Ebesu-Hubbard. 1998. Managing the outcomes of discovered deception. *Journal of Social Psychology* 138:677–89.

Bahrick, H. P., L. K. Hall, and S. A. Berger. 1996. Accuracy and distortion in memory for high school grades. *Psychological Science* 7:265–71.

Bandura, A. 2000. Exercise of human agency through collective efficacy. *Current Directions in Psychological Science* 9:75–78.

———. 2001. Social cognitive theory: An agentic perspective. *Annual Review of Psychology* 52:1–26.

Bandura, A., G. V. Caprara, C. Barbaranelli, C. Pastorelli, and C. Regalia. 2001. Sociocognitive self-regulatory mechanisms governing transgressive behavior. *Journal of Personality and Social Psychology* 80:125–35.

Bandura, A., and E. A. Locke. 2003. Negative self-efficacy and goal effects revisited. *Journal of Applied Psychology* 88:87–99.

Barash, D. P. 2002. Evolution, males, and violence. *Chronicle of Higher Education*, May 24, B7.

Barnett, O. W., and C. Y. Lee. 1997. Gender differences in attributions of self-defense and control in interpartner aggression. *Violence against Women* 3:462–82.

Barnett, R. 2000. *Realizing the university in an age of supercomplexity*. Buckingham, England: Society for Research into Higher Education/Open University Press.

Barrett, W. 1978. *The illusion of technique: A search for meaning in a technological civilization*. Garden City, N.Y.: Anchor Press.

Barron, K. E., and J. M. Harackiewicz. 2001. Achievement goals and optimal motivation: Testing multiple goal models. *Journal of Personality and Social Psychology* 80:706–22.

Batson, C. D., and E. Shannon. 1997. Perspective taking: Imagining how another feels versus imagining how you would feel. *Personality and Social Psychology Bulletin* 23:751–59.

Batson, C. D., E. R. Thompson, and H. Chen. 2002. Moral hypocrisy: Addressing some alternatives. *Journal of Personality and Social Psychology* 83:330–39.

Batson, C. D., E. R. Thompson, and G. Seuferling. 1999. Moral hypocrisy: Appearing moral to oneself without being so. *Journal of Personality and Social Psychology* 77:525–37.

Bauman, Z. 1997. *Postmodernity and its discontents*. New York: New York University Press.

Baumeister, R. F., J. J. Exline, and K. L. Sommer. 1999. The victim role, grudge theory, and two dimensions of forgiveness. In *Dimensions of forgiveness: Psychological research and theological perspectives*, ed. E. L. Worthington Jr., 79–104. Philadelphia: Temple Foundation Press.

Beck, R., and C. D. Miller. 2000. Religiosity and agency and communion: Their relationship to religious judgmentalism. *Journal of Psychology* 134:315–24.

Becker, E. 1973. *The denial of death*. New York: Free Press.

Becker, H. 1964. Values. In *A dictionary of the social sciences*, ed. J. Guld and W. L. Kolb, 743–45. New York: Free Press.

Bell, J. M. 1999. Therapeutic failure: Exploring unchartered territory in family nursing. *Journal of Family Nursing* 5:371–73.

Benjamin, O. 2003. The power of unsilencing: Between silence and negotiation in heterosexual relationships. *Journal for the Theory of Social Behaviour* 33:1–19.

Bennett, J. O. 1999. Selves and personal existence in the existentialist tradition. *Journal of the History of Philosophy* 37:135–57.

Benoit, W. L., and S. Drew. 1997. Appropriateness and effectiveness of image repair strategies. *Communication Reports* 10:153–63.

Berdahl, J. L., V. J. Magley, and C. R. Waldo. 1996. The sexual harassment of men? *Psychology of Women Quarterly* 20:527–47.

Berger, P. L., and T. Luckmann. 1996. *The social construction of reality: A treatise in the sociology of knowledge*. Garden City, N.Y.: Anchor Books.

Bergner, R. M. 1998. Therapeutic approaches to problems of meaninglessness. *American Journal of Psychotherapy* 52:72–87.

Berman, E. 1998. Structure and individuality in psychoanalytic training: The Israeli controversial discussions. *American Journal of Psychoanalysis* 58:117–33.

———. 2000. The utopian fantasy of a new person and the danger of a false analytic self. *Psychoanalytic Psychology* 17:38–60.

Berman, H., K. McKenna, C. T. Arnold, G. Taylor, and B. MacQuarrie. 2000. Sexual harassment: Everyday violence in the lives of girls and women. *Advanced Nursing Science* 22:32–46.

Bernstein, M. 1998. Well-being. *American Philosophical Quarterly* 35:39–56.

Bernstein, R. J. 1992. *The new constellation: The ethical-political horizons of modernity/postmodernity*. Cambridge, Mass.: MIT Press.

Berry, J. W., and E. L. Worthington. 2001. Forgiveness, relationship quality, stress while imagining relationship events, and physical and mental health. *Journal of Counseling Psychology* 48:447–55.

Besser, A., G. L. Flett, and R. A. Davis. 2003. Self-criticism, dependency, silencing the self, and loneliness: a test of a mediational model. *Personality and Individual Differences* 35:1735–52.

Best, D. L. 2001. Gender concepts: Convergence in cross-cultural research and methodologies. *Cross-Cultural Research: The Journal of Comparative Social Science* 35:23–43.

Bhui, K, and D. Bhugra. 2001. Transcultural psychiatry: Some social and epidemiological research issues. *International Journal of Social Psychiatry* 47:1–9.

Black, M. M. 1995. Failure to thrive: Strategies for evaluation and intervention. *School Psychology Review* 24:171–85.

Blum, A. 1996. Panic and fear: On the phenomenology of desperation. *Sociological Quarterly* 37:674–99.

Boleyn-Fitzgerald, P. 2002. What should "forgiveness" mean? *Journal of Value Inquiry* 36:483–98.

Boninger, D. S., F. Gleicher, and A. Strathman. 1994. Counterfactual thinking: From what might have been to what may be. *Journal of Personality and Social Psychology* 67:297–307.

Boon, S. D., and L. M. Sulsky. 1997. Attributions of blame and forgiveness in romantic relationships: A policy-capturing study. *Journal of Social Behavior and Personality* 12:19–55.

Bosson, J. K., and W. B. Swann Jr. 1999. Self-liking, self-competence, and the quest for self-verification. *Personality and Social Psychology Bulletin* 25:1230–41.

Bowman, M. L. 1990. Coping efforts and marital satisfaction: Measuring marital coping and its correlates. *Journal of Marriage and the Family* 52:463–75.

Bowman, T. 1999. Shattered dreams, resiliency, and hope: "Restorying" after loss. *Journal of Personal and Interpersonal Loss* 4:179–94.

Bozon, M. 2001. Sexuality, gender, and the couple: A sociohistorical perspective. *Annual Review of Sex Research* 12:1–32.

Bradbury, T. N., F. D. Fincham, and S. R. H. Beach. 2000. Research on the nature and determinants of marital satisfaction: A decade in review. *Journal of Marriage and the Family* 62:964–80.

Bradley, C. L., and J. E. Marcia. 1998. Generativity-stagnation: A five-category model. *Journal of Personality* 66:39–64.

Bradley, W. J., and K. C. Schaefer. 1998. *The uses and misuses of data and models: The mathematization of the human sciences.* Thousand Oaks, Calif.: Sage.

Braithwaite, J. 2000. Repentance rituals and restorative justice. *Journal of Political Philosophy* 8:115–31.

Brown, J. D., and K. A. Dutton. 1995a. The thrill of victory, the complexity of defeat: Self-esteem and people's emotional reactions to success and failure. *Journal of Personality and Social Psychology* 68:712–22.

———. 1995b. Truth and consequences: The costs and benefits of accurate self-knowledge. *Personality and Social Psychology Bulletin* 21:1288–96.

Brown, V. 1999. The "figure" of god and the limits of liberalism: A rereading of Locke's *Essay* and *Two Treatises. Journal of the History of Ideas* 60:83–100.

Burke, K. 1957. *The philosophy of literary form.* New York: Vintage Books (orig. pub. 1941).

Burke, P. J., and J. E. Stets. 1999. Trust and commitment through self-verification. *Social Psychological Quarterly* 62:29–51.

Burkitt, I. 1998. Bodies of knowledge: Beyond Cartesian views of persons, selves, and mind. *Journal for the Theory of Social Behaviour* 28:63–82.

Burleson, B. R. 1994. Comforting messages: Features, functions, and outcomes. In *Strategic interpersonal communication*, ed. J. A. Daly and J. M. Wiemann, 135–61. Hillsdale, N.J.: Lawrence Erlbaum.

Burleson, B. R., and W. H. Denton. 1997. The relationship between communication skill and marital satisfaction: Some moderating effects. *Journal of Marriage and the Family* 59:884–903.

Burleson, B. R., and C. M. Gilstrap. 2002. Explaining sex differences in interaction goals in support situations: Some mediating effects of expressivity and instrumentality. *Communication Reports* 15:43–55.

Burns, L. R., K. Dittman, N. L. Nguyen, and J. K. Mitchelson. 2001. Academic procrastination, perfectionism, and control: Associations with vigilant and avoidant coping. *Journal of Social Behavior and Personality* 16:35–47.

Byrne, R. M. J., and A. McEleney. 2000. Counterfactual thinking about actions and failures to act. *Journal of Experimental Psychology: Learning, Memory, and Cognition* 26:1318–31.

Caetano, A., J. Vala, and L. Jacques-Philippe. 2001. Judgeability in person perception: The confidence of leaders. *Group Dynamics* 5:102–10.

Cai, D. A., and E. L. Fink. 2002. Conflict style differences between individualists and collectivists. *Communication Monographs* 69:67–87.

Cameron, J. E. 2001. Social identity, modern sexism, and perceptions of personal and group discrimination by women and men. *Sex Roles* 44:743–67.

Cameron, L. 1998. Verbal abuse: A proactive approach. *Nursing Management* 29:34–37.

Camus, A. 1956. *The rebel*. Trans. Anthony Bower. New York: Vintage.

Cannon, D. R. 1999. Cause or control? The temporal dimension in failure sense-making. *Journal of Applied Behavioral Science* 35:416–38.

Carney, D. R., and J. A. Harrigan. 2003. It takes one to know one: Interpersonal sensitivity is related to accurate assessments of others' interpersonal sensitivity. *Emotion* 3:194–200.

Carson, C. L., and W. R. Cupach. 2000. Fueling the flames of the green-eyed monster: The role of ruminative thought in reaction to romantic jealousy. *Western Journal of Communication* 64:308–29.

Carver, C. S. 2004. Negative affects deriving from the behavioral approach system. *Emotion* 4:3–22.

Carver, C. S., J. W. Lawrence, and M. F. Scheier. 1999. Self-discrepancies and affect: Incorporating the role of feared selves. *Personality and Social Psychology Bulletin* 25:783–92.

Chang, E. C. 1998. Dispositional optimism and primary and secondary appraisal of a stressor: Controlling for confounding influences and relations to coping and psychological and physical adjustment. *Journal of Personality and Social Psychology* 74:1109–21.

Chang, E. C., and D. R. Strunk. 1999. Dysphoria: Relations to appraisals, coping, and adjustment. *Journal of Counseling Psychology* 46:99–109.

Chang, E. C., A. F. Watkins, and K. H. Banks. 2004. How adaptive and maladaptive perfectionism relate to positive and negative psychological functioning: Testing a stress-mediation model in black and white female college students. *Journal of Counseling Psychology* 51:93–102.

Chen, L. 2002. Perceptions of intercultural interaction and communication satisfaction: A study on initial encounters. *Communication Reports* 15:133–48.

Cheshier, D. M. 1997. Habermas' *Between facts and norms*: The domains and logics of public argument given cultural globalization. In *Argument in a time of change*, ed. J. F. Klumpp, 156–62. Annandale, Va.: National Communication Association.

Cheung, C. K. 1998. Sophistication in theorizing about social problems as a condition for the good life. *Genetic, Social, and General Psychology Monographs* 124:353–75.

Choo, P., and T. Levine. 1996. Gender, love schemas, and reactions to romantic break-ups. *Journal of Social Behavior and Personality* 11:143–58.

Clair, P. R. 1998. *Organizing silence: A world of possibilities.* Albany: State University of New York Press.

Clark, S. H. 1998. "The whole internal world his own": Locke and metaphor reconsidered. *Journal of the History of Ideas* 59:241–66.

Clarke, D. M., and D. W. Kissane. 2002. Demoralization: Its phenomenology and importance. *Australian and New Zealand Journal of Psychiatry* 36:733–42.

Cockburn, C. 1991. *In the way of women: Men's resistance to sex equality in organizations.* Ithaca, N.Y.: ILR Press.

Collins, N. L., and B. C. Feeney. 2000. A safe haven: An attachment theory perspective on support seeking and caregiving in intimate relationships. *Journal of Personality and Social Psychology* 78:1053–73.

Corcoran, K. O., and B. Mallinckrodt. 2000. Adult attachment, self-efficacy, perspective taking, and conflict resolution. *Journal of Counseling and Development* 78:473–84.

Cotter, D. A., J. M. Hermsen, and R. Vanneman. 1999. Systems of gender, race, and class inequality: Multilevel analysis. *Social Forces* 78:433–61.

Cozzarelli, C., and J. A. Karafa. 1998. Cultural estrangement and terror management theory. *Personality and Social Psychology Bulletin* 24:253–68.

Craig, R. T. 1990. Communication as a practical discipline. In *Rethinking communication: Paradigm issues,* ed. B. Dervin, L. Grossberg, B. J. O'Keefe, and E. Wartella, 1:97–122. Newbury Park, Calif.: Sage.

Crago, M. P., A. Eriks-Brophy, D. Pesco, and K. McAlpine. 1997. Culturally based miscommunication in classroom interaction. *Language, Speech, and Hearing Services in Schools* 28:245–55.

Cramer, K. M., and J. B. Nickels. 1997. Uncertainty of outcomes, prediction of failure, and lack of control as factors explaining perceived helplessness. *Journal of Social Behavior and Personality* 12:611–31.

Crane, J. K. 2003. Locke's theory of classification. *British Journal for the History of Philosophy* 11:249–59.

Crook, S. 1998. Minotaurs and other monsters: "Everyday life" in recent social theory. *Sociology* 32:523–40.

Crozier, W. R. 1998. Self-consciousness in shame: The role of the "other." *Journal for the Theory of Social Behaviour* 28:273–86.

Curzon-Hobson, A. 2002. Higher education in a world of radical unknowability: An extension of the challenge of Ronald Barnett. *Teaching in Higher Education* 7:179–91.

Dallmayr, F. 1999. Rethinking secularism (with Raimon Panikkar). *Review of Politics* 61:715–36.

Davies, M. F. 2001. Socially desirable responding and impression management in the endorsement of love styles. *Journal of Psychology* 135:562–70.

Davis, J. L., and C. E. Rusbult. 2001. Attitude alignment in close relationships. *Journal of Personality and Social Psychology* 81:65–84.

Debats, D. L. 1999. Sources of meaning: An investigation of significant commitments in life. *Journal of Humanistic Psychology* 39:30–58.

Deetz, S. A. 1992. *Democracy in an age of corporate colonization: Developments in communication and the politics of everyday life.* Albany: State University of New York Press.

De Looze, L. 1998. To understand perfectly is to misunderstand completely: "The debate in signs" in France, Iceland, Italy and Spain. *Comparative Literature* 50:136–54.

Demaris, A. 2000. Till discord do us part: The role of physical and verbal conflict in union disruption. *Journal of Marriage and the Family* 62:683–92.

Deppe, R. K., and J. M. Harackiewicz. 1996. Self-handicapping and intrinsic motivation: Buffering intrinsic motivation from the threat of failure. *Journal of Personality and Social Psychology* 70:868–76.

Donskis, L. 1998. The conspiracy theory, demonization of the other. *Innovation: The European Journal of Social Sciences* 11:349–61.

Dorian, B. J., Dunbar, C., Frayn, D., and P. E. Garfinkel. 2000. Charismatic leadership: Boundary issues, and collusion. *American Journal of Psychotherapy* 54:216–26.

Dunham, K., and C. Y. Senn. 2000. Minimizing negative experiences. *Journal of Interpersonal Violence* 15:251–61.

Dunkley, D. M. 2003. Self-critical perfectionism and daily affect: Dispositional and situational influences on stress and coping. *Journal of Personality and Social Psychology* 84:234–52.

Dunkley, D. M., and K. R. Blankstein. 2000. Self-critical perfectionism, coping, hassles, and current distress: A structural equation modeling approach. *Cognitive Theory and Research* 24:713–30.

Dunn, R. G. 1998. *Identity crises: A social critique of postmodernity.* Minneapolis: University of Minnesota Press.

Dunne, J. 1996. Beyond sovereignty and deconstruction: The storied self. *Philosophy and Social Criticism* 21:137–57.

Duval, T. S., and N. Lalwani. 1999. Objective self-awareness and causal attributions for self-standard discrepancies: Changing self or changing standards of correctness. *Personality and Psychology Bulletin* 25:1220–30.

Dykema, J., Bergbower, K., and C. Peterson. 1995. Pessimistic explanatory style, stress, and illness. *Journal of Social and Clinical Psychology* 14:357–71.

Eagly, A. H., and W. Wood. 1999. The origins of sex differences in human behavior: Evolved dispositions versus social roles. *American Psychologist* 54:408–23.

Ehninger, D., and G. A. Hauser. 1984. Communication of values. In *Handbook of rhetorical and communication theory*, ed. C. A. Arnold and J. W. Bowers, 720–28. Boston: Allyn and Bacon.

Eibach, R. P., L. K. Libby, and T. D. Gilovich. 2003. When changes in the self is mistaken for change in the world. *Journal of Personality and Social Psychology* 84:917–31.

Eliasoph, N., and P. Lichterman. 2003. Culture in interaction. *American Journal of Sociology* 108:735–94.

Elliot, A. J. 1999. Approach and avoidance motivation and achievement goals. *Educational Psychologist* 34:169–90.

Elliot, A. J., and K. M. Sheldon. 1997. Avoidance achievement motivation: A personal goals analysis. *Journal of Personality and Social Psychology* 73:171–85.

———. 1998. Avoidance personal goals and the personality-illness relationship. *Journal of Personality and Social Psychology* 75:1282–99.

Elliott, K. 2004. Error as a means to discovery. *Philosophy of Science* 71:174–97.

Elliott, T. R., and J. S. Richards. 1999. Living with the facts, negotiating the terms: Unrealistic beliefs, denial, and adjustment in the first year of acquired physical disability. *Journal of Personal and Interpersonal Loss* 4:361–82.

Enright, R. D., and J. North, eds. 1998. *Exploring forgiveness*. Madison: University of Wisconsin Press.

Epley, N., and D. Dunning. 2000. Feeling "holier than thou": Are self-serving assessments produced by errors in self-or social prediction? *Journal of Personality and Social Psychology* 79:861–75.

Erdley, C. A., and S. A. Asher. 1999. A social goals perspective on children's social competence. *Journal of Emotional and Behavioral Disorders* 7:156–67.

Espeland, W. N., and M. L. Stevens. 1998. Commensuration as a social process. *Annual Review of Sociology* 24:313–44.

Estany, A. 2001. The thesis of theory-laden observation in the light of cognitive psychology. *Philosophy of Science* 68:203–18.

Evnine, S. J. 2001. Learning from one's mistakes: Epistemic modesty and the nature of belief. *Pacific Philosophical Quarterly* 82:157–77.

Feeney, B. C., and N. L. Collins. 2001. Predictors of caregiving in adult intimate relationships: An attachment theoretical perspective. *Journal of Personality and Social Psychology* 80:972–94.

Feldman, C. M., and C. A. Ridley. 2000. The role of conflict-based communication responses and outcomes in male domestic violence toward female partners. *Journal of Social and Personal Relationships* 17:552–73.

Feldman, S. P. 1999. The leveling of organizational culture: Egalitarianism in critical postmodern organization theory. *Journal of Applied Behavioral Science* 35:228–44.

Fiedler, K., and G. R. Semin. 1995. Actor-observer bias in close relationships: The role of self-knowledge and self-related language. *Personality and Social Psychology Bulletin* 21:525–39.

Fine, M. A., and K. A. Olson. 1997. Anger and hurt in response to provocation: Relationship to psychological adjustment. *Journal of Social Behavior and Personality* 12:326–45.

Finfgeld, D. L. 1999. Courage as a process of pushing beyond the struggle. *Qualitative Health Research* 9:803–14.

Finkel, E. J., and W. K. Campbell. 2001. Self-control and accommodation in close relationships: An interdependent analysis. *Journal of Personality and Social Psychology* 81:263–77.

Finlay, B. 2002. The origins of charisma as process: A case study of Hildegard of Bingen. *Symbolic Interaction* 25:357–554.

Fischer, K. 1988. The functional architecture of adaptive cognitive systems with limited capacity. *Semiotica* 68, nos. 3–4: 191–248.

Fish, S. E. 1989. *Doing what comes naturally*. Durham, N.C.: Duke University Press.

Fitzpatrick, J., and D. L. Sollie. 1999. Unrealistic gendered and relationship-specific beliefs: Contributions to investments and commitment in dating relationships. *Journal of Social and Personal Relationships* 16:852–67.

Fletcher, G. J. O., J. A. Simpson, G. Thomas, and L. Giles. 1999. Ideals in intimate relationships. *Journal of Personality and Social Psychology* 76:72–89.

Flett, G. L., and P. L. Hewitt. 1998. Perfectionism in relation to attributions for success or failure. *Current Psychology* 17:249–63.

———, eds. 2002. *Perfectionism: Theory, research, and treatment.* Washington, D.C.: American Psychological Association.

Flett, G. L., P. L. Hewitt, J. M. Oliver, and S. MacDonald. 2002. Perfectionism in children and their parents: A developmental analysis. In *Perfectionism: Theory, research, and treatment,* ed. G. L. Flett and P. L. Hewitt, 89–132. Washington, D.C.: American Psychological Association.

Florian, V., and M. Mikulincer. 1998. Terror management in childhood: Does death conceptualization moderate the effects of mortality salience on acceptance of similar and different others? *Personality and Social Psychology Bulletin* 24:1104–12.

Follingstad, D. R., and D. D. Dehart. 2000. Defining psychological abuse of husbands toward wives: Contexts, behaviors, and typologies. *Journal of Interpersonal Violence* 15:891–920.

Fong, M. L., and K. A. Silien. 1999. Assessment and diagnosis of DSM-IV anxiety disorders. *Journal of Counseling and Development* 77:209–18.

Fornas, J. 2000. The crucial in between: The centrality of mediation in cultural studies. *European Journal of Cultural Studies* 3:45–65.

Fow, N. R. 1996. The phenomenology of forgiveness and reconciliation. *Journal of Phenomenological Psychology* 27:219–33.

Frank, D. A. 1998. Dialectical rapprochement in the new rhetoric. *Argumentation and Advocacy* 34:111–27.

Fraser, B. 1994. No conversation without representation. In *Pretending to communicate,* ed. H. Parret, 144–72. New York: Walter de Gruyter.

Freedman, S. 1998. Forgiveness and reconciliation: The importance of understanding how they differ. *Counseling and Values* 42:200–216.

Fritz, C., P. E. Morris, R. A. Bjork, R. Gelman, and T. D. Wickens. 2000. When further learning fails: Stability and change following repeated presentation of text. *British Journal of Psychology* 91:493–512.

Fry, P. S., and L. A. Barker. 2002. Quality of relationships and structural properties of social support networks of female survivors of abuse. *Genetic, Social, and General Psychology Monographs* 128:139–63.

Funder, D. C. 1995. On the accuracy of personality judgments: A realistic approach. *Psychological Review* 102:652–70.

Furr, R. M., and D. C. Funder. 1998. A multimodal analysis of personal negativity. *Journal of Personality and Social Psychology* 74:1580–92.

Gable, S. L., H. T. Reis, E. A. Impett, and E. R. Asher. 2004. What do you do when things go right? The intrapersonal and interpersonal benefits of sharing positive events. *Journal of Personality and Social Psychology* 87:228–45.

Gabriel, S., and W. L. Gardner. 1999. Are there "his" and "hers" types of interdependence? The implications of gender differences in collective versus relational interdependence for affect, behavior, and cognition. *Journal of Personality and Social Psychology* 77:642–55.

Gassin, E. A. 1998. Receiving forgiveness as moral education: A theoretical analysis and initial empirical investigation. *Journal of Moral Education* 27:71–87.

Geer, J. H., and G. M. Manguno-Mire. 1996. Gender differences in cognitive processes in sexuality. *Annual Review of Sex Research* 7:90–124.

Georgesen, J. C., and M. J. Harris. 2000. The balance of power: Interpersonal consequences of differential power and expectancies. *Personality and Social Psychology Bulletin* 26:1239–57.

Gilbert, D. T., R. P. Brown, E. C. Pinel, and T. D. Wilson. 2000. The illusion of external agency. *Journal of Personality and Social Psychology* 34:587–99.

Gilbert, P., M. Clarke, S. Hempel, J. N. V. Miles, and C. Irons. 2004. Criticizing and reassuring oneself: An exploration of forms, styles and reasons in female students. *British Journal of Clinical Psychology* 43:31–50.

Gill, M. J., and W. B. Swann. 2004. On what it means to know someone: A matter of pragmatics. *Journal of Personality and Social Psychology* 86:405–18.

Gille, Z., and S. O'Riain. 2002. Global ethnography. *Annual Review of Sociology* 28:271–95.

Gilovich, T., K. Savitsky, and V. H. Medvec. 1998. The illusion of transparency: Biased assessments of others' ability to read one's emotional states. *Journal of Personality and Social Psychology* 75:332–46.

Glenberg, A. M. 1997. What memory is for. *Behavioral and Brain Sciences* 20:1–55.

Glock, H. J. 1993. The indispensability of translation in Quine and Davidson. *Philosophical Quarterly* 43:194–210.

Goldenberg, J. L., T. Psyzczynski, J. Greenberg, and S. Solomon. 2000. Fleeing the body: A terror management perspective on the problem of human corporeality. *Personality and Social Psychology Review* 4:200–219.

Goldenberg, J. L., T. Pyszczynski, J. Greenberg, S. Solomon, B. Kluck, and R. Cornwell. 2001. I am not an animal: Mortality salience, disgust, and the denial of human creatureliness. *Journal of Experimental Psychology* 130:427–35.

Gollobin, I. 1998. Dialects and wisdom. *Science and Society* 62:483–97.

Gomory, T. 2001. A fallibilistic response to Thyer's theory of theory-free empirical research in social work practice. *Journal of Social Work Education* 37:26–50.

Gorsevski, E. W. 1998. The physical side of linguistic violence. *Peace Review* 10: 513–17.

Gove, W. R., and N. L. Malcom. 1997. Can sociology be a science? The issue of gender and sex-dimorphic characteristics. *American Sociologist* 28:9–31.

Grace, G. W. 1987. *The linguistic construction of reality*. London: Croom Helm.

Grant, H., and C. S. Dweck. 2003. Clarifying achievement goals and their impact. *Journal of Personality and Social Psychology* 85:541–53.

Graumann, C. F. 1998. Verbal discrimination: A neglected chapter in the social psychology of aggression. *Journal for the Theory of Social Behaviour* 28:41–61.

Gray, J. A., and N. McLaughton. 1996. The neurospychology of anxiety: Reprise. *Nebraska Symposium on Motivation* 43:61–134.

Greeff, A. P., and H. L. Malherbe. 2001. Intimacy and marital satisfaction in spouses. *Journal of Sex and Marital Therapy* 27:247–57.

Greenberg, J., J. Arndt, L. Simon, T. Pyszczynski, and S. Solomon. 2000. Proximal and distal defenses in response to reminders of one's mortality: Evidence of a temporal sequence. *Personality and Social Psychology Bulletin* 26:91–99.

Greenspan, T. S. 2000. "Healthy perfectionism" is an oxymoron! *Journal of Secondary Gifted Education* 11:197–209.

Gresham, F. M., and S. N. Elliott. 1989. The relationship between adaptive behavior and social skills: Issues in definition and assessment. *Journal of Special Education* 21:167–81.

Griffin, J. 1990. *Well-being: Its meaning, measurement, and moral importance.* Oxford, England: Oxford University Press.

Grossen, M., and D. Apotheloz. 1996. Communicating about communication in a therapeutic interview. *Journal of Language and Social Psychology* 15:101–32.

Habermas, J. 1979. *Communication and the evolution of society,* trans. T. McCarthy. Boston: Beacon Press.

———. 1984. *The theory of communicative action.* Vol. 1, *Reason and the rationalization of society,* trans. T. McCarthy. Boston: Beacon Press.

Hafer, C. L., and J. M. Olson. 1993. Beliefs in a just world, discontent and assertive actions by working women. *Personality and Social Psychology Bulletin* 19:30–38.

Hahn, J., and T. Blass. 1997. Dating partner preferences: A function of similarity of love styles. *Journal of Social Behavior and Personality* 12:595–610.

Halpern, D. F. 2000. *Sex differences in cognitive abilities.* 3rd ed. Mahwah, N.J.: Lawrence Erlbaum.

Hamberger, L. K., J. M. Lohr, D. Bonge, and D. F. Tolin. 1997. An empirical classification of motivations for domestic violence. *Violence against Women* 3:401–23.

Hamby, S. L., and D. B. Sugerman. 1999. Acts of psychological aggression against a partner and their relation to physical assault and gender. *Journal of Marriage and the Family* 61:959–70.

Hamlyn, D. W. 1974. Person-perception and our understanding of others. In *Understanding other persons,* ed. T. Mischel, 1–36. Oxford: Basil Blackwell.

Hardin, C. D., and E. T. Higgins. 1996. Shared reality: How social verification makes the subjective objective. In *Handbook of motivation and cognition: The interpersonal context,* ed. R. M. Sorrentino and E. T. Higgins, 3:28–84. New York: Guilford Press.

Harding, R., H. Kikko, and K. E. Arnold. 2003. Dynamics of the caring family. *American Naturist* 161:395–412.

Harley, E. M., K. A. Carlsen, and G. R. Loftus. 2004. The "saw-it-all-along" effect: Demonstrations of visual hindsight bias. *Journal of Experimental Psychology: Learning, Memory, and Cognition* 30:960–68.

Harris, S. R. 1997. Status inequality and close relationships: An integrative typology of bond-saving strategies. *Symbolic Interaction* 20:1–21.

Harris, W. 1990. The fabric of the imagination. *Third World Quarterly* 12:175–87.

Hart, R. P. 1984. The functions of human communication in the maintenance of public values. In *Handbook of rhetorical and communication theory,* ed. C. A. Arnold and J. W. Bowers, 749–91. Boston: Allyn and Bacon.

Harvey, D. L. 2002. Agency and community: A critical realist paradigm. *Journal for the Theory of Social Behaviour* 32:163–94.

Haselton, M. G., and D. M. Buss. 2000. Error management theory: A new perspective on biases in cross-sex mind reading. *Journal of Personality and Social Psychology* 78:81–91.

Hazan, C., and P. Shaver. 1987. Romantic love conceptualized as an attachment process. *Journal of Personality and Social Psychology* 52:511–24.

Heidegger, M. 1962. *Being and time,* trans. J. Macquarrie and E. Robinson. New York: Harper & Row.

Heller, A. 1990. *Can modernity survive?* Cambridge, England: Polity Press.

Heller, P. E., and B. Wood. 1998. The process of intimacy: Similarity, understanding, and gender. *Journal of Marital and Family Therapy* 24:273–89.

Hendrix, W. H., J. D. Rueb, and R. P. Steel. 1998. Sexual harassment and gender differences. *Journal of Social Behavior and Personality* 13:235–53.

Henry, J. 1999. Changing conscious experience—comparing clinical approaches, practice and outcomes. *British Journal of Psychology* 90:587–609.

Hermans, H. J. M. 2001. The dialogical self: Toward a theory of personal and cultural positioning. *Culture and Psychology* 7:243–81.

Hewitt, P. L., and G. L. Flett. 1991. Perfectionism in the self and social contexts: Conceptualization, assessment, and association with psychopathology. *Journal of Personality and Social Psychology* 60:456–70.

Hewitt, P. L., G. L. Flett, S. B. Sherry, M. Habke, M. Parkin, R. W. Lam, B. McMurtry, E. Ediger, P. Fairlie, and M. B. Stein. 2003. The interpersonal expression of perfection: Perfectionistic self-presentation and psychology distress. *Journal of Personality and Social Psychology* 84:1303–25.

Hickins, M. 1998. Reconcilable differences. *Management Review* 87:54–59.

Hirt, E. R., H. E. McDonald, G. M. Levine, R. J. Melton, and L. L. Martin. 1999. One person's enjoyment is another person's boredom: Mood effects on responsiveness to framing. *Personality and Social Psychology Bulletin* 25:76–91.

Hobfoll, S. E. 2002. Social and psychological resources and adaptation. *Review of General Psychology* 6:307–24.

Hobfoll, S. E., K. E. E. Schroder, M. Wells, and M. Malek. 2002. Communal versus individualistic construction of sense of mastery in facing life challenges. *Journal of Social and Clinical Psychology* 21:362–99.

Hodgins, H. S., E. Liebeskind, and W. Schwartz. 1996. Getting out of hot water: Face work in social predicaments. *Journal of Personality and Social Psychology* 71.300–14.

Hoffer, W. 1951. *The True Believer.* New York: Mentor Books.

Hoffman, R. M. 2001. The measurement of masculinity and femininity: Historical perspective and implications for counseling. *Journal of Counseling and Development* 79:472–86.

Hoffrage, U., R. Hertwig, and G. Gigerenzer. 2000. Hindsight bias: A by-product of knowledge updating? *Journal of Experimental Psychology* 26:566–81.

Holmes, J. G. 2000. Social relationships: The nature and function of relational schemes. *European Journal of Social Psychology* 30:447–95.

Horneffer, K. J., and F. D. Fincham. 1996. Attributional models of depression and marital distress. *Personality and Social Psychology Bulletin* 22:678–89.

Huemer, M. 1999. The problem of memory knowledge. *Pacific Philosophical Quarterly* 80:346–57.

Hunt, A. 1999. Anxiety and social explanation: Some anxieties about anxiety. *Journal of Social History* 32:509–28.

Hupka, R. B., and A. L. Bank. 1996. Sex differences in jealousy: Evolution or social construction? *Cross-Cultural Research* 30:24–60.

Hurley, J. R. 1998. Agency and communion as related to "Big Five" self-representations and subsequent behavior in small groups. *Journal of Psychology Interdisciplinary and Applied* 132:337–51.

Huston, T. L., and A. L. Vangelisti. 1991. Socioemotional behavior and satisfaction in marital relationships: A longitudinal study. *Journal of Personality and Social Psychology* 61:721–34.

Ingram, R. E., and N. A. Hamilton. 1999. Evaluating precision in the social psychological assessment of depression: Methodological considerations, issues, and recommendations. *Journal of Social and Clinical Psychology* 18:160–80.

Irani, G. E., and N. C. Funk. 1998. Rituals of reconciliation: Arab-Islamic perspectives. *Arab Studies Quarterly* 20:53–74.

Jamison, P. 1998. Human and ultimate consciousness: The pitfalls of rationalist cosmology. *Humanist* 58:33–34.

Jarvis, D. S. L. 1998. Postmodernism: A critical typology. *Politics and Society* 26:95–142.

Jaworski, A. 1993. *The power of silence.* Newbury Park, Calif.: Sage.

Johnson, K. L., and M. E. Roloff. 1998. Serial arguing and relational quality. *Communication Research* 25:327–44.

———. 2000. Correlates of the perceived resolvability and relational consequences of serial arguing in dating relationships: Argumentative features and the use of coping strategies. *Journal of Social and Personal Relationships* 17:676–86.

Johnson, L. M., M. Rehan, and C. L. Mulford. 2002. General versus specific victim blaming. *Journal of Social Psychology* 142:249–64.

Johnson, M. K., J. G. Bush, and K. J. Mitchell. 1998. Interpersonal reality monitoring: Judging the sources of other people's memories. *Social Cognition* 16:199–224.

Johnson, M. P., J. P. Caughlin, and T. L. Huston. 1999. The tripartite nature of marital commitment: Personal, moral, and structural reasons to stay married. *Journal of Marriage and the Family* 61:160–77.

Johnston, H., and S. Lio. 1998. Collective behavior and social movements in the postmodern age: Looking backward to look forward. *Sociological Perspectives* 41:453–72.

Jones, W. E. 1997. Why do we value knowledge? *American Philosophical Quarterly* 34:423–40.

Jordan, C. H., S. J. Spencer, M. P. Zanna, and E. Hoshino-Brown. 2003. Secure and defensive high self-esteem. *Journal of Personality and Social Psychology* 85:969–79.

Josselson, R., and A. Lieblich. 1996. Fettering the mind in the name of "science." *American Psychologist* 51:651–53.

Juni, S. 1998–1999. The defense mechanisms inventory: Theoretical and psychometric implications. *Current Psychology* 17:313–33.

Kane, R. 1998. Dimensions of value and the aims of social inquiry. *American Behavioral Scientist* 41:578–97.

Karelitz, T. M., and D. V. Budescu. 2004. You say "probable" and I say "likely": Improving interpersonal communication with verbal probably phrases. *Journal of Experimental Psychology* 10:25–41.

Karney, B. R., and N. E. Frye. 2002. "But we've been getting better lately": Comparing prospective and retrospective views of relationship development. *Journal of Personality and Social Psychology* 82:222–38.

Karremans, J. C., P. A. M. Van Lange, and J. W. Ouwerkerk. 2003. When forgiving enhances psychological well-being: The role of interpersonal commitment. *Journal of Personality and Social Psychology* 84:1011–26.

Kasser, T., and R. M. Ryan. 1993. A dark side of the American dream: Correlates of financial success as a central life aspiration. *Journal of Personality and Social Psychology* 65:410–22.

Katzko, M. W. 2003. Unity versus multiplicity: A conceptual analysis of the term "self" and its use in personality theories. *Journal of Personality* 71:83–114.

Kaufman, C. 1999. The unforced force of the more familiar argument: A critique of Habermas's theory of communicative rationality. *Philosophy Today* 43:348–61.

Kenaan, H. 1999. Subject to error: Rethinking Husserl's phenomenology of misperception. *International Journal of Philosophical Studies* 7:55–67.

Kenny, D. A. 1994. *Interpersonal perception: A social relations analysis.* New York: Guilford.

Kenny, D. A., and L. K. Acitelli. 2001. Accuracy and bias in the perception of the partner in a close relationship. *Journal of Personality and Social Psychology* 80: 439–48.

Kenny, T. A., B. A. Smith, and B. Donzella. 2001. The influence of sex, gender, self-discrepancies, and self-awareness on anger and verbal aggressiveness among U.S. college students. *Journal of Social Psychology* 141:245–75.

Kierkegaard, S. 1962. *Works of love,* trans. Howard Hong and Edna Hong. New York: Harper & Row.

Kim, P. H., D. L. Ferrin, C. D. Cooper, and K. T. Dirks. 2004. Removing the shadow of suspicion: The effect of apology versus denial for repairing competence-versus integrity-based trust violations. *Journal of Applied Psychology* 89:104–18.

Kincanon, E., and W. Powel. 1995. Chaotic analysis in psychology and psychoanalysis. *Journal of Psychology Interdisciplinary and Applied* 129:495–505.

King, G. A. 2004. The meaning of life experiences: Applications of a meta-model to rehabilitation sciences and services. *American Journal of Orthopsychiatry* 74:72–88.

Klacznski, P. A., and B. Robinson. 2000. Personal theories, intellectual ability, and epistemological beliefs: Adult age differences in everyday reasoning biases. *Psychology and Aging* 15:400–416.

Knaus, W. J. 2001. Procrastination, blame, and change. *Journal of Social Behavior and Personality* 16:153–67.

Knee, C. R. 1998. Implicit theories of relationships: Assessment and prediction of romantic relationship initiation, coping, and longevity. *Journal of Personality and Social Psychology* 74:360–71.

Knight, D. A. 1997. A poetics of psychological explanation. *Metaphilosophy* 28:63–80.

Knoll, M., and T. Charman. 2000. Teaching false belief and visual perspective taking skills in young children: Can a theory of mind be trained? *Child Study Journal* 30:273–303.

Kroska, A. 2001. Do we have consensus? Examining the relationship between gender ideology and role meanings. *Social Psychology Quarterly* 64:18–40.

Kruger, J., and D. Dunning. 1999. Unskilled and unaware of it: How difficulties in recognizing one's own incompetence lead to inflated self-assessments. *Journal of Personality and Social Psychology* 77:1121–34.

Kruger, J., and T. Gilovich. 1999. "Naive cynicism" in everyday theories of responsibility assessment: On biased assumptions of bias. *Journal of Personality and Social Psychology* 76:743–54.

Kunkel, A. W., and B. R. Burleson. 1999. Assessing explanations for sex differences in emotional support: A test of the different cultures and skill specialization accounts. *Human Communication Research* 25:307–40.

Kurdek, L. A., and W. D. Schnopp. 1997. Predicting relationship commitment and relationship stability from both partners' relationship values: Evidence from heterosexual dating couples. *Personality and Social Psychology Bulletin* 23:1111–19.

Kurtz, J. E., and J. L. Sherker. 2003. Relationship quality, trait similarity, and self-other agreement on personality ratings in college roommates. *Journal of Personality* 71:21–48.

Laing, R. D. 1969. *Self and others*. New York: Pantheon Books.

———. 1970. *Knots*. New York: Vintage Books.

Landau, I. 2003. Sexual harassment as "wrongful communication." *Philosophy of the Social Sciences* 33:225–34.

Landau, M. J., M. Johns, J. Greenberg, T. Pyszczynski, A. Martens, J. L. Goldenberg, and S. Solomon. 2004. A function of form: Terror management and structuring the social world. *Journal of Personality and Social Psychology* 87:190–210.

Landman, J., and J. D. Manis. 1992. What might have been: Counterfactual thought concerning personal decisions. *British Journal of Psychology* 83:473–78.

Larson, J. H., C. H. Hammond, and J. M. Harper. 1998. Perceived equity and intimacy in marriage. *Journal of Marital and Family Therapy* 24:487–506.

Larson, R. W., and S. Gillman. 1999. Transmission of emotions in the daily interactions of single-mother families. *Journal of Marriage and the Family* 61:21–37.

Latridou, S. 2000. The grammatical ingredients of counterfactuality. *Linguistic Inquiry* 31:231–71.

Leary, M. R., C. Springer, L. Negel, E. Ansell, and K. Evans. 1998. The causes, phenomenology, and consequences of hurt feelings. *Journal of Personality and Social Psychology* 74:1225–38.

Lee, D. 2000. Hegemonic masculinity and male feminisation: The sexual harassment of men at work. *Journal of Gender Studies* 9:141–56.

Lee, J. W., and L. K. Guerrero. 2001. Types of touch in cross-sex relationships between coworkers: Perceptions of relational and emotional messages, inappropriateness, and sexual harassment. *Journal of Applied Communication Research* 29:197–220.

Leeser, J., and W. O'Donohue. 1999. What is a delusion? Epistemological dimensions. *Journal of Abnormal Psychology* 108:687–94.

Lefley, H. P. 1997. Synthesizing the family caregiving studies: Implications for service planning, social policy, and further research. *Family Relations* 46:443–50.

Lewandowski, E. 2000. United language. *Capital Times*, February 12–13, 13a.

Li, H. Z. 2001. Cooperative and intrusive interruptions in inter- and intracultural dyadic discourse. *Journal of Language and Social Psychology* 20:259–84.

Linden, G. W. 1993. Excuses, excuses! *Individual Psychology* 49:1–12.

Lisak, D., and C. Ivan. 1995. Deficits in intimacy and empathy in sexually aggressive men. *Journal of Interpersonal Violence* 10:296–309.

Little, D. 1993. Evidence and objectivity in the social sciences. *Social Research* 60:363–397.

Locke, E. A., and G. P. Latham. 2002. Building a practically useful theory of goal setting and task motivation: A 35-year odyssey. *American Psychologist* 57:705–17.

Locke, J. 1659. *An essay concerning human understanding.* Oxford, England: Clarendon Press, 1975.

Lockwood, P. 2002. Could it happen to you? Predicting the impact of downward comparisons on the self. *Journal of Personality and Social Psychology* 82:343–58.

Loftus, E. F. 2003. Make-believe memories. *American Psychologist* 58:867–73.

Lounsbury, J. W., H. E. Tatum, W. Chambers, K. S. Owens, and L. W. Gibson. 1999. An investigation of career decidedness in relation to "Big Five" personality constructs and life satisfaction. *College Student Journal* 33:646–51.

Lowe, E. J. 2000. Locke, Martin, and substance. *Philosophical Quarterly* 50:499–515.

Lu, L. 1999. Personal or environmental causes of happiness: A longitudinal analysis. *Journal of Social Psychology* 139:79–90.

Luten, A. G., J. A. Ralph, and S. Mineka. 1997. Pessimistic attributional style: Is it specific to depression versus anxiety versus negative affect? *Behavioral Research and Therapy* 35:703–19.

Lyne, J. 1998. Knowledge and performance in argument: Disciplinarity and prototheory. *Argumentation and Advocacy* 35:3–10.

Lyubomirsky, S., and S. Nolen-Hoeksema. 1995. Effects of self-focused rumination on negative thinking and interpersonal problem solving. *Journal of Personality and Social Psychology* 69:176–91.

Macaskill, N. D., and A. Macaskill. 1999. Failure to diagnose depression in patients referred for psychotherapy. *International Journal of Social Psychiatry* 45:140–48.

Mackay, J. 2001. Global sex: Sexuality and sexual practices around the world. *Sexual and Relationship Therapy* 16:71–82.

Maio, G. R., and J. M. Olson. 1998. Values as truisms: Evidence and implications. *Journal of Personality and Social Psychology* 74:294–312.

Makoul, G., and M. E. Roloff. 1998. The role of efficacy and outcome expectations in the decision to withhold relational complaints. *Communication Research* 25:5–30.

Maltby, J., and L. Day. 2004. Forgiveness and defense style. *Journal of Genetic Psychology* 165:99–110.

Marczely, B. 1999. Mixed messages: Sexual harassment in the public schools. *Clearing House* 72:315–19.

Markert, J. 1999. Sexual harassment and the communication conundrum. *Gender Issues* 17:34–52.

Markova, I. 1997. Language and authenticity. *Journal for the Theory of Social Behaviour* 27:265–75.

Marks, D. F. 1999. Consciousness, mental imagery, and action. *British Journal of Psychology* 90:567–86.

Marsh, R. L., J. L. Hicks, and M. L. Bink. 1998. Activation of completed, uncompleted, and partially completed intentions. *Journal of Experimental Psychology: Learning, Memory, and Cognition* 24:350–61.

Marshall, L. L., R. Weston, and T. C. Honeycutt. 2000. Does men's positivity moderate or mediate the effects of their abuse on women's relationship quality? *Journal of Social and Personal Relationships* 17:660–75.

Martin, A. J., H. W. Marsh, A. Williamson, and R. L. Debus. 2003. Self-handicapping, defensive pessimism, and goal orientation: A qualitative study of university students. *Journal of Educational Psychology* 95:617–28.

Martin, R., C. K. Wan, J. P. David, E. L. Wegner, B. D. Olson, and D. Watson. 1999. Style of anger expression: Relation to expressivity, personality, and health. *Personality and Social Psychology Bulletin* 25:1196–1207.

McAdams, D. P., M. Lewis, A. H. Patten, and P. J. Bowman. 2001. When bad things turn good and good things turn bad: Sequences of redemption and contamination in life narrative and their relation to psychosocial adaptation in midlife adults and in students. *Personality and Social Psychological Bulletin* 27:474–85.

McCaw, J. M., and C. Y. Senn. 1998. Perception of cues in conflictual dating situations: A test of the miscommunication hypothesis. *Violence against Women* 4:609–24.

McClure, B. A. 1994. The shadow side of regressive groups. *Counseling and Values* 38:77–90.

McCullough, M. E. 2000. Forgiveness as human strength: Theory, measurement, and links to well-being. *Journal of Social and Clinical Psychology* 19:43–55.

McCullough, M. E., F. D. Fincham, and J. A. Tsang. 2003. Forgiveness, forbearance, and time: The temporal unfolding of transgression-related interpersonal motivations. *Journal of Personality and Social Psychology* 84:540–57.

McCullough, M. E., K. C. Rachal, S. J. Sandage, E. L. Worthington, S. W. Brown, and T. L. Hight. 1998. Interpersonal forgiving in close relationships: II. Theoretical elaboration and measurement. *Journal of Personality and Social Psychology* 75:1586–1603.

McCullough, M., E. L. Worthington, and K. C. Rachal. 1997. Interpersonal forgiving in close relationships. *Journal of Personality and Social Psychology* 73:321–36.

McGlynn, G. H. 2001. The facade of good intentions. *Peace Review* 13:281–86.

McGregor, I., and B. R. Little. 1998. Personal projects, happiness, and meaning: On doing well and being yourself. *Journal of Personality and Social Psychology* 74:494–512.

McGregor, I., and D. C. Marigold. 2003. Defensive zeal and the uncertain self: What makes you so sure? *Journal of Personality and Social Psychology* 85:838–52.

McIntosh, W. D., and L. L. Martin. 1997. Goal beliefs, life events, and the malleability of people's judgments of their happiness. *Journal of Social Behavior and Personality* 12:567–75.

Mei, L. S. 2002. Contextualizing intercultural communication and sociopragmatic choices. *Multilingua* 21:77–99.

Meloy, J. R. 2002. The "polymorphously perverse" psychopath: Understanding a strong empirical relationship. *Bulletin of the Menninger Clinic* 66:273–90.

Memon, A., L. Hope, and R. Bull. 2003. Exposure duration: Effects on eyewitness accuracy and confidence. *British Journal of Psychology* 94:339–55.

Mendieta, E. 1997. Identity and liberation. *Peace Review* 9:497–502.

Mesquita, B. 2001. Emotions in collectivist and individualist contexts. *Journal of Personality and Social Psychology* 80:68–74.

Metts, S. 1994. Relational transgressions. In *Communication and relational maintenance*, ed. D. J. Canary and L. Stafford, 217–39. San Diego, Calif.: Academic Press.

Miceli, M., and C. Castelfranchi. 1998. How to silence one's conscience: Cognitive defenses against the feeling of guilt. *Journal for the Theory of Social Behaviour* 28:287–318.

Mikula, G. 2003. Testing an attribution-of-blame model of judgments of injustice. *European Journal of Social Psychology* 33:793–811.

Miller, D. T. 2001. Disrespect and the experience of injustice. *Annual Review of Psychology* 52:527–54.

Miller, J., and K. Bukva. 2001. Intimate violence perceptions: Young adults' judgments of abuse escalating from verbal arguments. *Journal of Interpersonal Violence* 16:133–51.

Mills, R. B., and K. Malley-Morrison. 1998. Emotional commitment, normative acceptability, and attributions for abusive partner behaviors. *Journal of Interpersonal Violence* 13:682–99.

Montiel, C. J. 2000. Constructive and destructive post-conflict forgiveness. *Peace Review* 12:95–101.

Moomal, Z. 1999. The relationship between meaning in life and mental well-being. *South African Journal of Psychology* 29:42–49.

Moon, H., and D. E. Conlon. 2002. From acclaim to blame: Evidence of a person sensitivity decision bias. *Journal of Applied Psychology* 87:33–42.

Morreall, J. 1994. The myth of the omniscient narrator. *Journal of Aesthetics and Art Criticism* 52:429–35.

Morris, D. 2000. Privacy, privation, perversity: Toward new representations of the personal. *Signs: Journal of Women in Culture and Society* 25:323–52.

Mortensen, C. D. 1972. *Communication: The study of human interaction.* New York: McGraw-Hill.

———. 1976. A transactional paradigm of verbalized social conflict. In *Perspectives on communication in social conflict*, ed. G. R. Miller and H. W. Simons, 90–124. Englewood Cliffs, N.J.: Prentice Hall.

———. 1979. The problem of incommunicability. East-West Institute Seminar. Honolulu, Hawaii.

———. 1983. The symbolic killing of Ronald Reagan. Fourth International Conference on Structural and Semiotic Studies. University of Indiana, Indianapolis.

———. 1984. Public reactions to an attempted presidential assassination. Sixth Annual Conference of the International Society for the Study of Aggression, Turku, Finland.

———. 1987. *Violence and communication: Public reactions to an attempted presidential assassination.* Lanham, Md.: University Press of America.

———. 1991. Communication, conflict, and culture. *Communication Theory* 1:273–93.

———. 1994. *Problematic communication. The construction of invisible walls.* Westport, Conn.: Praeger.

———. 1997. *Miscommunication.* Newbury Park, Calif.: Sage.

———. 1998. Boundary crossing in miscommunication and problematic talk. Eighth Annual Meeting of the Society for Text and Discourse, Madison, Wisconsin.

———. 1999. Linguistic constructions of violence, peace, and conflict. In *Encyclopedia of violence, peace, and conflict*, ed. L. Kurtz, 2:333–43. San Diego, Calif.: Academic Press.

Mortensen, C. D., and P. H. Arntson. 1974. The effect of predispositions toward verbal behavior on interaction patterns in dyads. *Quarterly Journal of Speech* 60:421–30.

Mortensen, C. D., P. H. Arntson, and R. W. Lustig. 1980. Predispositions toward verbal behavior in task-oriented interaction. *Human Communication Research* 6:239–52.

Mortensen, C. D., and C. Ayres. 1994. Symbolic violence. In *Problematic communication: The construction of hidden walls*, ed. C. D. Mortensen, 177–200. Westport, Conn.: Praeger.

Mortensen, C. D., and K. K. Sereno. 1970. The influence of ego-involvement and discrepancy on perceptions of communication. *Speech Monographs* 37:127–34.

Mumford, M. D., R. A. Schultz, and J. R. Van Doorn. 2001. Performance in planning: Processes, requirements, and errors. *Review of General Psychology* 5:213–40.

Mummendey, A., S. Otten, U. Berger, and T. Kessler. 2000. Positive-negative asymmetry in social discrimination: Valence of evaluation and salience of categorization. *Personality and Social Psychology Bulletin* 26:1258–70.

Murphy, J. D., D. M. Driscoll, and J. K. Kelly. 1999. Differences in the nonverbal behavior of men who vary in the likelihood to sexually harass. *Journal of Social Behavior and Personality* 14:113–28.

Murray, S. L., G. M. Bellavia, P. Rose, and D. W. Griffin. 2003. Once hurtful, twice hurtful: How perceived regard regulates daily marital interactions. *Journal of Personality and Social Psychology* 84:126–47.

Murray, S. L., and J. G. Holmes. 1999. The (mental) ties that bind: Cognitive structures that predict relationship resilience. *Journal of Personality and Social Psychology* 77:1228–44.

Murray, S. L., J. G. Holmes, and D. W. Griffin. 1996. The self-fulfilling nature of positive illusions in romantic relationships: Love is not blind but prescient. *Journal of Personality and Social Psychology* 71:1155–81.

———. 2000. Self-esteem and the quest for felt security: How perceived regard regulates attachment processes. *Journal of Personality and Social Psychology* 78:478–98.

Nelson-Jones, R. 2002. Are there universal human being skills? *Counselling Psychological Quarterly* 15:115–19.

Neufeld, J., J. McNamara, and M. Ertl. 1999. Incidence and prevalence of dating partner abuse and its relationship to dating practices. *Public Health Nursing* 10:151–58.

Nickerson, R. S. 1998. Confirmation bias: A ubiquitous phenomenon in many guises. *Review of General Psychology* 2:175–220.

———. 1999. How we know—and sometimes misjudge—what others know: Imputing one's own knowledge to others. *Psychological Bulletin* 125:737–59.

O'Hare, E. A., and W. O'Donohue. 1998. Sexual harassment: Identifying risk factors. *Archives of Sexual Behavior* 27:561–80.

O'Hearn, R. E., and K. E. Davis. 1997. Women's experience of giving and receiving emotional abuse. *Journal of Interpersonal Violence* 12:375–94.

Okami, P., and T. K. Schackelford. 2001. Human sex differences in sexual psychology and behavior. *Annual Review of Sex Research* 12:186–241.

Oleson, K. C., K. M. Poehlmann, J. H. Yost, M. E. Lynch, and R. M. Arkin. 2000. Subjective overachievement: Individual differences in self-doubt and concern with performance. *Journal of Personality* 68:491–524.

Oliphant, M. 1999. The learning barrier: Moving from innate to learned systems of communication. *Adaptive Behavior* 7:371–84.

Oliver, M. B., and J. S. Hyde. 1993. Gender differences in sexuality: A meta-analysis. *Psychological Bulletin* 114:29–51.

Olson, B. D., and D. E. Evans. 1999. The role of the big five personality dimensions in the direction and affective consequences of everyday social comparisons. *Personality and Social Psychology Bulletin* 25:1498–1508.

O'Sullivan, L. F., E. S. Byers, and L. Finkelman. 1998. A comparison of male and female college students' experiences of sexual coercion. *Psychology of Women Quarterly* 22:177–95.

Overskeid, G. 2000. The slave of the passions: Experiencing problems and selecting solutions. *Review of General Psychology* 4:284–309.

Pacht, A. R. 1984. Reflections on perfection. *American Psychologist* 39:386–90.

Pankhurst, D. 1999. Issues of justice and reconciliation in complex political emergencies: Conceptualising reconciliation, justice, and peace. *Third World Quarterly* 20:239–56.

Parrett, H., ed. 1994. *Pretending to communicate*. New York: Walter de Gruyter.

Pellizzoni, L. 2001. The myth of the best argument: Power, deliberation, and reason. *British Journal of Sociology* 52:59–88.

Petty, R. E., P. Brinol, and Z. L. Tormala. 2002. Thought confidence as a determinant of persuasion: The self-validation hypothesis. *Journal of Personality and Social Psychology* 82:722–41.

Pickering, J. 1999. Consciousness and psychological science. *British Journal of Psychology* 90:611–24.

Pillemer, D. B. 2001. Momentous events and the life story. *Review of General Psychology* 5:123–34.

Pizarro, D. 2000. Nothing more than feelings? The role of emotions in moral judgment. *Journal for the Theory of Social Behavior* 30:355–75.

Platt, R. 1989. Reflexivity, recursion, and social life: Elements for a postmodern sociology. *Sociological Review* 37:636–67.

Polivy, J., and C. P. Herman. 2002. If at first you don't succeed: False hopes of self-change. *American Psychologist* 57:677–89.

Pontari, B. A., B. R. Schlenker, and A. N. Christopher. 2002. Excuses and character: Identifying the problematic aspects of excuses. *Journal of Social and Clinical Psychology* 21:497–516.

Poon, W. T., and S. Lau. 1999. Coping with failure: Relationship with self-concept discrepancy and attributional style. *Journal of Social Psychology* 139:639–53.

Porpora, D. V. 1997. The caterpillar's question: Contesting anti-humanism's contestations. *Journal for the Theory of Social Behaviour* 27:243–63.

Powell, C. M., and K. C. Heriot. 2000. The interaction of holistic and dyadic trust in social relationships: An investigative theoretical model. *Journal of Social Behavior and Personality* 15:387–99.

Pratt, M. W., R. Filyer, and J. E. Norris. 1999. Generativity and moral development as predictors of value-socialization narratives for young persons across the life span: From lessons learned to stories shared. *Psychology and Aging* 14:414–26.

Pronin, E., J. Kruger, K. Savitsky, and L. Ross. 2001. You don't know me, but I know you: The illusion of asymmetric insight. *Journal of Personality and Social Psychology* 81:639–56.

Purdon, C., M. M. Antony, and R. P. Swinson. 1999. Psychometric properties of the frost multidimensional perfectionism scale in a clinical anxiety disorders sample. *Journal of Clinical Psychology* 55:1271–86.

Quereshi, M. Y. 2000. The invariance of certain personality factors over four decades. *Current Psychology* 19:21–28.

Reevy, G. M., and C. Maslach. 2001. Use of social support: Gender and personality differences. *Sex Roles* 44:437–59.

Reiss, S. 2004. Multifaceted nature of intrinsic motivation: The theory of 16 basic desires. *Review of General Psychology* 8:179–93.

Rempel, J. K., M. Ross, and J. G. Holmes. 2001. Trust and communicated attributions in close relationships. *Journal of Personality and Social Psychology* 81:57–64.

Rice, K. G., and S. A. Mirzadeh. 2000. Perfectionism, attachment, and adjustment. *Journal of Counseling Psychology* 47:238–51.

Richardson, F. C., A. Rogers, and J. McCarroll. 1998. Toward a dialogical self. *American Behavioral Scientist* 41:496–515.

Ridgeway, C. L., and L. Smith-Lovin. 1999. The gender system and interaction. *Annual Review of Sociology* 25:191–216.

Riskind, J. H., N. L. Williams, T. L. Gessner, L. D. Chrosniak, and J. M. Cortina. 2000. The looming maladaptive style: Anxiety, danger, and schematic processing. *Journal of Personality and Social Psychology* 79:837–53.

Roberts, R. D., and L. Stankov. 1999. Individual differences in speed of mental processing human and cognitive abilities: Toward a taxonomic model. *Learning and Individual Differences* 11:1–21.

Robins, R. W., and J. S. Beer. 2001. Positive illusions about the self: Short-term benefits and long-term costs. *Journal of Personality and Social Psychology* 80: 340–52.

Roese, N. J. 1997. Counterfactual thinking. *Journal of Personality and Social Psychology* 121:133–48.

Rogers, M. J., and G. N. Holmbeck. 1997. Effects of interparental aggression on children's adjustment: The moderating role of cognitive appraisal and coping. *Journal of Family Psychology* 11:125–31.

Roland, C. E., and R. M. Foxx. 2003. Self-respect: A neglected concept. *Philosophical Psychology* 16:247–87.

Roloff, M. E., K. P. Soule, and C. M. Carey. 2001. Reasons for remaining in a relationship and responses to relational transgressions. *Journal of Social and Personal Relationships* 18:362–85.

Romig, C. A., and G. Veenstra. 1998. Forgiveness and psychosocial development: Implications for clinical practice. *Counseling and Values* 42:185–200.

Rosen-Grandon, J. R., J. E. Myers, and J. A. Hattie. 2004. The relationship between marital characteristics, marital interaction processes, and marital satisfaction. *Journal of Counseling and Development* 82:58–69.

Ross, D. 2003. Learning, cognition and ideology. *South African Journal of Philosophy* 2:139–56.

Roth, P. A. 2003. "Mistakes." *Synthese* 136:389–408.

Rotundo, M., D. H. Nguyen, and P. R. Sackett. 2001. A meta-analytic review of gender differences in perceptions of harassment. *Journal of Applied Psychology* 86:914–22.

Rusbult, C. E., J. M. Martz, and C. R. Agnew. 1998. The investment model scale: Measuring commitment level, satisfaction level, quality of alternatives, and investment size. *Personal Relationships* 5:357–91.

Russell, B. L., and D. L. Oswald. 2001. Strategies and dispositional correlates of sexual coercion perpetrated by women: An exploratory investigation. *Sex Roles* 45:103–15.

Ryan, R. M., and E. L. Deci. 2000. Self-determination theory and the facilitation of intrinsic motivation, social development, and well-being. *American Psychologist* 55:68–78.

Sacher, J. A., and M. A. Fine. 1996. Predicting relationship status and satisfaction after six months among dating couples. *Journal of Marriage and Family* 58:21–32.

Samter, W. 2002. How gender and cognitive complexity influence the provision of emotional support: A study of indirect effects. *Communication Reports* 15:5–16.

Sanford, K. 1998. Memories of feeling misunderstood and a schema of partner empathetic responding: New scales for marital research. *Journal of Social and Personal Relationships* 15:490–501.

Sanna, L. J., S. Meier, and E. A. Wegner. 2001. Counterfactuals and motivation: Mood as input to affective enjoyment and preparation. *British Journal of Social Psychology* 40:235–56.

Sarre, R. 1997. Justice as restoration. *Peace Review* 9:541–47.

Savitsky, K., N. Epley, and T. Gilovich. 2001. Do others judge us as harshly as we think? Overestimating the impact of our failures, shortcomings, and mishaps. *Journal of Personality and Social Psychology* 81:44–56.

Sbrage, T. P., and W. O'Donohue. 2000. Sexual harassment. *Annual Review of Sex Research* 11:258–85.

Scharfstein, B. 1993. *Ineffability: The failure of words in philosophy and religion.* Albany: State University of New York.

Scheff, T. J. 1990. *Microsociology: Discourse, emotion, and social structure.* Chicago: University of Chicago Press.

Schegloff, E. A. 2000. Overlapping talk and the organization of turn-taking for conversation. *Language in Society* 29:1–63.

Schimel, J., J. Arndt, and T. Pyszczynski. 2001. Being accepted for who we are: Evidence that social validation of the intrinsic self reduces general defensiveness. *Journal of Personality and Social Psychology* 80:35–52.

Schimel, J., T. Pyszczynski, J. Greenberg, H. O'Mahen, and J. Arndt. 2000. Running from the shadow: Psychological distancing from others to deny characteristics people fear in themselves. *Journal of Personality and Social Psychology* 78:446–62.

Schlenker, B. R., B. A. Pontari, and A. N. Christopher. 2001. Excuses and character: Personal and social implications of excuses. *Personality and Social Psychology Review* 5:15–33.

Schlenker, B. R., and S. A. Wowra. 2003. Carryover effects of feeling socially transparent or impenetrable on strategic self-presentation. *Journal of Personality and Social Psychology* 85:841–80.

Schmitt, D. P. 2002. A meta-analysis of sex differences in romantic attraction: Do rating contexts moderate tactic effectiveness judgments? *British Journal of Social Psychology* 41:387–402.

Schutz, A. 1998. Assertive, offensive, protective, and defensive styles of self-presentation: A taxonomy. *Journal of Psychology Interdisciplinary and Applied* 132:611–29.

———. 1999. It was your fault. Self-serving biases in autobiographical accounts of conflicts in married couples. *Journal of Social and Personal Relationships* 16:193–208.

Schutz, A. 1967. *The phenomenology of the social world.* Evanston, Ill.: Northwestern University Press.

Schutz, A., and R. Baumeister. 1999. The language of defense: Linguistic patterns in narratives of transgression. *Journal of Language and Social Psychology* 18:269–87.

Schwandt, T. A. 1999. On understanding understanding. *Qualitative Inquiry* 5:451–64.

Semin, G. R., and E. R. Smith. 1999. Revisiting the past and back to the future: Memory systems and the linguistic representation of social events. *Journal of Personality and Social Psychology* 76:877–92.

Sen, A. 2000. East and west: The reach of reason. *New York Review of Books* 47:33–38.

Sereno, K. K., and C. D. Mortensen. 1969. The effects of ego-involved attitudes on conflict negotiation in dyads. *Speech Monographs* 36:8–12.

Shackelford, T. K., G. L. LeBlanc, and E. Drass. 2000. Emotional reactions to infidelity. *Cognition and Emotion* 14:643–59.

Shamasundar, C. 1999. Understanding empathy and related phenomena. *American Journal of Psychotherapy* 53:232–45.

Sharpsteen, D. J., and L. A. Kirkpatrick. 1997. Romantic jealousy and adult romantic attachment. *Journal of Personality and Social Psychology* 72:627–40.

Shaver, P., J. Schwartz, D. Kirson, and C. O'Connor. 1987. Emotional knowledge: Further exploration of a prototype approach. *Journal of Personality and Social Psychology* 52:1061–86.

Shaw, J. C., E. Wild, and J. A. Colquitt. 2003. To justify or excuse: A meta-analytic review of the effects of explanations. *Journal of Applied Psychology* 88:444–58.

Sheftel, S. 2002. Regressive communication in intimate relationships. *Modern Psychoanalysis* 27:219–34.

Sherry, S. B., P. L. Hewitt, G. L. Flett, and M. Harvey. 2003. Perfectionism dimensions, perfectionistic attitudes, dependent attitudes, and depression in psychiatric patients and university students. *Journal of Counseling Psychology* 50:373–86.

Simmons, L. 1994. Three kinds of incommensurability thesis. *American Philosophical Quarterly* 31:119–32.

Simpson, J. A., W. Ickes, and T. Blackstone. 1995. When the head protects the heart: Empathic accuracy in dating relationships. *Journal of Personality and Social Psychology* 69:629–41.

Skaldeman, P., and H. Montgomery. 1999. Interpretational incongruence of value-profiles: Perception of own and partner's values in married and divorced couples. *Journal of Social Behavior and Personality* 14:345–65.

Slugoski, B. R., and A. E. Wilson. 1998. Contribution of conversational skills to the production of judgment errors. *European Journal of Social Psychology* 28:575–601.

Smith, P. 2000. Culture and charisma: Outline of a theory. *Acta Sociologica* 43:101–12.

Snapp, C. M., and M. R. Leary. 2001. Hurt feelings among new acquaintances: Moderating effects of interpersonal familiarity. *Journal of Social and Personal Relationships* 18:315–26.

Sneed, C. D., R. M. McGrae, and D. C. Funder. 1998. Lay conceptions of the five-factor model and its indicators. *Personality and Social Psychology Bulletin* 24:115–26.

Snodgrass, S. E., M. A. Hecht, and R. Ploutz-Snyder 1998. Interpersonal sensitivity: Expressivity or perceptivity? *Journal of Personality and Social Psychology* 74:238–49.

Sommerville, C. J. 1998. Secular society/religious population: Out tacit rules for using the term "secularization." *Journal for the Scientific Study of Religion* 37:249–54.

Spieker, C. J., and V. B. Hinsz. 2004. Repeated success and failure influences on self-efficacy and personal goals. *Social Behavior and Personality* 32:191–98.

Spitzberg, B. H. 2001. Obsessive relational intrusion, coping, and sexual coercion victimization. *Communication Reports* 14:19–31.

Sprecher, S. 1999. "I love you more today than yesterday": Romantic partners' perceptions of changes in love and related affect over time. *Journal of Personality and Social Psychology* 76:46–54.

Stack, S., and J. R. Eshleman. 1998. Marital status and happiness: A 17-nation study. *Journal of Marriage and the Family* 60:527–36.

Stanford, P. K. 1998. Reference and natural kind terms: The real essence of Locke's view. *Pacific Philosophical Quarterly* 79:78–97.

Statman, D. 1997. Hypocrisy and self-deception. *Philosophical Psychology* 10:57–78.

Stephan, W. G., R. Dias-Loving, and A. Duran. 2000. Integrated threat theory and intercultural attitudes: Mexico and the United States. *Journal of Cross-Cultural Psychology* 31:240–49.

Stevens, L. E., and S. T. Fiske. 2000. Motivated impressions of a powerholder: Accuracy under task dependency and misperception under evaluation dependency. *Personality and Social Psychology Bulletin* 26:907–22.

Stockdale, M. S. 1998. The direct and moderating influences of sexual harassment pervasiveness, coping strategies, and gender on work-related outcomes. *Psychology of Women Quarterly* 22:521–35.

Stucke, T. S., and S. L. Sporer. 2002. When a grandiose self-image is threatened: Narcissism and self-concept clarity as predictors of negative emotions and aggression following ego-threat. *Journal of Personality* 70:509–32.

Suls, J., R. Martin, and J. P. David. 1998. Person-environment fit and its limits: Agreeableness, neuroticism, and emotional reactivity to interpersonal conflict. *Personality and Social Psychology Bulletin* 24:88–98.

Swann, W. B., Jr., and M. J. Gill. 1997. Confidence and accuracy in person perception: Do we know what we think we know about our relationship partners? *Journal of Personality and Social Psychology* 73:747–58.

Szasz, T. 1998. The healing word: Its past, present, and future. *Journal of Humanistic Psychology* 38:8–20.

Szymanski, M. H. 1999. Re-engaging and dis-engaging talk in activity. *Language in Society* 28:1–23.

Takaku, S. 2001. The effects of apology and perspective taking on interpersonal forgiveness: A dissonance-attribution model of interpersonal forgiveness. *Journal of Social Psychology* 141:494–509.

Tang, Y. 1999. Language, truth, and literary interpretation: A cross-cultural examination. *Journal of the History of Ideas* 60:1–22.

Tanney, J. 1998. Investigating cultures: A critique of cognitive anthropology. *Journal of the Royal Antropological Instituts* 4:669–88.

Tauer, J. M., and J. M. Harackiewicz. 2004. The effects of cooperation and competition on intrinsic motivation and performance. *Journal of Personality and Social Psychology* 86:849–61.

Ter Laak, J. J. F., T. Olthof, and E. Aleva. 2003. Sources of annoyance in close relationships: Sex-related differences in annoyance with partner behaviors. *Journal of Psychology* 137:545–60.

Tetlock, P. E. 1998. Close-call counterfactuals and belief-system defenses: I was not almost wrong but I was almost right. *Journal of Personality and Social Psychology* 75:639–52.

Tetlock, P. E., O. V. Kristel, S. B. Elson, M. C. Green, and J. S. Lerner. 2000. The psychology of the unthinkable: Taboo trade-offs, forbidden base rates, and heretical counterfactuals. *Journal of Personality and Social Psychology* 78:853–70.

Thomas, G., and G. O. Garth. 2003. Mind-reading accuracy in intimate relationships: Assessing the roles of the relationship, the target, and the judge. *Journal of Personality and Social Psychology* 85:1079–94.

Thompson, S. C., W. Armstrong, and C. Thomas. 1998. Illusions of control, underestimations, and accuracy: A control heuristic explanation. *Psychological Bulletin* 123:143–61.

Thompson, V. A., and R. M. J. Byrne. 2002. Reasoning counterfactually: Making inferences about things that didn't happen. *Journal of Experimental Psychology: Learning, Memory, and Cognition* 28:1154–70.

Thomson, A., and N. Bolger. 1999. Emotional transmission in couples under stress. *Marriage and the Family* 61:38–48.

Tilly, C. 2004. Social boundary mechanisms. *Philosophy of the Social Sciences* 34:211–36.

Todorov, A. 1997. Another look at reasoning experiments: Rationality, normative models, and conversational factors. *Journal for the Theory of Social Behaviour* 27:387–417.

Totterdell, P., and S. Reynolds. 1997. Forecasting feelings: The accuracy and effects of self-predictions of mood. *Journal of Social Behavior and Personality* 12:631–53.

Toulmin, S. E. 1964. *The uses of argument*. Cambridge, England: Cambridge University Press.

Treadgold, R. 1999. Transcendent vocations: Their relationship to stress, depression, and clarity of self-concept. *Journal of Humanistic Psychology* 39:81–106.

Trigg, R. 1998. *Rationality and religion*. Malden, Mass.: Basil Blackwell.

Tugade, M. M., and B. L. Fredrickson. 2004. Resilient individuals use positive emotions to bounce back from negative emotional experiences. *Journal of Personality and Social Psychology* 86:320–33.

Twenge, J. M., K. R. Catanese, and R. F. Baumeister. 2003. Social exclusion and the deconstructed state: Time perception, meaninglessness, lethargy, lack of emotion, and self-awareness. *Journal of Personality and Social Psychology* 85: 409–23.

Ungar, S. 2001. Moral panic versus the risk society: The implications of the changing sites of social anxiety. *British Journal of Sociology* 52:271–92.

Urdan, T. 2004. Predictors of academic self-handicapping and achievement: Examining achievement goals, classroom goal structures, and culture. *Journal of Educational Psychology* 96:251–64.

Vaes, J., and R. A. Wicklund. 2002. General threat leading to defensive reactions: A field experiment on linguistic features. *British Journal of Social Psychology* 41:271–80.

van Berlo, W., and B. Ensink. 2000. Problems with sexuality after sexual assault. *Annual Review of Sex Research* 11:235–57.

Vangelisti, A. L. 1994. Messages that hurt. In *The dark side of interpersonal communication*, ed. W. R. Cupach and B. H. Spitzburg, 53–82. Hillsdale, N.J.: Lawrence Erlbaum.

Vangelisti, A. L., and L. P. Crumley. 1998. Reactions to messages that hurt: The influence of relational contexts. *Communication Monographs* 65:173–97.

Vangelisti, A. L., M. Knapp, and J. A. Daly. 1990. Conversational narcissism. *Communication Monographs* 57:251–74.

Velmans, M. 1999. When perception becomes conscious. *British Journal of Psychology* 90:543–66.

Vohs, K. D., and T. F. Heatherton. 2001. Self-esteem and threats to self: Implications for self-construals and interpersonal perceptions 81:1103–18.

Vorauer, J. D., J. J. Cameron, J. G. Holmes, and D. G. Pearce. 2003. Invisible overtures: Fears of rejection and the signal amplification bias. *Journal of Personality and Social Psychology* 84:793–812.

Voronov, M., and J. A. Singer. 2002. The myth of individualism-collectivism: A critical review. *Journal of Social Psychology* 142:461–80.

Wagstaff, G. F. 1998. Equity, justice, and altruism. *Current Psychology* 17:111–35.

Waldo, T. G., and R. Davis. 2000. Fantasy proneness, dissociation, and DSM-IV Axis II symptomatology. *Journal of Abnormal Psychology* 109:555–58.

Walen, H. R., and M. E. Lachman. 2000. Social support and strain from partner, family, and friends: Costs and benefits for men and women in adulthood. *Journal of Social and Personal Relationships* 17:5–30.

Wall, E. 2001. Sexual harassment as wrongful communication. *Philosophy of the Social Sciences* 31:525–37.

Wallace, H. M., and R. F. Baumeister. 2002. The performance of narcissists rises and falls with perceived opportunity for glory. *Journal of Personality and Social Psychology* 82:819–34.

Wallace, J. C., S. J. Kass, and C. J. Stanny. 2002. The cognitive failures questionnaire revisited: Dimensions and correlates. *Journal of General Psychology* 129:238–56.

Wallace, K., M. Martin, S. McMillan, and M. Mell. 1999. When strangers disagree: Expressive response styles and attitude change. *Journal of Social Behavior and Personality* 14:197–206.

Walmsley, J. 2000. The development of Lockean abstraction. *British Journal for the History of Philosophy* 8:395–418.

Walton, D. N. 1998. *The new dialectic: Conversational contexts of argument*. Toronto, Ontario: University of Toronto Press.

Washburn, M. 1990. Two patterns of transcendence. *ReVision* 13:3–16.

Watkins, D., S. Mortazavi, and I. Trofimova. 2000. Independent and interdependent conceptions of self: An investigation of age, gender, and culture differences in importance and satisfaction ratings. *Cross-Cultural Research* 34:113–35.

Watt, G. C. M. 1996. All together now: Why social deprivation matters to everyone. *British Medical Journal* 312:1026–30.

Weaver, A., and F. B. M. de Waal. 2002. An index of relationship quality based on attachment theory. *Journal of Comparative Psychology* 116:93–106.

Weber, N., and N. Brewer. 2004. Confidence-accuracy calibration in absolute and relative face recognition judgments. *Journal of Experimental Psychology: Applied* 10:156–72.

Wells, J. D., S. E. Hobfoll, and J. Lavin. 1999. When it rains it pours: The greater impact of resource loss compared to gain on psychological distress. *Personality and Social Psychology Bulletin* 25:1172–82.

Wells, A., and C. Papageorgiou. 1998. Relationships between worry, obsessive-compulsive symptoms, and meta-cognitive beliefs. *Behaviour Research and Therapy* 36:899–913.

Welsh, G., and J. E. Gruber. 1999. Not taking it anymore: Women who report or file complaints of sexual harassment. *Canadian Review of Sociology and Anthropology* 36:559–84.

Wiebe, R. E., and S. B. McCabe. 2002. Relationship perfectionism, dysphoria, and hostile interpersonal behaviors. *Journal of Social and Clinical Psychology* 21:67–90.

Wiederman, M. W., and L. LaMar. 1998. "Not with him you don't": Gender and emotional reactions to sexual infidelity during courtship. *Journal of Sex Research* 35:288–97.

Wiland, E. 2003. Psychologism, practical reason, and the possibility of error. *Philosophical Quarterly* 53:68–78.

Wilden, A. 1980. *System and structure: Essays in communication and exchange*. 2nd ed. New York: Tavistock.

Williams, C. L., P. A. Giuffre, and K. Dellinger 1999. Sexuality in the workplace: Organizational control, sexual harassment, and the pursuit of pleasure. *Annual Review of Sociology* 25:73–93.

Williams, J. E., and M. L. Munick. 1995. Psychological importance of the "Big Five": Impression formation and context effects. *Personality and Social Psychology Bulletin* 21:818–27.

Williams, P. J. 1991. *The alchemy of race and rights*. Cambridge, Mass.: Harvard University Press.

Winman, A., P. Juslin, and M. Bjorkman. 1998. The confidence-hindsight mirror effect: An accuracy-assessment model for the knew-it-all-along phenomenon. *Journal of Experimental Psychology: Learning, Memory, and Cognition* 24:415–31.

Wolters, C. A. 2004. Advancing achievement goal theory: Using goal structures and goal orientations to predict students' motivation, cognition, and achievement. *Journal of Educational Psychology* 96:236–50.

Woods, P. A. 2001. Values-intuitive rational action: The dynamic relationship of instrumental rationality and values insights as a form of social action. *British Journal of Sociology* 52:687–706.

Worthington, E. E., Jr., and J. G. Wade. 1999. The psychology of unforgiveness and forgiveness and implications for clinical practice. *Journal of Social and Clinical Psychology* 18:385–418.

Wright, D. B., G. Self, and C. Justice. 2000. Memory conformity: Exploring misinformation effects when presented by another person. *British Journal of Psychology* 91:189–202.

Yancey, A. K. 1992. Identity formation and social maladaptation in foster adolescents. *Adolescence* 27:819–32.

Yelsma, P. 1996. Affective orientations of perpetrators, victims, and functional spouses. *Journal of Interpersonal Violence* 11:141–61.

Zechmeister, J. S., and C. Romero. 2002. Victim and offender accounts of interpersonal conflict: Autobiographical narratives of forgiveness and unforgiveness. *Journal of Personality and Social Psychology* 82:675–86.

Zuckerman, M., S. C. Kieffer, and C. R. Knee. 1998. Consequences of self-handicapping: Effects of coping, academic performance, and adjustment. *Journal of Personality and Social Psychology* 74:1619–28.

Zulick, M. D. 1997. Generative rhetoric and public argument: A classical approach. *Argumentation and Advocacy* 33:109–19.

Zweig, J. M., L. J. Crockett, A. Sayer, and J. R. Vicary. 1999. A longitudinal examination of the consequences of sexual victimization for rural young adult women. *Journal of Sex Research* 36:396–410.

Index

About the Author

C. David Mortensen is professor of communication science in the Department of Communication Arts at the University of Wisconsin, Madison. His research involves the social scientific study of communicative difficulties in social and personal relationships. He teaches graduate and undergraduate courses in communication theory, interpersonal conflict, symbolic violence, miscommunication, the psychology of communication, perfectionistic communication, and optimal human relations.